PSEUDONYMOUS SHAKESPEARE

To the memory of my parents, Geoff and Bucky Gee,
and of my parents-in-law, Ralph and Nan McCarthy

Pseudonymous Shakespeare
Rioting Language in the Sidney Circle

PENNY McCARTHY
Honorary Research Fellow, University of Glasgow, UK

ASHGATE

Published by
Ashgate Publishing Limited
Wey Court East
Union Road
Farnham
Surrey, GU9 7PT
England

Ashgate Publishing Company
110 Cherry Street
Suite 3-1
Burlington
VT 05401-3818
USA

Ashgate website: http://www.ashgate.com

British Library Cataloguing in Publication Data
McCarthy, Penny
    Pseudonymous Shakespeare : rioting language in the Sidney circle
    1. Sidney, Philip, Sir, 1554-1586 – Friends and associates 2. Shakespeare, William, 1564-1616 3. English literature – Early modern, 1500-1700 – History and criticism 4. Anonyms and pseudonyms – England – History – 16th century 5. Literary forgeries and mystifications – History – 16th century
    I. Title
    820.9'003

Library of Congress Cataloging-in-Publication Data
McCarthy, Penny, 1943-
    Pseudonymous Shakespeare : rioting language in the Sidney circle / Penny McCarthy.
        p. cm.
    Includes bibliographical References (p.   ) and index.

1. Laneham, Robert, 16th cent. Letter. 2. Kenilworth Castle (Kenilworth, England)—Historiography. 3. Elizabeth I, Queen of England, 1533-1603—Travel—England—Kenilworth. 4. Sidney, Philip, Sir, 1554-1586—Friends and associates. I. Title.

DA690.K4L236 2006
820.9'003—dc22

2005017267

ISBN 978-0-7546-5508-4

MIX
Paper from
responsible sources
FSC® C003969

Transferred to Digital Printing in 2011

Printed and bound in Great Britain
by Printondemand-worldwide.com

Contents

List of Illustrations

List of Tables

Acknowledgements

The Berkeley Will Trust, the National Archives, the Shakespeare Birthplace Trust and the Warden and Scholars of Winchester College granted permission for the reproduction and publication of pages of manuscript. The British Library allowed me to reproduce and publish an image and a photograph; and the *New York Times*, a photograph by Edward Keating for the cover. To all these institutions, I am very grateful.

Preface

The list of people to whom I am indebted for help with this book is very short in one sense, and almost boundless in another. My study runs so counter to most interpretations of English literary works of the late sixteenth and early seventeenth centuries that it was not easy to consult anyone. And yet for so many of my findings, I owe a debt to some work or other that set me on the right road.

The few scholars who have read some former draft of a section of the study have mostly felt disabled from venturing comment, because they had no idea of the shape of the whole. Yet I thank Jonathan Crewe and Alan Sinfield for reading an early draft of Chapter 5. Alan's observation that wherever it was aiming to go, it was back-to-front, was both true and useful. Robert Cummings was willing to suspend disbelief on first hearing some of the arguments in Chapter 4. Richard Abrams answered questions whose import he could only guess at. Stanley Wells e-mailed an answer to a specific query within an hour of being asked. Henry Woudhuysen helped me decipher the manuscript scrawl of pages of Gabriel Harvey's *Letterbook*. Terence Cave and Richard Scholar suggested possible strategies. Park Honan and Clare Asquith offered encouragement.

My chief support in the academic world has been the reader for the Ashgate Press, whose copious initial comments helped to tighten and improve the study a great deal, and to whose open-mindedness the appearance of the book in print is mainly due. Heartfelt thanks are also due to the editor Erika Gaffney.

To my immediate family I owe a large practical as well as emotional debt. Callum, Tom and Melissa provided the help an author so needs and can hardly ever find – the critical gaze of intelligent and sensitive readers who are not experts in the field. All the early chapters benefited from their reactions and criticisms. Chris, being further off and busy, simply believed that my thesis would convince the world as soon as it was given a hearing, a loyalty just as useful. The freedom from financial worries that allowed me to concentrate on research I owe to Callum.

I am grateful to Glasgow University, whose grant of an honorary research fellowship allowed me to benefit from the collegiality of the English department, the library and associated internet facilities, and alleviated the loneliness of the independent scholar. The fellowship was thought up and implemented by Drummond Bone. The Shakespeare Association of America has provided stimulating conferences and the chance to meet scholars with shared interests; as has the Shakespeare Institute in Stratford. I thank Sussex University for the initiation into English literary studies in its MA and D.Phil. programmes. (The D.Phil. 'programme' was the mind and scholarship of Brian Cummings, an invaluable resource. Michael Hawkins gave me an induction into the reading of manuscripts, in his own time.)

I thank the archivists Jan Piggott and Allan Ronald at Dulwich College, David Smith at Berkeley Castle, Suzanne Foster at Winchester College, Robin Whittaker at Worcester County Records Office, Paul Johnson at the National Archives, and helpful librarians at the Society of Genealogists, the Bodleian Library, the London Library, the British Library, the library of Christ's Church College, Oxford, and the earl of Northumberland's library at Alnwick.

The type-script was scrupulously prepared by Pat FitzGerald, who has saved me weeks of time and energy.

Some of the argument of Chapter 7 has been published in the Shakespeare Yearbook, Vol. 14 (2004), edited by Douglas Brooks. It appeared as 'Some *quises* and *quems*: Shakespeare's True Debt to Nashe' in the volume entitled *New Studies in the Shakespearean Heroine.* I am grateful to Douglas for his tireless enthusiasm and generous scholarship.

For the rest, the ripples of gratitude run out and back in time to encompass: my London poetry group; Tony Lucas, Will Vaughan, Ron Taylor and others, who have honed my poetry-reading skills, as have Don Paterson, Colin Falck and George Szirtes; the radical work of Eric Sams on Shakespeare; Peter Dronke's re-imagining of mediaeval lyrics, which I have tried to emulate when dealing with early modern lyric; a class on Dante by John Freccero and one on philosophy by Ian Hacking; the works of Vladimir Nabokov. And further: my teachers in philosophy, translation, the classics – Philippa Foot, Elizabeth Anscombe, Mildred Taylor; and the historian Isobel Henderson, from whom I learned one sole thing, that the interest of any age in its own past is driven by contemporary concerns. And further back still, to James Cullen, Cynthia Gee and Mary Wilson, teachers at Benenden School, Kent; to my childhood friends and their games and word-play; to my parents, whose wit and gentleness is much missed ... and many, many more. ·

Penny McCarthy

List of Abbreviations

Journals

ELH	*English Literary History*
ELR	*English Literary Renaissance*
LRB	*London Review of Books*
MLR	*Modern Language Review*
MP	*Modern Philology*
N&Q	*Notes and Queries*
PQ	*Philological Quarterly*
SEL	*Studies in English Literature 1500–1900*
SP	*Studies in Philology*
TCBS	*Transactions of the Cambridge Bibliographical Society*
TLS	*Times Literary Supplement*

Reference works

CSP Spanish	Calendar of State Papers Spanish
STC	Short Title Catalogue of English Books, 1475–1640

Titles of works

DD	*Dom Diego*, by R.L.
PDH	*Poems in Divers Humors*, by Richard Barnfield
PP	*The Passionate Pilgrime*, 1599
PR	*The Poetical Rhapsody,* edited by Francis Davison. *'PR'* is utilized for the composite of the volumes of 1602, 1608, 1611, 1621.

Other

P.C.C.	Prerogative of the Court of Canterbury
PRO	Public Record Office, now the National Archives at Kew

What Song the *Syrens* sang, or what name *Achilles* assumed
when he hid himself among women, though puzzling questions
are not beyond all conjecture.

Thomas Browne. *Urn-Burial.* 1658.

Introduction – Highways and Labyrinths

A certain critic writing for students of Vladimir Nabokov's *Ada or Ardor: a Family Chronicle* advised his readers to skip the first three chapters of the novel on a first reading.[1] This was because he knew the students would find these pages immensely complicated and mystifying, and he thought the information contained in them did not materially contribute to the understanding of the subsequent events in the novel. In fact, they contain vital clues that serve as a key to later understanding.

In an ideal world, I would make a similar recommendation to all readers who enjoy being mystified by a detective story; but the recommendation is for the opposite reason. I would advise such readers to jump from page xvi to page xviii of this introduction, for these pages will only *de*mystify, prematurely. These readers should also expunge any expectations already raised by the title.

But this is not an ideal world; and most potential readers will want to know in advance how the book will proceed, and what it will cover. To what use will the investigation of pseudonyms be put? Which sixteenth- and early seventeenth-century English authors will feature in the study? What claims will be made about the Sidney circle? For both kinds of reader, I sketch the barest outline of the book, before offering a choice between 'The Highway', which spells out the precise nature of the content, and 'The Labyrinth', which illustrates modes of interpretation, without giving away the core secret.

This is a study of a particular pseudonym, R.L., found in or attached to diverse works written and published between 1575 and 1601. The question posed is whether this pseudonym could attach to one particular author, and the answer given is that it does. It is equally an investigation into sixteenth-century modes of 'indirection'. The pursuit of R.L. provides the narrative line on which to hang the devices used by early modern English writers to perplex and mislead their readers while simultaneously offering them the clues to solve the enigmas posed. Many of the devices are newly identified in this study; and the question of R.L.'s identity has not been raised for decades, and certainly not solved. I claim that he is someone in whose biography many have been interested, and whose works are still generally admired.

The R.L. trail leads from an account of Queen Elizabeth's 1575 visit to Kenilworth, penned by an R.L. purporting to be Robert Langham; through R.L. the author of *Diella* and *Dom Diego and Gyneura* (sonnets with a narrative poem, published in 1596); to two R.L.s who produced single poems – one a poem in the anthology *A Paradyce of Dayntie Devises* (1576), the other a dedicatory poem to Michael Drayton's *Matilda* in 1594. Richard Linche's name and his translations of Italian versions of classical mythology, published at the turn of the century, are scrutinized with suspicion. The next R.L. is addressee, not author: the man to whom Richard Barnfield addressed a poem about poetry and music in a volume of 1598, a poem that found its way into *The Passionate Pilgrime* of 1599. Finally there is the odd Richard Lichfield, the 'Barber of Trinity College' whom Thomas Nashe addressed in his *Have With You to Saffron Walden* (1596) and who replied to Nashe the next year in *The Trimming of Thomas Nashe*, a work whose authorship has never been satisfactorily settled.[2]

These R.L.s are dealt with in the four chapters 1, 3, 5, 7. Even-numbered chapters (2, 4, 6, and 8) are devoted to a series of 'Supposes', dealing with the implications of the material in each preceding chapter. Chapter 9 gathers up the threads into a new narrative of R.L.'s life, which differs in radical respects from all traditional (and all recent) biographies of this person. An envoi sums up the ways in which the book is aligned with respect to current mainstream views, and suggests how it might affect various fields of early modern studies.

I follow R.L.'s identity as it transmogrifies into other authorial pseudonyms – A.W., Humphrey King and some others. There is one name that hovers doubtfully between pseudonym and true name: 'William Smith' straddles the literary and the real worlds. Other nicknames for R.L. are ones used by his contemporaries to refer to him. These covert references are mined in the poetry of George Gascoigne, Philip Sidney, John Lyly, Edmund Spenser, Christopher Marlowe, George Chapman, Robert Armin, Ben Jonson, John Davies of Hereford and some others. Prose works of Gabriel Harvey, Thomas Nashe, Robert Greene, William Covell, William Kemp and John Harington are also found to be a fruitful source of covert reference, as are dedicatory poems, prose prefaces, epigraphs and marginalia. The investigation extends into works published in the early decades of the seventeenth century. Some of these were genuine seventeenth-century compositions; but others, it is argued, were written long before they were published, and are essentially sixteenth-century works.

As the roll-call of names may suggest, the Sidney circle looms large in this enquiry. This is widely understood to comprise Philip Sidney and his sister Mary Sidney (later Herbert, the Countess of Pembroke), and the writers enjoying their patronage and that of their powerful uncle Robert Dudley, Earl of Leicester. Its contours will be somewhat redefined here; and not one, but two great poets will be added to it.

R.L. was in this coterie. The secrecy shrouding this fact was necessitated in part by the scandal of his low birth and cross-class liaisons, in part by the 'daungerous' politics. The poetry of the Earl of Leicester's protégés is saturated with covert *anti*-Elizabethan sentiment, as I shall show. Shared terms of reference and sleights of hand learned from each other meant that much was left opaque in the work of Sidneian writers, intended to be deciphered only by 'understanders' – those in the inner circle. My aim is to put modern readers in the position of that inner circle, rather than that of benighted outsiders.

For the purposes of this study, the subtext – that which is concealed under the bland surface of the text – is the important text. This does not involve ignoring what each work appears to be 'about' – what its matter is – but it does pay particular attention to what it is 'about' – what its designs on us are. Accordingly, I pay much attention to puns, for they are a prime means of masking an author's intent: it requires an act of attention on the reader's part to notice their presence.

Censorship is another useful hermeneutic tool in the study. It is treated as a potential marker of a concealed meaning that 'authority', of whatever kind, was attempting to suppress. I draw into its orbit those texts that the Stationers' Company stipulated should be 'lawfully authorized' before publication, even if publication was not long delayed. This was an unusual demand, and has a particular implication, I shall argue.

Because I do not pause to theorize the use of pseudonyms in the course of my narrative, I offer here a brief theoretical backing to the proposition that the multiple occurrences of the sign 'R.L.' could have been intended to convey the existence of a single authorial hand.

The phenomenon of the persona in the work appearing to be the that of the historical author – as Astrophel is (really) Philip Sidney – paves the way for an easy transition to believing that an author could use the same ploy for his or her signature when it is dubious, when it is a mark designed to half-conceal while half-revealing his or her identity. If R.L. appears as the 'speaker' in some works, as he does in the *Letter* from Kenilworth and the Barber's reply to Nashe, or is not differentiated from the speaker, as in the *Diella* sonnets, then he is a quasi-literary entity, and his name must be motivated by something.

The contemporary habit of calling an author after his best-known work can serve as an additional persuasive argument for seeing the author-name in the light of an adopted persona. It happens even when the author is clearly not the protagonist in the work: Sir John Harington becomes known as 'Ajax' following his publication of *The Metamorphosis of Ajax* (1596), though the protagonist, properly speaking, is 'A jakes', or privy, and the author is hostile to the concealed contemporary Ajax whose morals and politics he wishes to reform. Though the two types of naming – internal character and external pseudonym – are not logically linked, the use of the first as the author's nickname must have helped to blur the line between the inside and the outside of the text and would have facilitated the reading of the second in the same light.

Sometimes there appears an author-name with no apparent extra-literary identity, so that the name might as well be a pseudonym. 'Humphrey King' is one such, with numerous 'walk-on' parts, as author and as addressee. In his case as in the ones above, when a reader kept meeting the same nickname on different types of texts, he or she might well have suspected that the same real person was involved. The suspicion could have been right or wrong, of course: coincidence might have played a part. But we should keep open the possibility that writers might knowingly have played on the belief in their readers' minds, signing off very diverse texts with a telling clue.

Those who prefer to puzzle out solutions themselves should now turn to page xviii. Those who are unwilling to read on unless they are given more information as to who R.L. will turn out to be and why the texts chosen for investigation might be supposed to yield more information than has been previously gleaned from them should read the next section.

The Highway

There is a mystery about the authorship of the account of the Queen's visit to Kenilworth. Though no author is given on the title page, references are dropped at intervals in the text purporting to identify him as Robert Langham. But Langham, a real official attendant on the Progress, complained about the publication, and a William Patten appeared to accept responsibility for its composition. Internal evidence, however, suggests that the voice of the narrator is not that of Patten either. I shall argue that the writer must be a lowly servant in the household of Robert Dudley, Earl of Leicester, and is very young. The contents of the library of 'Captain Cox', a local man, have informed his mind – as they informed the mind of another local boy also very young in 1575, William Shakespeare. Shakespeare's plays abound with allusions to tales in manuscripts in Captain Cox's library. Some disguised punning on 'will' lends support to the nearly-novel hypothesis that the page boy co-author (with Patten) of 'Langham's Letter' is in fact William

Shakespeare (of Stratford, son of John Shakespeare and Mary Arden, none other).

Thereafter, following William Patten's lead, other writers in Leicester's circle of patronage try surreptitiously to promote the talented proletarian youth in their midst. By means of various literary tricks, they present him under one guise or another. The use of pseudonyms, variously derived and invented, is one of the chief means of this disguising. But the repertoire of 'indirection' is much wider.

The upshot of my investigation is the reinterpretation, to a small or large degree, of many texts by Shakespeare's contemporaries; a considerable ante-dating of the existence of contemporary allusion to the historical Shakespeare; and the advancement by many years of the dates of first reference to several of his works.

Clearly, therefore, this study will argue for much earlier dates of composition for most of Shakespeare's known corpus. I shall insist on a strict application of the 'terminus ante quem', for two reasons. Abundant evidence exists for long intervals between composition and publication of works of all kinds in the sixteenth century. And mention is a haphazard phenomenon: there is one sole record of the existence of *As You Like It* (in the Stationers' Register of 1600) before its publication in the First Folio of 1623. These two probabilistic reasons are given firm backing by my findings of a wealth of oblique references to Shakespeare's person and his plays at dates earlier than the currently accepted dates of composition.

I re-order Shakespeare's plays chronologically, suggesting that internal evidence can be invoked to work out, from the likely state of his imagination, understanding, general knowledge and loyalties at different times of his life, a more plausible order of composition. I reject the whole notion of a late period of romance.

I add to Shakespeare's corpus, identifying his lost juvenile occasional poems, lyrics, and elegies, his juvenile accounts of progresses and a poetic 'entertainment'. I further identify as his two sonnet sequences; a poetic romance; more mature poems of all kinds; dedicatory poems; a pamphlet; a prose translation; a pseudo-historical treatise.

The meaning of Shakespeare's known works is partially reinterpreted. I find a hidden agenda of anti-Tudor sentiment and promotion of the would-be rulers of England, the Dudley/ Sidneys, in the plays of Shakespeare, and of others who collaborated with him in a series of history plays to promote the Dudley cause. This antagonism to the monarch was deeper and longer-lasting than has been supposed. There is, conversely, a strongly autobiographical element in many of Shakespeare's plays, relayed by means of a persona he adopted for himself. His *Sonnets* and narrative poems are hardly touched on, for they require much more space than I could allow them in this study.

An unfamiliar picture of our protagonist emerges: an almost motherless boy by reason of his transfer from his own family to the aristocratic milieu of the Dudleys (a Protestant milieu), he received an extraordinary if erratic education under the best scholars and poets of the day, writing masques and poetry – much of it non-dramatic – in that coterie. He was promoted by his contemporaries, even by Robert Greene (who was not jealous of him), and especially by Nashe, who trusted his talent and urged him to publish. (My reading of Nashe's works differs considerably from that of previous criticism.) Our protagonist travelled to Italy when young. He 'enjoyed' an uneasy social status, was not quite a Cambridge undergraduate, and perhaps not quite a law student (or perhaps he was one). He taught in the country, enjoyed serially Sir Edward Denny's, Sir John Salusbury's and Sir John Harington's protection. He turned his early compositions to good use in the citizens' theatre. He was more deeply involved in the Burbages' venture of the Globe than we previously imagined. His family situation was more complicated than has been supposed; and it inflects his plays from the earliest to the latest.

Rejoin the chapter at page xxii, where a short defence of my philosophical approach is offered.

The Labyrinth

Jorge Luis Borges, that consummate story-teller, gives his readers what looks like a simple detective story, or even simpler ghost story, in his 'Abenjacán el Bojarí, muerto en su laberinto'.[3] The Penguin translator Andrew Hurley entitles the story 'Ibn-Hakam al-Bokhari, Murdered in His Labyrinth'.[4] One of the difficulties of translation is that in cases where words do not velcro exactly on to each other in two different languages, we are often forced to plump for a single word that loses a nuance, or abolishes a fruitful ambiguity, of the original. 'Muerto' can mean 'dead' or 'murdered'. It looks as though Abenjacán was murdered by the ghost of his vizier. But if ghosts cannot murder, then 'dead' might be more correct; or perhaps we should conclude 'then the labyrinth was not *his*, Abenjacán's'; or, 'then the victim was not Abenjacán'.

These conundrums are integral to the telling of the detective story that frames the uncanny story of al-Bokhari told by a young Englishman, Dunraven, to his friend Unwin, in Cornwall in 1914. But Borges is of course doing more with his double tale than appears on the surface. He is leading us to understand something about all tales, their tellers and their hearers. We know that tellers of tales can be unreliable because duplicitous; but they can also be sincere and wrong, even when the tale involves elements they have witnessed, or was told by witnesses they trust. Though the teller seems to have control of the tale, it is possible for a stubborn hearer to react (as Unwin does) with 'That must be wrong'; and to be right, or more right than the teller. It is possible for the hearer, on reflection, to come up with a more coherent tale, based on nothing more than the details of the story itself, that is, without using historical props (witnesses), but bringing into play a knowledge of human motivation.

I shall narrate the Borges tale in some detail, because I too want to tell a simple detective story that may have implications for the reading of a great many stories – stories we tell about the meaning of the literature of sixteenth- and early seventeenth-century England. I also want to object that some of *those* stories must be wrong as told. And I need to indicate how attention to minute detail is important. My primary tale, as I have indicated, concerns the identity of 'R.L.', author of an account of Elizabeth I's visit to Kenilworth, seat of her powerful subject Robert Dudley, Earl of Leicester, in 1575. Retold, it expands into a web of tales about the contemporary uses of pseudonyms. The retelling requires an attentive ear for irony, teasing attempts to mislead, and other subtextual meanings in the writings of authors long dead, who cannot confirm or rebut our interpretations.

In 'Abenjacán el Bojarí', Dunraven tells a tale to Unwin about the massive bright red brick building in front of them, on 'the land of his ancestors' in Cornwall. Twenty-five years ago, when Dunraven was still a child, a chieftain or king from somewhere along the Nile died in the central and only chamber of this building at the hands of his cousin, Zaid. The mystery remained unsolved. On Unwin's asking why this was so, Dunraven gives multiple reasons: because the building was a labyrinth; because Abenjacán was guarded by a slave and a lion; because a secret treasure disappeared at the same time; because the assassin was already dead at the time of the murder; because .... Unwin cuts off the recital of mysteries, on the grounds that solutions are always simple.

Unwin agrees to accompany Dunraven into the labyrinthine building, with the aim of reaching the centre. As they progress, Dunraven tells the tale of its construction. As a child, he saw Abenjacán arrive by boat in Pentreath – a man of impressive bearing, attended by a black man and a golden lion. He told his family he had seen a king arrive by boat. Abenjacán hired bricklayers to build a house with no rooms and miles of corridors.

The local rector Allaby used to describe Abenjacán's previous history as told to him by the man himself, says Dunraven. It ran as follows.

Abenjacán had ruled his people with a rod of iron; they had rebelled; he had fled with his cousin Zaid, a slave, and the treasure extorted during his reign. Waking one night from a terrible dream caused by the brushing of a spider's web against him, the king became angry that Zaid, who was a coward by nature, slept calmly beside him. He reflected that the treasure was not infinite, and that Zaid might demand his share. He slit Zaid's throat. In his agony, Zaid burbled something Abenjacán could not catch. Zaid was certainly dead, but he might come to life, feared Abenjacán. He ordered the slave to obliterate the corpse's face with a rock. He and the slave wandered till they came to the sea. Abenjacán considered that a dead man would not be able to cross water, and set sail. The fist night at sea, he dreamed the murder over again, but this time he heard the dead man's words: 'As you slay me now, so shall I slay you'. He had sworn to foil that threat: he was going to hide in a labyrinth so that the ghost should lose its way!

Allaby sifted what he had heard. He first thought that the Moor was mad, and the labyrinth a sign of his madness. Then he thought that while such an explanation fitted the building of the labyrinth and the Moor's story, it was not backed by the impression Abenjacán himself had made. Perhaps it was the sort of story told in that culture .... However, Allaby read back numbers of *The Times* in London, establishing the truth of the rebellion against Abenjacán and his vizier, who did indeed have a reputation as a coward.

The workmen finished; the Moor installed himself. After the space of three years, a ship called the *Rose of Sharon* entered the harbour. That very evening, Abenjacán burst into the rectory, crying that his slave and lion had perished. He asked whether the authorities could protect him; then he fled. Allaby reflected in amazement that this terrified man had ruled iron tribes, fought battles and murdered a fellow human being.

The next day, the Rose of Sharon had sailed away. Allaby thought he had better look into the death of the slave. Abenjacán's story seemed to him fantastic – but in the labyrinth he came across the lion, dead; the slave, dead; and in the central chamber, 'el Bojarí', whose face was mutilated. A pearl-inlaid treasure-chest lay at the foot of the corpse. Someone had forced its lock, and there was not a coin left.

Unwin senses that Dunraven has often told this tale, often reached this climax, 'with identical aplomb and inefficacity'. To simulate interest, he asks how the lion and slave had met their deaths. Dunraven's 'incorrigible voice' replies: 'Their faces were smashed in too'. As if exacting a debt from Unwin, he asks whether the story is not inexplicable. 'I don't know if it's explicable or inexplicable', replies Unwin. 'I do know it is wrong.' Dunraven flies into a fury, invoking the testimony of the rector's older son (Allaby being now dead) and all the inhabitants of Pentreath. They sleep in the building, in the sole room, at the centre: it has a trap-door in the floor. Unwin sleeps well, Dunraven stays awake, haunted by lines of poetry he knows to be excruciatingly bad: 'Faceless the sultry and overpowering lion,/ Faceless the stricken slave, faceless the king' (in English in the original).

Although he had not thought his interest engaged by the tale, Unwin wakes with the conviction that he has deciphered it. Two days later, he meets Dunraven in a pub in London, and says to him, 'Your facts were right, or could be right, but told the way you told them, they were wrong, quite obviously wrong. Let's start with the incredible labyrinth. A fugitive does not hide in a labyrinth, a labyrinth built on the coast, a bright crimson labyrinth that can be seen from afar by sailors.'

Unwin relates how the solution started to present itself when he thought of the Minotaur (a natural progression of thought, as he observes, when labyrinths are under consideration). Dunraven, who would really rather preserve a mystery, considering how banal solutions usually are, how much they depend on a sleight-of-hand, prevaricates for a moment over whether the Minotaur was a man with a bull's head, or a bull with a man's head. 'It could have been either', Unwin allows. 'The important thing is to have a monster to go with a monstrous construction. The Minotaur justified the construction of the mythical labyrinth. No one could say the same of a threat sensed in a dream. All the same, I confess I did not understand that that ancient figure was the key, and therefore your subsidiary story about the spider's web was vital. It would not surprise me at all if the spider's web was what suggested to the assassin his plan.'

Unwin then gives his version of the events. The king, who was brave, had slept that night when he fled with his vizier. It must have been the vizier who stayed awake, because he was a timid man. He did not dare kill the king, either; but instead, he called the slave, they buried part of the treasure there, and made their way to England. He built the red labyrinth not to hide but to lure el Bojarí and then kill him.

When el Bojarí entered the labyrinth, his vizier killed him as he was mounting the steps to the central chamber. The slave must have killed the lion, and then been killed himself by another bullet. Then Zaid disfigured the visages of all three victims. He had to do so, because one dead person alone with a mutilated face would have suggested a questionable identity. Contrariwise, the 'dead lion, dead slave, dead king' sequence sets up a series, and people would argue from the first two terms to the last. No wonder the vizier was in a state of terror at Allaby's house: he had just done the dreadful deed, and was ready to flee England and collect the treasure.

Dunraven greets this with a pensive silence. Then he accepts its correctness, in essence. He accepts the switching of identities: 'such metamorphoses are classic conceits of the genre, conventions whose observance is demanded by the reader'. But he sticks in his heels at the notion of a return to collect the treasure. The vizier would have taken it all: there had been no time to bury it. Perhaps not a coin was found in the treasure-chest in Cornwall because the bricklayers had used it all up. 'Then we would have Abenjacán crossing the sea to reclaim a squandered treasure.'

'Not *squandered*' objects Unwin in his turn. '*Invested*'. (Note that Unwin too is prepared to give way to another's counter-interpretation.) Zaid had invested in an enormous circular trap to catch and kill his victim. The vizier had discovered that his true motive was to destroy Abenjacán. He pretended to be Abenjacán, he murdered Abenjacán and at last he was Abenjacán. Dunraven assents to this. 'He was a wanderer who, before becoming a non-person in death, would remember having once been a king or having pretended to be.'

* * *

The story is mysterious, taken as a whole. The reader has to work hard at the level of the simple tale itself to get the wider meaning or meanings. She has to try to distinguish between true and false leads. For instance, Borges is careful about the naming and description of the vizier and the king at each stage of his story. 'Abenjacán' and 'el Bojarí' look interchangeable, but I suspect they are not totally so. It may be that both men bore the name el-Bojarí (meaning 'from Bokhara') but only one the name Abenjacán. We are led to forget that the vizier was first described as a cousin to the king, and therefore might have looked very like him. The bearing of the first one to arrive in Cornwall was kingly; the man who burst into Allaby's house after the death of the slave and the lion (and the man? we do not know for sure – that could have occurred later that night) was cowardly. The classical story of the Minotaur provides a clue, though in a disingenuous manner: it does matter which head is on which body. A simple solution (which we have been warned is often the right one) is that the old story was right after all, in essence, and once stripped of its mysticism.

Just as the Abenjacán story was 'owned' by Dunraven by virtue of his ancestors' possession of the land on which the brick labyrinth stood, the story I want to tell about Elizabethan literature is also already owned – by postmodernists, mainly, who would rather one did not try to 'tell it how it was', but prefer to retain indeterminacy and mystery. A story about the use of pseudonyms as a phenomenon, about collaboration in the telling of tales (plays, poems, anything in print), about inter- or super- or hyper-subjectivity in writing practice, about secrets with no content (like the empty chest), would lure them into a labyrinth. A story called 'Who was R.L.?' would not. Postmodernists are Dunravens, with their 'incorrigible voices'.

The Unwins, historicists, want to unravel the tale, but have made some slips in translation. We have seen how the smallest wrong nuance can have a baneful effect, framing the tale the wrong way, or not quite the right way.

My simple tale must function as Unwin's retelling functioned – to overthrow the accepted version. It might be objected that there is not a single accepted 'version' of early modern literature. But as Angus Fletcher has argued, postmodernist, materialist, historicist, Lacanian approaches 'paradoxically ... hold the centre of a decentring academic study of literature.'[5] They dovetail to form a solid rampart, holding out against any account that pays attention to the poem, poiesis, the author, and his or her imagination and intention, though these are the very concepts under which the writers of the works under consideration would have conceived of their art. Comparison of 'poems' ('things made') becomes impossible, as 'individual works of art disappear, as forms, into general statements of the sociopolitical dynamic'.

Fletcher implies, I think, that part of the motive for the shift to the newer story or stories is a desire to be seen as more scientific. He makes the point that the choice of an over-arching theory is far from simple even in the domains of the sciences themselves: we can ask for a Popperian, a Duhemian, or a Kuhnian approach. 'Theory' can itself be naïve about its scientific underpinning. Though the practitioners of most of the above-mentioned highly theoretical approaches to early modern literature think of themselves as anti-positivist, in fact their theories tend to favour some explanations of the empirical facts over others. Witness the newly fashionable account of the play *Pericles*: death-of-the-author theories, and anti-elitism, and the preference for collaborative enterprise have resulted in the conclusion (a remarkably positivist one) that while Shakespeare contributed to it, George Wilkins wrote this play.[6] My plodding detective work will suggest that is not true.

My thesis does subject itself to the demands of scientific accountability. It invites Popperian analysis, in being strongly stated with obvious conditions of falsifiability. It fulfills Imré Lakatos's requirement that a theory be 'test-worthy', and potentially fruitful in generating a new paradigm or the elucidation of more facts (indicating a 'progressive' not a 'degenerative problemshift').[7] Being test-worthy does not entail that a theory cannot eventually be refuted.

So to my story of R.L. Strange to say, it too turns out to be a tale about a man who played kingly parts; a wanderer or traveller; a humble servitor and a lion. Taking a leaf from the book of William Shakespeare, who played with two incompatible but identically worded versions of his chosen motto 'Non Sanz Droict' ('Not without justification') and 'Non. Sanz Droict' ('No! Without justification'), I choose as my *impresa* 'Not without a pinch of salt'; or alternatively 'No! Without a pinch of salt'; that is, 'All is true'.

Notes

1   Vladimir Nabokov, *Ada or Ardor: A Family Chronicle* (1969; London: Penguin, 1990). David Rampton, *Vladimir Nabokov* (Basingstoke: Macmillan, 1993), p. 113.
2   Full biographical details of all these texts are given at the points at which they are subjected to detailed examination.
3   Jorge Louis Borges, 'Abenjacán el Bojarí, muerto en su laberinto', in *El Aleph* (1949), *Obras Completas*, 4 vols (Barcelona: Emecé, 1996), 1.600–606.
4   Jorge Luis Borges, 'Ibn-Hakam al-Bokhari, Murdered in His Labyrinth', in *The Aleph*, trans. Andrew Hurley (London: Penguin, 1998), pp. 95–104.
5   Angus Fletcher, 'On Shakespeare and Theory', in *The Shakespearean International Yearbook* (Aldershot: Ashgate, 2002), pp. 3–19.
6   Gordon McMullan, in 'The Invention of Late Writing: Shakespeare, Biography, Death', a paper presented to the Shakespeare Association of America, March 2002, spelled out the interdependence of the authorship 'finding' and the aforementioned theoretical approaches.
7   Imré Lakatos, 'Changes in the Problem of Inductive Logic' (1968) in *Mathematics, Science and Epistemology*, ed. J. Worrall and G. Currie (*Philosophical Papers*, 2 vols) (Cambridge: Cambridge University Press, 1978), 2.128–200, 178.

Chapter 1

First Candidate – Robert Langham, 'El Prencipe Negro'

'The Black Prince' is the title adopted by the author of a detailed account of Queen Elizabeth I's visit to Kenilworth Castle in 1575.[1] The author also describes himself as 'R.L.', and is therefore the first candidate for the post of 'the person who really was R.L.' – the quarry pursued throughout this book. This chapter could be summarized as an attempt to discover why this R.L. should have claimed to be the Black Prince. I shall show why it is highly unlikely that Robert Langham had anything to do with the work: his name was simply purloined. Then I shall cast doubt on the hypothesis that William Patten was the sole author. I advance a third solution: that Patten had a guiding hand in the work, but it was in the voice of, and was actually mainly written by, a talented servant in the Kenilworth household, a young page. In his case, there is a plausible reason for his self-description as 'the Black Prince'.

In the course of the chapter, I hope to reveal a depth of opposition on the part of the Leicester faction to the Queen that has been previously underestimated. As a preliminary, it must be stressed (as previous studies have stressed) how critical a moment this July of 1575 was for the Dudley/Sidney fortunes. Robert Dudley had serious hopes of marrying the Queen, and it is clear that some of the events had been planned with a view to giving her an opportunity to accept him.[2] The fact that he had secretly married Lettice, formerly Countess of Essex, was not an obstacle. Dudley had already repudiated one former wife; and it is clear from the fact that Lettice's family insisted on a marriage ceremony for her in 1578 that they had had doubts about the strength of her claim. Had Dudley become the Queen's consort, Philip Sidney, his nephew and heir, would have become effectively heir to the throne. The Queen was too old for child-bearing, and in any case, the point of the marriage would have been to let power pass peacefully to the Dudley clan, as they had for two generations believed it should.[3]

Edmund Dudley had served his monarch as right-hand man; and John Dudley had been effectively uncrowned king in Edward VI's reign. Both had come to grief. Edmund had been executed in 1510, accused of plotting to seize power from the King and Council. John (Robert's father) put Lady Jane

Grey on the throne for nine days when Edward VI died, after marrying her to his son Guildford. Both John and Guildford were executed as a result.[4] What the Dudleys now wanted was a guarantee of future power without having to raise open rebellion.

It is only if one listens to the subtext of the works of the Dudley coterie that one can hear the implacable resistance. Close textual analysis will demonstrate the necessity of keeping 'on one's toes' at all times, to face the challenge thrown out to the reader by the author(s) to 'understand', in the coterie sense of grasping the unspoken sense. The other Elizabethan word for this is interesting: it is the Latin 'subauditur' – 'it is heard *beneath* (the words)'.

Anyone who reads George Gascoigne's account of the great progress of the Queen to Kenilworth is sure to enjoy, vicariously and at whatever temporal distance, the splendours of the entertainment offered over nineteen June days. Gascoigne was the Earl of Leicester's soldier-poet, deviser of many of the masques and events on that occasion. Leicester had laid on an extraordinary programme for the Queen, who as she entered his castle ('his' because she had granted it to him) entered an Arthurian fairy world, complete with legendary figures, carefully staged 'impromptu' events, lavish gifts and Italian fireworks – as well as the customary banquets, hunting, dancing, bear baiting, juggling, and music. Gascoigne published his account in due course, a year later, as *The Princely Pleasures at the Courte at Kenelwoorth.*[5]

But anyone who reads the parallel account known familiarly as 'Langham's Letter'[6] feels as though the intervening space of time had been suddenly dissolved, and she were standing by the Mere to watch the Lady of the Lake float over the water and Triton with a mermaid scud past; as though she could hear the guns 'pealing' and the fireworks flashing when the Queen retired to rest on the night of her arrival; as though she felt a shudder of horror when the Savage Man's club snapped and frightened her Majesty's horse – and the relief when the Queen cried 'No hurt, no hurt'. For the vivacity of the author's style is such that one cannot but feel in the thick of events which took place so many centuries ago; cannot but be struck by his personality, with which most have been delighted, though some have been scandalized.

Here is how he introduces himself ostensibly to his friend, Master Humfrey Martin, but more likely to the intended general reader, at the beginning of his *Letter*.

> Understand ye, that syns through God and good freends, I am placed at Coourt heer (as ye wot) in a worshipfull room [respected position]: Whearby, I am not only acquainted with the most, and well knoen too the best, and every

officer glad of my company: but also have poour [power, licence], a dayz (while the Councell sits not) to go and too see things sight woorthy, and too be prezent at any sheaw or spectacl, ony whear whear this Progress reprezented untoo her highnes: And of part of which sportez, having taken sum notez and observationz (for I can not be idl at ony hand in the world) az wel too put fro me suspicion of sluggardy, az too pluk from ye doout of ony my forgetfulnes of freendship: I have thought it meet to impart them untoo yoo, az frankly, az freendly, and az fully az I can. Well wot ye the blak Prins waz never stained with disloyaltee of ingratitude toward ony, I dare be his warrant, hee wyll not begyn with yoo, that hath at hiz hand so deeply dezerved.[7]

The spelling – odd even by Elizabethan standards[8] – the cocksure air, the energy, both of language and character, the ease of the syntax, the natural-sounding alliteration ('frankly … friendly … fully') and the extraordinary adoption of the title 'the Black Prince' are immediately intriguing.

Walter Scott was one of those scandalized rather than beguiled. His reaction is worth recording, because it is typical of many subsequent responses. In one scene in his *Kenilworth*, he has Leicester graciously greeting courtiers as he makes his way through an anteroom at Greenwich.[9] Scott cares not a jot for anachronism, so he has Leicester greet the poet Edmund Spenser and exchange a word about his 'Irish petition' (Spenser could not have gone to Ireland before 1577); progressing immediately to a 'Ha, Will Shakespeare – wild Will! Thou hast given my nephew, Philip Sidney, love-powder – he cannot sleep without thy Venus and Adonis under his pillow!' *(Venus and Adonis* was first printed in 1593); and finally being approached by:

> … a person quaintly dressed in a doublet of black velvet, curiously slashed and pinked with crimson satin. A large cock's feather in the velvet bonnet, which he held in his hand, and an enormous ruff, stiffened to the extremity of the absurd taste of the times, joined with a sharp, lively, conceited expression of countenance, seemed to body forth a vain hare-brained coxcomb, and small Wit; while the rod he held, and an assumption of formal authority, appeared to express some sense of official consequence, which qualified the natural pertness of his manner. A perpetual blush, which occupied rather the sharp nose than the thin cheek of this personage, seemed to speak more of "good life," as it was called, than of modesty; and the manner in which he approached to the Earl confirmed that suspicion.
>
> 'Good even to you, Master Robert Laneham,' said Leicester ….[10]

Scott had only the evidence of the *Letter* to draw on for this sketch, and as we shall see, he is faithful to the details. His unflattering characterization would be perfectly just – if it were indeed Robert Langham/Laneham (both spellings are found in the original) who wrote the *Letter*. But concerning this there is, or ought to be, grave doubt. There are a number of discrepancies, some obvious, some apparently minute but with great potential for disrupting the identity between the historical Langham and the author of the *Letter*. There is also some external evidence that Langham objected to the authorship foisted upon him. But before appealing to the external evidence and to the work of predecessors who have expressed misgivings about the *Letter*'s authenticity, I shall continue with Scott's imaginary Kenilworth for a moment longer.

In the conversation imagined by Scott, Laneham has a suit to Leicester. '"And what is it, good master keeper of the council-chamber door?"' asks the Earl. '"*Clerk* of the council-chamber door",' Laneham corrects him. '"Well, qualify thine office as thou wilt man," replied the Earl; "what wouldst thou have with me?"' It turns out that Laneham is requesting permission to attend at Kenilworth during the forthcoming visit of the Queen, to keep order at the door of the Council Chamber when the Privy Council meets, and to chase away prying listeners at crannies.

Scott has noticed something of importance here: it is the quibble on the correct title of Laneham's office. But the importance of the point lies not where Scott placed it, in the distinction between Keeper and Clerk, but in something else. Robert Langham is described in the Acts of the Privy Council documents as 'Keeper of the Council Chamber'.[11] There was no such post as Keeper or Clerk of the Council Chamber *Door*. Yet that is precisely how the author of the *Letter* describes himself. Langham's post involved the provision of the mundane necessities for the Privy Council's meetings: flowers, fire-tongs and such-like. Yet what the author of the *Letter* describes himself as doing in *his* office is rather different.

> Noow syr, if the Councell sit, I am at hand, wait at an inch I warrant yoo. If any make babling, peas (say I) woot ye whear ye ar? If I take a lystenar [catch anyone listening] or a priar in at the chinks, or at the lokhole, I am by and by in the bonez of him: but noow they keep good order, they kno me well inough: If a be a freend, or such one az I like: I make him sit doun by me on a foorm, or a cheast, Let the rest walk a Gods name.[12]

The writer clearly is what he says he is – a keeper of the door. He preserves quiet outside when the Council is in session. Could his title be a joke, deriving from that which Langham actually held?

Something about the way he carries out his work, as he describes it, jars with the figure Langham should have presented to those with whom he had dealings. Langham had been admitted to the Mercers' Company in 1557. Since admittance depended on the completion of a seven-year apprenticeship, which he would have started at around the age of fifteen, he must have been born in about 1535. His widow drew his last Keeper's wage in 1579/80. He must have been a married man of about forty when he carried out his duties at Kenilworth in 1575.[13]

Contrast that with the impression given by the doorkeeper. Thanks to his languages, he says, he can chat with the ambassadors' men when their masters are in Council, and answer 'roundly' to the ambassadors themselves when they bid him call their lackeys or ask him what o'clock it is. The languages he commands, or more probably, of which he has picked up scraps, for he seems inordinately proud of his foreign phrases, are French, Spanish, Dutch, Latin, and German. At first glance, all this seems perfectly compatible with the figure that might have been cut by Langham. He carried, presumably, enough authority to speak roundly to ambassadors. What jars is the revelation that the ambassadors and their men marvel to see such a fellow there. Why is this? It must be that they too perceived something quite incongruous in the figure before them, with his grasp of foreign phrases and his confidence. There must be something about this figure that is odd in a way that we would dearly like to understand.

It has long been suspected that the *Letter* might be spurious, that is, not really a letter to the Master Humfrey Martin it addresses, and not by its ostensible author.[14] The strongest piece of evidence is a letter addressed to the Lord Chancellor, Lord Burghley, apologizing abjectly for involving Langham in the original farce. This letter is by a William Patten, a literary man called in as part of Leicester's 'creative team' to compose poetry for the occasion.

Patten had heard 'hoow the book waz too be supprest for that Langham had complayned upon it, and ootherwize for that the honorabl enterteinment be not turned intoo a iest'.[15] He assures Burghley that no more than six copies have been sent out to known notables, one being Burghley himself. 'I have not let three more pass me, but have and suppress them all.' He even reveals that he had asked the Master of Requests, Dr Wilson, to give Langham a copy, and adds 'sory I am that he takez it so noow.' It could hardly be more plain that Langham had not been able to take a joke – the *Letter* – put out in his name, for which Patten holds the true responsibility.

The letter to Burghley was written on 10 September, from London, by which time the Queen's Progress had reached Woodstock, in Oxfordshire. The visit to Kenilworth, which lies between Warwick and Coventry (with Stratford-upon-Avon a mere fourteen miles to the southwest), had lasted from 9 to 27

July. The final date on the *Letter* is 'the xx. of August.1575' and the place of despatch is given as 'the Coourt. At the citee of Worcester'.

Clearly the book had been hurried into print, it seems by Patten, who would have had access to printers in London. He was a seasoned author, having published *The Expedicion into Scotlande of ... Edward, Duke of Somerset* in 1548, and an erudite *Calender of Scripture* earlier in 1575, mostly in Latin, giving the derivation of names in the Bible.

Immediately, the *Letter* fell foul of the authorities, and we see in Patten's letter the results: Burghley attempted to retrieve all the copies.[16] Equally clearly, it was a surreptitious publication. Normally, though not invariably, a text would have the author's name or a foreword by the publisher in lieu. The printer, sometimes the bookseller and very often the place of sale would be stated on the title page. The omissions of the second set in particular prove the irregularity of the publication. The timescale suggests that the book could not possibly have been licensed by the Stationers' Company, who in a case touching state affairs would probably have stipulated the need for authorization by the ecclesiastical powers.

I strongly suspect that the bookseller Richard Jhones published the *Letter* in 1575, with the title 'The Pastime of the Progresse'. In his original preface to Gascoigne's *Princely Pleasures*, the account published in 1576, Jhones describes the pressure put on him and other printers by 'yong Gentlemen and others' eager to know what had taken place at Kenilworth. He took pains to get 'very true and perfect copies' and now publishes Gascoigne's account of them:

> ... the rather, because a report thereof lately imprinted, by the name of The Pastime of the Progresse; which (in deede) doth nothing touch the particularitie of every commendable action, but generally reherseth hir Majestie's cheerefull entertainment in all places where shee passed: togither with the exceeding Joye that her subjects had to see hir: which report made very many the more desirous to have this perfect copy: for that it plainelye doth set downe every thing as it was in deede presented, at large ....[17]

So 'desirous' is Jhones to deprecate the previous publication and absolve the current one from suspicion that he never achieves a main verb in this sentence. His description of 'The Pastime' does indeed match 'Langham's' emphasis on the Queen's reactions and the joy her presence brought to all. Its author mentioned the Sibyl's declaration 'hoow great gladnes her gracious prezenz brought into every steed whear it pleazed her to cum'; gave the Porter's similar reaction; reported the savage Man's rehearsal of 'the incredibl joy that all estatez in the land have allweyz of her highnes whear so ever it cums'.[18] But

Jhones is lying through his teeth about the 'particularities': the particularities, in fact, must have been the root of the trouble.

In spite of the rather compelling evidence of Langham's innocence, indeed outrage ('sory I am that he takez it so noow', adds Patten), the theory of his authorship remains an article of faith for some. Roger Kuin clings to it in 1985. Katherine Duncan-Jones shows no awareness of the precariousness of his identification in her biography of Philip Sidney, published in 1991.[19]

The Langham hypothesis is based on two instances of the surname Langham, one of 'Ro. La.' and one of 'R.L.' in the text of the *Letter.* (There are two simultaneous printings, and in one, 'Laneham' replaces 'Langham'.) On page 58, our author speaks of the lively delight with which music can pierce into its hearers' hearts, and quoting a French 'sententia' about 'la tresnoble Science de Musique' implies to his friend Master Martin that with this he has told him a 'great matter'. He goes on to remark on the 'small skyl in muzik' he has been blessed with – '(ye know it iz sumwhat)' – claiming it entitles him to 'set the more by my selfe whyle my name iz Lanham' (sic).[20] He is clearly good at music, as the other passage 'revealing' his surname proves. For 'allweyz amoong the Gentlwemen by my good wyll (O, ye know that cumz allweyz of a gentle spirit)' he so delights them with his songs that they cry 'anoother good Langham anoother'.[21]

The third occasion of 'name-dropping' occurs in the penultimate paragraph. Giving his regards to Master Denman ('a Mercer ye wot az we be'), the author says 'he iz woont too summon me by the name of Ro. La. of the coounty of Nosingham Gentleman'[22] – a joke on red noses and the drinking of sack, which has occurred in the text immediately preceding. And finally there is the signing off in the last paragraph: 'Yoour countreeman, companion, and freend assuredly: Mercer, Merchauntaventurer, and Clark of the Councell chamber doore, and also kepar of the same: *El prencipe* (sic) *negro. Par me.* R.L. Gent. Mercer'.[23] It is certainly distinctive in style, and would seem to justify Walter Scott's characterization of the author as vain and hare-brained. Why *does* he refer to himself as the Black Prince, this time in Spanish?

It is time to investigate the persona of the author in more detail. Bear in mind, if you will, when reading the following account of the form and contents of the *Letter*, that what modern commentators take themselves to be doing when they consider the question of authorship is to decide between the claims of Robert Langham and William Patten. Patten is a prime suspect for authorship, because as we have seen he had control of the distribution, he is known to be have attended the Kenilworth festivities, he was a writer, scholar and poet, and he wrote to Burghley in the same hand as that of some marginal

notes in some copies of the *Letter* and with the same very distinctive spelling
– the long vowels being the most salient features. The technical aspects of
this 'dialect' or 'orthography' (and much depends on the question of which
it is) are to be found in articles cited by Kuin in his edition of 1983. Kuin's
own summary is that what we have does not amount to a reforming system of
spelling such as was being practised by some contemporary grammarians.[24]
This finding is important, because it tilts the evidence back in favour of the
view that what is represented in the *Letter* is a dialect. It might turn out to be
the authentic voice of the true author.

Let us turn first to the known biographies of the two people who are usually
taken to be the candidates for authorship. (As I shall be arguing that neither
of them will fit the bill, I shall reserve the name 'R.L.' for the putative real
author of the *Letter*.)

All the salient facts of Langham's life have been given above. He was a
London mercer who in virtue of his appointment followed the Court in its
summer progresses.

William Patten was currently Teller of the Exchequer and Customer of
London Outward, that is to say, he had reached prestigious heights in the
mercantile life of London.[25] He must have been at least fifty years old, for his
Expedicion into Scotlande, an account in diary form, was published in 1548, as
I have mentioned. He knew Burghley well as a comrade on that campaign. He
describes himself on the title page as 'Londoner': he was not a Warwickshire
man. This casts the spotlight back on the question of dialect forms.

Though there are some mild instances of the double 'o' in his text, the
Patten of *The Expedicion* does not go to the extremes of R.L., nor indulge
in 'z' for 's'. David Scott, who champions his authorship of the *Letter*,
professes to find a number of similarities apart from the spelling, but in my
view, the points of comparison he draws are either inevitable or insignificant
or wrong.[26] It is true that Patten and R.L. share a diary format; there are one
or two shared items of vocabulary ('importabl', for modern 'insupportable';
'duddle' for 'confuse'); and there is some overlap of interest in historiography,
etymology and numerology. But the differences between the two are greater.
Patten has a deep interest in history, offering pages of background to the
1548 campaign. His use of alliteration is not as marked as that in the *Letter*.
His viewpoint is not naïve and his descriptions not superb *(pace* Scott). His
powers of dramatization are negligible. On all counts, R.L. presents a very
different profile, as the following discussion will show.

After his flamboyant opening, the writer of the *Letter* devotes a page or two
to the geographical and historical situating of Kenilworth, which he calls by its

local name 'Killingworth'. He locates it by its distance from London, Coventry and Warwick, and describes it lapped on three sides by a great 'Pool'. His descriptive powers are in evidence even in this section, as when he describes the Chase lying to the north and west of the Castle, 'beautified [by the Earl of Leicester] with many delectabl, fresh and umbragioous Boowerz, arberz, seatz, and walks, that with great art, cost, and diligens wear very pleazauntly appointed: which also the natural grace by the tall and fresh fragrant treez and soil did so far foorth commend, az *Diana* her self might have deyned thear well inough too raunge for her pastime'.[27] ('Beautified' and 'umbragious' are first uses, according to the *OED*.) His humour – or is it his naïvety? – is apparent in his remark that 'the Castl hath one auncient strong and large Keep that iz called Cezarz Toour, rather (az I have good cauz too think) for that it iz square and hy foormed after the maner of Cezarz Fortz then that ever he bylt it'.[28]

His 'history' is of the briefest possible (unlike Patten's background information to the *Expedicion*). Having mentioned the founding Saxons Kenulph and Kenelm in his geographical section, he assigns Kenilworth to its historical region Mercia, and lists its bishoprics. A second paragraph investigates the etymology of 'worth', deriving it (wrongly, it seems) from the German 'Werd', meaning 'island' or 'peninsula'. He cites the German scholar '*Althamerus*', a commentator on Tacitus, in confirmation, and adds in the margin a few items of German vocabulary to prove the point that German 'wer' tends to become English 'wor'. Interestingly, in view of Patten's known scholarly interests, Andreas Althamer had published in 1530 the *Sylva biblicorum nominum*, an analogue and forerunner of Patten's own *Calender of Scripture*.

With a blithe 'thus proface ye with the preface', R.L. then abandons further learned preamble, to launch into the account of the Queen's visit. The 'proface/preface' pun is all his own. 'Prou fasse' – 'may it do you good' – was in use as a term of welcome or good wishes for a meal, but it was not used reflexively, as here.

From the moment of the Queen's riding up to the Castle on the hot summer evening of 9 July, coming from the south across parkland to the hillock called the 'Brays', opposite the double gates leading into the Tiltyard, the impressionable R.L. describes the staged 'happenings' and the main activities day by day until the last seven days, when his notes ran out! At this point (line 1067 out of a total length of 1672), he makes an excursus on the number seven (as did Patten in his *Calender*); then on the manner in which the Olympian gods and other deities could be said to have presided over the festivities; on the gardens which Leicester had laid out; on the number one; and on the number two, which would seem to be his favourite, as his account is more extended and given application to Kenilworth and the Visit. He proceeds with mention of the great tent in which Her Majesty dined on the day of 9 July before proceeding to Kenilworth, and of a 'great Chyld' there presented to the Queen – a simpleton supposedly six years old, as large as a lad of eighteen. This leads naturally into the theme of 'greatness' – of Leicester's munificence, in particular his kindness to the author himself. The author seizes the opportunity to describe his daily round at Kenilworth. Finally he explains how it is that he appears so 'bookish', mentions his education as far as the fifth form, commends himself to friends he and Master Martin have in common in London, and signs off, as we have seen.

In fact, even the earlier part of the *Letter*, the narration of the Visit itself, had contained one or two divagations, one being the famous detailed listing of the tales, romances and ballads possessed by a certain Captain Cox, the leader of the Coventry men who performed the Hock Tuesday play before the Queen. The other takes off from a 'device' which should have been presented to her Majesty, had time been found for it. An ancient minstrel should have sung a ballad of King Arthur. But R.L. has heard the performance before in company, and what is more, he remembers every detail of the minstrel's dress, his account of the meaning of his horn-spoon scutcheon, the banter which ensued when someone present contradicted the explanation the minstrel gave, the calming of the minstrel, and his launching into the Arthurian ballad. R.L. copies out some stanzas in the text of his *Letter*, having borrowed a copy, but not for long enough, it seems, to copy out the rest: 'More of the song iz thear, but I gat it not'.[29]

A suspicion begins to take root. It seems unlikely that the London mercers Langham or Patten had been in the vicinity of Kenilworth long enough to hear the local minstrel perform. Is R.L. perhaps a local? Another part of his account suggests that he is.

Describing the leader of the mummers who came to perform before the Queen, R.L. writes, with dramatic flourish: 'But aware, keep bak, make room noow, heer they cum. And fyrst captin Cox, an od man I promise yoo: by profession a Mason, and that right skilfull: very cunning in fens [fencing], and hardy as Gawyn, for hiz tonsword hangs at his tablz eend: great oversight hath he in matters of story: For az for king Arthurz book, Huon of Bordeaus ...'. And on he rattles, with a great list of romances; and then, having mentioned but not listed Captain Cox's books of moral and natural philosophy, he adds a list of poetry, plays and ballads which the Captain has 'fayr wrapt up in Parchment and boound with a whipcord'.[30]

There is no way this writer could have seen the two-handed sword hanging at the table end, or the parchments, or read the titles of the latter, unless he had visited Captain Cox's house. Now the question of who he was becomes a burning one.

'One day (Maister Martin) az the Gardin door waz open, and her highnes a hunting, by licens of my good freend Adrian, I cam in at a bek [peeking], but woold skant oout with a thrust: for sure I waz looth so soon too depart.'[31] R.L. knows the gardener by name: he is a friend of Adrian's, but can be kicked out of the garden at will by this – presumably senior – personage. Is it likely that Patten or Langham would have called the gardener 'friend', or been subject to the indignity of being 'thrust' by one of Leicester's servants? The hierarchical nature of sixteenth-century society strongly suggests not.

In describing the garden, with its beautifully constructed cage containing birds, R.L. refers to the fountain which was adorned with statues of naked deities such as might inflame the mind, and asks: 'but whoo so waz foound so hot in desyre, with the wreast of a Cok waz sure of a coolar: water spurting upward with such vehemency, az they shoold by and by be moystened from top too to'.[32] He is over-impressed with the 'rude' parts of statues and loves turning the water-cocks full on to fool in the spraying water. What kind of person have we here? A senior (both elevated and elderly) member of the Mercers' Company? An august friend of Lord Burghley's?

For his friend Humfrey Martin's benefit, the author describes his daily round.

> At mornings I rize ordinarily at seaven a clok: Then reddy, I go intoo the Chapell: soon after eyght, I get me commonly intoo my Lords Chamber, or intoo my Lords prezidents. Thear at the cupboord after I have eaten the manchet [small loaf of fine wheat bread], served over night for lyvery (for I dare be az bolld, I promis yoo, az any of my freends the servaunts thear ....[33]

'My friends the servants'? Is this perhaps one of the servants himself, helping himself in the morning to his bare allowance of a loaf of bread?

> It pleazed his honor [Leicester] too beare me goodwill at first, and so to continu. To have given me apparail eeven from hiz bak, to get me allowauns in the stabl, too advauns me unto thiz woorshipfull office so neer the most honorabl Coouncell ... too permit my good Father to serve the stabl. Whearby I go noow in my sylks, that els might ruffl in my cut canvas: I ryde noow a hors bak, that els many timez might mannage it a foot: am knoen too theyr honorz and taken foorth with the best, that els might be bidden to stand bak my self: My good Father a good releef, that he farez mooch the better by.[34]

In similar vein, the writer praises the Lady Sidney, Leicester's sister, as 'a Noblwooman, that I am az mooch boound untoo, az ony poor man may be untoo so gracioous a Lady'.[35]

The last two passages indicate someone of very humble birth, rescued from poverty by the goodness of the Lord Leicester. Yet Patten had been a friend of Burghley's since his campaigning days. He was not a permanent part of Leicester's household, but an independent London man. The phrase 'serve the stable' in the former passage probably indicates the provisioning of the stables. The *OED* definition of 'serve' given under sense 38 seems the most applicable: 'To supply, provide, or furnish with something requisite or necessary. Also, to furnish (a person, town, etc.) with a regular or continuous supply'. Langham's father would presumably have been in his sixties; Patten's in his eighties. With their successful gentlemen sons well placed, they would hardly have aspired to serve the stables at Kenilworth (assuming that they were still alive). Nor would they have been able to do so from a distance of a hundred miles. R.L.'s father must have lived in the vicinity of Kenilworth.

A profile very different from that of either of our two candidates is assembling itself for R.L. the *Letter* writer. It is that of a young Warwickshire servant taken into the household of the earl at Kenilworth, and spoiled by all because of his talents.

How young was he? How small? In fairy lore the Black Prince was the diminutive Fairy Prince, consort to the Fairy Queen. A Black Prince was being advertised in 1710, with his wife the Fairy Queen, as a marvel to be seen at Charing Cross.[36] He was 'a little *Black-Man* being but 3 Foot high, and 32 Years of Age … distinguish'd by the name of the *Black-Prince*', with 'his Wife, the *Little-Woman*, NOT 3 Foot high, and 30 Years of Age … commonly called the Fairy Queen'.

Is that why R.L. can call himself the Black Prince: because he is no more than three feet high? *Is he a child?* A page-boy with a talent for music, a passion for romances and ballads – and little interest in moral and natural philosophy? Good at picking up languages, passionate about stories and histories?

> Storeyz I delight in, the more auncient and rare, the more lykesum untoo me: If I tolld ye, I lyked Wylliam a Malmesbery so well, bicauz of hiz diligens and antiquitee, Perchauns ye woold conster it bicauz I loove Malmzey so well, but I feyth it iz not so: for sipt I no more Sak and Suger … then I doo Malmzey, I shoold not blush so mooch a dayz az I doo, ye kno my minde.[37]

Malmesbury/Malmsey is a puerile pun: but that is precisely what we should expect from a precocious young boy. If that is what R.L. was, it would explain the rather bumptious, cocksure air that almost everyone has noticed in his account.

Picture him, re-envisage him, rather, hanging about by the Council chamber door, bossing the other boys, startling everyone with his proficiency in languages, swinging his legs as he sits on the chest or form onto which he has hauled some even shorter-legged boy who has tried to peep in at the chinks of the Council chamber. Picture him sneaking into the garden, sniggering and splashing in the fountains. He is the darling of the women, who demand endless songs. He is especially keen to impress Mistress ... he almost gives her name away. '(A, see a mad knave, I had allmost tolld all).' He wants her to praise his singing and dancing: 'that shee gyvez onz but an eye or an ear: why then, man I am blest: my grace, my coorage, my cunning iz doobled'.[38]

R.L. describes how she does sometimes praise him for his musical performance.

> She sayz sumtime she likez it, and then I like it mooch the better, it dooth me good to heer how well I can do. And too say the truth: what, with mine eyz, az I can amoroously gloit it with my spanish sospires, my french heighes, mine Italian dulcets, my dutch hovez, my doobl releas, my hy reachez, my fine feyning, my deep diapason, my wanton-warblz, my running, my tyming, my tuning and my twynkling, I can gracify the matter az well az the proudest of them.[39]

It is a little unlikely that the prestigious and elderly Patten or the married Langham (who never wrote a word of literature, as far as we know) would have allowed themselves to become figures of fun by swooning over some noble lady in a furious effort to impress her by singing and dancing.

The idiolect or personal vocabulary of the *Letter* writer contains far more dialect than Patten's previous works, though, strangely, Patten's subsequent writing is more assimilated to that of the writer of the *Letter*. The spelling in his letter to Burghley apologizing for the trick on Langham, in a mourning ditty of 1579, in a letter to Francis Walsingham of 1580, and in the *Deus Iudicium* of 1583 is in every case closer to that of R.L. of Kenilworth than the spelling in his *Expedicion* or his *Calender of Scripture*, the latter of which, it should be noted, was published only shortly before the Kenilworth progress. Some compelling cause must be found for his sudden change of practice.

Editors who have had doubts about the probability of Patten being R.L. have tended to revert to the notion that Robert Langham was after all the true author. But this is the wrong move to make. We should rule out Langham first, on the basis of Patten's letter to Burghley, and the mismatch of Langham's persona to R.L.'s. Two items not yet investigated should serve to give this mismatch even greater prominence. One is the remark near the end of the *Letter* 'ye marvell perchaunce to see me so bookish'.[40] In the course of his *Letter*, the author has shown himself well-versed in mythology, has quoted Latin, cited authorities for his brief introductory history of Kenilworth. Clearly, readers were likely to find this puzzling when they compared it with what they knew of the historical Langham, and the (pseudo)-explanation is thrown in to deflect suspicion. The other is the matter of Langham's apprenticeship. R.L. remarks that his master was called 'Bomsted'.[41] Christopher Bompsted *could* have been Langham's master when he was an apprentice in the Mercers, but in fact he was not. Langham was apprenticed to William Leonard.[42] The writer of the *Letter* seems rather hazy on the facts of his own life – perhaps because the life he purports to be recalling is not his.

We should then proceed to rule out Patten as well. And yet … Patten does seem to have had a hand in the affair.[43] I suggest the cause of his taking up the Warwickshire dialect so suddenly was his shared authorship of R.L.'s *Letter*. He took on the persona and voice of the literary page boy, partly because he assumed responsibility for the *Letter*, partly because he wrote some parts of it himself, and had to chime with the voice of the boy who wrote the bulk of it; and he was then stuck with using the odd orthography for the sake of consistency.

There are two pieces of internal evidence relevant to the degree of Patten's involvement. One is marginal – literally. It is a marginal note in the Huntington Library copy of 'Langham's Letter'. To the side of the paragraph on the ballads is written, opposite 'Bonny lass upon a green', 'Watkyn a miller is 'tis?' i.e. 'Is "Bonny lass upon a green" the same ballad as "Watkyn a miller"?'[44] The handwriting (of this and the rest of the handwritten notes, which are trivial corrections) appears to be the same as that of the letter of apology from Patten to Burghley. Therefore, we deduce, it is Patten who asks: is ballad x the same as ballad y? Why would he need to ask this? Because he, unlike the musical boy who had read them in Captain Cox's house, *did not know*. Unless there are two individuals involved, the question is incomprehensible. Recall the strong hint given that in telling Master Humfrey of his musical ability, R.L. has told him 'a great matter' ('Percyve ye me?' he asks, with a nudge and a wink). It was, presumably, a sure clue to his true identity.

The second item bearing on the question is this. We know from George Gascoigne's account, *The Princely Pleasures*, that it was Patten who devised one of the Latin poems describing in order the gifts 'from the gods' which the Queen had inspected in passing across a platform bridge set over dry land, leading from the Base Court to the inner gate.[45] The poem had been inscribed on a great Tablet, in white Roman letters on black, set over the Castle gate.[46] R.L. was later able to take it down in writing *only because the board on which it was written had not been removed.* Patten would not have had to rely on such luck to copy it 'at leyzure and pleasure': he must have had it in his own tablets or note-book, or by heart. The person who wrote this part of the *Letter* appears therefore to be another individual.

There is a possible 'last ditch' argument left for those who want to retain Patten as sole author for the Kenilworth *Letter.* Perhaps he wrote it *as though he were* a young Warwickshire boy snatched from near penury and given his chance in life shortly before 1575. Perhaps he imitated the Warwickshire voice of such a boy, and imaginatively recreated many details of his supposed life as a humble page of Leicester's, appointed to watch the door and manage the errands of the Council. To the question: 'Why might he have adopted this strange conceit?' one might conceivably answer: 'To obscure his identity'.

The supposition strikes me as marginally more credible than the arguments of creationists who believe God planted false fossil 'evidence' for evolution. Patten's identity is already obscured by the pretence that he is Langham. It complicates matters enormously to suppose that Patten only pretended to pretend to be Langham, while actually pretending to be Leicester's page. It would involve setting aside the plausible belief that in using the strange spelling system and novel vocabulary, the *Letter*'s writer spoke in his own voice, a Warwickshire dialect with a Warwickshire accent to match; and clinging to the implausible belief that Patten had suddenly decided, two months after finishing his *Calender*, to experiment with a new orthographical system.

More implausibility would follow. Patten must either have invented the persona of the sprightly page, or modelled it on a page boy currently in the household. The former is just possible, though the insight displayed by the elderly and elevated Patten into the mind and tastes of a lowly child is nearly incredible. To add to the factors already mentioned which seem to drive a wedge between Patten and the true author (the marginal note raising a question about the ballad; the need for a lucky opportunity to copy Patten's poem from the board), there is the evidence of the title page. It contains three lines of verse – two and a half lines of poorly made Latin hexameters, with a half-line from Virgil's eclogues tacked on. The half-line, 'Rumpantur et [orig. ut] ilia Codro', is interesting for its original context. In Virgil's eclogue 7, Thyrsis and Corydon stage a singing contest. Corydon begs the nymphs to endow him with a song as good as the ones Codrus sings. Thyrsis begs 'Arcadian shepherds' to crown a budding poet with ivy, so that 'Codrus may burst his guts with envy'.[47]

It could be that Patten is elegantly and economically introducing a budding new poet ('crescentem poetam', also referred to as 'vates futurus' – a future poet) to his public, under his (Patten's) aegis and guidance. *He* cannot be that incipient poet – he is an established writer, good enough to be on occasions a semi-official poet in Leicester's own 'court'.

, Who is this unknown genius? A second possible explanation for Patten's strange procedure (on the supposition that he was the author of the whole *Letter*) swings into focus here at the same time as it renders itself unlikely. Suppose Patten modelled his imaginary page on an actual page in the household: does that not *eo ipso* suggest that the real-life model had the literary and dramatizing skills shown in Patten's 'imaginary' page? Why not suppose, then, that a real boy had a hand in writing the *Letter* which is in his voice? Why not accept the statement at the opening of the *Letter* that he was given licence to be present at the events, on which he made notes; and the later statement that his notes on the festivities ran out, causing him to supplement the narrative with an account of his diurnal round?

Because a young page could not have displayed quite as much geographical, literary and historical knowledge as he does in the course of the account, it will be answered. Because he could not have engineered the work into print. Because no young boy could have written so well. Let me take the last point first.

Boys as young as eleven could write supremely polished letters in Elizabethan England. Edgar Fripp gives an example in Latin, with his own English translation, of one penned by the eleven-year-old Richard Quiney to his father Richard Quiney of Stratford, probably in 1598.[48] Even in the English translation, it is possible to grasp the sophistication of the little boy, and it is a marvel to think of his competence in Latin. He has even thrown in a quotation from Cicero, 'a teneris ... unguiculis', 'from tender soft nails', meaning 'from one's tenderest youth'.

> To his most loving father, Master Richard Quinye,
> Richard Quinye the son bids very good health.
> With all respect, nay, rather with filial affection towards thee, my father, I give thanks for all those kindnesses which thou hast bestowed upon me; also I pray and beseech thee that thou wouldst provide for my brother and me two paper books, which we very much want at this present time; for if we had them we should truly find great use for them; and moreover, I give thee thanks that 'from tender soft nails', as they say, unto this day thou hast instructed me in the studies of Sacred Learning. Far from my poor words be even a suspicion of flattery, for I deem not any one of my friends to be dearer

or more loving of me than thou art. And earnestly I pray that that surpassing love of thine may remain as always hitherto; and although I am not able to repay thy kindnesses, nevertheless I shall wish thee from my heart of hearts all prosperity. Farewell.

Thy little son most obedient unto thee
Richard Quinye.

The brother mentioned as needing a writing book was probably Thomas, even younger, nine and a half, and a good penman.

It is therefore by no means improbable that a lowly-born page in Leicester's service, one who could 'not be idl at ony hand in the world', as we read in the *Letter*'s opening, and therefore lapped up all he could learn, could have produced an account such as the *Letter* in collaboration with a mentor (Patten). He does not have the polished spelling of the son of a gentleman, he is not writing in a classic style. But that is what we should expect from someone whose education was proceeding somewhat erratically.

The other two objections to my hypothesis on R.L.'s identity have, in a way, been dealt with already. I have allowed that Patten played a large part in the publication of the *Letter*, and he may have done so in its composition too. His would have been the guiding hand in the historical account of Kenilworth; his too the inspiration for the numerological reflections on the number one and the number two.

I do not mean to imply that the page boy's existence, still less his shared authorship, has passed straight from being merely postulated to being proved. At the beginning of the next chapter, I shall set out the conditions which the hypothesis would have to meet before becoming acceptable. At this point, I take the licence of temporarily treating the hypothesis as true, and sketching the ways in which collaboration between the learned Patten and the bright unlearned page could have operated. For there is a third aspect of the work, its semi-concealed antipathy to the Queen, in which it is difficult to know how much irony to ascribe to the young author, and how much to the more worldly Patten.

Susan Frye has described the tensions between Leicester and his monarch during the 1575 visit as 'the competition for representation'.[49] I have just alluded to them as the 'antipathy' of the Leicester faction, which implies something more seditious than the struggle of wills between Elizabeth and Dudley discerned by Frye. Let me give Frye's examples first with the added commentary of R.L., before adding an item from the *Letter* which Frye did not notice, and which might vindicate the harsher label for the Leicestrian attitude to Elizabeth.

One incident from the Kenilworth festivities which Gascoigne dared not include but referred to as too plain to need explication was the mock-wedding of the country bride, so clearly, as Frye notes, a burlesque on Elizabeth and her would-be husband Leicester. R.L. has no such inhibitions, and goes into the 'particularities'.

A country girl, neither young nor beautiful, and her bumpkin groom proceeded on ambling horses in the sweating heat to be presented to the Queen.[50] The groom wore a straw hat with a crown 'steepl wyze' on his head, harvest gloves to signify his good husbandry, a tawny jacket of his father's, and at his girdle a muffler for a napkin (kerchief) lent by his mother. He had a pen and inkhorn at his back 'for he woold be knowen to be bookish'. A red-headed yokel was plucked from the crowd to act as cup-bearer to the couple. He was found to be 'a meet actor for hiz office', probably because of his red head: for the red-headed Philip Sidney was currently cup-bearer to the Queen. The Queen would not watch all this, we learn, ostensibly because she was still watching dancing in the hall, and the couple arrived too early – 'yet waz it a four a clok', says R.L. knowingly.[51] Here it seems quite possible that the page would have understood the satirical nature of the ceremony, and why the Queen might have made the feeble excuse.

In the second example, R.L. seems less socially aware. The Kenilworth troupe kept trying to put on a play about the nymph Zabeta, who graciously agreed to a marriage. The real '[Eli]Zabeta' seems to have done everything to avoid having this staged: marriage to Leicester was not on *her* agenda. On the day it should have been performed, says R.L., there was 'such earnest tallk and appointment of remooving that I gave over my notyng, and harkened after my hors'.[52]

R.L. gives no hint that he connects the non-performance of the Zabeta play with the talk of 'removal' – of the Queen's, and with her the Court's, premature departure. He ascribes the non-performance of the play to the inclement weather, as does George Gascoigne; but the latter overdoes his explanation to such an extent that it is clearly done tongue-in-cheek. 'This shewe was devised and penned by M. Gascoigne, and being prepared and redy (every Actor in his garment) two or three dayes together, yet never came to execution, The cause whereof I cannot attribute to any other thing, then to lack of opportunitie, and seasonable weather. The Queenes Majestie hasting her departure from thence ....'[53] It is actually in Gascoigne's account, in this case, that we perceive the degree of the Queen's fury over the pressure to marry. He connects her departure with the play by the simple expedient of juxtaposing two sentences in his text. Later he depicts himself running along at her stirrup, improvising poetry as he does so, trying to dissuade her from leaving in a huff.

The phenomenon of the clocks on two sides of the tower known as Caesar's Tower is reported by R.L. only. It shows very clearly how offence is subtly offered to the Queen in the *Letter* under the guise of homage: but whether R.L. or Patten should be held responsible for the tone in this case is hard to divine. The bell of the clock in the Tower had apparently been silenced for the duration of the Queen's stay. What R.L. professes to find somewhat miraculous is this: the two hands of the clock-faces that adorned the east and south sides of the Tower at Kenilworth had also stopped, 'poynting too just too a clok, still at too a clok'. R.L. sees this as highly significant:

> That thiz thing amoong the rest waz for full signifiauns of hiz Lordships honorabl, frank, freendly and noble hart toward all estatez. Which, whither cum they to stay and take cheer, or streight to returne: too see or too be seen: cum they for duty to her Majesty or loove too hiz Lordship, or for both: Cum they early or late: For hiz Lordships part, they cum allweyz all at too a clok, een jump at too a clok: That iz to say, in good hart, good acceptauns, in amitee, and freendly welcome.[54]

How is the number 2 connected with welcome? Or with frankness? R.L. has, to be sure, shown that things that come in pairs, such as 'appls and pearz', signify 'freendly conjunction'; though sometimes, as he admits, they signify 'contraryez'. Suddenly we get the point: his example is ironic. 'Two-faced' is the opposite of frank. Leicester is in fact double-dyed in falsehood: his two-faced clocks (pointing to two o'clock) face two ways. His 'welcome' involved an attempt to force the Queen into marriage. Add to this the potential *lèse majesté* of the suggestion that the population comes to see the Queen out of duty, and to see Leicester out of love, and we begin to understand the degree of outrage caused by the lively account. The 'calling in' of copies was probably *not* due to the umbrage taken by the unimportant Langham.

The balance of probability suggests the existence of a young page from a humble background, with musical and literary talent, at Kenilworth, in 1575, with the pseudonym R.L. Can we guess his real name? Perhaps, if we are prepared to take puns seriously. After the great linguistic flight concerning his music-making and dancing to impress his mistress, R.L. takes his bow with: 'And thus have I tolld ye most of my trade the leeve long day: what wyll ye more, God save the Queen, and my Lord, I am well I thank yoo.'[55] The almost juxtaposed 'wyll' and 'well' recall the odd exclamation in an earlier sentence already quoted, 'allweyz amoong the Gentlewemen by my good wyll

(O ye know that cumz allweyz of a gentle spirit)'. Is that perhaps word-play on 'will' also? And now that we reflect on it, was not the other instance of his name in the text oddly phrased: 'Ile set the more by my selfe whyle my name iz Lanham'? 'Whyle' is yet another possible Will. So is 'I'll' ('I will'). And possibly too a joke lies concealed in the suggestion that his name 'Lanham' is temporary.

The best clue comes last in the text. After the final signature – 'R.L. Gent. Mercer' – there is a four-line Latin poem. Its heading is 'DE MAIESTATE REGIA', and on the line below that is the word 'Benigno'. Kuin translates: 'Of the Queen's Majesty', correctly; and then 'In gratitude' – incorrectly, I think. 'Benignus' means 'well-intentioned' or 'kindly'. My translation would be 'for' or 'by Good Will'.

Curiouser and curiouser, as Lewis Carroll's Alice said. For there was another young Will, aged eleven in 1575, living not far off in Stratford – a boy called William Shakespeare. He too had a great poetic gift – at least he had when in his late twenties, according to the consensus. It beggars belief that he should not have displayed some glimmerings of it at an early age. He was musical too, the composer of some of the most beautiful songs in the language ('Fear no more the heat o' the sun' in *Cymbeline*; 'When that I was but a little tiny boy' in the play punningly subtitled 'What you will'). He declared that 'the man that hath no music in himself,/ Nor is not mov'd with concord of sweet sounds,/ Is fit for treasons, stratagems, and spoils'.[56]

Vladimir Nabokov wrote: 'Some law of logic should fix the number of coincidences, in a given domain, after which they cease to be coincidences, and form, instead, the living organism of a new truth'.[57] In the cases of R.L. and William Shakespeare we are nearing that critical point at which the missing law of logic should dictate that the coincidence is no coincidence: that the page R.L. and William Shakespeare of Stratford, son of John Shakespeare and Mary Arden, are one and the same person. Unfortunately, no such Nabokovian law to circumscribe the sphere of the non-coincidental has been officially declared.

Notes

1   *A Letter whearin, part of the entertainment untoo the Queenz Maiesty, at Killingwoorth Castl, in warwik Sheer, in this soomerz Progress. 1575, iz signified: from a freend officer attendant in Coourt, untoo hiz freend a Citizen, and Merchaunt of London* (no publication details). *Robert Langham, A Letter*, ed. R.J.P. Kuin (Leiden: E.J. Brill, 1983).

2   Kuin, *Letter*, Introduction, pp. 1–3; Katherine Duncan-Jones, *Sir Philip Sidney, Courtier Poet* (London: Hamish Hamilton, 1991), pp. 87–91. Derek Wilson believes Dudley was

encouraging the Queen to marry Alençon at this point, though the evidence he cites plainly contradicts his own view, and points to Dudley as the intended consort: *Sweet Robin: A Biography of Robert Dudley, Earl of Leicester, 1533–1588* (1981; London: Allison and Busby, 1997), pp. 221–4.

3   See Jean Wilson, 'Why Fotheringhay? The Location of the Trial and Execution of Mary, Queen of Scots', *Renaissance Journal* 2.2 (June 2004), pp. 3–31, esp. 9, 17–18.

4   Wilson, *Sweet Robin*, pp. 6–7, 38–44, 54–65.

5   George Gascoigne, *The Princely Pleasures at the Courte at Kenelwoorth* (London: Richard Jhones, 1576). The edition is lost, the first reprint being the source document for modern readers: *The Whole Woorkes of George Gascoigne* (London: Abel Jeffes, 1587). *Princely Pleasures* is unpaged, but following from p. 296. Late eighteenth- and early nineteenth-century editors such as J. Nichols *(The Progresses ... of Queen Elizabeth*, London, 1788), vol. 1; *Kenilworth Illustrated* (Chiswick: C. Whittingham, 1821), extracted from Wm Dugdale, *The Antiquities of Warwickshire* (London: Thomas Warren, 1656); and *British Stage*, vol. 6 (1821) (London: F. Marshall, 1822), still had access to Jones's edition. Reference here will be to John W. Cunliffe's two-volume *Complete Works of George Gascoigne* (Cambridge: Cambridge University Press, 1907–10), 2, pp. 91–131.

6   Kuin's edition is the text used for reference. Occasional reference is made to *Robert Laneham: A Letter (1575)*, ed. R.C. Alston (Menston: Scolar, 1968), a facsimile of the Huntington copy. It reproduces Edition B of the original, retaining hand-written marginal notes, while Kuin follows Edition A. These were probably two almost-contemporaneous printings.

7   Kuin, *Letter*, p. 36.

8   As noted by E.J. Dobson in his *English Pronunciation 1500–1700*, 2 vols (1957; Oxford: Clarendon Press, 1968), 1.88–93.

9   Sir Walter Scott, *Kenilworth* (1821), ed. Ernest Rhys (1906; London: Dent, 1929), pp. 198–200.

10   Scott, *Kenilworth*, p. 199.

11   *Acts of the Privy Council*, ed. J.R. Dasent, 32 vols (London: HMSO, 1890–1907), n.s. 11, 445.

12   Kuin, *Letter*, p. 77.

13   *Letter*, Introduction, pp. 13–15.

14   William A. Jackson was the first sceptic, in *The Carl H. Pforzheimer Library. English Literature 1475–1700*, 3 vols (New York: privately printed, 1940), 2.600. Brian O'Kill argued strongly that William Patten was the author: 'The Printed Works of William Patten (c.1510–c.1600)', *TCBS* 7.1 (1977), pp. 28–45. Simultaneously, David Scott dealt the Langham hypothesis what should have been a death blow. See his 'William Patten and the Authorship of "Robert Laneham's *Letter*" (1575)', *ELR* 7.3 (Autumn 1977), pp. 297–306.

15   David Scott, 'William Patten', 301, cites Hatfield House MSS, Cecil Papers 8/52. (B.L. microfilm M.485/2).

16   Kuin argues that Patten's letter to Burleigh must refer, not to Langham's *Letter*, but to some no-longer-existing parody by Patten of an original by Langham. See 'The Purloined Letter: Evidence and Probability Regarding Robert Langham's Authorship', *The Library*, 6th series, vol. 7.2 (June 1985), pp. 115–25. The timing makes Kuin's theory extremely precarious.

17   Not reproduced in Cunliffe's edition. See Kuin, *Letter*, intro., pp. 9–10.

18   *Letter*, pp. 39, 39–40, 46.

19   Kuin, 'The Purloined Letter'; Duncan-Jones, *Courtier Poet*, pp. 92–4.
20   The name is here spelled 'Lanham' in Kuin's A edition (copies at the Bodleian, Harvard, and Emmanuel College, Cambridge), 'Laneham' in Kuin's B (copies at the British Library, the Bodleian, Huntington, Illinois and elsewhere).
21   Kuin, *Letter*, p. 78.
22   *Letter*, p. 80.
23   Ibid.
24   Kuin has the backing of the investigation of E.J. Dobson, who in his *English Pronunciation* also concluded that the *Letter*'s spelling was rather loose and inconsistent to be a serious attempt at a reformed spelling system. See note 8 above.
25   O'Kill does an excellent job of reclaiming his biography. See note 14 above.
26   For Scott's article, see note 14 above.
27   Kuin *Letter*, p. 37.
28   *Letter*, p. 74.
29   *Letter*, p. 64. The minstrel episode occupies pp. 59–64.
30   *Letter*, pp. 53–4.
31   *Letter*, p. 71.
32   *Letter*, p. 72.
33   *Letter*, p. 77.
34   *Letter*, p. 76.
35   *Letter*, p. 78.
36   British Library, N. Tab. 2026/25. (19).
37   Kuin, *Letter*, p. 79.
38   *Letter*, pp. 78–9.
39   *Letter*, p. 79. 'Gloit' is probably a dialect word, otherwise unknown but comparable with the word 'gloat', defined in the *OED* as casting flirting sidelong glances. 'Gracify' is unique, but occurs twice in the *Letter*.
40   *Letter*, p. 79.
41   *Letter*, p. 36.
42   Muriel Bradbrook, *The Rise of the Common Player: A Study of Actor and Society in Shakespeare's England* (London: Chatto and Windus, 1962), ch. 6, p. 145 and note p. 301.
43   O'Kill lists the following items common to Patten's earlier works and the *Letter*: the belief that English is mainly derived from German; the deriving of 'Elizabeth' from the Hebrew 'seventh of our God'; the interest in numerology, and abstruse Anglo-Saxon vocabulary. He plausibly suggests the jokes against inhabitants of Islington in a section of the *Letter* could have been prompted by Patten's having established himself as Lord of the Manor of neighbouring Stoke Newington.
44   *A Letter (1575)*, ed. Alston, p. 35.
45   *Princely Pleasures*, in *Works*, p. 4.
46   Kuin, *Letter*, p. 42.
47   *Virgil: The Eclogues and Georgics*, ed. R.D. Williams (1979; London: Duckworth for the Bristol Classical Press, 1996), p. 17, lines 21–8.
48   Edgar Fripp, *Shakespeare's Stratford* (London: Oxford University Press, 1928), pp. 34–5.
49   Susan Frye, *The Competition for Representation* (New York and Oxford: Oxford University Press, 1993).
50   The passage comes from Kuin, *Letter*, pp. 49–52.
51   *Letter*, p. 55.

52 *Letter*, p. 59.
53 Gascoigne, *Works*, p. 120.
54 Kuin, *Letter*, p. 74.
55 *Letter*, p. 79.
56 William Shakespeare, *Merchant of Venice*, V.1.83–5. All Shakespeare citations will be from the modern Arden editions.
57 Nabokov, *Ada*, p. 283.

Chapter 2

Supposes

Though it is admitted by all Shakespeare scholars that we know nothing of William Shakespeare's early life, the idea that the bright son of a humble but respected burgher of Stratford and his socially more elevated wife could have been placed in service nearby with the Earl of Leicester at the tender age of nine or ten will be resisted fiercely. It already has been resisted by the critic Brian O'Kill. Pondering Patten's authorship of 'Langham's Letter', O'Kill confesses he feels there is some deeper joke which he cannot grasp: 'I am already, heaven help me, beginning to wonder about the significance of the reputed presence at the Kenilworth festivities of an imaginative youngster from nearby Stratford'.[1] Daunted by the enormity of the implications, O'Kill does no more wondering.

The thought repressed so firmly by O'Kill will be given leave to blossom in the rest of this book. Suppose the ambitious parents John Shakespeare and Mary Arden *did* place their brilliant son where he would have a chance of advancement in life – in the 'court' of the greatest courtier in the land, who happened to be their local patron. Suppose young William *did* start writing early, under the tutelage of the best writers in the land. Suppose he came to inhabit a peculiar position in that caste society, recognized as an equal talent to the revered poet Philip Sidney, yet irredeemably proletarian by birth. Suppose he supported not the Tudor dynasty but the Leicestrian cause. The two would coincide only if Leicester succeeded in marrying the Queen.

I shall now begin to examine those 'Supposes', dealing in this chapter with material that relates to 1572–78. In giving a list of the things that would have to hold true if the suppositions are right (as promised in the previous chapter), I am in fact sketching the contents of this chapter.

We should expect the historical evidence on the state of John Shakespeare's finances in 1575 to be compatible with the Kenilworth R.L.'s remarks on his 'poor father'. This point will be addressed first: evidence assembled by Park Honan will be used to illuminate John Shakespeare's situation.[2]

We should expect Shakespeare's plays to contain some memories of the Kenilworth events of 1575 and of R.L.'s life in the Kenilworth household. *Midsummer Night's Dream* and *Macbeth* answer to this expectation, and will constitute the second section of the chapter. Reflections on *Macbeth* will lead directly into literary texts relating to Philip Sidney's death, *Hamlet* being one such work.

Then we might expect to find Shakespeare's hand in some of the later Leicestrian masques written for the Queen's Progresses; and some notice of the young prodigy in the work of Leicester's *de facto* master of ceremonies, Gascoigne. The third section of this chapter deals with these points. I look at an anonymous entertainment called 'The Queenes Majesties entertainment at Woodstock' from later in 1575, together with its relationship to George Gascoigne's *Hemetes the Heremyte* (Hermit) performed on the same occasion, and a poem, *The Hermits Tale*, printed much later.

Philip Sidney must quickly have become aware of the presence of the budding poet in his uncle's 'court', if the main hypothesis is correct. (Philip had returned from his European travels only shortly before the 1575 royal visit to Kenilworth.) I shall go on to suggest a developing relationship between the anonymous author of the Woodstock entertainment and Philip; and a much altered appreciation of R.L. on Philip's part in the masque he devised for another royal visit in 1578, the 'Lady of May'. The character 'Espilus' is the focus of suspicion here.

Gabriel Harvey, the socially ambitious Cambridge don whose literary pretensions were mocked by Thomas Nashe, was already in the Earl of Leicester's service in 1578. So he joins the group of writers whom we must suppose should have noticed Shakespeare, if the latter was a young servant of Leicester's. Though published long after 1578, one of Harvey's pamphlets, *Pierces Supererogation* (1593), is here investigated because it appears to look back to Shakespeare's childhood – and to place him where our Suppose places him, in the heart of the Dudley/Sidney nexus. I examine the *Supererogation*'s relation to Shakespeare's *Dream* and his *Comedy of Errors.*

Two more general propositions about the attitudes one would expect to find permeating plays written by one who served Dudley and was right at the centre of the charmed Sidney circle will receive some discussion at the end of this chapter, though more material on each is reserved for Chapters 4, 6 and 9.

The first is this: we would expect to find a strongly Protestant slant to Shakespeare's earliest plays, since Dudley, his putative master, was so fervent in the Protestant cause. Secondly, considering the 'great expectations' of Philip Sidney,[3] whom Dudley had made his heir at a time when Dudley himself hoped to become the Queen's consort, the young Shakespeare would surely have pinned his hopes on the coming to power of a dynasty that would eventually bring about a Golden Age ruled by a philosopher- or poet-King (Philip Sidney) with young Mary Sidney as quasi-consort. We might suppose that Shakespeare would love to portray banished or self-exiled rulers and their courts. And so he does.[4]

A brief explanation of my choice of the noun 'Supposes' should be supplied, before I start the trail of detection that leads through each 'Suppose'. The word was used by George Gascoigne in the title of his translation of *I suppositi* by Ariosto. (Gascoigne completed *The Supposes* in 1566, published it in 1573, and it was reprinted in the first edition of Gascoigne's complete works in 1587.) It is particularly applicable to my theme for two reasons. The first reason is Gascoigne's own definition of the word, which is cognate with 'substitution'. He defines it as the mistaking of identity, 'a mystaking or imagination of one thing for an other'. Many of the pseudonyms in this study are purloined names or aliases. Secondly, as is well known, *The Supposes* is the source for the sub-plot of Shakespeare's *Taming of the Shrew*, an early play of which the framing story is pure Warwickshire. The rustic Christopher Sly found in a drunken state as the play opens insists on his identity as a humble denizen of Warwickshire, citing the existence of his neighbours in the villages around Stratford, and the inner story that constitutes the main plot is all set notionally within the household of the Warwickshire lord where poor Christopher is gulled into believing he is a noble.

Our first Suppose falls in the non-literary domain of Stratford records. The Kenilworth R.L.'s father was 'relieved' and 'fared much better' when appointed to serve the Kenilworth stables, we noted. It looks as though he had been in financial straits. So if R.L. was William Shakespeare, John Shakespeare's fortunes should have followed a similar pattern. They did.[5]

John had risen to prominence in Stratford, holding office as an alderman in 1565 and High Bailiff of the borough in 1568. He was still a justice and deputy bailiff in 1572, but apparently held no office after that. There are signs of trouble before 1572. He was accused twice in 1570 of breaking usury laws. This may not have set him back him too much, but it was followed in 1572 with two summonses before the Royal Exchequer for illegal wool dealing, and a summons for a debt of £30 in 1573. Yet in 1575, John paid £40 to Edmund and Emma Hall for two houses with gardens and orchards at Stratford. He had already inherited, bought or leased a large amount of land, twenty-two acres of it being grazing land.

Honan follows other historians in presenting the 1575 purchase as part of John's continuing pattern of acquisition. But John had bought nothing new for some years, and the purchase from the Halls could as easily be represented as the result of a sudden resurgence in his fortunes after some difficult years of litigation and a decline in public prestige since 1572. It was in 1575 or 1576 that he applied to the College of Heralds for a grant of arms as a gentleman. That application came to nothing at that time, and John's fortunes declined sharply from 1576.

If John did indeed see a temporary bettering of his position around 1575, such as to enable him to think of himself (a humble glover, wool trader, and grazier, for all that he had held public office) suddenly as a potential gentleman, his candidacy for the position of father to the R.L. of Kenilworth gains credibility. A prominent but financially encumbered grazier from Stratford could well have provided horses, or other goods for that matter, to Robert Dudley's stables. We might pause to wonder, though, whether one who had not gained the status of a gentleman could have placed his son in quite such a privileged position as page in the Kenilworth household. Shakespeare's social rank is a matter that will become gradually plainer as this study progresses.

A late piece of evidence concerning Shakespeare's entry into service of some sort comes from the seventeenth-century chronicler David Lloyd. Writing of Fulke Greville, the poet friend of Philip Sidney's who became Lord Brooke, Lloyd remarks on Greville's 'desiring to be known to posterity under no other notions than of Shakespear's and Ben Johnson's Master, Chancellor Egerton's patron, Bishop Overal's Lord, and Sir Philip Sidney's friend'.[6] There seems no possible ulterior motive for Lloyd's remarking on what he obviously took to be common knowledge. And the labels are suggestive: 'patron' to the more gentlemanly Egerton; 'Master' to the two well-known writers, who were humbly born. Presumably Greville claimed to have set them up in life, opened the route to their first employment.

Greville took a keen interest in the affairs of Stratford, to the extent of persuading his cousin Edward Greville, Lord of the Manor of Stratford, to withdraw his opposition to a bailiff elected in 1592.[7] In a society which functioned through patronage, it is quite conceivable that he should have searched out likely boys to employ, and to press into the service of the greatest local lord. We have a restricted understanding of the nets of affiliation that then operated. We tend to think of linear employment; whereas it is clear that one could at that time be a student, for instance, at Oxford or Cambridge, and still be 'Lord Somebody's man' (as Marlowe clearly was). Even teachers at the universities were sometimes 'signed off' for a period, and sent out on some lord's employ, as Richard Madox, a Fellow of All Souls, Oxford, was in 1582.[8]

So it makes sense to think of Shakespeare as finding a niche within this system. We know how he later made bids for the Earl of Southampton's favour, by dedicating his narrative poems *Venus and Adonis* and *Lucrece* to him in

1593 and 1594. By that time, all the powerful male Dudleys and Sidneys were dead, and he must have needed a new source of protection. But before that, he must have been part of some patronage circle, for nobody was completely outside one.

Meredith Skura has remarked how Shakespeare tends to set his plays not in the capital, as we might expect from one who (so all believe) worked in London from an early age as an actor, but rather in great country houses.[9] She imagines it was a matter of habit with playwrights of the 1590s to hark back to an era when plays were constructed for performance in the great houses, when one lord's servants would take their entertainment on tour to the houses of other peers. Far from being a nostalgic throwback, I am arguing, Shakespeare composed and performed some of those comedies much earlier, when still in a great house. The settings of those comedies that were written later were not selected to flatter the aristocrats who were to hear the plays, but arose from the depths of Shakespeare's psyche: they reverberate with his own recollections of childhood.

One tiny clue is of huge potential importance in this respect: Honan has noticed that the single building most often mentioned by Shakespeare is Julius Caesar's Tower.[10] Editors take this to mean the Tower of London, and wonder why it had such a hold on Shakespeare's imagination. I suggest it was because the Kenilworth tower, the one with the two-faced clocks, was also called 'Caesar's Tower'. In *Richard III*, the young prince Edward asks childlike but probing questions about 'Julius Caesar's Tower' (the Tower of London): How do we know it is Caesar's? Did Caesar build it? Is it a question of recorded history or oral tradition?[11] Young R.L. too had pondered the derivation of the name, as we saw above. The repetition (for that is what I claim it to be) is one of those involuntary little betrayals of one's private frame of reference that a writer finds it impossible to avoid.

We turn now to search for echoes of the Kenilworth events in Shakespeare's plays. Various editors of *Midsummer Night's Dream* have observed that young William could perhaps have witnessed some of the events of 1575. They are prompted to this observation by Oberon's description of a mermaid on a dolphin's back. It is highly reminiscent of a 'happening' that took place at Kenilworth on the evening of 18 July 1575, a fantastic display on the Mere that lapped the castle on two sides. Here is R.L.'s description.

After hunting, 'her highness returning: cam thear upon a swimming Mermayd (that from top too tayl waz an eyghteen foot long) *Triton, Neptunes* blaster', i.e. a Triton figure, who is Neptune's trumpeter, and either is a mermaid shape, or, we later find, is riding on a mermaid '... whoo, with his trumpet foormed of a wrinkled wealk [whelk], az her Majesty waz in sight, gave soound very shrill and sonoroous, in sign he had an ambassy too pronoouns'.[12] Her Majesty deigning to approach the lake, the Lady of the Lake appeared and offered the Queen a gift:

> ...which was *Arion* that excellent and famouz Muzicien ... ryding aloft upon hiz olld freend the Dolphin, (that from hed too tayl waz a foour and twenty foot long) and swymd hard by theez Ilands: heerwith Arion ... after a feaw well coouched woords untoo her Majesty of thanks gyving ... beegan a delectabl ditty of a song wel apted too a melodioous noiz, compoounded of six severall instruments al coovert [hidden], casting soound from the Dolphins belly within, *Arion* the seaventh sittyng thus singing (az I say) withoout.[13]

Here is Shakespeare's version. Oberon says to Puck –

> My gentle Puck, come hither. Thou remember'st
> Since once I sat upon a promontory,
> And heard a mermaid on a dolphin's back
> Uttering such dulcet and harmonious breath,
> That the rude sea grew civil at her song,
> And certain stars shot madly from their spheres
> To hear the sea-maid's music.
>   (II.1.148–54)

It might be objected that a mermaid on a dolphin's back cannot be a poetic reminiscence of a triton on a mermaid compounded with Arion on a dolphin. But poetry can blend events either inadvertently (as memory often does) or for poetic effect. And in all cases of semi-covert allusion, as Annabel Patterson has argued, the writer making the allusion is likely to aim off exactitude in order not to be too blatant.[14] If the attitude of Leicester's servants to their monarch was as disaffected as I have begun to suggest, the obliquity of reference should become as comprehensible to us as it was necessary to the writer. Fear of making too patent an allusion to events at Kenilworth, on stage or in print, would have persisted throughout Elizabeth's reign

Shakespeare had, when older (whatever he comprehended as a boy), intimate knowledge of the fraught politics of the 1575 Kenilworth visit. To be sure, he could have learned of many details of the visit without having been present – from locals, or from Gascoigne's 1576 publication. But it is unlikely, in my view, that had he been a mere plebeian outsider, he could have tuned in quite so acutely to the vibrating tensions in the Kenilworth atmosphere as I

hope to show he does in the *Dream* and in *Macbeth.* The *hoi polloi* were banned
from all observation of the events, we learn from R.L.'s account. Speaking
of the gods who presided so benevolently over the proceedings, R.L. has
Saturn's niece Pallas make sure that 'no unruly body or disquiet, disturb the
nobl assemblee, or els ons be so bolld too enter within the Castl gatez'.[15] (It
is clear that R.L. is casting the noble Dudleys as Olympian gods here. Saturn
must be Ambrose Dudley, Robert's brother, since R.L. gives him a lame leg,
which Ambrose did have, but Saturn did not. 'Pallas' must be young Mary
Sidney.) R.L. was granted 'poour … to be prezent at any sheaw or spectacl'
– he was given *special* permission, and witnessed things that ordinary local
people could not have witnessed.

Yet Shakespeare the dramatist not only knows of the events, but also seems
to grasp their political import. The passage on the mermaid quoted above
becomes still more evocative of that evening at Kenilworth in July 1575 as
Oberon proceeds to recall how 'that very time, I saw, though couldst not/Cupid
…'. The love god took a shaft and fired it at an 'imperial votaress' who passed
on, fancy-free. (Could it be that 'Puck' could not see this incident because he
was then a mere child, ignorant of the swirling emotions and intrigues around
him?) What a gracious compliment to Elizabeth, say the critics. The poet
recalls, obliquely, the suit of Leicester to the Queen, and delicately by-steps
the failure of the Earl's ambitious marriage plans. But maybe the poet was
recalling something much more sinister.

There was an assassination attempt during the Kenilworth visit. The Spanish
agent was there, and he mentions it twice in dispatches. Someone shot with
a crossbow at the Queen while she was hunting. The agent not only reports
this, but follows it up with the remark that he can get little information about
the prisoner (the man arrested for the attempt) as no-one dares say a word.[16]
Historians are strangely loath to believe the agent. Frye says there is no
corroborating evidence. Kuin speculates that the awkward incident when the
Savage Man stepped out and snapped his stick, causing the Queen's horse to
shy, and the Queen to cry 'No hurt', must have given rise to a garbled tale about
an attack.[17] But consider the following items from the Kenilworth catalogue
of 'happenings' during the July visit, and ask yourself whether they do not
remind you of another play of Shakespeare's.

When the Queen reached the first gate of the Castle on her arrival, a
doorman acted the role of a grumpy porter. He complained about all the toing
and froing, the noise and the knocking, and then, seeing the Queen, pretended
to start and declared that he could not refuse entrance to such a virgin.[18]
Referring to Gascoigne's account, we find that the Porter is supposed to be

Hercules, and that his speech included a claim to be 'a Porter, not a Paper (i.e. papist).[19]

Much later in his account, R.L. mentions something he quite forgot to relate in its proper place. There were three 'hags' who greeted the Queen on the first night, acting the Parcae (the three Fates of the classical world). 'The Parcae (az earst I shoold have sayd) the first night of her Maiestiez cumming: they heering & seeing so precious adoo heer at a place unlookt for, in an uplondish cuntree so far within the Ream [realm] ....'[20]

A monarch comes to the castle of the greatest subject of the realm, and is welcomed most kindly. There are three weird sisters in uplandish country. There is a Porter unwilling to open the doors: he rails against papists.

The porter in *Macbeth* pretends to be the porter of the gates of Hell (as was Hercules). Disturbed by all the knocking at the door on the morning after Duncan's murder, he rails against various types including 'equivocators', who are Jesuits. 'I pray you, remember the porter' are his final words. Shakespeare did, it seems, with his anti-papist porter. He remembered the three weird sisters. He remembered an assassination plot.

These innuendoes are quite misplaced, Shakespeareans will say. *Macbeth* was written in 1605/6 to please James I.[21] Banquo was supposedly James's ancestor, and Banquo is blameless in Shakespeare's story (though not in the histories). The porter's Jesuits and their equivocations are an allusion to the Gunpowder Plot of 1605, the blame for which was being placed on Catholics.

But *Macbeth* was not written in 1606. It was written before 1600. For William Kemp undoubtedly refers to it in his *Kemps Nine Daies Wonder*, an account of a nine-day journey he made from London to Norwich, jigging and dancing all the way.[22] The book contains an appended humble request to 'the impudent generation of Ballad-makers and their coherents', and opens 'My notable Shakerags'. The proper noun sounds like a plural, and appears at first sight to be the 'generation' and their 'coherents'. But it is strongly evocative of one particular surname. Since Robert Greene could use 'Shake-scene' in the confident knowledge that his audience would discern Shakespeare in the text, it is likely that Kemp knew his audience would recognize this 'Shakerags'.[23]

Kemp, in his own story, is looking for someone who had maligned him. His search turns towards 'a proper vpright youth, onely for a little stooping in the shoulders: all hart to the heele, a penny Poet whose first making was the miserable stolne story of Macdoel, or Macdobeth, or Macsomewhat: for I am sure a Mac it was, though I never had the maw to see it' (D3v). The witty substitution of 'maw' for the expected 'stomach', continuing the 'mac' pun, distracts us from one important clue here: the word 'see'. It implies a performance rather than a text.[24]

The 'vpright youth' directs Kemp to the Bankside – clearly we are in the sphere of plays and actors. A fat filthy apprentice heaps abuse on the youth in his absence. Kemp is astounded: 'I hardly beleeved, this youth that I tooke to be gracious, had bin so graceles: but I heard afterwards his mother in law was eye and eare witnes of his fathers abuse by this blessed childe on a publique stage, in a merry Hoast of an Innes part' (D3v).

It is difficult to get the precise gist of the jokes at this distance. But it does seem that the youth, whose first work was 'Macdobeth', is here supposed to have been maligning his own father *in a play* (a Falstaffian play, where the hostess of an inn features largely?) Later in this study, external evidence from two other literary sources will help place the composition of *Macbeth* before 1592, which would explain why the youth who wrote it is in Kemp's eyes now rather an *old* lad, stooping in the shoulders. But for now I draw attention to two aspects of the work itself, one stylistic, one concerning its motivation.

The language is very Senecan, as Kenneth Muir has observed.[25] There are speeches of Lady Macbeth's corresponding closely to speeches of the Clytemnestra of Seneca's *Agamemnon* and of his Medea in the eponymous play. Macbeth himself echoes speeches of Seneca's Cassandra. To me, such imitation implies the authorship of a young dramatist still rather dependent on his models, before he finds his own vernacular voice.

Though the rationale in terms of topical reference to James's reign usually given for the play's contents sounds plausible, a much earlier set of events maps into the plot equally well, if not better. Elizabeth I (Duncan) visits the seat of her chief subject Leicester (Macbeth), married to the wicked Lettice (Lady Macbeth); and is (almost) assassinated. Leicester then assassinates his companion Philip Sidney (Banquo) whose children are destined to rule, on the assumption that a marriage between Leicester and the Queen would have been a barren one, and power would have devolved to Philip, as Leicester's heir. Historically, Banquo was as much implicated in the rebellion against Duncan as Macbeth was. But Shakespeare wants to exonerate his hero Sidney from any taint of treason. Macbeth and Lady Macbeth were childless, yet, notoriously, Lady Macbeth refers to babies to whom she has given suck. Robert Dudley and Lettice had no surviving children: but a young son Robert died aged 4 in 1584, and Lettice had earlier had children.

In October 1586, Philip, the Banquo figure, died while in his uncle's care in Zutphen in the Netherlands. The evidence that his contemporaries believed

Philip had been killed by Leicester is ubiquitous, and it is remarkable that it has escaped notice.

Edmund Molyneux reports Sidney's desperate letter to his physician Weir written the night before he died: 'My dear Weir, come, please come, my life is in danger, I can say no more'. Weir was an authority on poisoning. Molyneux mentions that three Sidneys died within six months of each other in places where they could 'pretend no interest' – yet Philip was surrounded by kinsmen, his uncle Leicester, his brother and his wife.[26] Is Molyneux implying that Philip's nearest and dearest worked *against* his interest? I think he is.

At Philip's death, his contemporaries at New College, Oxford, applied to the Chancellor of Oxford, Leicester himself, for permission to publish a collection of elegies for him, mostly in Latin, The lament written by Sir John Hoskyns for this anthology, *Peplus*, contains some startling lines.[27] Translated from the Latin, they run: 'So I shall mourn, since he was killed by a poisoned bullet. It is no secret that poison offers a way to heaven – a well-worn way, especially well worn in our age. Gaul has her Medea, if you were in any doubt Alcides experienced this, so did his heir. The son of Philyra feels it, and his child too'. Medaea was a poisoner; Alcides is Hercules, who was killed with a poisoned shirt. 'Phyllirides', 'son of Philyra', is a nickname for Philip.

Spenser's compendium anthology *Astrophel*, also containing elegies for Philip, came out much later, in 1595. Included in it is an elegy by Lodowick Bryskett that is in fact a translation of an elegy for the *poisoned* Duke Gonzaga of Mantua. In that publication there is an elegy by Matthew Roydon, who speaks of 'Astrophill by envie slaine'.[28]

Thomas Nashe was among the crowd of the suspicious. In his *Pierce Penilesse* (1592), he tells a story of a wicked bear enticing a horse to his death.[29] (Philippos means 'lover of horses', and Philip plays on his own 'horseness' in the opening of his *Defence of Poesie*.[30] The 'son of Philyra' was the centaur.) Nashe's story becomes strangely entangled with that of the forester poisoned by the Bear, who is clearly really a human. Nashe's modern editor, McKerrow, accepts that Leicester, whose *impresa* was the Bear and Ragged Staff, is the target of the reference. The fables occur in the context of 'Hypocrisie', of 'Italionate conveyances, as to kill a man, and then mourne for him', as Leicester seems to have done in authorizing the Oxford anthologies. In his *Terrors of the Night* (1594), Nashe has a peculiar account of a man dying in suspicious circumstances, after drinking a 'quintessence' 'in the Countrey some threescore myle off from London'.[31] We are led to believe that this refers not the countryside of England, but to Holland. 'The house where this Gentleman dwelt, stood in a low marish ground, almost as rotten a Clymate as the Lowe Countreyes.'[32] Nashe manages to work into the text not only 'Molenax' (supposedly an allusion to the constructor of a great globe, but probably in fact to Edmund Molyneux), but also 'the Virgines of *Marie Magdalens* order in Rome' and 'the chast daughters of Saint *Philip*'. We have no excuse for not spotting the frame of reference.

So when Shakespeare inserts the poison theme (for it was not in the original tale) into his most famous tragedy, *Hamlet*, which itself contains a play about the poisoned Duke 'Gonzago', I am tempted to see Hamlet's intensity as *in part* a reflection of Shakespeare himself, cursing himself for his cowardice in having merely put on a play (*Macbeth*) in the aftermath of Sidney's death, rather than executing vengeance on the murderers of his 'sweet Prince'.

Though my mapping of *Macbeth* and *Hamlet* onto Dudleian history may seem fanciful, I would suggest that is because my mapping is unfamiliar. It should not be: the critic G. French noted parallels between the Sidneys and the Hamlet family, such as the fact that the father died five months and twelve days before the son, in both cases.[33]

The objection that some items in the text of *Macbeth* do imply a Jacobean context (the twofold balls and triple sceptres of Banquo's descendants in Act 4, Scene 1; the reference to the King's Evil in Act 4, Scene 3) should be ruled out of court in view of growing evidence that Shakespeare revised his own plays.[34] Topical references could have been added, in this case any time after James's accession in 1603.

Besides, there could have been good reason for not referring *overtly* to an early *Macbeth* or *Hamlet*. (The first mention of *Macbeth* relates to a performance stated to have been in 1610, perhaps a mistake for 1611.) If the plays lauded Sidney while attacking Dudley, they were full of 'daunger' as the Elizabethans would have said – likely to bring down wrath on their author. The subversive charge of the original might account for the extreme superstition that persists in the acting world concerning the playing of *Macbeth*. The distaste of Kemp ('I never had the maw to see it') for *Macbeth* also tends to suggest something reprehensible in the author's undertaking the subject. Perhaps Kemp found disloyalty to Dudley, or stupidity in Shakespeare's hinting at murder among his patrons.

The Queen proceeded to Woodstock in September 1575 after she had visited Kenilworth and Worcester, and the Court progressed with her. The entertainments continued. Their theme was that of a hermit who had been struck blind, a lowly suitor and his lovely lady, and a prophecy that each would gain his desire (sight, or the love of the beloved) at the moment when the lowly one fought the hardiest knight in the land before the eyes of the most beauteous Lady in the land. This last, of course, turns out to be the Queen before whom the duel is being enacted. The lovely lady is lost again, and found, is torn between her duty to marry well and her love for the lowly suitor. The case is magnanimously referred to the Fairy Queen (the watching Queen Elizabeth, in this case) by the lowly suitor, who renounces all claims to his lovely lady.

Rather as in the case of Kenilworth, we have two overlapping accounts of the drama as it was presented. One is Gascoigne's *Hemetes the Heremyte* (Hermit), a prose account which delivers the story as far as the resolution of the duel. The other is a quarto volume not published until 1585, *The Queenes Majesties entertainment at Woodstocke*.[35] This too is a prose account of the Woodstock visit, in the form of a letter to another who was not present at the festivities. It runs from the point reached by Gascoigne and leads into a verse drama of the next instalment of the lowly suitor saga. It is anonymous. The two accounts constitute the arena in which we can vindicate the propositions that Shakespeare's apprenticeship in writing occurred in the Dudley orbit when he was extremely young, and that Gascoigne was one of his mentors.

Some features of the anonymous work demand attention before we can attempt to determine its authorship. Its whole first sheaf – four pages, eight sides – is unfortunately missing. It opens in mid-sentence on page B1, with the Hermit's interruption of the duel between the lowly knight and the hardy knight: '... followeth brought no lesse like to the Queenes maiestie: and al the rest that were present: for at his coming hee caused them to dismount themselves and said: You must fight no more ...'.[36] It is clear from the first word that there had been a previous act. The sentence must have begun something like 'This scene that followeth'. We presume that the previous scene was equivalent to Gascoigne's narrative of the prophecy and its fulfilment.

Gascoigne ended his narrative with a brief statement that the Hermit led the Queen to his grotto, bade her farewell and retired to his orisons. 'Anon' (if we may use this shorthand, for there is no indication of authorship in the quarto) continues from this point with detailed description of the posies with which the grotto was hung. 'The which posies, with some perfect note of their pictures, I would haue presented vnto you: but because the Allegories are hard to be vnderstood, without some knowledge of the inuentors, I have chosen my tyme rather when my selfe shall be present.'[37]

There are more posies in this account. They are presented to various ladies when the Fayry Queen arrives with a gift and some verses of *sesta rima* poetry which she declaims to the real Queen. As the writer is about to describe the mottoes of each posy he declines to give the Queen's because hers was in

Italian. 'Whiche because I neither vnderstoode it nor scarce canne write it
to be vnderstood I leaue also till my next coming to visite you.'[38] He notes
down all the others, ending 'I think (good sir) I have within little repeated
the names …'.[39]

So far, we can deduce that Anon is writing to someone superior in status;
that he does not comprehend the lore of emblems as well as this person; and
that he does not understand Italian. These are important points, to which I
shall return.

Anon then relays to his recipient the incident of the 'Song in the Oke', in
which a voice from within an oak tree appealed to the Queen. The singer of
the song is described as 'the excelentest now living'. It is likely that the singer
was Sir Edward Dyer (friend and companion poet to Philip Sidney) for there
are puns in the Song on 'dying'. Anon had had some trouble getting a copy of
the Song, for he relates that had 'hardly gotton [it] to present you withal'.[40]

He had no trouble, it seems, getting the copy of the Comedy which is the
next item in his text. It is the continuation of the lowly suitor saga, as given
above. It is in verse, and ends with a sad song of 'Thysby' and Pyramus, as the
suitor renounces his beloved. The Queen and ladies were deeply moved by the
play, reports Anon, 'in such sort, that her Graces passions, and the other Ladies
could not but show it selfe in open place more then ever hath beene seene'.[41]
It was 'as well thought of, as anye thing ever done before her Maiestie' he
says – *proudly*, one is tempted to say. Could he have written it himself?

There was a convention in these entertainments according to which
the protagonists represented themselves and their own interests under the
fantastic guise they had chosen. Dyer did so from the oak, it is generally
agreed; in the next section, we shall see Philip Sidney putting forward his
sister Mary's case in 1578 in a masque. Gascoigne, it is clear, himself played
the part of the Hermit struck blind, for he prefaces his narration with an
apology for having to speak of himself. He was probably trying to undo a
terrible gaffe he seems to have made at Kenilworth, when playing the part
of the Wild Man.

He had said to the Queen 'I never ioyd [joyed] so much:/ As when I might
behold your face,/ because I see none such'. A marginal note in one version of
Gascoigne's *Princely Pleasures* tells us that 'Here the Queene saide that the
Actor was blind'.[42] This sounds a very fraught exchange: surely the Queen
must have said something like 'You must be blind if you can see no one to rival
me'. That it was fraught is corroborated by a link directly relating this point in
the proceedings with lines assigned to the Wild Man's son in the play 'Zabeta'
prepared for performance at Kenilworth. In the text of this play (performance

of which the Queen successfully blocked), the son pleads for the removal of a film from the Wild Man's eyes, which had been *caused by* 'such words as hyr highnesse dyd then use unto him'.[43] A marginal note here refers us to the end of the Wild Man's exchange with Echo, exactly the point at which the Queen said he must be blind. The son's next words suggest the depths of the peril into which Gascoigne had plunged himself: the son explains that his father had declared 'God put mine eyes out cleane,/ Ere choice of change in England fall,/ to see another Queene'. Not only is the thought of a rival Queen treacherous, but the word 'change' carried a tremendous charge to Elizabethans – it implied revolution. It is further evidence of the near-treasonous attitude of the Leicestrian retainers towards their monarch. Gascoigne apparently succeeded in recovering the Queen's favour two months later at Woodstock. As the blind Hermit, he ascribed his blindness to a different cause, a visit to Venus's temple.

Gascoigne's example is instructive, and emboldens me to propose that the second act of the 'Lowly Suitor', the so-called 'Comedy', shows Anon representing his own case likewise. He makes no attempt to indicate the authorship, as he does with the 'Song in the Oke'; he reports no difficulty in acquiring the text; and he addresses his recipient in a subservient manner. These three facts strengthen the hypothesis that he was speaking on his own behalf. If he was, the case for Gascoigne's authorship or that of Sir Henry Lee is correspondingly weakened, because, as we shall see, what he pleads does not appear to match their concerns.[44] The proposal of the modern editor of *The Queenes Majesties entertainment*, A.W. Pollard, that the drama is an allegory of Leicester's marriage suit to the Queen, is also undermined.[45] My scepticism about the other candidates for authorship and the point of the drama needs defending.

Gascoigne clearly identifies himself with the Hermit, as we saw: but Anon refers to the Hermit as 'he'. This drives a wedge between Gascoigne and Anon. Besides, there are features of his publication *Hemetes the Heremyte* that suggest to me that Gascoigne gives credit for Act 1 of the drama of the Hermit and the Lowly Suitor to someone else.

Gascoigne claims to have 'translated' *Hemetes* for the Queen. Yet the work is clearly a continuation of some of the motifs of Kenilworth. He offered it to the Queen on New Year's Day 1576, in manuscript, in four versions, Latin, French, Italian, and – strangely, since it was presumably performed in English – English![46] Whom is he 'translating'? Is his 'English translation' a transcription, perhaps from verse to prose? Gascoigne praises the original highly: 'nott that I thinke any of the same translacõns any waie comparable with the first invencõn/ for if yor highnes compare myne ignorance wth thauctors skyll, or have regard to my rude phrases compared with his well polished style, you shall fynde my sentences as much disordered, as arrowes shott owt of ploughes/ and my theames as inaptly prosecuted, as hares hunted wth oxen/ for my latyne is rustye, myne Itallyan mustye, and my french forgrowne'.[47] The implication is that the Queen somehow knew the original and could compare Gascoigne's redaction with it.

Gascoigne's manuscript text has no title page. We are confronted first with a drawn frontispiece. It shows a raftered room, graced by the Queen sitting in state on a canopied dais. Before her kneels Gascoigne presenting his book, with a tall spear in his left hand, a sword girt at his side, and a pencil in his ear. The verse that follows on the next page rather compounds our confusion over his many accoutrements.

> Beholde (good Queene) A poett with a Speare
> (straundge sightes well markt are understoode the better)
> A Soldyer armde, with pensyle in his eare
> With penn to fighte, and sworde to wryte a letter,
> His gowne haulffe of, his blade not fully bownde …

This is hardly enlightening (where is the pen?), and some mystery is hinted at in the line on 'straundge sightes'. The kneeling figure has two weapons: he is 'A poett with a Speare' and 'a Soldyer armde'. Could he be two people in one? The divine hand reaching down from a serendipitous hole in the rafters to dangle over him the motto 'Tam Marti quam Mercurio' ('As much for Mars as for Mercury') might in fact be aiming for two poets, one called Mars and one called Mercury, in spite of the fact that the motto was frequently used by Gascoigne alone.

'Then peereles prince, employe this willinge man/ In your affayres to do the beste he cann', concludes Gascoigne. The reader naturally supposes that the willing man is Gascoigne. But if Gascoigne is presenting someone else's work, which he has translated, to the Queen, is he not *ipso facto* presenting this other to the Queen? This other is no less a 'willing' man. And he might well be the poet (with a spear) from whom Gascoigne has 'translated', and who is credited with a 'well polished style'. This anonymous poet might be a willing shake-spear.

The most I can claim is that the hypothesis is plausible, and makes better sense than the alternatives. Sir Henry Lee, Francis Yates's candidate, was put forward on the strength of the fact that an original of the 1585 account,

2.1   Gascoigne wood-cut. © British Library 12270DD12. (Taken from *The Complete Works of George Gascoigne*, edited by John W. Cunliffe (Cambridge: Cambridge University Press, 1907–10), vol. 2, p. 472)

including the play, is to be found in the Ditchley manuscript, which has other work of Lee in it. But if the theory of self-representation and special pleading on the part of the deviser and protagonist of masques is correct, no knight or noble could have written the play. A humble deviser is needed to put forward the case of the lowly suitor. And if the author of the Comedy is the same as the author of the framing narrative, as I suggested, Henry Lee is ruled out because we know he had visited Italy on numerous occasions, whereas the one who described the posies could not understand Italian.[48] The same reasoning rules out Gascoigne as the author, for he could write Italian, while Anon did not understand it.[49] Lee had the title of Queen's Champion: he must have been deeply versed in emblem lore, which Anon was not.

As for the theory that the Comedy must be an allegory concerning the Queen, her marriage and Leicester, as argued by A.W. Pollard, that too is somewhat implausible. Pollard argued that the Queen would see herself in the Lady, being 'granted permission' to give up her faithful Leicester, and marry for reasons of state. The French Ambassador was in the audience, and the little play could be the start of the suit which the Duc d'Alençon was to pay to the Queen over the next few years.

Two things militate against this. In the play, the Queen is not the potential bride: she is being flattered as the wise one who can offer protection and arbitrate. In this case, she appears to be the wise Fairy Queen to whom appeal is made about the rights and wrongs of marrying the Lowly Suitor. The other contra-indication is the continued and bitter opposition of the Leicester faction to the Queen's French marriage. It is improbable that two months after trying to put on the Zabeta play at Kenilworth urging marriage with Dudley on the Queen, they should commission a playlet 'allowing' her to abandon him, especially when one considers the intransigence of their opposition over the next four years.

I therefore suppose that just as Gascoigne and Dyer had done, the author writes from personal motives, to bring his own plight and that of his lady to the Queen's notice. I do not think the Ladies and the Queen would have been moved to tears over such a presentation if they had taken it as political allegory. I believe they were moved by the pathos of the real-life story they were being shown in allegory, and by the youth and sweetness of the protagonists.

Mary Sidney's future was at this time potentially blighted with a marriage of convenience to Henry Herbert, an old man of forty, married twice before. I suggest Mary is to be seen in the play, torn between a dutiful marriage and her childhood sweetheart, who is far too low-born to be considered a fit partner for her.

None of this – the reflection that someone capable of writing this little drama could have written the original of the earlier instalment 'translated' by Gascoigne, and that that person might be a Poet with a Spear, nor the speculation that, *if* Shakespeare was in Leicester's household, he *might* have loved young Mary – can be taken to prove his involvement in writing the narrative and the Comedy published in the 1585 quarto. But an extraordinary after-light is cast on the Woodstock literature by a publication of 1613.

In that year, the copyright of *The Hermites Tale* was assigned by Edward Blount to Thomas Thorpe for its third printing.[50] The poem itself is a disappointing mish-mash of satirical thoughts in a variety of metres, including the clumping 'fourteener'. It lambasts usurers and other miscreants. It does make reference, as if to something in the dim and distant past, to the amours of Phyllida, Coren and Herpilus. There is a hint in one of the dedicatory verses that the old story was not a 'Tale' but 'Truth'. It is not at all clear that this has any connection with the tangled story of the Woodstock Hermit's Tale. But certain details of its circumstances of publication, its title, its preface, and its author's name, 'Humfrey King', are intriguing. So is the name of one of the characters.

It was Thomas Thorpe who published Shakespeare's *Sonnets* in 1609. So Thorpe was not unknown to Shakespeare.[51] The title 'A half-penny-worth of wit …' evokes Greene's 'Groatsworth of witte', the title of the pamphlet in which Greene mentions the Shake-scene. And *The Chapman of a peniworth of Wit* was seen by R.L. in Captain Cox's library.

The preface contains self-mockery about the poet's lack of learning ('I am no Scholler'). We have the solid evidence of Ben Jonson that this was a common gibe against Shakespeare. In his tribute to Shakespeare in the First Folio, Jonson declared that his addressee had 'small *Latine and lesse Greeke*'. The *Hermites Tale* author supposedly cannot even spell: '*I am a very bad writer of* Orthography, *and can scarce spell my Abcie if it were laid down before mee. The* Printer *may helpe mee to deliuer to you true* English' (A3v). This is a little like having a Cretan tell you 'All Cretans are liars': if you can manage the word 'orthography', you are not an ignorant writer. There is no odd spelling in the subsequent text, so either the printer did correct it, or it was not faulty in the first place. What is intriguing is that a writer of a work with the same title as a masque performed at Woodstock in September 1575 should be associated with bad orthography, like the writer of the account of the Kenilworth visit two months before.

The name 'Humphrey King' will reappear frequently in our study. Nashe's *Lenten Stuffe* (pub. 1599) has a dedication to 'Lustie Humfrey, King of

Tobacconists *hic et ubique*' who is unlearned, yet a poet.[52] The publisher
of Anthony Chute's treatise on tobacco of 1595 appears in his preface to be
addressing a kind of proletarian king – Humphrey King, the 'sovereigne of
Tobacco'.[53] It sounds as though Humphrey is called King because he is a king,
a king of tobacconists (i.e. tobacco users). It recalls John Davies of Hereford's
epigram on Shakespeare:

> Some say (good *Will*) which I, in sport, do sing,
> Had'st thou not plaid some kingly parts in sport,
> Thou hadst bin a companion for a *King*;
> And, beene a King among the meaner sort.[54]

In another pamphlet, Nashe refers rather mysteriously to a youth 'that could not
vnderstand a word of Latine', whose vengeance on Chute has been prevented
by Chute's death (his *Tabaco* was published posthumously).[55] Nashe seems
to be saying that the Latin-less youth had a bone to pick with Chute over his
book *Tabaco*. But the book was aimed at Humphrey King: is he the Latin-less
youth? We shall return to Humphrey in the chapter on Nashe's work, Chapter
7, to solve this conundrum.

One of the characters in the *Hermites Tale* has the odd name 'Herpilus'. It
is comparable with the odd 'Espilus' in the masque called 'The Lady of May',
composed for the Queen's visit to Wanstead in 1578. Philip Sidney's modern
editors accept this masque as his work.[56] Latin 'pilum' is a javelin, lance or
spear. 'Her Spear' and 'S-spear' are, to say the least, evocative names; and the
Greek for a spear-wielder is 'engchespalos'. Both Herpilus and Espilus are of
low birth. The Espilus in the Wanstead masque is at first said to be rich, but
this is rather contradicted by his Lady's statement that 'his fortune hath not
been to do me great service'; and also that he 'has very small deserts'. In his
own wooing song, though he pleads for her love, Espilus warns the Lady to
take heed of submitting herself to one 'that hath no wealth'.[57]

Just as telling as the joke name is the wording of his rival's challenge to
Espilus.

> Come, Espilus, come now declare thy skill,
> Show how thou canst deserve so brave desire,
> Warm well thy wits, if thou wilt win her will,
> For water cold did never promise fire.[58]

'Warm *well* thy wits, if thou *wilt* win her, *Will*'? No poet could be so tone-
deaf as to be unaware of such insistent sound-repetition. Since the vagaries

of Elizabethan pronunciation could make homonyms of 'will' and 'well', we could also read 'Warm, Will, thy wits ...'.

It is admitted in the masque that the Lady is already married, but this does not seem to impinge on her right to decide between two rival suitors. Once more, as at Woodstock, the Queen (an unmarried woman) is the arbiter of the love affair of another woman. Things have moved on from 1575, but I would argue that the female protagonist is the same – Mary Sidney, now Herbert, Countess of Pembroke. She was present at Wanstead in 1578, as Duncan-Jones shows.[59] Helpfully for my case, Duncan-Jones also doubts whether Sidney was urging state policy on the Queen, rather than a private cause.[60]

I suggested above that Gabriel Harvey, once he was drawn into the Leicester circle, would have known William Shakespeare, and had a hand in the education of this talented servant of his own patron. In his *Pierces Supererogation* (1593), intended as a stinging reply to Nashe's parodying attack on him in *Pierce Penilesse*, Harvey mocks a certain Apuleius, ostensibly Nashe, the 'Ass'. There is an elusive quality to Harvey's style, and one often suspects other subjects have crept in at some point. The following passage speaks of Apuleius in a markedly more sympathetic tone than normal.

> Peerless young Apuleius, that from the swathing bandes of his infancie in Print, was suckled of the sweetest nurses, lulled of the deerest groomes, cockered of the finest minions, cowled of the daintiest paramours, hugged of the enticingest darlinges, and more then tenderly tendered of the most delitious Muses, the most-amiable Graces, and the most-powerfull Vertues of the said vnmatchable great A. the graund founder of Supererogation, and sole Patron of such meritorious clients.[61]

Can this Apuleius be Nashe? Why is he now 'peerless' and a 'meritorious client', after being so execrated? Much later in the work, we find that Harvey is implying the existence of *two* Apuleii. '[T]hey clapp their hands that have heard the Comedie of *Adelphi*, or the two Asses: a more notable Pageant, then the Interlude of the two sofias, or the two Amphitryos, or the two Men(d)echmi, or the two Martin Guerras; or any such famous Paire of the true person, and the counterfait.' Harvey thinks it ironic that 'the true man should be the counterfait; and the false fellow the true Asse'.[62]

He is fooling, of course, with the conceit of the *Metamorphoses* of Lucius Apuleius, a Latin romance translated as *The Golden Asse* by William Addington in 1566. The character Lucius is there transformed into an ass. Harvey is playing too with the notion of doppel-gangers – 'suppositi' or impersonators. His conjoining of the 'ass theme' with the 'doubles theme' makes our impulse to see the Apuleius who was suckled and hugged as someone *other* than Nashe appear justified. But there may be a further implication. Harvey could be implying the existence of a current play about doubles, a 'pageant' which is more notable than all its predecessors in any genre, including Plautus' *Menaechmi*, on which Shakespeare modelled the *Comedy of Errors.* He could actually be referring to the *Comedy*; and with his sly juxtaposition of the two themes – asses and doubles – he could be implying that one of his Apuleii is Shakespeare. If that is what Harvey is doing, the Apuleius who was so petted by the Dudley nobles as a child will surely be the one in question.

Many will see this as drawing too many deductions from a text which says much less at a superficial level. But Harvey *designed* his pamphlet to be ambiguous, to be teased out. Context and juxtaposition are offered to the reader as aids to a solution; and if a suspicion is raised in the reader's mind, it is likely that Harvey meant to raise that suspicion. 'His infancy in Print' may legitimately, I think, be pressed to yield the meaning that the favoured Apuleius was an 'infant' when he first broke into print (or that his infancy was described in print).

Now Nashe was twenty-two when he first appeared in print in 1589, no more than four years previously. Besides, Nashe was brought up rather privately in Norfolk, and Harvey is unlikely to have known anything of his youth. Contrariwise, the Apuleius we suspect Harvey has smuggled in, the author of the *Comedy of Errors*, had a childhood about which Harvey could have known, and had been in print – briefly – at the age of eleven.

Pierces Supererogation, I have argued elsewhere, is a surreptitious defence of Mary Sidney against Nashe.[63] Its Sidneian credentials are in any case evident, as Margaret Hannay and others have observed.[64] In the light of this, the education of the childish Apuleius (a Bottom-like 'Ass') among the sweetest Muses is highly significant, for the reference is most likely to the Sidney circle itself. In this connection, one tiny stage direction from the *Comedy of Errors* (known to Harvey, it now appears, before its first recorded performance in 1594), yields an exciting clue. The stage 'houses' out of which the twins in the *Comedy* appear are called 'Phoenix' and 'Centaur'. The phoenix symbol is used so often to indicate either Mary or Philip that it is practically synonymous with either.[65] As for 'Centaur', we saw how Hoskyns addressed the dead Philip as 'Phyllirides', the centaur being the son of Philyra in mythology.

Imagine two red-headed, similar-featured actors on the raised grass stage in the garden at Penshurst, the Sussex home of the young Sidney siblings. (Philip and Mary were very alike, says John Aubrey, the biographer, though Philip's hair was a little darker, inclining to amber.)[66] They are playing the

twins in the *Comedy*, adapted from the *Menaechmi* of Plautus – adapted by a
young 'servant' before 1586 when Philip was killed. Such a scenario would
be impossible on the consensus view of Shakespeare's youth, according
to which the future playwright was still in Stratford aiding his father the
grazier and glover. But that consensus lacks any basis in evidence, as even
its proponents admit.

A Sidneian or Leicestrian flavour can be traced in more of Shakespeare's
early plays. I undertook to link his staunch Protestantism to the Earl of
Leicester's faction, and his love of the theme of a court in Arcadian exile to
the aspirations of the Sidneys, to round off this chapter.

Commentators on *King John* and *Henry VI, Part 1*, observe, correctly, how
fiercely anti-Catholic the plays are.[67] (*The Troublesome Reign of King John*, a
forerunner of *King John*, is even more so. Eric Sams offers convincing reasons
for including *Troublesome Reign* in Shakespeare's oeuvre.)[68] Those modern
critics who believe that Shakespeare was a Catholic because his father was one
must account for his apparent trajectory in the wrong direction – from youthful
Protestant fanaticism to more positive portrayal of Catholic characters, and a
general tone of reconciliation. If he was removed from his close family at an
early age, as I postulate, the hypothesis of a Catholic John Shakespeare and a
fervently Protestant young William is entirely credible. The late seventeenth-
century note on Shakespeare by Richard Davies 'He died a papist', even if
correct, implies late conversion, not a life-long practice.[69]

The court-in-exile in *Love's Labour's Lost* belongs to the quasi-secessionist
state of Navarre. The Countess's 'court' in *All's Well that Ends Well* is placed
in Roussillon, France's other quasi-secessionist state at the time. Though the
Countess is not in exile, she is not the power centre, which is occupied by the
King. This important point has been missed by commentators, but I am sure
it reflects the way the Sidney faction conceived of its situation in the 1570s
and 1580s.[70] Sometimes Shakespeare portrays the relinquishing of the idyllic
Arcadian setting as almost unwelcome, even though it constitutes a justified
return to power (*The Tempest*). Shakespeare's obsessive treatment of the
theme might imply either that the plays antedate the deaths of Philip in 1586
and Robert Dudley in 1588; or that having 'imprinted on' the Dudleys in his
childhood, Shakespeare wrote such plays even in his more mature years, when
all realistic hopes of the Dudleys' gaining supreme power had evaporated.

Not all Shakespeare's comedies have high matters of state as an underlying
theme. I return to the *Shrew*, a very early comedy. It is interesting that
Shakespeare should have turned to a work of Gascoigne's for one of his early
sub-plots. It is perhaps even more interesting that the main plot is related to

the old folk tale 'The wife lapt in a Morels skin', a copy of which was seen in Captain Cox's library by R.L. Interesting, too, is the linking of *The Shrew* to Pembroke's Men. Henry Herbert, second Earl of Pembroke and husband of Mary Sidney, maintained players. *The True Tragedie of Richard Duke of Yorke* ('source', 'forerunner', or early version of Shakespeare's *Henry VI, Part 3*) had been 'sometimes acted by the Right Honourable the Earle of Pembrooke his seruants'. So had *Titus Andronicus*; and so had *A Taming of A Shrew* (which Eric Sams argues is the same play as *The Taming of The Shrew*, and by the same author). This close and early connection of Shakespeare with Mary Sidney's husband's players argues a close and early connection with the Sidney family itself.

What is the theme of the *Shrew*? Something extremely personal to its author, I suggest. It is the flattering dream of a Warwickshire yokel of winning, by kindness, an imperious and aristocratic woman. Tricked by cruel courtiers into believing himself high-born and beloved of a lady, he is 'in sleep a king, but waking, no such matter', like the Shakespeare of Sonnet 87.

Notes

1   O'Kill, 'The Printed Works of William Patten', p. 43.
2   Park Honan, *Shakespeare: A Life* (Oxford: Oxford University Press, 1999), Ch. 3.
3   Alluded to by Philip Sidney himself, in his twenty-first sonnet of *Astrophel and Stella* (London: Thomas Newman, 1591). William Ringler, ed., *The Poems of Sir Philip Sidney* (Oxford: Clarendon Press, 1962), pp. 163–237, 175.
4   Jane Kingsley-Smith has also noticed this phenomenon. See *Shakespeare's Drama of Exile* (Basingstoke: Palgrave Macmillan, 2003).
5   I follow Honan's *Shakespeare*, where numerous documentary sources are given, and the work of previous biographers cited.
6   David Lloyd, *The Statesmen and Favourites of England Since the Reformation* (London: J.C. for Samuel Speed, 1665), p. 504.
7   F. Halliday, *A Shakespeare Companion: 1550–1950* (London: Duckworth, 1952), p. 268, s.v. 'Stratford-on-Avon'.
8   See *An Elizabethan in 1582: The Diary of Richard Madox, Fellow of All Souls*, ed. Elizabeth Donno (London: The Hakluyt Society, 1976), series 2, vol. 147.
9   Meredith Skura, *Shakespeare the Actor and the Purposes of Playing* (Chicago: University of Chicago Press, 1993), pp. 31–2; 243, notes 8–11.
10 Honan, *Shakespeare*, p. 98.
11 *Richard III*, III.1.69–78.
12 Kuin, *Letter*, p. 56.
13 *Letter*, p. 57.
14 Annabel Patterson, in *Censorship and Interpretation* (Wisconsin: University of Wisconsin Press, 1984), pp. 181–2, cites the example of a seventeenth-century writer (William Barclay,

author of *Argenis*) explicitly plotting to mix real historical events with 'fained' events and 'inventions that cannot possibly agree to those that I entend to point at', in order to lead the reader into an interpretative maze.

15 Kuin, *Letter*, p. 65.

16 18 July 1575, *CSP Spanish*, 2. 497–9. See Frye, *The Competition*, pp. 56–7.

17 Kuin, *Letter*, p. 91.

18 *Letter*, pp. 39–40.

19 Gascoigne, *Works*, p. 92.

20 Kuin, *Letter*, p. 68.

21 Editors have been prepared to place it in 1603, and one critic, Daniel Amnaeus (*The Mystery of Macbeth* (Alhambra, CA: Primrose, 1983)), suggested 1599. Robert Fleissner, in 'The "Upstart Crow" Reclawed: Was it Kemp, Wilson, Alleyn, or Shakespeare', *The Upstart Crow*, 15 (1995), pp. 143–9, seems to accept the relevance of William Kemp's *Nine Daies Wonder* (London: E. Allde for N. Ling, 1600), to dating the play before 1600, while G.B. Harrison, ed., *Kemps Nine Daies Wonder* (New York: Dutton, 1923), pp. 30–31, does not.

22 Kemp, *Wonder*, D3r–D4v.

23 Robert Greene, *Greene's Groatsworth of Witte* (London: William Wright, 1592), F1. *Life and Complete Works of Robert Greene*, ed. A.B. Grosart, 15 vols (Huth Library) (Manchester: privately printed, 1881–86), 12.95–150, 144. Anthony Holden assumes Kemp's reference is to Shakespeare, but he fails to see the implication for the date of *Macbeth*: Anthony Holden, *William Shakespeare: His Life and Work* (1999; London: Abacus, 2000), p. 174. Robert Fleissner, in *Names, Titles, and Characters by Literary Writers – Shakespeare, 19th and 20th Century Authors* (Lampeter: Edwin Mellen, 2001), p. 67, recognizes the Shakespearean reference, but does not spell out the dating implications.

24 H.H. Furness Jr. cites J.P. Collier, who noticed this long ago. See *A New Variorum Edition of Shakespeare, Macbeth*, 8th edn (Philadelphia and London, 1915), pp. 359–60; 360.

25 Kenneth Muir, ed., *Macbeth* (introductory material 1962 and 1984, Methuen; London: Arden, 2001), intro., p. xlii.

26 Edmund Molyneux, *Historical Remembrance of the Sidneys, father and son.* In Raphael Holinshed, *Third Volume of Chronicles* (1587). Katherine Duncan-Jones, *Sir Philip Sidney* (Oxford: Oxford University Press, 1989), pp. 311–14.

27 *Peplus* (Oxford: J. Barnes, 1587), pp. 14–18, 17, lines 91–8.

28 Lodowick Bryskett, 'A pastorall Aeglogue upon the death of Sir Phillip Sidney Knight', in *Astrophel*, in *Colin Clouts Come Home Againe*, Edmund Spenser (London: T. Creede for William Ponsonby, 1595). *Spenser: Poetical Works*, ed. J.C. Smith and E. De Selincourt (1912; Oxford: Oxford University Press, 1989), pp. 554–5. Matthew Roydon, 'An Elegie, or friends passion, for his Astrophill', ibid., *Works*, pp. 556–8, line 222.

29 Thomas Nashe, *Pierce Penilesse His Supplication to the Divell* (London: Richard Jones, 1592; also Abel Jeffes for John Busbie, 1592). Ronald B. McKerrow, *The Works of Thomas Nashe*, 5 vols (1904–10), revised by F.P. Wilson (Oxford: Blackwell, 1958), I.149–245, 221–3.

30 Philip Sidney, *The Defence of Poesie* (London: William Ponsonby, 1595), n.p. *Miscellaneous Prose of Sir Philip Sidney*, ed. Katherine Duncan-Jones and Jan van Dorsten (Oxford: Clarendon Press, 1973), pp. 73–121, 73.

31 Thomas Nashe, *The Terrors of the Night* (London: J. Danter, 1594). *Works*, I.339–86, 378.

32 *Works*, I.382.

33 Cited by H.H. Furness, ed., *Hamlet: A New Variorum Edition*, 2 vols (New York: Dover, 1963), 2.238–40.

34 See Grace Ioppolo, *Revising Shakespeare* (Cambridge, MA and London: Harvard University Press, 1991); E.A. Honigmann, *The Stability of Shakespeare's Text* (Lincoln, NE: University of Nebraska Press, 1965), esp. pp. 12, 90.

35 *The Queenes Maiesties Entertainment at Woodstock 1575* (London: Thomas Cadman, 1585). Citations are from the edition of A.W. Pollard, *The Queen's Majesty's Entertainment at Woodstock. 1575* (1903; Oxford: Daniel and Hart, 1910).

36 Pollard, *Entertainment*, B1a.

37 *Entertainment*, B4b.

38 *Entertainment*, C1b.

39 *Entertainment*, C2a.

40 *Entertainment*, C2b.

41 *Entertainment*, C3a.

42 This marginal note and the next exist only in *Kenilworth Illustrated*, the 1821 version of events published by C. Whittingham, who had the earliest edition of the *Princely Pleasures* in front of him (that of Jhones of 1576). See *Kenilworth Illustrated*, pp. 51–80. This note is on p. 60, the next on p. 63.

43 Gascoigne, *Works*, p. 107.

44 Francis Yates, *Astraea: The Imperial Theme in the Sixteenth Century* (London: Routledge, 1975), pp. 96–7, proposes Sir Henry Lee as the author. I understand that the AHRB group of scholars at the Centre for the Study of Renaissance Elites and Court Cultures at the University of Warwick is shortly to publish a proposal that a scholar of St John's College, Oxford, was the author.

45 Pollard, *Entertainment*, p. xiii.

46 Cunliffe prints the first manuscript version, *Works*, pp. 473–510.

47 Ibid., pp. 476–7.

48 E.K. Chambers, *Sir Henry Lee* (Oxford: Clarendon Press, 1936), pp. 32–6.

49 Pollard, *Entertainment*, p. vii.

50 Humfrey King, *An Half-penny-worth of Wit, in a Penny-worth of Paper, or, The Hermites Tale* (London: Thomas Thorpe, 1613).

51 Though Brian Vickers still holds that publication of the *Sonnets* was not authorized by Shakespeare, the arguments of Katherine Duncan-Jones to the contrary are far more convincing. See Brian Vickers' letter, *TLS* (21 January 2005), p. 15; Duncan-Jones, ed., *Shakespeare's Sonnets* (1997; London: Arden, 1998), intro., pp. 32–41.

52 Thomas Nashe, *Nashes Lenten Stuffe* (London: N.L. for C.B., 1599). *Works*, III.147.

53 *Tabaco.* Gathered by A.C. (London: A. Islip for F. Barlow [Barley], 1595). F.P. Wilson, ed. and intro. (Oxford: Basil Blackwell, 1961), Aiiv.

54 John Davies, *The Scourge of Folly* (London: E. Allde for F. Redmer, *c.* 1611), Epigram 159, p. 76. *The Complete Works of John Davies of Hereford*, ed. A.B. Grosart, 2 vols (Edinburgh: Chertsey Worthies' Library, 1878), 2.26.

55 Thomas Nashe, *Have With You to Saffron Walden* (London: John Danter, 1596). *Works*, III.3–139, 106.

56 Sidney, *Poems*, pp. 1–5.

57 *Poems*, p. 4.

58 *Poems*, p. 3.

59 Duncan-Jones, *Courtier Poet*, p. 152, citing HMC De L'Isle and Dudley, i.250.

60 *Courtier-Poet*, pp. 148–9.

61 Gabriel Harvey, *Pierces Supererogation* (London: J. Wolfe, 1593), 121. *Works of Gabriel Harvey*, ed. A.B. Grosart, 3 vols (Huth Library) (Manchester: privately printed, 1884–85), 2.1–346, 212.

62 Harvey, *Works*, 2.250.

63 Penny McCarthy, '"Milksop Muses" or Why Not Mary?', *SEL* 40.1 (Winter 2000), pp. 21–39.

64 Margaret Hannay, *Philip's Phoenix: Mary Sidney, Countess of Pembroke* (New York and Oxford: Oxford University Press, 1990), pp. 140–42.

65 Hannay, *Philip's Phoenix*, passim.

66 *John Aubrey: Brief Lives*, ed. J. Buchanan-Brown (London: Penguin, 2000), p. 304.

67 For *King John*'s anti-catholicism, see E.A. Honigmann's Arden introduction (1954), p. xxix. For that of *Henry VI, Part 1*, see Leah Marcus, *Puzzling Shakespeare: Local Reading and Its Discontents* (London: University of California Press, 1988), pp. 83–94.

68 *The Troublesome Raigne of King John* (London: Samson Clarke, 1591). Eric Sams, *The Real Shakespeare: Retrieving the Early Years, 1564–1594* (New Haven and London: Yale University Press, 1995), pp. 146–53.

69 See Ian Wilson, *Shakespeare: The Evidence* (London: Headline, 1993), p. 411, where the manuscript evidence, from the library of Corpus Christi College, Cambridge, is reproduced.

70 The whole topic of Arcadia, as well as Philip Sidney's own *magnum opus*, urgently needs re-evaluation.

Chapter 3

Second Candidate – Dom Diego

The book containing the character Dom Diego comprises a sonnet sequence, *Diella*, and a verse narrative, the *Poeme of Dom Diego and Gyneura*.[1] Its author being one R.L., Gent., it belongs in this enquiry. This R.L. is the main focus in this chapter; but he draws others in his wake. Questions have been raised as to whether he could be identical with the author of a poem signed R.L. in *The Paradyce of Dayntie Devises*, 'Being in Love he complaineth';[2] or with the Richard Linche who wrote The *Fountaine of Ancient Fiction*, a translation from an Italian work by Vincenzo Cartari;[3] or the Richard Lynche, Gent., of *The Historical Treatise of the Travels of Noah into Europe*;[4] or the 'R.L. Esquire' who praised Michael Drayton's narrative poem *Matilda*.[5]

I shall first treat these R.L.s here in order of publication. I shall then introduce another writer, William Smith, author of the sonnet sequence *Chloris.* He is implicated in the search for R.L. because of a rare formal feature shared by his sequence and *Diella*. Other works by this Smith and their links with Spenser are investigated. Ben Jonson's nostalgic glance at the Kenilworth of 1575, his *Masque of Owles* of 1624, implicates a 'Spanish don'. I ask whether the don could be 'el prencipe negro' or Diego.

The current understanding of the relation of the R.L.s mentioned above to each other and to Linche or Lynch is neither deep nor informed by much curiosity. Edward Utterson, editor of an 1841 edition of *Diella*, notes that the *Paradyce* poem 'Being in Love' has a 'similar signature'.[6] (The signature is identical). W.C. Hazlitt ascribes *Diella* to 'Linch' or 'Lynch' and connects the author to what he seems to think are two separate sonnets praising Drayton, prefacing the latter's *Matilda* of 1594 and his *Robert Duke of Normandy &c.* of 1596 which contains a reprint of *Matilda*. (In fact, the same sonnet is reprinted).[7] A.B. Grosart is wary of Hazlitt's identification, but pronounces himself satisfied that *Diella* is by the same Linche as the author of the *The Fountaine* and *The Treatise*.[8] Thereafter, editors tend to agree with Grosart; but little interest has been shown in tying in the authors of the occasional poems.

The poem by R.L. in the 1576 *Paradyce of Dayntie Devises* is in heavy-handed 'fourteeners'. Its subject is the tale of Troilus and Cressida, and in the 1580 reissue of the *Paradyce*, R.L.'s poem is actually in the voice of 'Troylus', with an answering poem by 'Cressida'. Others beside Shakespeare knew the tale from Chaucer and Lydgate, so no particular conclusions about R.L.'s imagination should be built on this fact. What may be significant, however, is that the printer and bookseller is R. Jones, the publisher of Gascoigne's *Princely Pleasures* in the same year, and (if I am right) of the aborted 'Langham's Letter' called 'The Pastime of the Progress' the autumn before. And no-one disputes that the *Paradyce* is full of poems from the Sidney circle.

The dedicatory poem to Drayton is pleasing enough, beginning 'Teares in your eyes, and passions in your harts,/ With mournfull grace vouchsafe *Matildas* story'. Drayton himself dedicated his own early collection to Mary Sidney in 1594, in which there are hints that he is *au fait* with Sidneian secrets. *Ideas Mirrour*'s Poem 51 refers to her as Minerva, in close conjunction with a Dorus.[9] This connection of Dorus to Mary Sidney was, apparently, something that needed to be excised from subsequent editions of Drayton's works, for it does not appear in any but the first edition. Dorus is the name taken by the companion of the hero Pyrocles in Philip Sidney's *New Arcadia*. He is Musidorus – 'gifted by the Muses' – in the *Old Arcadia*, as he is at the beginning and the end of the *New Arcadia*, where he turns out to be a prince, Palladius. 'Palladius' means one loyal to Pallas Athena, or Minerva. This neatly completes the circle connecting Dorus with Minerva (that is, Mary) in Drayton's dangerous poem. Whether we should read off anything particular from the fact that Dorus is 'Muse-endowed' is more doubtful. Yet one cannot but be struck by the fact that the Arcadian Dorus is the one who takes on the disguise of a lowly herdsman – the implication being that the real-life character he masks (since the work is allowed by all to be *roman-à-clef*) is humbly born.

It is a little unlikely that there should have been more than one poet signing himself 'R.L.' in the Sidney circle at the time. Therefore it is tempting to compress the R.L.s of the single poems into one writer. And the reflections in the preceding two paragraphs make it tempting to absorb the humble boy diarist from Kenilworth, also an R.L., into this composite figure.

Diella's R.L. also appears to have been close to the heart of the Sidneian coterie. The book was published by Henry Olney, whose only other venture into publishing was Philip Sidney's *Apologie for Poetrie*, of 1595.[10] Olney's involvement with *Diella* is therefore a matter to be pondered. Why should he have interested himself in this obscure poet R.L., at the same time as he was aiming for the heights with his publication of the *Apologie?*

Equally noteworthy is the interest the obscure little book raised among contemporaries. Thomas Nashe refers to it in a letter to William Cotton:

'Don Diego & Brokkenbury beshitt pouls [i.e. St Paul's]'.[11] Nashe's editor McKerrow takes this literally, as though a Spaniard called 'Diego' had fouled himself in St Paul's. St Paul's was the book-sellers' area, and it seems plain to me that Nashe means his words metaphorically: a book called 'Don Diego' had brought the book-trade into disrepute. John Webster jokes to the same effect in his play *The Famous History of Sir Thomas Wyatt*. 'Brett: And what is a Dondego? Clown: A Dondego is a kind of Spanish stock fish or poor-John. Brett: No, a Dondego is a desperate Viliago, a very Castilian. God bless us, there came but one Dondego into England, and he made all Paul's to stink again.'[12] Thomas Heywood repeats the by-now worn joke in his *Fair Maid of the West*, published in 1631: 'But for these Spaniards, now you Don Diegoes,/ You that made Paules to stinke'.[13]

Why this animus against the romance of *Dom Diego*? Could the eponymous lady of the accompanying sonnets, Diella, be a conglomeration of 'Delia' (to whom Samuel Daniel, tutor to Mary Sidney's children, wrote sonnets) and 'Stella' (Philip Sidney's Muse)? If so, the secret cause of disgust might be the 'scandal' of a liaison between the 'real' Don Diego and the 'real' Diella. Perhaps all three poetic mistresses were, in historical reality, the same woman.[14]

The bare facts of the publication of *Diella* are these. The sequence and its attached romance were published with the customary details, even as to the place of sale in Olney's shop 'in Fleetstreete, neer the Middle-temple gate'. Olney dedicated the work – 'a few passionate Sonnets intermingled with the Loves of Dom DIEGO and GYNEURA' – to the Lady Anne Glemnham, who was the eldest daughter of Thomas Sackville, later Earl of Dorset. Olney describes it as having been 'conceived in the brain of a gallant Gentleman'. The title page gives the author's name as 'R.L., Gentleman'; with the *impresa* or motto 'Ben balla, á chi fortuna suona'. ('He dances well, for whom Fortune plays the tune.' The first word is of course short for 'bene' – 'well', homonym of 'Will'.) R.L. has advanced in status, it seems, from Esquire in 1594 to Gentleman in 1596. So had Shakespeare: the 'grant of arms' for which his father had once applied had been reapplied for in 1596 and (most probably) granted that year.[15]

Diella consists of 38 sonnets. They contain much classical mythology; the verse-form is the 'Shakespearean' sonnet (three quatrains rhyming abab cdcd efef, and a couplet gg); the lady addressed is 'Diella', and the poet is an unnamed 'I'. The individual sonnets are fairly unremarkable. They are not usually picked for inclusion in selective anthologies of sixteenth-century sonnets.

Diella's thirty-eighth sonnet introduces the *sesta rima* narrative poem *Dom Diego and Gyneura.* The whole therefore follows the pattern of sequences of the time (or should one say, 'of the Sidney circle'?), which typically comprise sonnets to a particular mistress, followed by a Complaint (as in Daniel's *Delia and the Complaint of Rosamund*) or by Songs (as in the original *Astrophel and Stella*) or by an *Epithalamium* (appended by Spenser to his *Amoretti* sonnets).[16]

Dom Diego, in contrast with *Diella*, does show originality and liveliness of vocabulary. It is 'intermingled with' the sequence quite tightly. The last of the sonnets spells out the connection to the story which is to follow: 'Harken awhile, (*Diella*) to a storie/ that tells of beauty, love, and great disdaine!' It is to tell of the 'suspect' under which Diego fell, and of how, when his mistress Gyneura finally discovered he had always been true, she 'loved him now, as when he first did woo her'. The moral is that Diella too should learn 'to quench hate's fuel' and 'be to me, as She to Him, a friend'.

The tale was one of those European stories that were passed on orally and in literary collections. The Italian storyteller Matteo Bandello has it in the first volume of his *Novelle;* the French author François Belleforest translated many Bandello tales, this one among them.[17] Rather than being straight translations, Belleforest's versions are transformations into longer and much more moralistic tales, of which Geoffrey Fenton translated a number in *Certaine Tragicall Discourses* (1567).[18] Fenton dedicated the work, in which 'Dom Diego' is the final story, to the older Mary Sidney (Dudley), mother of Mary and Philip. Another Englishman, William Painter, translated 'Dom Diego' in his *Palace of Pleasure*, tales from a variety of sources.[19] Painter dedicated his first edition to Ambrose Dudley, and the title page shows the Bear and Ragged Staff. This translation, like Fenton's, seems to derive from Belleforest's long adaptation. Belleforest/Bandello tales underlie a large number of plots and subplots in Shakespeare's plays, including *Othello*, *Twelfth Night*, *Cymbeline*, *The Winter's Tale*, *Romeo and Juliet*, and *Much Ado About Nothing.*

The question of R.L.'s possible sources is important to this study for the information it might be able to yield about his practice and his knowledge of languages. It is probable that he had all the antecedent versions to hand, since he includes details from each that are lacking in each of the others. He derives from Belleforest, Fenton or Painter a 'blazon' of Diella's beauty feature by feature.[20] (The details are not in Bandello.) Only in Painter is there a beautiful dawn, the description of which R.L. imitates. The form of the heroine's name he takes from Bandello or Painter, who call her 'Gineura'. (Belleforest converts her into 'Genievre', Fenton into 'Genivera'.) That this is not just a matter of chance orthography (for printed u and v are interchangeable) is proved by the first full rhyme R.L. uses for the name: he rhymes 'Gyneura' with 'Liguria'. Yet he later rhymes her with 'Minerva', to match 'Ginevra', closer to the French and to Fenton. He must have thought of her under both pronunciations.

The point to stress is R.L.'s direct knowledge of Bandello, for it implies competence in Italian. (Such competence would not rule out identifying this R.L. with the author of the Woodstock drama: all that is required is time for him to have learned the language since 1575.) One very specific detail of phrasing and the general tone of the narrative strongly suggest dependence on Bandello's account.

When some hunters appear on the scene in which Diego is alone and has lost his way, R.L. describes them thus: 'as Knights, so Ladies', meaning '[hunters] both knights and ladies'. Bandello too describes them as 'una compagnia di donne e d'huomini'. But on reading Belleforest and Fenton, where they are described merely as 'hunters', one does not immediately envisage ladies being part of the company.[21] Only when Gyneura and her mother are mentioned as sending to know who the stranger (Diego) is does it transpire that ladies formed part of the company. In Painter, too, the phrasing is unlike Bandello's, though in this case, Gineura's mother certainly and perhaps Gineura herself is among the hunters. Diego, 'hearing a certayne noyse of Hunters, thinking they had been his People, resorted to the same, who in deede were the servaunts of the Mother of Gineura with the golden Locks, which in company of their Mistresse had hunted the Hare'.[22]

The other English translators take their moralizing tone from Belleforest. Children come to grief if they do not follow their parents' wishes when marrying; women are prone to fits of jealousy and madness, because they are subject to the changes of the moon; to marry below one's station will inevitably incur disaster; and so on. Bandello does not moralize: he simply tells the facts. And R.L. does not draw morals in the sense of offering moralistic homilies to the reader: he too tells the tale straight.

All the sources tell a story whose main events are as follows. In Catalonia, there lived a widow with a beautiful daughter, Gineura/Genivera/Genievre, and another widow with a sole son, Diego. Diego won the favour of Philip of Austria, and was knighted by him. Yet he did not go to Court, but stayed at home. Out hunting one day, Diego rode ahead of his companions and lost his way. He spotted some hunters, who likewise caught sight of him, and enquired who he was. He was invited to their castle, and fell in love with Ginevra and she with him. The mothers approved, but unwisely did not set about arranging the marriage. Diego fell under suspicion in Ginevra's eyes because, in the long interval of quasi-betrothal, another woman became enamoured of Diego, and sent him a hawk as a present, which he quite innocently adored and took everywhere with him.

Some malicious person told Ginevra that Diego was not faithful: she should ask him about the hawk he wore on his hand. Diego compounded his mistake by saying in front of Ginevra that the hawk was one of the things he held most dear in the world. She was furious; he destroyed the hawk and tried to explain in letters (which she would not read); he left for the wilderness to become a hermit.

Nearly two years pass, and Ginevra falls in love with a steward of unsuitably low rank. She plans to elope with him. Meanwhile, Diego's faithful friend, Roderigo, finds Diego living as a 'wild man', and plans to reconcile him with Ginevra. Roderigo hears of the planned elopement, ambushes the escaping lovers, kills the steward, violently kidnaps Ginevra and leads her to Diego. She at first refuses to accept her old suitor. But Roderigo threatens to kill her two servants, and then to kill her. As she pleads for the servants' lives, Diego humbly releases her from her 'obligation' to love him. She sees him as he used to be, and loves him once more. The moral is: Lo, what can faithful friends and a persevering love achieve!

R.L. varies the story considerably. He de-historicizes it: there is no Philip of Austria or any particular period setting. He concentrates all attention on the two protagonists and their thoughts. (Diego's mother does not feature at all). He dramatizes, giving Gyneura, for example, a speech equivalent to Diego's on the night following the first encounter of the two (D8r). Though Bandello gestures towards her thoughts, describing both lovers as being 'in simul labirinto' (94), 'in like turmoil', and Painter says she 'fantasied no fewer devises than passionated Dom Diego' (315v), only R.L. gives her a voice. He varies the 'rivalry' theme: contrary to his sources, he has no female rival for Diego's love, but there is a male rival for Gyneura's love, who craftily tells her of the hawk given to Diego. Gyneura does read Diego's letters, but is unmoved by them. (Like Julia in *Two Gentlemen of Verona*, Gyneura rejects the first letter when the servant brings it, but reads it subsequently.)

R.L. excises the entire strand of the story of Gyneura's loving the steward, the elopement, ambush, murder and enforced confrontation with Diego in the wilderness. He simply has Roderigo find Diego, and act as ambassador to Gyneura. Gyneura is persuaded, and follows Roderigo to be reconciled with Diego. This may be because of R.L.'s narrowing of focus to concentrate on the two lovers. It may also be to avoid the medieval barbarity of the whole incident, which the moralizing of Fenton (following Belleforest) on women's being 'voide of raison' because they are influenced by the changes of the moon and will not accept a new suitor, under threat of death, days after the brutal murder of an old one, makes particularly unpleasant reading.[23] But R.L.'s omission might also be from lack of sympathy with that part of the tale that deplores falling in love with a social inferior. (The steward was a 'gentleman', but without means.)

At the end of the story, R.L. reinforces *his* lesson, which is that his Diella too should 'impose some end to undeserved ruth', as he put it in the lead-in thirty-eighth sonnet. This he does with an extra couplet added to the last six-line stanza of the narrative: 'Then (deerest love) Gyneuryze at the last,/ And I shall soone forget what ere is past'. There follows a single sonnet in Shakespearean form, like the sonnets of *Diella* itself, which perhaps significantly contains the rhyme-syllable '-ill' in two different quatrains, the first and the third – a signature?

There are a number of Will-like (in the sense of being typical of Shakespeare) features of *Dom Diego*. The habit of dramatizing by putting direct speech into the characters' mouths has been pin-pointed. It is of a piece with Shakespeare's dramatization in his narrative poem *Lucrece*, which is the sole version to give Tarquin a voice or a mind by endowing him with long psychologically intricate soliloquies.[24] *Lucrece* provides other parallels with *Dom Diego*. I could go into the equal balancing of speeches for the female and male protagonist, the immediacy of the opening in both poems, in which we are plunged straight into the story, and the interest in internal psychological conflict. But I shall concentrate on two very Shakespearean traits R.L. demonstrates.

He has, firstly, a fondness for Shakespearean clusters of imagery. Critics have drawn attention to the evocation in Macbeth's 'dagger' speech of the passage in *Lucrece* when Tarquin stalks through the chambers at night towards his victim's curtained bed, when 'the eye of night is out'.[25]

> Now o'er the one half-world
> Nature seems dead, and wicked dreams abuse
> The curtain'd sleep; now witchcraft celebrates
> Pale Hecate's offerings; and wither'd murder,
> Alarum'd by his sentinel, the wolf,
> Whose howl's his watch, thus with his stealthy pace,
> With Tarquin's ravishing strides, towards his design
> Moves like a ghost.

Now compare the language of Macbeth in that speech with the language of the following stanza of R.L.'s *Dom Diego*.

The gloomy Curtaines of the tongue-lesse night,
  Were drawne so close as day could not be seene,
Now leaden-thoughted Morpheus dyms each sight,
  Now murder, rapes, and robberies begin:
Nature crav'd rest, but restlesse Love would none,
Diego, Loves young prentice, thus gan mone.

(D7v)

Caroline Spurgeon was the first to identify in Shakespeare's writing the recurrence of 'thought clusters', and a recognizable grouping is observable in these three cases: night falling ... curtains ... sleep/Morpheus ... Nature dead or resting ... someone who stays awake ... murder, rapes, robberies.[26] To spell it out: the R.L. of *Dom Diego* makes the imaginative associations typical of early Shakespeare.

A second Shakespearean trait in R.L. is the hugely innovative vocabulary. The daring of that English coinage 'Gyneuryze', 'act as a (true) Gyneura', is typical of Shakespeare. The large number of first uses of words as given in the *OED* (and some which antedate the *OED*'s first given date of occurrence) is striking. I present the evidence of the poet's 'idiolect' or personal idiosyncrasies of speech under headings in Table 3.1.

One candidate sometimes canvassed for authorship of *Diella* and *Dom Diego* is Richard Linche, who clearly knew Italian well, since his *Fountaine of Ancient Fiction* is a translation from a genuine Italian work. Nothing is known of Linche or Lynche except his translations, which comprise the *Fountaine*, some translations from Latin and from the Italian of Claudianus, and a pseudo-translation, *The Historical Treatise of the Travels of Noah into Europe*, which is by far the most interesting. This last could not possibly be a translation, though the author, R. Lynche, Gent., claims on the title page that it was 'Done into English'. It draws, he says in his dedication, on the work of Berosus, who was a scholar in the hermetic tradition. So one would expect some syncretism – and indeed, the mythography in which Lynche interested himself was a peculiar blend of classical and medieval material. But Lynche takes this to ludicrous extremes.

The *Travels of Noah* starts with Noah living in Phoenicia. An incomprehensible and quite impossible family tree follows, on which the author himself frequently gives up, with phrases such as '... which now to recite, were tedious and impertinent to our purpose' or '... and many others, now too long to recite'. Pandora is the wife of one of Noah's sons: Triton is one of his distant descendants. At the end, the author simply runs out of energy:

Table 3.1   R.L.'s idiolect

Pre-*OED* first recorded words
adamantick (*OED* first use 1605), *DD* 78.
tapistred (*OED* first use 1630), *DD* 66.
simpathize meaning 'feel as one with' (*OED* first use 1605 – but it is a favourite Shakespearean word, occurring in similar uses in *Richard II*, *Lucrece*, *Henry V*, *Love's Labour's Lost*, *Sonnets*), *DD* 51.
'*agravate* my spight': this should be the first use in the sense of 'intensify an evil', but *OED* gives 1597. *DD* 64. Shakespeare has this use in *Edward III*.

First use recorded by *OED*
conglomerate, *DD* 74.
impassionated, *DD* 52: compare *compassionate*, which occurs in *DD* 73 and 81, in *Titus Andronicus*, and *Richard II* (*OED* first use is 1587, *Mirror for Magistrates*) (cf. 'Langham's Letter', p. 22, line 1565, *compassiond* with me – a unique use).
ymedicable, *Diella* 1.

No parallel in use, or nonce word
cookerie ('drudge and toile'), *DD.* 73.
inquisitive (in the sense of 'asking questions, like an inquisitor'), *DD* 77.
flintfull heart, *DD* 65.

'Rare' according to *OED* (which gives only this example)
irresisted force, *DD* 67.

Used by Shakespeare
disgorge thy hate, *DD* 80 (*Tr. and Cr.* Disgorge passengers from a ship).
metamorphize, *DD* 65, in *Two Gentlemen* (*OED* first use).
ruminate, *DD* 52, used by 'Langham', also *1 Henry VI*, V. 5. 101. (But *OED* gives even earlier instances.)
they murder hope, *DD* 75. Figurative use of 'murder' occurs earlier in the phrase, 'murder souls', but that is very close to the literal. Only Shakespeare uses the verb completely figuratively before the eighteenth century: 'murdered this poure heart of mine' (*Venus and Adonis*); 'Macbeth does murther Sleepe' (*Macbeth*).

Table 3.1 (cont'd)

In current use but very Shakespearean
inexorable, in conjunction with tigers both in *Romeo and Juliet* V. 3. 38, and *DD* 75.
indissoluble (*Macbeth* III. 1. 17), *DD* 67.
invocates, earlier in religious contexts, but nowhere else secular except Shakespeare's *Sonnets*, and *1 Henry VI. DD* 49 and 59.

Formation of a verb with the prefix 'en'
The *OED* notes this use in Shakespeare (including *Edward III*) and in John Florio in the sixteenth century. Florio coins such words to translate an Italian 'in', e.g. 'to enlead' for 'impiombare'; 'to insope' for 'insaponare'.
endip (first use), *DD* 82.
eniourney (nonce-word), *DD* 82.
[*imparadiz'd*, used in print in 1592 by Samuel Daniel and Henry Constable]

Note: references given are the page numbers of Grosart's edition, since the stanzas are not
          numbered, and the original book is hard to obtain.

> And for this time (beeing indeed forced by an extraordinarie occasion) I must thus on the suddaine abruptly breake of; desiring and wishing very earnestly, that if this small peece of paines of mine shall fortune ever to bee publickely impressed (which leaving behind mee, it will not bee in my power to prevent) it may indifferently passe uncensured, till the returne of his fortune-beaten father may aunswere for the innocencie of the child, and bee able a little better to protect him in his afflictions. (O3r)

The cheeky jibe at the usual disclaimers of writers who claim their work was 'bewrayed' to printers against their wishes and the casualness of the whole enterprise is of a piece with his extraordinary cheek in dedicating the whole to Peter Manwood, who was an antiquary with a great interest in collecting and transcribing books.[27] It may also be a deliberate joke against the protestations of 'Richard Linche', author of the *Fountaine*, whether this personage is Lynche's own previous self, or another, a worthily dull translator of genuine Italian works. The author of the *Fountaine* had claimed that his work 'happened into the hands of a stranger', and when he saw it was 'irrevocably escaped' he 'chose to father it' (A2r). He 'never imagined [it] to have been now subiect to the error-searching sight of a generall eye, being only pend and translated for mine owne exercises and private recreations' (A2v).

The Fountaine is a rather selective and slightly distorted prose translation of Vincenzo Cartari's *Le imagini de I dei de gli antichi*.[28] It has some pedantic Latinate vocabulary, such as 'suppeditate' (to supply), 'decurtaile and cut away', 'redemyted' (wreathed), the last two of which may be coinages – the *OED* does not contain the words. But it does not match the lively and inventive *Diego* at all, whereas the treatise on Noah's travels has something of the same spirit. There was something not quite right about the *Travels*, it seems, for it was reissued in 1602 with the title page cancelled. The Phoenician setting gives it a strongly Sidneian flavour, allying it to the Phoenix theme of the Sidney siblings. And the flavour is intensified when we recognize that Adam Islip, the printer and publisher, used as his title-page *impresa* a palm tree – which is likewise a 'phoinix'. Islip was hand-in-glove with John Wolfe, often passing off his (Wolfe's) imprints as his own.[29] In 1579, Wolfe described himself as 'servitore de l'illustrissimo signior Filippo Sidnei'.[30]

The balance of probability on the identity or otherwise of Lynche and Linche is not easy to determine. That the author of *Fountaine* spelled his name Linche and the author of *Travels* spelled his Lynche is of course not relevant to the question, since such laxity was common. It is tempting to reason as follows.

A certain author, R.L., who had co-written a lively prose account of the Kenilworth festivities in 1575 and a sonnet sequence and romance when still quite young, wrote also a spoof genealogy in prose, to amuse the Sidney circle. When the scholarly Richard Linche published his translation *The Fountaine of Ancient Fiction*, taken from the Italian of Cartari, the cheeky R.L. seized on the opportunity offered by Linche's initials to publish his pseudo-mythology about Noah and his descendants, which he claimed was also translated. He used the same publisher, the same format of title page, and called himself Lynche. When he did so, Linche objected – a familiar sequence of events – and the book was temporarily withdrawn, and reissued without the name Lynche, or indeed any name or title page.

But a recently published article on Shakespeare's knowledge of Italian mythographers such as Cartari alters the balance somewhat. John Mulryan demonstrates Shakespeare's debt to the legends as transmitted by Cartari and his fellow mythographer Conti.[31] It is not part of Mulryan's thesis that Shakespeare necessarily knew the works at first hand. But that is after all the most economical theory. It would set up an intimate connection between Shakespeare and the learned Linche who translated Cartari's *Fountaine*. It might even be enough to establish identity: for if Shakespeare had had to wait till 1599 for the English version of the *Fountaine* to appear in print, we should be hard pressed to account for the close acquaintance with the 'Italian' mythography that is revealed in his early plays. Better to suppose that he *was* Linche.

There is another sonnet sequence, also published in 1596, that contains a rare formal feature to be found in the *Diella* sequence. William Smith's *Chloris, or The Complaint of the passionate despised Shepheard*, consisting of fifty sonnets, was published by Edmond Bollifant.[32] The anomaly is a doubled thirteenth sonnet. In *Diella*, Sonnet 13 forms a single sonnet with its successor, also labelled 'Sonnet XIII'. The whole has quite an intricate and formal rhyme, being abab bcbc cdcd de/de efef fgfg hh. There is a textual break after 14 lines, a new heading 'Sonnet XIII', and the second d-e pair launches a twelve-line quasi-sonnet. Obviously one complete poem has been arbitrarily split in two midway through the fourth quatrain. A normal sonnet, 'Sonnet XIV', follows. The thirteenth sonnet of *Chloris* is likewise doubled in length, with twenty-six lines arranged as six quatrains and a couplet. It has its own title – 'Corin's dreame of his faire Chloris'.

In an age of intrigue and false personae, of anonymous and semi-anonymous publication, an indicator such as an anomalous sonnet of the same form in the same position in two disparate sequences must have carried great weight. To treat the feature as coincidental, a fortuitous similarity of two practitioners, would not have occurred to a sixteenth-century reader; nor should it to us. Either the author is the same in both cases, or one is paying homage to, or copying, another. The immediate tasks before us, then, are to see what can be gleaned from the contents and the circumstances of publication of Smith's *Chloris* and of R.L.'s *Diella*. Are we dealing with authorial identity, an act of plagiarism or an act of homage?

The entry in the Stationers' Register of Smith's *Chloris* on 5 October 1596 contains a particular condition, that the publisher 'procure it to be laufully aucthorised before he prynt yt'.[33] This means that Bollifant had not already obtained the 'allowance' of the ecclesiastical authorities – nominally the Archbishop of Canterbury or the Bishop of London, but often someone to whom they had delegated the task; and that the Wardens of the Stationers' Company did not want to authorize publication ('license' it) without that allowance. Such a system of authorization had formally come into being in 1586.[34] The ecclesiastical authorization was intended to block publication of anything subversive of Church or State; but the Wardens did not always require it – many more works were 'licensed' by them than were 'allowed'. A dozen plays were referred in this way between 1591 and 1606,[35] but no other sonnet sequences were – though Gascoigne's romance *The Adventures of F.J.*

in 1576 and Philip Sidney's *Astrophel and Stella* in 1591 had been subject to direct intervention by the Privy Council.

It is difficult to see why sonnets should be thought dangerous to the interests of the Queen or of religion; and it is clear that highly placed individuals could lean on the licensing authorities to prevent publication of something noxious to or risky for them personally, as happened in 1586 when Greville prompted Walsingham to lean on Warden Cosin and the archbishop to block the licensing or allowing of Sidney's *Arcadia*.[36] Indeed, Sidney family interest is to be suspected also in the case of both *The Adventures of F.J.* and *Astrophel and Stella*.[37] I would therefore claim that the most likely explanation for the condition attached to *Chloris* is an attempt to avoid, yet again, a scandal involving the Sidneys.

Chloris was the chief nymph in the 'Aprill' eclogue of Spenser's *Shepheardes Calender*, published in 1579.[38] I shall suppose as a working hypothesis that Smith's Muse is the same woman as Chloris the chief of the Ladies of the Lake in 'Aprill'. One scholar has already remarked that the setting of 'Aprill' seems to recall the events at Kenilworth, thus extending the link backwards in time.[39] The glosses of E.K. on Spenser's 'Aprill' can perhaps pave the way for a forward link to Smith's publication. This mysterious commentator E.K., who is known only by his initials, alludes to without quite explaining the fact that the classical Chloris, goddess of green things, transmogrified into Flora, goddess of flowers.[40] If we turn back to 'March', we find a very odd footnote of E.K.'s on 'Flora'.

> Flora, the Godddesse of flowres, but indede (as saith Tacitus) a famous harlot, which with the abuse of her body having gotten great riches, made the people of Rome her heyre: who in remembraunce of so great benefice, appointed a yearely feste for the memoriall of her, calling her, not as she was, nor as some doe think, Andronica, but Flora ....[41]

Nobody ever called Flora 'Andronica': what is E.K. up to? He is, I think, planting a clue that the daughter of Titus Andronicus, Lavinia, the only female member of the Andronici, is to be identified with the real-life correlate of Flora/Chloris in the coterie literature. This is startling, but what are we to make of it? For the moment, I shall confine myself to suggesting that it shows the theme of the Andronici to be part of the mental furniture of the Sidney circle in 1579; and it is not hard to see how that might have come about. The Andronici (in the wildly a-historical prose history that must have been Shakespeare's source for the early play *Titus Andronicus*, according to G. Harold Metz)[42] were the bulwark of Rome, but they voluntarily give up office, only to be decimated by the ruling family. The recent history of the Dudley family with its triumphs and disasters (described at the beginning of Chapter 1) mirrors that of the legendary Andronici.

Smith's Chloris, then, with her suggestive links to Flora and Andronica, would have caused a furore had she been publicly identified as poor 'Corin's' mistress at the time he was addressing her. We have confirmation of this from the last sonnet, number 50. Smith writes:

> *Colin* I know that in thy lofty wit
> Thou wilt but laugh at these my youthfull lines,
> Content I am, they should in silence sit,
> Obscur'd from light, to sing their sad designes:
> But that it pleased thy grave shepherdhood
> The Patron of my maiden verse to bee,
> When I in doubt of raging Envie stood,
> And now I waigh not who shall *Chloris* see.[43]

There are clearly two different time-scales involved, marked by the 'youthfull lines' of line 2, the contrasting 'now' of line 8, and the change of tense after line 4. This sonnet is an 'envoi', a packaging up and sending into the world of the work of his youth, now that it is safe, or safer, to do so. But who was 'William Smith', that his adoration of Chloris should be found so outrageous?

He was clearly someone in the heart of Spenser's circle, for the appeal in sonnet 50 to Colin would have been understood by contemporaries as an appeal to Spenser. There are also two linked prefatory sonnets 'To the most excellent and learned Shepheard Collin Cloute'. And as Smith's editor Grosart wrote: 'It seems strange that one who faced the world with his simple name on his title page, and was evidently known to and apparently cared for by Spenser, should have passed out of contemporary memories and records'.[44]

It is more than strange. But is there no historical William Smith who might fit the bill? We need to find one who had some connections with Spenser when the latter was in the Sidney orbit (effectively, before 1589, since Spenser was more or less continuously in Ireland after that); a literary person who (ideally) is known to have written poetry.

There is a William Smith with exactly the right characteristics. He once presented the Countess of Pembroke, Mary Sidney, with a New Year's gift of a poetic 'posy', or 'poesy', of flowers. It is a little home-made pamphlet entitled 'A newyeares Guifte made upon certen Flowers', and is to be found in the British Library manuscript room.[45] It has a patterned cover. Inside the cover page are the words: 'A posie made upon certen flowers'; and on page 3, 'Presented To the right noble, honourable and the singuler good Ladie, the Countesse of Pembrooke'. Below this are seven couplets of verse, ending: 'Through wch; My Muse presumes to offer you,/ although unknowne, yet pretious love, and trewe'. Subscript: 'William Smith'. Seven pleasing little poems in *sesta rima* on various flowers, in a clear italic hand, fill the rest of the simple book.

The editors of the *Collected Works* of Mary Sidney read the declaration at the end of the verse dedication as meaning that Smith did not know Mary.[46] This may be so, though the poet might mean that his Muse (his talent) is unknown, or that he is unknown to the wider world, or that his love is not known to Mary. ('His love' may of course be the respectful duty owed by a humble dependent.) But another poem by Smith, also in *sesta rima*, found by Kent Talbot van den Berg in the Yale University Library, likewise suggests that the poet is unknown to his addressee.[47] Van den Berg believes the addressee of this Osborn Manuscript is once again Mary Sidney. The booklet is in the same hand and the same format as the 'Newyeares' Guifte' and is headed by a prose preface addressed to 'Madam'. It is signed: 'your Ladyshippes devoted servante as a stranger. William Smythe'.

It is puzzling that Smith should offer a 'precious love and true' to one whom he did not know at all; even more puzzling that he should claim to be unknown on a *second* occasion – whether the second was that of the 'Guifte' or the offering of the Osborn MS. It sets one searching for alternative explanations. Perhaps the devoted servant who offers this booklet is estranged from himself – writing under a pseudonym?

Why 'Smith'? A William Smith lived in Henley Street, near John Shakespeare. The two families were close, and Edgar Fripp believes Smith could have stood as godfather to John's son William.[48] The practice of 'Supposes' (impersonations) in the Sidney circle makes the supposition (guess) that young William Shakespeare borrowed the name of his godfather plausible. It makes the line of Berowne's in *Love's Labour's Lost*: 'And every godfather can give a name', take on a humorous resonance – perhaps unintended, perhaps not.[49] However that may be, the Osborn manuscript demands further investigation.

It is 396 lines long, and concerns the figure of Time vindicating himself before a parliament of all living creatures. It is, as van den Berg points out, quite like the pleading of Mutability in Spenser's *Mutabilitie Cantos* in *The Faerie Queene*. Indeed, it seems at one point that Time will win his case to hold sway in the sublunary world only, not in heaven, just as Mutabilitie does. But in fact Time makes out a better case, and is adjudged powerful everywhere. Time is then asked to give a fuller account of himself, in answer to his creatures' questioning. His wife is Opportunity, he replies; her servants are Humility and Thankfulness. He has three daughters, Experience, Patience and Truth, who is naked. He himself has servants, Providence, Diligence and Prudence. His neighbours are five: Love, Temperance, Justice, Liberality, Fortitude. Taxed by his interlocutors to admit that he has been economical with the truth ('queintly glosed'), Time admits he once fell for the strumpet 'Fancie', and fathered three illegitimate children, Excuse, Protraction and Deceit. 'Fancie's' servants are Pride and Unthankfulness.

Though clearly indebted to past iconography, William Smith's ethics are also very much his own. Ingratitude figures large (as it does in Shakespeare's beautiful song 'Blow, blow, thou winter's wind'). Whereas the classical cardinal virtues are Justice, Temperance, Prudence, Fortitude, Smith has removed Prudence to servant rank, elevated Liberality, and, most appealingly, placed Love first. The presentation of Time and Opportunity in a semi-metaphysical dissertation in poetry is paralleled by Lucrece's meditation on Night, Opportunity and Time in Shakespeare's *Rape of Lucrece*.[50]

Here, then, is a Smith who *is* a poet, in the very heart of the Sidney circle, with Shakespearean interests. It is quite possible that the presentation pamphlets are the autograph books of the William Smith of *Chloris*, the poor Corin who nurtured an impossible love. He entered our story because he has an intimate relationship of some kind with the R.L. of *Diella* through the formal link of their lengthened thirteenth sonnets. We questioned whether the link constituted evidence of identity, or of influence. A later case casts light on this question.

There is an anomalous 'sonnet' in Shakespeare's sonnet sequence of 1609: number 126, 'O thou my lovely Boy', is only twelve lines long, and consists of couplets. William Smith's Sonnet 27 is of the same form. Shakespeare's sonnet is about the inexorable progress of Time, whose fickle glass, sickle and hour the lovely boy has only temporarily stolen. The Osborn Manuscript author likewise meditates on Time, who is portrayed there with his sickle and hourglass.

It would seem extraordinarily unlikely that Shakespeare should imitate the idiosyncratic habit of including a non-sonnet in a sonnet sequence, and that he should imitate exactly the *same form* of non-sonnet, the *douzain*, from some obscure poet who faded from public notice. Shakespeare shares this poet's initials and first name. He shares his obsessions. It would be fair to conclude: he is this poet. We begin to suspect that the little 'posie' is far more precious than the British Library knows; and the almost forgotten manuscript in the Yale University Library perhaps equally precious.

The pressure of space prevents me from analysing William Smith's sonnets in detail, to see how they compare with Shakespeare's. But there is one (Sonnet 18) I cannot resist quoting as a small taster, for it expresses that suspicion of 'making comparisons' (in the sense of trying to pin down the beloved's essence with similes) that is so prevalent in Shakespeare's *Sonnets.*

> My Love, I cannot thy rare beauties place
> Under those formes which many writers use.
> Some like to stones compare their mistres' face;
> Some in the name of flowers do love abuse;
> Some make their love a goldsmith's shop to be,
> Where orient pearles and pretious stones abounde.
> In my conceite these farre do disagree,
> The perfect praise of beautie foorth to sounde.
> O Chloris thou dost imitate thy selfe;
> Self's imitating passeth pretious stones,
> Or all the Easterne Indian golden pelfe:
> Thy red and white with purest faire attones:
>> Matchlesse for beautie nature hath thee framed,
>> Onely unkinde, and cruell thou art named.

The discovery that Shakespeare used a formal device, the *douzain*, to flag his identity (retrospectively) with William Smith can serve to conflate the identities of William Smith and R.L. also, who flagged their identities with their doubled thirteenth sonnets. The differing quality of the two 1596 sonnet sequences strongly suggests that the *Diella* sonnets were composed even earlier than those of *Chloris*, which were themselves written in the poet's youth. R.L.'s are stiffer and more conventional in imagery than those of Smith, whose sonnets do occasionally get included in selections. The progression towards the intricate and marvellous sonnets published in 1609 is nevertheless exciting to observe.

In 1624, a great many years after the Kenilworth visit, Jonson presented *A Masque of Owles at Kenelworth. Presented by the Ghost of Captaine Coxe mounted in his Hoby-horse.*[51] It is rather an odd little piece, with six owls taking the speaking parts, and recalling the Queen's visit of 1575. The fifth stanza is especially odd.

> But here was a defeat
> Never any so great,

Of a Don, a Spanish Reader,
Who had thought to have bin the Leader
(Had the Match gon on)
Of our Ladyes one by one,
And triumpht our whole Nation
In his *Rodomant* fashion:
But now since the breach,
He has not a Scholler to teach.

No Spanish Reader featured in the Kenilworth narratives: but a Spanish 'principe negro' featured large in his own account. Could this be the Don to whom Jonson obliquely refers? Could he be connected with Diego? A nonsense poem by a witty writer John Sanford, published in 1611 with nonsense notes attached, suggests the answer in both cases is 'Yes'.[52] Sanford explains that Don Diego was 'a famous reader in the Bay of Mexico'. Here is our Spanish Reader, who parades as a ghostly owl years after the Kenilworth visit. If we find that the Rodomant and the schoolmaster can be likewise hooked onto the thread of Shakespeare's biography, we shall justifiably conclude that Jonson is offering us a reverse-telescopic glimpse of a series of young Shakespeares, right back to the child starstruck by Captain Cox and his hobby horse.

Notes

1   R.L. (Gent.), *Diella, Certaine sonnets, adioyned to the amorous Poeme of Dom Diego and Gyneura* (London: James Robert for Henry Olney, 1596). A.B. Grosart, ed., *Occasional Issues of Unique or Very Rare Books*, 17 vols (Edinburgh: privately printed, 1877), 4b.
2   *A Paradyce of Dayntie Devises* (London: R. Jones for H. Disle, 1576), L2r–v. Hyder E. Rollins, ed. (Cambridge, MA: Harvard University Press, 1927), number 93, p. 81.
3   Richard Linche, *The Fountaine of Ancient Fiction. Done out of Italian into English* (London: Adam Islip, 1599), a translation of Vincenzo Cartari's *Imagini de I dei de gli antichi* (Venice [Venetia]: F. Marcolini, 1556).
4   Richard Lynche, *An Historical Treatise of the Travels of Noah into Europe* (London: Adam Islip, 1601).
5   Michael Drayton, *Matilda* (London: J. Roberts for J. Busby, 1594), A4r. *Michael Drayton, Works*, ed. J.W. Hebel, 5 vols (1941; Oxford: Basil Blackwell, 1961), 1. 209–46, 213.
6   Edwd. Utterson, ed., *Diella* (London: Beldornie Press, J.N. Lyall for Edwd. V. Utterson, 1841), note on the colophon.
7   W.C. Hazlitt, *Hand-book to the Popular, Poetical and Dramatic Literature of Great Britain* (London: John Russell Smith, 1867), s.n. Linch, p. 335. Drayton's *Matilda* was included in the volume entitled *Robert Duke of Normandy* (London: J. Roberts for N. Ling, 1596), and the poem reappears on fol. P3v.
8   Grosart, *Occasional Issues*, 4, intro., pp. v–vii.

9   Michael Drayton, *Ideas Mirrour* (London: J. Roberts for N. Ling, 1594), H2r. *Works*, 5.17.

10 It is the same work as *The Defence of Poesie* published by Ponsonby in the same year.

11 Nashe, *Works*, 5.194–5.

12 Thomas Dekker and John Webster (and others?), *The Famous History of Sir Thomas Wyatt* (London: E[dward] A[llde] for Thomas Archer, 1607). John S. Farmer, ed. (London: Tudor Facsimile Texts, 1914), E2r–E2v.

13 Thomas Heywood, *Fair Maid of the West or, A Girl Worth Gold* (London: Richard Royston, 1631), part first, p. 51.

14 See below, Chapter 5.

15 Samuel Schoenbaum, *William Shakespeare: A Compact Documentary Life* (1977; Oxford: Oxford University Press, 1987), pp. 38–9; 227–32.

16 See J. Kerrigan, ed. and intro., *Shakespeare: The Sonnets and a Lover's Complaint* (London: Penguin, 1986), pp. 1–15.

17 Matteo Bandello, *Novelle*, 3 vols (1554; Venice: C. Franceschini, 1566), vol. 1, Chapter 25. François Belleforest, *Histoires Tragiques* (1564), story 18, in *The French Bandello*, ed. and intro. Frank S. Hook (Columbia: University of Missouri Studies, 1948), pp. 83–128.

18 Geoffrey Fenton, *Certaine Tragicall Discourses of Bandello* (London: Thomas Marshe, 1567), fols 265–306.

19 William Painter, *The Palace of Pleasure*, 2 vols (London: H. Bynneman for N. England, 1567), Tome 2, novel 29, fols 309v–350r.

20 Belleforest, pp. 86–7; Fenton, fols 268–9; Painter, fol. 313r–v.

21 R.L., *Diego*, D6; Bandello, fol. 93v; Belleforest, p. 86; Fenton, fol. 267.

22 Painter, fol. 312v.

23 Belleforest, p. 116; Fenton, fol. 294. Painter likewise speaks of Gyneura's 'fickle fragillitie' connected to the phases of the moon, fol. 338v.

24 William Shakespeare, *The Rape of Lucrece* (London: Richard Field, 1594). Reference is to *Shakespeare: The Narrative Poems*, ed. M. Evans (London: Penguin, 1989).

25 *Lucrece*, lines 169–378. *Macbeth*, II.1.49–56.

26 Caroline Spurgeon, *Shakespeare's Imagery* (1935; Cambridge: Cambridge University Press, 1965), pp. 192–9.

27 See Henry Woudhuysen, *Sir Philip Sidney and The Circulation of Manuscripts, 1558–1640* (Oxford: Clarendon Press, 1996), pp. 129–33.

28 See note 3.

29 Ronald B. McKerrow, *Printers' and Publishers' Devices in England and Scotland, 1485–1640* (London: Chiswick, 1913), no. 226.

30 *Short Title Catalogue of English Books, 1475–1640*, ed. A Pollard and G. Redgrave, 2nd edn revised by W. Jackson and F. Ferguson, completed by K. Pantzer, 3 vols (Oxford: Oxford University Press, 1986), s.v. 'Acontius', no. 92.

31 John Mulryan, 'Shakespeare and the Italian Mythographers', *The Shakespearean International Yearbook 2002*, ed. W.R. Elton and John M. Mucciolo, 2 vols (Aldershot: Ashgate, 2002), 2.305–17.

32 William Smith, *Chloris, or The Complaint of the passionate despised Shepheard* (London: Edm. Bollifant, 1596). Citations will be from the original and the edition of A.B. Grosart, *Occasional Issues*, 3c.

33 *Records of the Court of the Stationers' Company*, ed. W.W. Greg and E. Boswell, 5 vols (London: Bibliographical Society, 1930), 3.71.

34 See Peter Blayney 'The Publication of Playbooks' in *A New History of Early English Drama*, ed. John Cox and David Scott Kastan (New York: Columbia University Press, 1997), pp. 383–422.

35 E.K. Chambers, *The Elizabethan Stage*, 4 vols (Oxford: Clarendon Press, 1923), 3.169. I exclude two of Chambers' candidates whose right to copy was in question.

36 See Sidney, *Poems*, p. 530.

37 Cyndia Susan Clegg, *Press Censorship in Elizabethan England* (Cambridge: Cambridge University Press, 1997), pp. 103–22. For *Astrophel and Stella*, see Germaine Warkentin, 'Patrons and Profiteers: Thomas Newman and the "Violent Enlargement" of "Astrophil and Stella"', *The Book Collector* 34.4 (1985), pp. 461–87.

38 Edmund Spenser, *The Shepheardes Calender* (London: Hugh Singleton, 1579). *Works*, pp. 415–67.

39 Richard McCoy, 'Eulogies to Elegies: Poetic Distance in the April Eclogue', *Soundings of Things Done: Essays in Early Modern Literature in Honor of S.K. Heninger Jr.*, ed. P. Medine and J. Wittreich (London: Associated University Presses, 1997), pp. 52–69, esp. 58–66.

40 The iconography of 'Aprill' alludes to Botticelli's 'Primavera'. The figure of Hermes/Mercury dominates the foreground in Botticelli, and is not mentioned by Spenser. But for reasons which will become apparent in chapter 6, it is an absence which cries aloud.

41 Spenser, *Works*, p. 430.

42 G. Harold Metz, *Shakespeare's Earliest Tragedy: Studies in Titus Andronicus* (London: Associated University Presses, 1996), pp. 150–89.

43 *Chloris*, 50, lines 1–8; Grosart, *Occasional Issues*, 3.30.

44 Grosart, *Occasional Issues*, 3.8.

45 BL Additional MS 35186.

46 *The Collected Works of Mary Sidney Herbert, Countess of Pembroke*, ed. M. Hannay, N. Kinnamon, and M. Brennan, 2 vols (Oxford: Clarendon Press, 1998), 1.28–9.

47 Osborn MS, Yale University Library. Kent Talbot van den Berg, 'An Elizabethan Allegory of Time by William Smith', *ELR* 6.1 (Winter 1976), pp. 40–59.

48 Edgar Fripp, *Shakespeare Man and Artist*, 2 vols (1938; London: Oxford University Press, 1964), 1.39. See also his *Shakespeare's Stratford*, p. 15.

49 *Love's Labour's Lost*, I.1.93.

50 *Lucrece*, lines 764–1029.

51 *The Workes of Benjamin Jonson. The Second Volume* (London: Richard Meighen, 1640), pp. 125–8 of Masques section. *Ben Jonson*, ed. C. Herford, P. Simpson and E. Simpson, 11 vols (Oxford: Clarendon Press, 1925–50), 11.781.

52 John Sanford, 'A Sceleton or bare Anatomie of the *Punctures and Junctures of Mr. Thomas Coryate of Odcombe*', in *Coryats Crudities* (London: William Stansby, 1611), sigs li(v)–lii(v). See Noel Malcolm, *Origins of English Nonsense* (London: Fontana, 1997), pp. 130–36, 134.

Chapter 4

More Supposes

In this chapter, I trace the involvement of Harvey and Spenser in William Shakespeare's education as a poet in the late 1570s. If it was Shakespeare who masked himself as the R.L. investigated in the previous chapter, we need to account for his acquisition of Italian. If William Smith is the same historical person, we need to account for his tribute to Spenser as the poetic mentor of his youth. R.L.'s connections with the Sidney circle and Sidneian publishers demand explanation. I shall take up the 'William Smith' skein to pursue them through Spenser's *Shepheardes Calender*; a Paper Book associated with the *Calender*, which contains work by a mysterious A.W.; a catalogue of A.W.'s poems; further texts by A.W.; a sonnet in Smith's *Chloris* related to a settina of A.W.'s; and the 'Three Familiar Letters' 'passed between' Harvey and Spenser in 1579/80. This trawling expedition nets more pseudonyms for Shakespeare.

William Smith had his *Chloris* published by Edmond Bollifant in 1596. In 1585, Bollifant had published a translation of 'Aesopz fablz', in the same peculiar orthography as that of the Kenilworth R.L.[1] The Kenilworth R.L. might be identical with the R.L. who wrote *Diella*, whom we linked with the *Chloris* Smith by means of the 'extended thirteenth sonnet' phenomenon. This is an interesting epicycle on the R.L. system.

The translator of *Aesopz Fablz*, a William Bullokar, explains that his work is in effect a 'crib': he could have written in more gracious English, but he has stuck closely to the Latin phraseology to help learners. Part of his aim, he says, is the introduction of 'tru ortographie'. He had published a book on the amendment of orthography in 1580 with a different publisher, and was to publish some rules of grammar, again with Bollifant, in 1586.

There is no compelling reason to doubt William Bullokar's bona fides. But an odd coincidence makes me wonder whether a process of identity snatching has not occurred. Spenser refers to Aesop's Fables in a gloss on his 'Februarie' eclogue in an incomprehensible way, mentioning Erasmus, clerks, fatherly godfathers and good old fathers. And Edgar Fripp, Shakespearean biographer, records that a William Smith of Stratford-upon-Avon inherited a copy of Aesop's Fables from the Stratford schoolmaster John Brechtgirdle, in 1565.[2] I shall combine these apparently disparate facts to try to vindicate my suspicion that a genuine Bullokar (the one published in 1580) had his identity usurped by a frivolous imitator.

The alderman to whose sons the schoolmaster bequeathed books was a William Smith, linen draper and mercer; and he had two sons called William. His oldest son, aged about seven in 1565, was a William and so was his youngest, a mere baby christened apparently in November 1564.[3] The younger William and a daughter received from Brechtgirdle not a book, but a shilling. To the older child William, the schoolmaster left *Aesop's Fables* together with the *Apophthegmata*, notable sayings from Greek and Roman literature (the former translated into Latin) and from the philosophers and sophists, collected for schoolchildren by Erasmus.

William Smith was indeed a common name in Stratford at the time. There were two others of the generation older than Shakespeare besides Alderman Smith: a haberdasher Smith, and a corviser (shoemaker) Smith. Then in Shakespeare's generation, besides the two sons of the mercer, there was a junior William in the haberdasher's family. Edgar Fripp has a Suppose of his own, which is that the haberdasher was William Shakespeare's godfather.[4] Though he warns his readers not to confuse the mercer and the haberdasher, Fripp makes it difficult for them not to do so, since he habitually calls the haberdasher 'Alderman' – which indeed he was, at a slightly later date than Smith the mercer! (The corviser hardly enters the picture, and is easy to distinguish in any case because he is 'Smith alias Hood' or 'Wood'.) The haberdasher was on the Stratford Council as a 'burgess' when mercer Smith was an alderman. The mercer was obviously wealthier: his tithes and taxes are much greater. But not all aldermen are referred to as 'Mr': the mercer was, and the haberdasher was not. The haberdasher's name appears in the common secretary script. The mercer's is the sole signature in an educated italic – not surprisingly, since he had been educated at Oxford.[5] He probably became acquainted there with John Watson, whose sister he married in a second marriage (for both spouses). Watson was a fellow of All Souls, and later became Bishop of Winchester.

The three Stratford William Smiths of Shakespeare's generation just mentioned lived within the orbit of potential Kenilworth patronage. Should any of them be preferred as candidate for the mysterious William Smith of the unique New Year posies presented to the Countess of Pembroke, or the William Smith of *Chloris*, who was in Spenser's orbit?

It was in 1579 that Spenser published his *Shepheardes Calender* with the publisher Hugh Singleton, who had that very year incurred suspicion for printing John Stubbs's *Discovery of a Gaping Gulf*, a pamphlet urging the

Queen not to marry the Duc d'Alençon. The Dudley clan were still violently opposed to the royal marriage: Philip Sidney was deputed by them to address a letter to the Queen to dissuade her from accepting Alençon. It seems likely that Singleton was protected by this powerful faction, for while Stubbs lost his right hand in punishment for the *Discovery*, Singleton miraculously came off scot-free, and was later to rise to the position of Printer to the City of London, from 1584–93. The title-page dedication of the *Calender* to 'M. Philip Sidney' corroborates its Dudley affiliation, as do the contemporaneous *Familiar Letters* between Spenser and Harvey intended to advertise the *Calendar*, in which compliments are sent to Sidney and Spenser's residence at Leicester House is ostentatiously mentioned.[6]

The obscurity of the *Calender* eclogues, one for each month, of the Epistle to Gabriel Harvey signed 'E.K.', of the General Argument and E.K.'s critical apparatus are notorious. Even the question of authorship was left somewhat obscure. No author appeared on the title page, and the note there 'entitling', rather than 'dedicating' the work to Philip Sidney left George Whetstone, for one, with the impression that Sidney wrote it.[7] Sidney's own notice of the publication is rather disparaging. He condemns the archaic style in his *Defence of Poesie*, saying somewhat contradictorily that there is good poetry in the eclogues.[8] George Puttenham too made a mystery of the author's identity, calling him 'that other Gentleman who wrate the late shepheardes Callender'.[9] The authorship should still be a matter of doubt, but strangely it is not. All take it that Spenser wrote it all. Yet apart from the facts just mentioned, there are two or three other considerations that should have given pause for thought.

Many critics now believe that the mysterious E.K. is Spenser himself; and I have argued that Spenser has given us unmistakable clues that this is so.[10] If it is, there are problems of 'voice'. The 'voice' of the Epistle (ostensibly E.K.'s) addressing his good friend Gabriel Harvey commends his own labour and 'the patronage of the new Poete'. He has high praise for the new poet. Are we to imagine Spenser is recommending and praising himself? Before jumping to the conclusion that he utilizes the E.K. device to distance himself from himself in order to blazon his own talents, or reverting to the hypothesis that E.K. is not after all Spenser, we should entertain the possibility that Spenser is promoting someone else.

As the 'Januarie' eclogue opens, the authorial voice describes a shepherd's boy called 'Colin Clout', as pale and wan as his flock. After two stanzas, the boy breaks into direct speech, and sings his plaintive song. Though he is loved by an older man, Hobbinol, he himself loves Rosalind – in vain. The last line of the penultimate stanza of 'Januarie' returns us unobtrusively from

Colin's speech to that of the narrator: 'So broke his oaten pype, and down did lye'. Whom are we to visualize as narrator, and whom as boy? There seem to be two figures here; and E.K., Harvey's 'singular good frend', as he called himself in his apostrophe to Harvey, compounds the mystery by the way he ends the Epistle. 'And thus recommending the Author unto you, as unto his most special good frend, and my selfe unto you both, as one making singuler account of two so very good and so choise frends, I bid you most hartely farwel ....'[11]

'Making singular account of two choice friends': Spenser has made one out of two. Let me suggest that Spenser cannot be seen in the guise of a shepherd's boy singing his first poems for his public. In 1579, he was about twenty-seven years old, which hardly counted then as youthful. He was not much younger than Harvey, who, a gloss to 'September' tells us unequivocally, is the real Hobbinol. Spenser had published (anonymously, admittedly) a work of translation, *A theatre ... Devised by S. John vander Noodt*, ten years before in 1569.[12] Many contemporary writers won reputations through translation, so it cannot be assumed that a lack of published 'original' work means that Spenser would have been perceived as a novice ten years later. His extended period of university education was far behind him and he was well launched on a prestigious career in the Leicester/Sidney circle on the strength of his humanist talent. He was of an age to set up house separately as a married man, which he did in 1580.[13]

The poet being launched by E.K. is first presented in the *Calender* as a shepherd's boy, young enough to be pursued by Hobbinol in a 'paederastice' love.[14] The pederastic theme is already present in E.K.'s Epistle: he offers up to Harvey the 'maydenhead of this our commen frends Poetrie,' though it has, apparently, previously been offered to Ma. Phi. Sidney.[15] The sexual metaphor (if it was mere metaphor)[16] is inappropriate to Spenser himself.

There is a strong suggestion, therefore, that another and younger poet is being introduced by Spenser, and incorporated somewhat surreptitiously ('sup-posed') into his *Calender.* This is achieved by a sleight of hand involving spelling. Spenser turned to his own advantage the common Elizabethan expectation that wide variation in the spelling of names was acceptable.[17] He used it to smuggle in extra characters, to write about someone other than the ostensible subject. This is a novel claim, and it underpins a novel hypothesis.

The hypothesis is that Colin the author of the lyrical songs in the *Calender* – in 'Aprill', 'August' and 'November' – is not the Collin who declares in 'June' that he 'connes no skill' of Muses (doesn't 'do' lyric.) The latter is no longer a boy: he refers twice to his past youth and his present 'riper' years. His plaint is not primarily a love plaint: he laments the death of 'Tityrus', and only as an afterthought accuses some lass of infidelity. He speaks in a very Spenserian stanza, as does his interlocutor Hobbinol. It is the Spenserian stanza of *The Faerie Queene* without the final hexameter line, and with only two rhymes per stanza. It is in the gloss to this eclogue that E.K. evokes a line of *The Faerie Queene*, attributing it to the 'Pageaunts' of 'thys same Poete'.[18] I think we can assume that this more prosaic and less lovelorn Collin (with a double 'll') is Spenser, particularly because an allusion to epic, in the form of an allusion to the opening of the Aeneid, attaches to him: 'But I unhappy man, whom cruell fate,/ And angry Gods pursue from coste to coste …'.[19]

The Elizabethans felt a deep divide between pastoral and epic. True, they felt it incumbent on them to make the 'Virgilian progression' from the first to the second. 'E.K.' utilizes this very expectation to pull wool over his readers' eyes about the *Calender* authorship. In the Epistle, he claims that his Author, perhaps doubting his poetic 'habilitie', followed previous poets who, like young birds just crept out of the nest, tried eclogues before attempting greater flights. 'So flew Theocritus', he says, 'as you may perceive he was all ready full fledged'. *The very first example contradicts rather than supports his thesis of natural poetic progression.* Theocritus is the lyric poet *par excellence*. E.K. goes on to cite Mantuan ('not full somd' [summed], but for all that, most famous for his pastoral); Virgil (of course); Petrarch and Boccaccio, surely more famous for their love poetry and tales than for epic; Marot and Sannazzaro (pastoral poets) 'whose foting this Author every where followeth, yet so as few, but they be wel sented can trace him out'. With this admission that there is a hidden figure in the work, Spenser also lets us know that the Author we have to decipher is not a poet about to launch on epic, but one who already shows talent in pastoral.

He is the other Colin (with a single 'l'), the Colin with the great lyrical gift that Collin lacks. It is this Colin whom Spenser and Harvey, I claim, mean to promote in both the *Calender* and the Letters. His songs are sometimes sung by others, once by himself. The first, in 'Aprill', is 'Ye dayntye Nymphs'. Hobbinol sings it, saying it was made by Colin. The next, from 'August', 'Ye wastefull woodes', was made by Colin and is sung by Cuddie. The third, 'Vp then Melpomene', comes in 'November' and is sung by Colin its maker. The three songs comprise the sum total of Colin's true songs in the *Calender*, for the January plaint was a simple continuation of the *sesta rima* of its context, and as we saw, melded back with it at its close. It was not distinguished by a capital letter at its start, in contrast with all Colin's songs, the song of Willy and Perigot in 'August', and the tales of Thenot in 'Februarie' and Piers in 'Maye'.[20] The tales are performances rather than songs, continuing with the same metre as their framing eclogues.

An odd gloss of E.K.'s in 'Aprill' compounds the suspicion that the three songs composed by Colin are by someone other than Spenser. Glossing the archaic 'yblent', E.K. explains that it means 'blinded', and that 'Y, is a poeticall addition'. He had not troubled to explain the archaic prefix when it occurred earlier in the same eclogue, in 'yclad'. If we are alert to the way he both misinforms and conveys secret information in his glosses, we can make a guess that he is hinting that a (capital) 'Y' indicates a 'poetical addition', some work by a different poet. Two of Colin's songs begin with 'Y', and one with 'V' for 'U' – the Greek upsilon which we transcribe as 'y', as in 'psyche'. The surrounding verses would be Spenser's own – a hypothesis which would give some sense to Sidney's peculiar observation that there is good poetry *in* the eclogues (an observation rather damning to Spenser). It would also imply that Puttenham's mention of 'that *other* Gentleman who wrate the late shepheardes Callender' could have a double meaning. It is interesting in this connection that the song in the 'August' eclogue is entirely without E.K.'s glosses, and so is most of the verse spoken by Colin in 'Januarie'. It could be that these 'blocks' of poetry had had a previous existence and were being incorporated whole.

That there really are two Colins in question is strongly hinted by the puzzling lack of an emblem in 'December'. At the end of all the previous eclogues, each contributing character pronounced a little posy, or emblem, summing up the sense of the eclogue, or his part in it. At the end of 'December' is printed 'Colins Embleme', but no emblem is given. Or so it seems. The Gloss gives an explanation of the emblem, however, from which it becomes plain that, firstly, the emblem is the sentiment that 'though all thinges perish and come to theyr last end ... workes of learned wits and monuments of Poetry abide for ever'; and secondly it is a *twinned* emblem. The words in which it is framed were uttered differently by Horace and by Ovid. The relevant lines of either are given in the Gloss – Horace's 'exegi monumentum aere perennius', and Ovid's 'grande opus exegi quod neque Iovis ira nec ignis ... poterit ... abolere'.[21]

Parallel with the two-faces-under-one-hood device, when we believe there is but one and there are really two, we are given a strong hint in a later gloss (on the name 'Cuddie' in the 'October' eclogue) that sometimes when we believe there are two, there is in fact only one. 'Some doubt' whether Cuddie the neatherd and Colin the shepherd's boy are different people, says

E.K., on the grounds that in 'August', Cuddie sang a song of Colin's.[22] The argument to 'August' tells us that 'Cuddie, a neatheards boye ... reciteth also himselfe a proper song, whereof Colin he sayth was Authour'.[23] 'Proper' can mean 'one's own'. In the Epistle, E.K. remarks, apparently to mislead but actually to alert the canny reader to the truth, that *Colin* compares the English Tityrus to the Roman one, Virgil. The comparison is in fact made by *Cuddie* in 'October'.[24] On the line immediately below the gloss that seeds the doubt on Cuddie's identity in this eclogue, we are given an unnecessary gloss on 'whilome', a word that has appeared before in 'Aprill'; while an adjacent gloss *in Latin* on the readily comprehensible 'oaten reedes' tells us it means 'Avena'. Like subliminal advertising, this sets up a subconscious association: 'William' + 'Avon'.

This is a new Suppose indeed, that Spenser composed the *Calender* to show his own talent, to be sure, and promote notice of Harvey's works; to flatter Sidney, and beg for his patronage and financial support; but *also* to give a platform to a very young and humble poet in the Sidney entourage. A lost 'Paper Book', a 'Paper Book bound wth ye Shepheards Calender', provides the arena in which the proposal may be tested.

This reference to a Paper Book is in Egerton Brydges' edition of *A Poetical Rapsodie*,[25] a collection of verse made by Francis Davison containing the poems of himself, his brother, and a mysterious A.W., the first extant edition of which is dated 1602. Brydges was the first to note that a manuscript (Harleian 280) contained a list in the hand of Francis Davison of all the poems known to him written by this A.W.[26] On folio 102a is a heading in a clear italic hand which is accepted by modern editors as Davison's: 'Catalog of all the Poems in Ryme or measured Verse by A.W.' There follows on folios 103, 104 and 105r a long list of poems identified by their first lines, many of which (but not all) are printed in full in the *PR*. The list ends with the contents of the Paper Book, four poems, as follows:

1. Eglog. A little Heard-Groom for hee was no bett.
2. Eglog. Upon the death of Sr. Ph: Sidney,
    Perin areed what new mischance betide.
3. Eglog a fragment, concerning ould Age.
    For when thou art not as thou wont of yore.
    A sestine of 8. Yee gastly Groves that heare my wofull cryes.[27]

Not only is it intriguing that these poems were apparently once bound and published with the *Calender*, but three of the four do look *prima facie* something like eclogues we know from that 1579 publication. Item 1 awakes echoes of 'A Shepheards boye (no better doe him call)', the line which opens the *Calender*'s 'Januarie' eclogue. The metre and the subordinate clause are the connectors here. A sestina of 8 (eight-line stanzas) beginning 'Yee gastly Groues' sounds not unlike Colin's sestina of 6 beginning 'Ye wastefull woodes' in the 'August' eclogue. Item 2 looks at first glimpse unpromising: since Philip Sidney did not die until 1586, and the *Calender* was published in 1579, surely no *Calender* poem can be said to relate to his death? But though the subject matter is different, there are other links. The character Perigot (a name not unlike Perin) in the *Calender*'s 'August' eclogue is associated with the words 'areed' and 'new mischance', words appearing in the first line of the elegy for Sidney, according to the Paper Book citation. 'Areed', meaning 'tell', is used twice in 'August': Willy first asks Perigot to 'reede me, what payne doth thee so appall?' and later tells Cuddie to 'areede uprightly' who has won the singing contest between himself and Perigot.[28] And Willy picks up Perigot's 'My old musick mard by a newe mischaunce' with 'Mischiefe mought to that newe mischaunce befall'.[29]

So far, then, we have threads of possible interconnection as follows:-

Paper Book	*Calender*
1 (A litle Heard-Groom)	— 'Januarie' ('A Shepheards boye')
2 (Elegy for Sidney: 'Perin areed')	— 'August' (Perigot + 'areed' + 'new mischance')
A sestine of 8: 'Yee gastly Groves'	— 'August' sestina 'Ye wastefull woodes'

The question posed by these links is: what might be the relationship between A.W. and the Colin of the *Calender*? To answer it, a rather daunting investigation of the full text of the Paper Book poems as they appear in Davison's *Poetical Rhapsody* is required. It will throw up yet more initials and pseudonyms; and to make matters worse, these are not consistent in the two first editions, the *Rapsody* (1602) and the *Rapsodie* (1608). (Two later editions are irrelevant to the argument for the moment.) I start by charting the contents of the relevant sections of these two editions of *PR*. I attach 'connector hooks' (thus: ꝛ) to any item that will require weaving into the complex in the subsequent argumentation. These 'hooks' indicate the target item in either the *Paper Book* or the *Calender* onto which the *PR* item will grapple.

Let us take first the relations between the Paper Book and the *PR*, setting aside the *Calender*. It is initially tempting to take Paper Book 1, 'A Shepheard

Table 4.1 Poetical Rapsody/Rapsodie, Paper Book and Shepheardes Calender

1602 I Eglogue. A Shepheard poore, Eubulus call'd he was	(cf. I by F.D. in 1608)
(Printed signature in body of the text: Francis Davison)	♪ Paper Book 1 ♪ 'Januarie'
III (sic) Eglogue. Made long since upon the death of Sir Phillip Sidney (Printed signature: A.W.)	(cf. unnumbered Eglogue in 1608) ♪ Paper Book 2 ♪ 'August' ♪ 'Aprill'
II (sic) Eglogue. Shepheard Heard-man (Printed signature: Ignoto)	(cf. II unsigned in 1608)
IIII Eglogue. Concerning olde Age. The beginning and end of this Eglogue are wanting. (Printed signature: Anomos)[30]	(Cf. IIII in 1608, unsigned) ♪ Paper Book 3 ♪? 'Februarie'?
1608 – 'A Complaint of which all the staves end with the words of the first, like a Sestine.' Subscript 'F.D.'[31]	♪ Paper Book: A sestine of 8 ♪ 'August' (Colin's sestina, sung by Cuddie)
I Eglogue. A Shepheard poore, Eubulus call'd he was (Printed signature F.D.)	(cf. I in 1602) ♪ Paper Book 1 ♪ 'Januarie'
I. Eglogue intituled CUDDY A Litle Heard-groome (for he was no bett)	♪ Paper Book 1 ♪ 'Januarie'
The Christian Stoick 'The virtuous man . .'	♪? 'August': Cuddie's emblem, 'felice chi può'
An Eglogue made long since upon the death of Sir Philip Sidney (Printed signature: A.W.)	(cf. III in 1602) ♪ Paper Book 2 ♪ 'August' ♪ 'Aprill'
II. Eglogue Shepheard ... Heardman (Unsigned)[32]	(cf. II in 1602, signed 'Ignoto')
IIII Eglogue. Concerning olde Age. The beginning and end of this Eglogue are wanting. (Unsigned)	(cf. IIII in 1602) ♪ Paper Book 3 ♪? 'Februarie'?

poore, *Eubulus* …', as an analogue of the 'I Eglogues' in both 1602 and 1608. But when we find an exact match in the *second* Eglogue numbered I in 1608, we have to rethink. Our thoughts might run something like this:– The Paper Book items are all said to be by A.W. The second Eglogue I in 1608 is apparently identical with item 1 of the Paper Book, but it is 'intituled CUDDY'. If 'intituled' implies authorship (as George Whetstone believed in the case of the *Calender*), Cuddy is not to be distinguished from A.W. Whatever the implication (and the fact that an emblem for Cuddy is printed after the eglogue suggests he *was* the author), Cuddy and A.W. must be closely related. Secondly, Eglogue I proper is signed by Francis Davison in both editions. This could mean not that he is muddying the waters of ascription, but contrariwise that he genuinely is the author of 'A Shepheard poore'. Whatever relation Davison's poem bears to 'A little Heard-Groome', Eubulus, the protagonist of Davison's poem, is of some interest to the quest for A.W.'s identity. 'eu' means 'well' or 'good'; and 'boule' might derive from 'boulomai', 'I wish or will', rather than 'bouleuomai', 'I counsel'. Arguably, Eubulus is a 'Good Will'.

Item 2 of the Paper Book is the elegy for Philip Sidney, plainly matched by the 'Eglogue made long since upon the death of Sir Philip Sidney' in both the 1602 and the 1608 *PR*. The full text does indeed begin 'Perin areed'. This is the only poem unequivocally attributed to A.W. across the board, that is, in the Paper Book, in 1602, and in 1608. It contains an embedded lyric "Yee Nimphes that bath your bodies in this Spring'. This sounds like Colin's 'Aprill' song, 'Ye dayntye Nymphs that in this blessed Brooke/ doe bathe your brest'; but inspection shows that it diverges in form and content after the first line.

Item 3 in the Paper Book, the fragment on old age, looks like *PR*'s fragmentary IIII Eglogue whose 'beginning and end are wanting', entitled 'Concerning olde Age'; and inspection confirms that it is. Though it is unsigned in 1608, it is attributed to Anomos in 1602. This again contradicts the ascription given by the Paper Book list. Davison has much to say about Anomos in his preface, as we shall see. By far the most plausible deduction is that the Anomos Davison was so keen to anthologize is identical with the A.W. whose poems he so carefully listed (and indeed modern editors do make this assumption).

Item 4, 'Yee gastly Groves', is, we can confirm from the full text, 1608's Complaint 'like a Sestine'. Here we have a genuine dilemma of ascription. 'F.D.' claims the Complaint; it is undoubtedly the Paper Book's 'Gastly Groves'; yet everything in the Paper Book is ascribed by F.D. himself to A.W. I am inclined to give priority to the Paper Book claim, and suppose that the subscript F.D. is a printer's mistake. But other interpretations are also possible: F.D. did not write 'Yee gastly Groues' but did claim it; F.D. did write it, and mistakenly included it in the Paper Book contents; F.D. (or the printer) is trying to confuse us.

This leaves us with two loose strands: II Eglogue ('Shepheard – Heard-man') in both 1602 and 1608, and the 'Christian Stoick' in 1608 have no apparent counterparts in the Paper Book. Yet the very fact that they are printed in the correlative clusters of poems suggests that Davison saw them as A.W.'s. This applies especially to II Eglogue, since it has a number in the series. Neither puzzle can be addressed until we turn to the *Calender* connections.

A possible rationale for the 'Christian Stoick's' inclusion in the poem cluster in *Rapsodie* 1608 lies in the emblem Cuddie chooses when he wins the 'August' contest: 'felice chi può'. E.K. allows that this is ambiguous, because truncated. 'Happy he who can ...' what? The 'Christian Stoick' is on the traditional theme of 'felix qui poterit ...' – 'Happy the man who can remain virtuous under life's vicissitudes'. Knowing that readers will know the *topos*, E.K. may well be leaving it to them to make the identification with the Stoick's author.

There is in the *Calender* a debate between a shepherd and a herdsman, constituting a contest between youth, championed by young Cuddie, and old age, championed by Thenot. It occurs in 'Februarie'. But it is not, on inspection, like Eglogue II or Eglogue IIII (on old age) in form or content. Nor are the characters the same in the correlative eclogues. However, the same *cast* of characters features in the two works in different combinations. In the *PR* eglogue on old age, young Perin debates with old Wrenock. Wrenock is mentioned as a 'good olde shephearde' in the *Calender*'s 'December'. Perin is linked by name and details of vocabulary to the Perigot of 'August' – who accompanies the very Willy (Sidney) whose death will be mourned in A.W.'s elegy in *PR*. Thenot also appears in A.W.'s elegy for Sidney, speaking to Perin. These links are closer than a mere plagiarist of pastoral sentiment would bother with – they are intricately woven into the fabric of that imaginary-but-real world as though predetermined in their outward reference. It is telling that Cuddie is a herd-boy, not a shepherd, in both *PR* and *Calender*.

It is through studying 'August' that we become most acutely aware of interconnections between *Calender* and *PR*. Shared vocabulary and linked names have been mentioned: in addition, we find that the 'August' song 'Ye wastefull woodes' is intimately connected with the sestine of 8 printed in 1608, 'Ye ghastly groves' (sic in *Rapsodie*). The phrase 'gastfull grove' actually occurs in 'August' in line 170. The variation in both sestinas follows the same pattern: the end-word of the last line of one stanza becomes the end-word of the first line of the next, but thereafter the end-words follow in the same order. The scheme is not as complex as a modern sestina. The two sestinas have some end-words in common: 'cries' and an '-ent' rhyme ('lament') in the sestine of 8, and 'cries' and 'augment' in 'August's' song. Both contain a capitalized Echo; the Philomel of the *Rapsodie* sestina finds a counterpart in the Nightingale of line 183 of the 'August' song; both harp on weeping all night and all day. These last items are hardly unique in love laments. Yet to find all three together in both poems suggests another sort of 'cluster', one comprising identical images and vocabulary, and produced by the mind of a single writer whenever the same mental chords are struck, perhaps over otherwise disparate material, distanced in time.[33]

Here are the two poems for comparison

a) Colin's 'August' song from *The Shepheardes Calender*, 1579

Ye wastefull woods beare witnesse of my woe,
Wherein my plaints did oftentimes resound:
Ye carelesse byrds are priuie to my cryes,
Which in your songs were wont to make a part:
Thou pleasaunt spring hast luld me oft a sleepe,
Whose streames my trickling teares did ofte augment.
 Resort of people doth my greefs augment,
   The walled townes do worke my greater woe
   The forest wide is fitter to resound
   The hollow Echo of my carefull cryes,
   I hate the house, since thence my loue did part,
   Whose waylefull want debarres myne eyes from sleepe.
 Let stremes of teares supply the place of sleepe:
   Let all that sweete is, voyd: and all that may augment
   My doole, drawe neare. More meete to wayle my woe,
   Bene the wild woddes my sorrowes to resound,
   Then bedde, or bowre, both which I fill with cryes,
   When I them see so waist, and fynd no part
 Of pleasure past. Here will I dwell apart
   In gastfull groue therefore, till my last sleepe
   Doe close mine eyes: so shall I not augment
   With sight of such a chaunge my restlesse woe:
   Helpe me, ye banefull byrds, whose shrieking sound
   Ys signe of drery death, my deadly cryes
 Most ruthfully to tune. And as my cryes
   (Which of my woe cannot bewray least part)
   You heare all night, when nature craueth sleepe,

Increase, so let your yrksome yells augment.
Thus all the night in plaints, the daye in woe
I vowed haue to wayst, till safe and sound
She home returne, whose voyces siluer sound
    To cheerefull songs can chaunge my cherelesse cryes.
    Hence with the Nightingale will I take part,
    That blessed byrd, that spends her time of sleepe
    In songs and plaintiue pleas, the more taugment
    The memory of hys misdeede, that bred her woe:
And you that feele no woe, / when as the sound
    Of these my nightly cryes / ye heare apart,
    Let breake your sounder sleepe / and pitie augment.

**b) 'Complaint' signed F.D. from the *Poetical Rhapsodie,* 1608. In the
Paper Book, it is called the 'sestine of 8', and assigned to A.W.**

A Complaint
Of which all the staues end with the
words of the first, like a
Sestine

1

YE ghastly groues, that heare my wofull cries
Whose shady leaues do shake to heare my paine
Thou siluer streame that dost with teares lament
The cruell chance that doth my greefe increase:
Ye chirping birds whose cheereles notes declare
That ye bewaile the woes *I* feele in minde,   **[Italicized capital I**
Beare witnesse how with care *I* do consume,   **in original]**
And heare the cause why thus I pine away.

2

Loue is the cause that makes me pine away,
And makes you heare the Eccho of my cries
Through griefes encrease: And though the cause of paine
which doth enforce me still thus to lament
Proceed from loue, and though my paine encrease
By dayly cries which doe that paine declare,
And witnesse are of my afflicted minde,
Yet cry I will, till crying me consume.

3

For as the fire the stubble doth consume,
And as the winde doth driue the dust away,
So pensiue hearts are spent with dolefull cries,
And cares distract the minde with pinching paine.
But all in vaine I do my cares lament,
My sorrow doth by sobs, sighes, teares, encrease:
Though sobs, sighes, teares, my torments doe declare,
Sobs, sighes, nor teares moue not her flintie minde.

4

I am cast out of her vngratefull minde
And she hath sworne I shall in vaine consume,
My wearie daies my life must wast away,
Consum'd eith paine, and worne with restles cries,
So *Philomele* too much opprest with paine
By his misdeed that causeth her lament,
Doth day and night her mournfull layes encrease,
And to the Woods her sorrowes doth declare.

5

Some ease it is, hid sorrowes to declare,
But too small ease to such a grieued minde,
Which by repeating woes doth more consume:
To end which woes I find at all no way,
(A simple salue to cure so great a paine)
But to deaths deafened eares to bend my cries.
Come then ye ghastly owles help me lament,
And as my cryes, so let your shrikes encrease.

6

For as your shrikes (the tunes of death) encrease
When sun is set and shaddowes do declare   **[a full-stop here,**
The nights approach, so I from my darke minde   **but clearly wrong]**
Since my bright Sun is fled, in cries consume   **[comma here – wrong]**
My night of woes, and though you flie away
Soone as the day returnes and cease your cries,
Yet *I* by day find no release of paine,
But day and night so foule a change lament.

7

But while I thus to sensles things lament
Ruth of my case in them thereby d'encrease

Which she feeles not, with scoffs she doth declare
My pangs to him, who first her wanton minde
From me did win: Since when I still consume
Like wax gainst fire, like snow that melts away
Before the sun: Thus thus, with mournful cries
I lyuing die, and dying, liue in paine.

8

And now adiew delight, and farewell paine
Adiew vaine hope I shall no more lament
Her fained faith which did my woes encrease,
And yee to whom my greefes I thus declare,
Yee which haue heard the secrets of my minde,
And seing then my lingring life in paine consume,
GROVE, BROOK, and BIRDS adiew, now hence away   **[comma here**
By death *I* will, and cease my deadly cries.   **– wrong]**

F.D.

Enter, from the wings, William Smith. He too has a version of 'Ye wastefull woodes'. It seems to have slipped out of the consciousness of the scholarly world that the twentieth sonnet of *Chloris* is closely related to the 'August' sestina. Maurice Evans's *Elizabethan Sonnets*, for instance, includes the sonnet with the note 'A sonnet heavily indebted to the pastoral eclogues of the *Old Arcadia*', unaware of the criticism of Herbert E. Cory, who saw it as a crude plagiarism of 'August'.[34] The opening two lines are identical, except for the last words of the second lines, naturally, as the sonnet and sestina form start to diverge. The '-ent' rhyme of the sestina's 'augment' is matched by 'disparagment' and 'sent' in the sonnet's second quatrain. In the third quatrain appears 'resoundeth,' where the sestina has 'resound'. Further, line 9 of the sonnet – 'The eccho of my still-lamenting cries' – hardly differs from line 160 of 'August' – 'The hollow Echo of my carefull cryes'. The capitalization hints at a person, and the hint is reflected in the couplet of the *Chloris* sonnet, where the nymph Echo is mentioned.

c) Sonnet 20 from *Chloris*, by William Smith, pub. 1596

Yee wastefull woods bear witness of my woe,
Wherein my plaints doe oftentimes abound:
Yee carelesse birds my sorrowes well doe knoe,
They in your songs were wont to make a sound.
Thou pleasant spring canst record likewise beare

Of my designes and sad disparagement,
When thy transparent billowes mingled weare
With those downfalls which from mine eies were sent.
The echo of my still-lamenting cries.
From hollow vaults in treble voice resoundeth,
And then into the emptie aire it flies,
And backe againe from whence it came reboundeth.
    That Nimphe vnto my clamors doth replie,
    Being likewise scorned in loue as well as I.

Plagiarism? Homage? Authorial revision? Davison's care in attribution, discussed below, tends to support the notion that authorial rights mattered, which would rule out plagiarism. It will be clear from what I said above about clusters that I think we have here a case of authorial revision, which carries the implication that Colin/Cuddie, A.W. and William Smith are identical.

A.W. can, I believe, be proved to be a Smith. In the library of the Earl of Northumberland at Alnwick there is a unique copy of a rather pious work, *A Speciall Remedie against the furious force of lawlesse Love ... by W.A.*[35] It is the third work in a bound book of English Poetry of 1578–79. It is dated 1579, and was published by Richard Jones. Jones (as Jhones) was the first publisher of Gascoigne's *Princely Pleasures of Kenilworth*, and, we suspected, of the ill-fated first edition of Langham's Letter. This W.A. is A.W., as the entry of the *Speciall Remedie* in the Stationers' Register reveals. It was entered in July 1578 as written by 'A.W., Artificer'. Reversal of initials is not at all uncommon.

'Artificer' is a pointless descriptive if it means merely 'writer'. I think there is more to it than that. An 'artifex' is the same as a 'faber', a smith. Two other publications show that the pseudonym was used by a William Smith, with the Latin derivation in mind. *Gemma fabri* is a collection of biblical extracts made by a William Smyth who was born, he says in his Latin introduction, not only during but actually at the commencement of Elizabeth's reign – that is, in 1558.[36] He offers the booklet to the Queen in the first instance, but more surreptitiously in a second epistle, to the Earl of Essex, commending these 'tela Vulcania' to the latter. Both this expression and the title spell out 'Smith'. The title means 'Smith's Jewel'; and 'tela Vulcania' are 'Vulcan's weapons', Vulcan being the lame smith god.

This William Smith does not have great literary powers, or he would presumably have composed something to offer the Queen and Essex, rather than make compilations of the Scriptures, or recycle his sermons. I believe he was the same Smith as the Smith who wrote and published a sermon, *The Blacksmith*, in 1606.[37] Here again, the author makes great play with the notion of Smiths as smiths – goldsmiths, ironsmiths, carpenters. I suggest he was William the elder son of Alderman Smith, and has comparatively little to do with our story.[38] His interest for us lies in the fact that he uncovers before our eyes the rationale of the label 'Artificer', namely, that it can stand for 'Smith'.

A.W.'s *Remedie* is no masterpiece, it must be said. It is in iambic quatrains, full of Protestant sentiment. It is followed by various shorter poems: 'The Discription of Love' and 'The Discription of a Lover', both in fourteeners; 'A Vision of rawe [rare] devise' in quatrains; 'An Epitaphe written upon the death of his deare friend' – who is female, but seems genuinely to be friend, not a beloved lady; 'A short admonition written to a friende' (almost a sonnet, comprising two sixains and a final couplet); a sonnet entitled 'Being requested to write two or three verses upon this theame, Ubi amor, ibi oculus'; a poem in quatrains 'Of the vanities of womens abuses'; 'What pleasure men place in the vaine showe of beautie' in fourteeners; and finally 'A Prayer of a repentant Sinner, bewailing his sins, and craving for mercy' in bad iambic pentameter quatrains.

These are hardly the poems one hoped young Shakespeare would have written. But if the trail can be shown to lead back to Shakespeare, they should not be excluded on the grounds of their quality from his corpus. What exactly would one expect a young adolescent (or child – for the poems could have been written some while before publication) to produce on demand? Some of these are clearly occasional poems. The devout Protestantism accords with the supposition that the young Shakespeare was influenced by his patron's religious affiliation. Besides, there is a faint flicker of an identifier in the dedication to the author's friend 'I.A.' (could this be Adam Islip, publisher of both the works of Richard Lynche investigated in the previous chapter?), in the dedication to the reader, and in the *Remedie* itself, which covers eight pages: it is a recurrent 'goodwill'.

There are two more pseudonyms in *PR* attached to poems supposedly by A.W., namely 'Ignoto' and 'Anomos'. 'Ignoto' is given as the author of the 'Shepheard – Heardman' poem in 1602, which is unsigned in 1608. What difference is implied between a blank where a signature might be, and the mark 'Ignoto', meaning 'Unknown'? Marcy North raises the question in other contexts – the anthologies *Phoenix Nest* and *England's Helicon*.[39] Two poems that in the *Nest* were non-attributed appeared in *Helicon* with the initials S.W.R., for Sir Walter Ralegh. Subsequently, these initials were pasted over with paper cancels inscribed 'Ignoto'. North goes through some of the possible reasons for this. Ralegh might be disavowing authorship because the poems belonged to another (whose name was probably unavailable, she thinks). Or the slips might indicate that Ralegh wants recognition, but only among the cognoscenti who knew that it was he who lurked under Ignoto's mask.

Certain possibilities are omitted in this account. It could be that Ralegh is disavowing authorship; that the poems belonged to another who was not untraceable; and that it is this other who has appropriated the pseudonym 'Ignoto'. I can offer some evidence that there was such another, and give one or two clues to his identity.

Four poems attributed by Davison to A.W. in the extended catalogue in Harleian 280 (preceding the Paper Book list), and printed in 1602 with the signature 'Anomos', were published in the *England's Helicon* of 1614 as by Ignoto. The William Smith of the New Year gifts was 'unknown' to the Countess of Pembroke in ways we could not fathom, since he addressed her *twice* in booklets in which he declared himself a devoted servant, though a stranger. Perhaps he was saying he was her 'Ignoto'. The first word of the dedicatory Epistle to the *Calender* is 'Uncouth', or 'Unknown'. It is a Chaucerian 'proverb', says E.K., which well applies to 'this our new Poete, who for that he is uncouthe (as said Chaucer) is unkist, and unknown to most men, is regarded but of few'. (The reference is to Chaucer's *Troilus and Crisseyde.*) The new Poet is perhaps both truly unknown to most, and also 'Ignoto' to most.[40] The songs covertly inserted into the *Calender* under Spenser's aegis would, on this supposition, be Ignoto's. That is, Ignoto would be yet another pseudonym used by William Shakespeare.

What of the odd pseudonym 'Anomos'? Dedicating the *Rapsody* of 1602 to William Herbert, son of Mary Sidney, Davison offers 'his owne, his Brothers, and *Anomos* Poems, both in his owne, and their names' (A2r). (In fact, poems by other well-known poets are included: poems by Philip and Mary Sidney are foregrounded early in the volume.) Davison refers in the 'Epistle to the reader' to his publishing 'some [poems] written by my deere frend *Anomos*, and my deerer *Brother* ... Both without their consent, the latter being in the low Country Warres, and the former utterly ignorant thereof' (A3v). Quite clearly, Anomos is here a single individual.

In the 1608 edition, however, Anomos has multiplied and transmogrified. The parallel passage in the epistle (there is a blank below the dedication to Herbert) reads: '*some written by my deere friends* Anonymoi'. Instead of 'the latter ... the former', we read '*the latter ... the rest*'. Not only is there now more than one friend, but Davison gives the impression that the friends have the generic label 'Anon'. Yet there is an admission in his explanation which completely subverts this impression. 'My friends names I concealed; mine owne and my Brothers, I willed the Printer to suppresse, as well as I had concealed the other' (A3r). The fact that Davison admits to *concealing* names refutes the *PR* editor Rollins's belief that Davison was listing poems whose authors were unknown to him. So does the way Davison's manuscript list divides the A.W. material into three categories: that in an autograph folio – 'In folio, written with ye Authors own hand'; those in loose pages of quarto; and those in 'the Paper Book bound wth ye Shepheards Calender'. The existence of the first category gives the lie to Rollins's picture of an editor assembling the works of anonymous writers.[41]

Turning to the lay-out of successive *Poetical Rhapsodies*, we find further evidence of a flesh and blood A.W. in the gradual changes effected in each new edition. In both 1602 and 1608, a whole clearly defined section of 'Sonets, Odes, Elegies and other Poesies' is included, with its own title page. In one surviving copy of 1602, this tile page (F12r) has an *impresa* and the name 'Anomos'.[42] In the Bodleian copy, Malone 348, the page is missing, and a later interleave has been inserted. In 1608, the page contains the heading only, no motto and no name.[43] Comparison of the charts given above for the 1602 and 1608 sections with the Paper Book contents shows a similar process of elision of identifiers. In two later editions, all indicators attempting to mark out the work of Anomos as an integral whole have vanished.

The first printing did not follow Davison's instructions on preserving his and his brother's anonymity, he reveals. (It almost sounds as though there was an edition antedating the so-called first edition; or perhaps Davison is being deliberately misleading about the time-scale of production, as North believes.)[44] But in any case, it is a policy which he now regrets, 'for if their Poems be liked, the praise is due to their inventions'.[45] So much for the lack of an early modern concept of authorship, that notion so dear to late twentieth-century commentary.

Did the printer and Davison preserve or 'bewray' Anomos's identity, after all? 'My friends names I concealed; mine owne and my Brothers, I willed the Printer to suppresse, as well as I had concealed the other.'[46] The sentence is possibly punning on a particular name: note the verb 'to will' and its close conjunction with 'well'. Davison did neither one thing nor the other: he revealed the name *while* concealing it.

A glance at the first three (linked) sonnets of Anomos's part of the *Rapsody* will serve to confirm his Shakespearean credentials.[47] The sonnets appear effortless in style. They explain the rationale for the poet's poetry: while some men write driven by a natural gift, some for praise, some for gain, 'Me, neither Nature hath a Poet made,/ Nor love of Glory ... nor thirst of Golde'. 'What moved me then? Say Love, for thou canst tel'. He goes on to record that his motivation, love, explains his immense freedom in matters poetic: 'I those lawes refuse/ Which other poets in their making use'. For 'all kinde of Stiles doo serve my Ladies name': 'the lofty Verse ... Sweet Liricks . . the tender Elege . . mournefull Tragicke Verse ... Comicke'.[48]

There is a limited number of people who could make such a boast circa 1602, and make it with such a show of independence. What has previously been lacking is material justification for Francis Meres' placing of Shakespeare in his lists of excellence for lyric poetry as well as comedy and tragedy.[49] If A.W.'s (and Cuddie's and Colin's) poetry is Shakespeare's, the lack is supplied.

Why would Shakespeare have taken the initials A.W.? For a reason connected with his adoption of the pseudonym R.L., I suggest. Though this seemed to be determined by the opportunity afforded by the existence of Robert Langham as Clerk to the Council Chamber, it is in fact *over*determined, as pseudonyms often are. The young Kenilworth page's master was Robert Leicester: the initials R.L. adorn the chimney breasts, furniture and cushions of the great house.[50] His other master in the early days was Ambrose Warwick, head of the whole Dudley clan by seniority, if not as powerful as Robert. It must remain a guess that the two lords underlie the choice of initials. But it is not an unreasonable guess.

The 1580 publication *Three Proper, and Wittie, Familiar Letters* is intimately linked with the *Calender*, as Henry Woudhuysen has argued.[51] There are in fact three Familiar followed by two Commendable Letters, purporting to be a correspondence between Spenser and Harvey. Their aim is patently to promote Spenser's recent work and hint at the future publication of *The Faerie Queene;* to promote Harvey similarly, giving him scope to show off his skill; and to demonstrate that both enjoy the patronage of 'M. Philip Sidney' and 'Maister Dyer'. But I think there is a further aim that has not been identified by previous commentary: to promote the recent work of the Cuddie figure, and discuss his talent, education, projects and prospects.

The *Calender*'s herdboy Cuddie 'whose person is secrete' (so we are told in a Gloss to 'Februarie'), has, apparently, the greatest lyrical talent in the group. The Willy and Perigot of 'August' are no mean singers. Yet after Cuddie has adjudicated Willy's and Perigot's singing contest, and rather tactfully (considering that Willy is Sidney, and Cuddie several degrees below him) split the prize between them, he obtains permission to sing Colin's sestina 'Ye wastefull woodes'. The 'emblems' of the two previous singers make it clear that they yield their prizes to Cuddie, though E.K.'s gloss strives to give exactly the opposite impression: 'Perigot by his poesie [motto] claiming the conquest, and Willye not yeelding'. What Perigot said was 'Vincenti gloria victi', that is 'The kudos of the conquered passes to the conqueror'. Willy said in Italian 'Vinto non vitto' ('To the conquered there is no crown'?).

Cuddie is quoted by Harvey in his Familiar Letter (the third). 'What saith *M. Cuddie, alias* you know who?' he asks, and quotes two stanzas from the tenth *Calender* eclogue ('October'), adding:

> But Master *Collin* (sic) *Cloute* is not everybody, and albeit his olde Companions, *Master Cuddy*, and *Master Hobbinoll* be as little beholding to their *Mistresse Poetrie*, as ever you wilt: yet he peradventure, by the meanes of hir special favour, and some personall priviledge, may happely live by *dying Pellicanes*, and purchase great landes, and Lordshippes, with the money, which his *Calendar* and *Dreames* have, and will afforde him.[52]

Harvey is here implying that while Cuddy was right to say in 'October' that poetry earns its practitioners nothing, Spenser may in fact earn a great deal from it, unlike his two companions Cuddy and Harvey himself. There is no reason to suppose Cuddy any less real than Hobbinol. The Argument at the head of the 'October' eclogue gives us a ghostly intimation of this real person. The eclogue itself gives us a sharper profile. And the 'October' gloss 'bewrays' him.

In the Argument to the eclogue, E.K. (we presume) declares: 'In Cuddie is set out the perfecte paterne of a Poete'.[53] The perfect Patten of a poet, perhaps? It is not impossible that such a joke could be lurking in E.K.'s words. Compare his statement in the 'August' gloss that Cuddie is 'Patron' of his own cause. Compare his gloss in 'Februarie' on the word 'galage', used by Cuddie: 'a startuppe or clownish shoe'. He does not give the alternative 'a patten', but the ghost of the word hangs there.

As Paul McLane has noticed, 'October's' Cuddie is shown as a poet on the lower reaches of his career.[54] He cannot be Spenser, McLane opines, for Spenser had already started on his epic. He could be Edward Dyer. What McLane has not noticed is that the poet in question is young (which Dyer was not in 1579) and his ambitions lie in *dramatic* poetry: he longs to 'reare the Muse on stately stage,/ And teache her tread aloft in bus-kin fine'.[55] Patrick Cheney, who has written with insight on other aspects of the *Calender*, notices this line relating to Cuddie, but believing Cuddie figures Spenser's ambitions here, manipulates the sense. 'Tragedy here [has] a distinctly epic cast', he declares.[56] But we must be tied by what Spenser actually wrote, which is that Cuddie longs to be a playwright. Piers, Cuddie's interlocutor in the eclogue, encourages him to 'abandon then the base and viler clown' and raise his sights to 'advaunce the worthy' whom Piers connects to the white bear and stake. E.K. explains, in case we are dull-witted, that this refers to the Earl of Leicester.[57] Cuddie is to leave his meaner topics and style, and write to advance the Earl's cause, which Piers believes calls for 'bigger notes' (of poetry) than singing of 'fayre Elisa'.

Those who are convinced that the 'Aprill' song celebrates the Queen as Eliza will surely find Piers' remark verging on treason: Leicester greater than Eliza? But in fact 'Aprill' celebrates Elisa – the woman crowned in the song is spelled 'Elisa' throughout the song. At the end, dame Eliza, with a 'z', is said to thank the nymphs for her song, which was indeed addressed to her, but (I think) was not about her, for all that E.K. labours in a gloss to insist that the song means to celebrate the daughter of Henry VIII. The sixth stanza features a Cynthia who shows herself with her silver rays, and is 'dasht' when 'she' – *another* she – displays the beams of her beauty. Cynthia (the Queen) has a rival who outshines her. The Sidneians had their own Queen, a faerie one: Elisa, not Eliza.

Cuddie starts to be persuaded by Piers that writing drama might be a possible course; but then he recalls that Maecenas is dead and gone, and there are no generous patrons left in the world. But suddenly, carried away in a kind of 'enthusiasmos', he bursts out

> O if my temples were distained with wine
> And girt in girlonds of wild Yvie twine,
> How could I reare the Muse on stately stage,
> And teache her tread aloft in bus-kin fine,
> With queint Bellona in her equipage.
> (110–14)

The gloss on 'queint Bellona' cites a myth about Pallas, Bellona's Greek incarnation. It then invents some nonsense to add to the myth, and in so doing, provides us with the true identity of Cuddie.

> Strange Bellona; the goddesse of battaile, that is Pallas, which may therefore wel be called queint for that (as Lucian saith) when Iupiter hir father was in traveile of her, he caused his sonne Vulcane with his axe to hew his head. Out of which leaped forth lustely a valiant damsell armed at all poyntes, whom seeing Vulcane so faire and comely, lightly leaping to her, proffered her some cortesie, which the Lady disdeigning, shaked her speare at him, and threatned his saucinesse. Therefore such straungenesse is well applyed to her.[58]

As a justification for applying the epithet 'quaint' to her, it leaves something to be desired. But as a means of introducing a hidden pun, it is highly successful. The pun in 'shaked her speare', which would have been seized on with glee had it occurred ten years later, has been invisible to readers of later ages because it is inconceivable to them that it should encode Shakespeare so early. But for what other purpose could E.K./Spenser have dragged in such a patently false explanation, to gloss those very words in an eclogue about a perfect pattern of a poet which concern the ambitions of that young poet to write for the stage? To which we might add: Cuddie had surely started writing plays, or no one would have urged him to make his name as a playwright. As for Vulcan, we might recall that he was a Smith.

Having promoted Cuddie as the subject of the *Calender* and author of its best lyrics, I must account for the fact that it is Immerito whom Spenser promotes in the *Calender*, and Harvey in the Letters and a manuscript Letterbook intimately related to the published correspondence.[59] We start with the *Calender*, and its verse envoi 'Goe little book', in which the signatory, Immerito, fears 'Envie' will bark at this 'child whose parent is unkent' (unknown – or Unknown).

There are two intriguing things about this Immerito, one of which has not been observed by modern scholarship, while the other has been remarked but ignored. The first is that he is plural. In the dedication of a Latin poem addressed by Spenser to Harvey in the first Commendable Letter the grammar makes this irrefutable. 'Ad Ornatissimum virum, multis iamdiu nominibus clarissimum, G.H. Immerito sui, mox in Gallias navigaturi, εὐτυχεῖν.'[60] 'To G.H. [Gabriel Harvey], a most honoured man, long famous for many titles, his (nominative plural) Immerito, about-to-sail (plural participle) to Gauls (plural), wish[es] farewell.' The Greek, being an infinitive, avoids any determination of whether the subject of 'wish' is singular or plural.

Immerito is the name always adopted by Harvey's correspondent in the Familiar and Commendable Letters. But, we learn from Harvey's Letterbook, he may also have been the 'bewrayer' of some of Harvey's 'virelays' (rhyming verses) to the public. I say he 'may have been', because Harvey himself appears to have changed his mind on the matter. And herein lies the second intriguing thing about Immerito: Harvey keeps scoring out his name in manuscript, and substituting for Immerito some version of the name 'Will'.

From folios 34b to 70a, Harvey drafts and redrafts letters which either concern the published correspondence, or came to constitute parts of it. On folio 35b he writes: 'To his verie friendlie [scored out] unfriendly frende that procurid ye edition of his so slender, and extemporall Devises'. Above and to the left, in the margin, are the words 'Verlayes and other my firste exp ...', which is presumably an alternative for 'extemporall Devises'. He continues 'Magnifico Signior Benevolo, Bihoulde What millions of thankes I yelde [scored] recount unto you, and ... ehoulde, gentle Master Imerito [last three words scored out, plus an inserted 'ungentle' above 'gentle' and above 'Imerito' a scored 'volens nolens']. On folio 37b he again addresses Signior Immerito and adds 'Benivolo' in darker ink above 'Immerito'. Many pages later (folio 48b), he writes out a rough version of a dedication for someone to use when publishing his verlayes. The dedication is to 'Master Edwarde Diar', and is to be offered by 'Benivolo Volens Nolens', the last two words being lightly scored. To the side of 'Benivolo' is a scored 'QuodvultDeus', meaning 'WhatGodwill'.

Harvey is anticipating the 'unauthorised' publication of some of his rhymes, and perhaps some other things, by someone. This someone is constantly flagged as 'Goodwill' or 'Godwill', or 'Willy Nilly'.

Now it can hardly be a coincidence that the preface of the 'Familiar Letters' is by a self-confessed 'Welwiller' of the two authors. The virelays and extemporal devises which Harvey professes to be unwilling to see in print look as though they will turn out to be the verse experiments of his which the Well-willer of the preface apologizes for printing – for there are a number of these given in the course of the 'Letters'.

It is not only in the preface that this Will-figure lurks. Spenser performs a neat trick with his name at the beginning of the first Commendable Letter. 'Good Master *G.* I perceive by your most curteous and frendly Letters your good will to be no lesse in deed, than I alwayes esteemed.'[61] Harvey's previous letter was the third Familiar.[62] Was Good Will mentioned there? There were various characters whose relevance to the correspondence was doubtful: an affected Italianate dandy; a young Brother (sic) of Harvey's, John, whom he is tutoring in versifying; and a friend 'now an honest Countrey Gentleman, sometimes a Scholler'.

The Italianate dandy appears in a hexameter verse entitled 'Speculum Tuscanismi', which concerns someone who is *'No man, but Minion, Stowte, Lowte, Plaine, swayne, quoth a Lording'.*[63] Some 'lording' despises him as lowly, and casts aspersions either on his age and size, or perhaps his sexuality. It was the Earl of Oxford, it seems, who did so. Many at the time and subsequently have believed Harvey was calling the Earl a minion. This is extremely unlikely, and contrary to the overt sense; yet Harvey *was* slighting the Earl in some way. It was perhaps the insulting use of 'lording' that brought Harvey within the furious Earl's sights, as we know it did.[64]

A truncated version of the 'Speculum' is inscribed on folio 52a of the manuscript Letterbook. The last nine lines of the poem as it appears in the Familiar Letter are omitted; but conversely, some additional lines of what are obviously the same poem have overflowed onto the next page of manuscript, where Harvey has scribbled:

> What should I speak of Inglishe Edwardes   Henrys
>   Talbotts, Brandons, Grays, with a thousand
>   Such and such? Lett [scored through, with another indecipherable word]
> [many? or may? scored]   Lett Edwards goe:
>   Letts
>   blott ye remembraunce,
>
> Of
> puissant Henryes: or letts exemplify
>   theyre Actes Etc.[65]

This is a cast list of Shakespeare's early history plays. The Talbots are the heroes of *Henry VI, Part 1* (entered as a play about the Talbots); there is a Sir William Brandon in *Richard III*, and a Brandon in *Henry VIII;* there is Sir Thomas Grey in *Henry V*, and Lady Grey who attains royal status in *Henry VI, Part 3*.[66] *Edward III* is now allowed into the Shakespearean canon.

I am not suggesting that *all* these or their prototypes had been written by 1579/80. We shall see in a moment that there is reason to suspect some of them had. But this could be Harvey's programme for the Italianate minion. It is the same programme, in effect, as that suggested to Cuddie in the 'October' eclogue. It was a Leicestrian programme, for Charles Brandon, Duke of Suffolk, married Henry VIII's sister and was grandfather to Lady Jane Grey; Greys married into the Dudley family more than once; and Talbots had married Greys.

The Italianate minion has only recently become Italianate, it seems. The last line of the poem in manuscript is 'This, nay more than this doth practise of Italy in one year'. In the printed Letter it continues: 'None doe I name, but some doe I knowe, that a peece of a twelvemonth:/ Hath so perfited outly, and inly, both body and soule,/ That none for sense, and senses, halfe matchable with them'. I believe we have here the solution to the puzzle of how and when Shakespeare became proficient in Italian, and gleaned his knowledge of its cities. It was in the year preceding the publication of the Familiar Letters. Harvey, having described the minion as eyed like a linx (Lynch?), winged like Mercury, nosed like Naso (Ovid), sums him up as a 'Travailer most blessed and happy'. In the subsequent course of this book, we shall accumulate reasons to connect Mercury, Ovid, and a Traveller with the 'minion' Shakespeare.

A considerable part of the third Familiar Letter is devoted to a young Brother of Harvey's, as mentioned above. Harvey describes how he sets the youth various poetic exercises, the results of which he sets out in full, and reports that the youth has made a start on some composition of great promise. Harvey did indeed have a younger brother, John, who later published some works. But the Brother does not sound at all like this John. 'See how I taske a young Brother of myne, (whom of playne *Iohn*, our *Italian* Maister hath Cristened his *Picciolo Giovanbattista*), Lo here (and God will) a peece of hollydayes exercise ...' and here Harvey describes how he gave the youngster some Ovid to translate into measured English verse.[67]

The poet with whom one would connect Giovanbattista (Cinthio) is not John Harvey, who wrote almanacs and treatises on prophecy, but William Shakespeare, which perhaps accounts for the inappropriate interjection 'and [if] God will'. Parts of the plots of *Twelfth Night*, *Othello*, and *Antony and Cleopatra*, and the main plot of *Measure for Measure* are taken from Cinthio's *Hecatommithi*. The suspicion that this Brother is the young Shakespeare is compounded when we hear whom he takes as his models for the more ambitious work he is engaged on: 'both *Master Collinshead*, and *M. Holli(n)shead* too'. Collinshead (note the double 'll') is of course Spenser: Holinshed was, as is well known, Shakespeare's source for a large number of his historical plays.

Extraordinary as it may seem, Spenser and Harvey between them thus not only give us hints that they knew young Shakespeare in the heart of the Sidney circle in 1579/80, but they actually describe his education. He was being steeped in Ovid and Cinthio; he was being encouraged by one (Spenser) whom later ages have thought of as the poet laureate of the Elizabethan age; and trained daily by one of the most prestigious university teachers of his day (Harvey) in poetic practice. Because of his talent, he was being groomed by them to become the court poet of the lord who they still hoped might rule England. They want him to write the plays for which he in fact became famous in due course. They drop hints referring to these plays, not only in private letter-books, but *publicly*, in glosses to the *Calender.*

The false attribution of the name 'Andronica' to the goddess Flora in 'March' has been noted already. But what does it imply? I put forward one hypothesis: possibly the members of the Sidney circle compared the Dudleys of sixteenth-century England to the Andronici of late Roman times, whose history was similar. If such was the coterie conceit, was it a notion shared by Spenser and the young Shakespeare? Or did one suggest it to the other? If so, which to which?[68]

Given the disingenuousness of E.K.'s note and the tortuous way he leads up to the critical name, I favour the thesis of 'literary allusion' on Spenser's part. 'Calling her, not as she was, nor as some do think, Andronica, but Flora' is hardly comprehensible. Does E.K. mean Flora *was* Andronica, or some think she was, but she was *not?* The confusion distracts the reader from asking the pertinent question 'Why bring that name in at all?'

A less misleading, more meandering, gloss on 'frendly faeries' in 'June' might lead us to doubt E.K.'s motives for leading up to Talbot, Earl of Shrewsbury. 'The Talbot' is of course the hero of Shakespeare's play, *Henry VI, Part 1*. Shakespeare characterizes him just as E.K. does. In the play, Talbot is 'the terror of the French,/ The scarecrow that affrights our children so'.[69] To the Countess of Auvergne he is 'the scourge of France ... the Talbot so much fear'd abroad/ That with his name the mothers still their babes'.[70] In the *Calender* gloss, E.K. weaves a path from friendly fairies, via elves and goblins, to Guelphs and Ghibellines, to threatening naughty children that the Guelph or Ghibelline is coming for them, to French mothers threatening their children with 'The Talbot cometh'. Common historical knowledge could account for the presence in both Shakespeare and Spenser of the last piece of folklore. Spenser is not necessarily making a covert allusion to a proto-*Henry VI*. But the gloss is undoubtedly contrived, which tends to suggest that he is doing so.

A third gloss, involving an incident that occurs in *Richard III*, looks innocent enough. It comes from the commentary to 'Maye'. Lord Hastings' horse stumbles 'twise or thrise' (E.K.)/ 'three times' (Shakespeare), riding towards the Tower of London (E.K.)/ when he looked at the Tower (Shakespeare), an ominous event that was indeed followed by the execution of Hastings. Spenser's account of the horse's stumbling is as given in Edward Halle's chronicle and the *Myrrour for Magistrates*.[71] What is odd, though, is that the learned E.K. should make a mistake in a different matter involving Hastings. In the sources and in Shakespeare, it was Stanley who had a prognosticating dream of the boar (signifying Richard) who 'razed his helm'. E.K. thinks it was Hastings' dream. When E.K. gives mistaken information, it flags some secret, as his giving the sign of the fish as November's zodiac sign probably signals that the death of 'Dido' actually occurred in February, and is that of Ambrosia Sidney (in 1575). The secret in the 'Maye' case could be that he alludes to a play by his 'new poet'.

My fourth and last case has not been previously remarked as being in any way odd, to my knowledge. But it is as telling a case of 'indirection' as the first. It is the gloss on 'the Widowes daughter of the glenne', a phrase in the 'Aprill' eclogue. 'He calleth Rosalind the Widowes daughter of the glenne, that is, of a country Hamlet or borough'.[72] The egregious piece of misinformation – a glen is not a hamlet, and if it were, it could not also be a borough – should alert readers to a hidden significance. (So should the capital H, but since it is usually taken for granted that Elizabethan authors could not influence the printers' practice, it will not.) E.K.'s remark certainly *feels like* an insider's joke. And a widow's daughter, in juxtaposition with 'Hamlet', sounds like Polonius's daughter Ophelia. But the fixed critical consensus that Shakespeare's *Hamlet* was written probably close to 1603, combined with the equally fixed notion of a *non*-Shakespearean 'Ur-Hamlet', makes it hard to argue for the possibility that E.K./Spenser could be referring to a Shakespearean Ur-Hamlet in 1579. Critics might prefer to conclude that Hamlet and his story were part of the mental furniture of the Sidney circle in 1579, and somehow became part of Shakespeare's mental furniture later. It is much harder, in this case, completely to divorce Shakespeare from any Sidneian affiliation. But it is possible, at a cost, to reject the conclusion that Spenser promotes Shakespeare and his plays, by taking each case in isolation and without presupposing the context this chapter has gradually been outlining.

With that context admitted, it becomes hard to deny the superior plausibility of the hypothesis of covert allusion to his 'new poet' on Spenser's part. Bear in mind that what he is alluding to could be unpolished first versions of *Henry VI, Part 1*, *Richard III*, *Titus Andronicus* and *Hamlet*, not the texts that have come down to us.

I began the chapter with a suspicion about William Smith and the copy of Aesop's Fables he inherited. Aesop's tales feature in two of the *Calender*'s eclogues. The Tale of the Fox and the Kid in 'Maye' is taken from Aesop, as E.K. notes. The Tale of the Oak and the Briar is told by Thenot in 'Februarie'. But it is the gloss E.K. gives on an emblem in 'Februarie' that makes one's hair stand on end. E.K. explains the meaning of Cuddie's chosen emblem, 'Niuno vecchio spaventa Iddio' ('No old man fears God'), by means of another Aesop's fable, that of the Ape who on first meeting the Lion, was aghast, but lost his fear through familiarity. He adds, 'Although it please Erasmus (sic) a great clerke and good old father, more fatherly and favourablye to construe it in his Adages for his own behoofe, That by the proverbe Nemo Senex metuit Iovem, is not meant, that old men have no feare of God at al, but that they be furre from superstition and Idolatrous regard of false Gods, as is Iupiter'.[73]

How much did Spenser know of his young protégé's circumstances? Here we have a conjunction of Cuddie, Aesop, Erasmus' works and a peculiar joke on a 'good father' who behaves in a fatherly manner. Which young William

Smith was it, we begin to wonder, who actually came to possess Brechtgirdle's books. Which older William Smith was Shakespeare's godfather? Was he an immoral, old, clerkly, fatherly godfather? We shall see in due course.

Of all the new personae of Shakespeare in this chapter, 'M. Cuddie alias you know who' is perhaps the most appealing. He is also one of the most useful, in that he holds the key to the decipherment of other pseudonyms, such as Colin and Ovid. We can observe this last Shakespearean label in its moment of crystallization from a fluid simile to a fixed pseudonym. First Harvey described the minion as 'nos'd like to Naso'. We then find Francis Meres metaphorically placing 'the sweet wittie soule of Ovid ... in mellifluous and hony-tongued Shakespeare'.[74] But it becomes clear that Meres treats 'Ovid' as a name pertaining particularly to Shakespeare when he speaks of the inspiration of poetry, making appeal to the Cuddie of the *Calender* as he does so:

> 'Celestiall instinction' ... which Poets themselves do very often and gladly witnes of themselves, as namely *Ovid in 6. Fast.* 'Est Deus in nobis agitante calescimus illo etc.' And our famous English Poet Spenser, who in his Shepheards Calender lamenting the decay of Poetry at these dayes, saith most sweetly to the same. 'Then make thee wings of thy aspiring wit ...'. (278v)

Here Meres quotes Ovid on divine inspiration, citing the line which Cuddie takes as his emblem for 'October'. Meres claims that Spenser *said to the same* 'Then make thee wings ...'. To the same effect, or to the same poet? Ostensibly the former; but actually, I think, to the latter. That is, Spenser spoke to 'Ovid' saying 'make thee wings ...'. But Spenser was speaking to Cuddie: so Cuddie is 'Ovid'. And Cuddie, we claim, is Shakespeare. Ergo, Ovid is Shakespeare. It is the very act of making the name a coterie secret that reveals it to be that contradiction in terms – a true pseudonym.

Notes

1   *Aesopz fablz*, trans. William Bullokar (London: E. Bollifant, 1585).
2   Brechtgirdle's will is reproduced in Fripp's *Shakespeare Studies* (London: Oxford University Press, 1930), pp. 23–31.
3   Ibid.
4   See above, p. 64.
5   His distinctive signature can be seen in *Minutes and Accounts of the Corporation of Stratford-upon-Avon and Other Records: 1553–1620*, transcribed by Richard Savage, ed. with notes by Edgar Fripp (Oxford: Ed. Hall for the Dugdale Society, 1921), facing p. 134. The same photo is in *Shakespeare's Stratford*, facing p. 26; and *Shakespeare Studies*,

facing p. 56. Haberdasher Smith's signature is reproduced in *Minutes and Accounts* facing p. 25.

6   Spenser, *Works*, pp. 623, 638.
7   George Whetstone, *Sir Phillip Sidney, His Honorable Life, His Valiant Death, and true Vertues* (London: Thomas Cadman, n.d.), B2v.
8   Sidney, *Miscellaneous Prose*, pp. 71–121, 112.
9   George Puttenham, *Arte of English Poesie* (London: Richard Field, 1589). Gladys Willcock and Alice Walker, eds (1936; Cambridge: Cambridge University Press, 1970), p. 63.
10 Penny McCarthy, 'E.K. Was Only the Postman', *N&Q*, n.s. 47.1 (March 2000), pp. 28–31.
11 Spenser, *Works*, p. 418.
12 Printed as 'Epigrams and Sonnets' in *Works*, pp. 605–8. The original publication was undertaken by Henry Binneman, who later habitually gave his address on title pages as 'by Baynards Castle', flaunting his proximity to the Pembrokes, whose London seat it was.
13 This is signalled by the given dates of two of the *Three Proper and Wittie Familiar Letters* (London: Henry Binneman, 1580) in Spenser, *Works*, pp. 609–45. The one dated April 1580 (the first Familiar) is written from Westminster, the parish where Spenser was married; the one dated October 1579 (the first Commendable) is written from 'Leycester House'. See *Works*, pp. 612, 638.
14 'Januarie' gloss on 'Hobbinol', *Works*, pp. 422–3.
15 Spenser, *Works*, p. 418.
16 Rambuss, *Spenser's Secret Career*, pp. 44–8, points out that a close relationship – probably involving a sexual element – with an aristocratic patron provided one route to advancement. See also Jonathan Goldberg, *Sodometries: Renaissance Texts, Modern Sexualities* (Stanford: Stanford University Press, 1992), pp. 63–81.
17 A.C. Hamilton suggests that Spenser deliberately varied spelling to emphasize the etymology of words, writing 'Geant', for example, to emphasize Orgoglio's descent from Gea. See his *Spenser: The Faerie Queene* (London: Longman, 1977), pp. 14–15.
18 Glossing 'Many Graces', E.K. tells us that 'thys same Poete in his Pageaunts sayth: "An hundred Graces on her eyeledde satte. &c"'. Spenser writes in *FQ* II.3.25 'Upon her eyelids many Graces sate'.
19 Spenser, *Works*, p. 441, lines 14–15.
20 Though variously decorated in different editions, the capitalization of these letters is constant.
21 Spenser, *Works*, p. 467.
22 *Works*, p. 458.
23 *Works*, p. 448.
24 *Works*, pp. 416, 457.
25 Egerton Brydges, ed., *A Poetical Rapsodie* (1608 edn) 3 vols (Kent: Lee Priory Press, 1814–17), 3.6.
26 I shall be referring to the first two of the four editions of the *Poetical Rhapsody: A Poetical Rapsody* (London: Valentine Simmes for John Baily, 1602); and *A Poetical Rapsodie* (London: Nicholas Okes for Roger Jackson, 1608). Page references to Hyder E. Rollins's edition: *A Poetical Rhapsody, 1602–21*, 2 vols (Cambridge, MA: Harvard University Press, 1931–32) are also given. The abbreviation '*PR*' will be used for the composite, i.e. when it is immaterial which version is consulted.
27 BM Harleian MS 280, f. 105r. (Rollins, 1.54–60.)

28   Spenser, *Works*, pp. 448, 450; 'August', lines 15, 130.

29   Ibid., lines 12–13.

30   *Rapsody*, B10r–C12v. Rollins, 1.25–53.

31   *Rapsodie*, pp. 31–33. Rollins, 1.259–61.

32   *Rapsodie*, pp. 59–85. Rollins, 1.25–30; 1.287–91.

33   The concept derives from Spurgeon, *Shakespeare's Imagery*. See above, page 57, and note 26, page 68.

34   *Elizabethan Sonnets*, ed. Maurice Evans, revised Roy Booth (1977; London: Dent, 1994), p. 265. Herbert E. Cory, *Edmund Spenser: A Critical Study* (Berkeley: University of California Press, 1917), pp. 27–9.

35   W.A., *A Speciall Remedie against the furious force of lawlesse Love*. In *Three Collections of English Poetry of the Latter Part of the Sixteenth Century* (London: R. Jones, 1578–79), in the Earl of Northumberland's Library at Alnwick. Reprinted by The Shakespeare Press (William Nicol for the Roxburghe Press, 1844).

36   William Smyth, *Gemma fabri* (London: F. Kingston for J. Porter, 1598).

37   William Smith, *The Blacksmith* (London: Ed. Allde for Martin Clarke, 1606). The STC assigns these two Smith works to the same individual.

38   See below, Chapter 9, for evidence from the Stratford birth register aligning this William Smith with the Alderman's eldest son.

39   Marcy North, *The Anonymous Renaissance: Cultures of Discretion in Tudor-Stuart England* (Chicago and London: University of Chicago Press, 2003), pp. 76–7.

40   North recognizes that Spenser's 'Ignoto' implies both 'not yet prominent' and 'covert'. See *Anonymous Renaissance*, p. 52.

41   Jeffrey Masten may be technically correct in claiming that 'Anonymous' did not at this period apply to a work bearing no author's name. But the use of 'Anomos' and 'Ignoto' as subscripts to individual poems, and of 'Anomos' on the title page of one section of the 1602 *Rapsody*, invalidates his general point that the notion of authorship, and therefore of anonymity, had not yet emerged. See Jeffrey Masten, *Textual Intercourse: Collaboration, Authorship, and Sexualities in Renaissance Drama* (Cambridge: Cambridge University Press, 1997), chapter 1.

42   Rollins, 1.125. It is the Folger copy. A third copy is in private hands, and Rollins gives no details. The *impresa* is 'splendidis longum valedico nugis', which is the subscript to 'Leave me oh love', the last sonnet in Philip Sidney's *Certaine Sonnets* (1598). I believe that sonnet is Shakespeare's.

43   Rollins, 1.331.

44   North, *Anonymous Renaissance*, pp. 84–5.

45   *Rapsody*, A3v; *Rapsodie*, A3r. (Rollins, 1.3.)

46   Ibid.

47   *Rapsody*, G1–G2r. Rollins, 1.127–9.

48   *Rapsody*, G2r. Rollins, 1.129.

49   Francis Meres, *Palladis Tamia: Wits Treasurie. Being the Second part of Wits Commonwealth* (London: P. Short for C. Busbie, 1598), fols 282v–284r.

50   Some of the furniture is to be found in Warwick Castle, having been removed from Kenilworth.

51   See note 13, above. Henry Woudhuysen, 'Leicester's Literary Patronage: A Study of the English Court' (D.Phil.) (Oxford, 1980), pp. 161–79.

52   *Works*, p. 628.

53   *Works*, p. 456.

54 Paul McLane, *Spenser's Shepheards Calender: A Study in Elizabethan Allegory* (Notre Dame, IN: University of Notre Dame Press, 1961), pp. 262–79.

55 Spenser, *Works*, p. 458, 'October', lines 112–13.

56 Patrick Cheney, *Spenser's Famous Flight: A Renaissance Idea of a Literary Career* (Toronto and London: Toronto University Press, 1993), p. 44.

57 Spenser, *Works*, p. 457, lines 37–48; gloss p. 458.

58 *Works*, p. 459.

59 Letterbook. BM MS Sloan 93. See *Letterbook of Gabriel Harvey*, ed. Edward J.L. Scott (London: Camden Society, 1874), pp. 55–143.

60 Spenser, *Works*, p. 637.

61 *Works*, p. 635.

62 In 'E.K. Was Only the Postman' I argue that the printed order of the letters is also their chronological order, contrary to the impression created by the (false) dates given.

63 Spenser, *Works*, p. 625.

64 V. Stern. *Gabriel Harvey. His Life, Marginalia and Library* (Oxford: Clarendon Press, 1979), pp. 65–6.

65 BM MS Sloane 93, f. 53r. Scott (see note 59 above) transcribes them into the hexameters they were intended to be. Henry Woudhuysen has assured me that the lines are part of the poem on the preceding manuscript page.

66 For my early dating of *Henry VIII*, see Chapter 9, p. 223.

67 Spenser, *Works*, p. 626.

68 Arthur Golding had translated *The historie of Leonard Aretine, concerning the warres betwene the Imperialles and the Gothes for the possession of Italy* (London: Rowland Hall for George Bucke, 1563). But Shakespeare followed more closely an English prose history of Titus Andronicus, according to Metz, *Shakespeare's Earliest Tragedy*.

69 *1Henry VI*, I.4.41–2.

70 *1Henry VI*, II.3.14–16.

71 Edward Halle, *The Union of the Two Noble Families of Lancaster and York* (1548) (Menston: Scolar Press, 1970), CCii(v)–CCiii(r). *Mirror for Magistrates* (1563 edn), ed. Lily B. Campbell from the Huntington Manuscript (Cambridge: Cambridge University Press, 1938), pp. 267–96, Tragedy 21, lines 381–600, lines 446–8.

72 Spenser, *Works*, p. 433.

73 *Works*, p. 427.

74 Meres, *Palladis Tamia*, 281v–282r.

Chapter 5

Third Candidate –
Friend of Richard Barnfield

The poem with which Richard Barnfield opens his *Poems in Divers Humors*, published in 1598, is a sonnet 'in praise of Musique and Poetrie'.[1] It is addressed to 'his Friend Maister R.L.'. Who is this R.L.? Is he connected with the R.L.s previously discussed? What motivates the sonnet? Is there a hint of a Shakespearean connection? This chapter provides some tentative answers to those questions.

The current state of interest in the relation of Barnfield's R.L. to other R.L.s could be summed up as 'meagre'. George Klawitter's note on Barnfield's dedicatee identifies him with R.L. the author of *Diella*, whom he identifies with 'Richard Linche'; but Klawitter allows that the evidence for the identification is slim.[2] The nineteenth century and the early twentieth were marginally more curious. Grosart conflates the R.L. of *Diella* and Barnfield's friend; the Beldornie editor simply notes that Barnfield's friend is known by the same initials as *Diella*'s author. Hazlitt does not mention the Barnfield tribute to R.L. Sidney Lee ascribes *Diella* to Richard Lynche but doubts whether *Diella*'s author is Barnfield's musical friend R.L.[3]

Let us turn to the sonnet itself, the spring-board for this chapter's inquiry into the R.L. who has a role in Barnfield's life and work.

> If Musique and sweet Poetrie agree,
> As they must needes (the Sister and the Brother)
> Then must the Love be great, twixt thee and mee,
> Because thou lov'st the one, and I the other.
> *Dowland* to thee is deare; whose heavenly tuch
> Upon the Lute, doeth ravish humaine sense:
> *Spenser* to mee; whose deepe Conceit is such,
> As passing all Conceit, needs no defence.
> Thou lov'st to heare the sweete melodious sound,
> That *Phoebus* Lute (the Queene of Musique) makes:
> And I in deepe Delight am chiefly drownd,
> When as himselfe to singing he betakes.
> One God is God of Both (as Poets faigne).
> One Knight loves Both, and Both in thee remaine.

The text alone does not give many leads. It is only if we are already predisposed to think of R.L. as a music lover (like the Ro. La. of the Kenilworth festivities) that we might be struck by the fact that Barnfield's friend adores music. If we are hyper-sensitive, we might have our antennae alerted by mention of Apollo as brother to Music. He is brother to Artemis, but she is not patron of music: it is Apollo who is usually portrayed as patron of both music and poetry, leader of all the Muses. Perhaps the conceit is Barnfield's own invention. He contradicts it somewhat by reverting to the classical notion of one god (Apollo, we presume) as god of both Music and Poetry, at the end of the sonnet. The hyper-sensitive might begin to wonder whether under the confusion there lurks an allusion to Philip Sidney, so often described as an Apollo, and his sister Mary. But the casual reader would hardly pause to worry over such details.

When the sonnet is set in the context of its fellows in the collection, however, and of Barnfield's earlier work; when certain dedications by and to Barnfield are duly considered; when the affiliation of his works becomes plain; when the reasons for the inclusion of the sonnet to R.L. in another publication – *The Passionate Pilgrime* – are investigated, the simple-looking text can be made to reveal considerably more. It will be most convenient to start with the last point; deal with earlier work, dedications, affiliations next; and finally to come back to the poem in the context of its own 1598 collection.

As a publication event, *The Passionate Pilgrime* of 1599 requires more explanation than it has received to date. It was printed by William Jaggard, who in the first edition attributed authorship of its contents to William Shakespeare. Five poems of the twenty in *PP* are definitely by Shakespeare: numbers 1, 2, 3, 5 and 16. They are: a version of his Sonnet 138, 'When my love swears that she is made of truth'; a version of his Sonnet 144 'Two loves I have of comfort and despair'; and three poems from *Love's Labour's Lost*, which was published in 1598 – 'Did not the heavenly rhetoric of thine eye'; 'If love make me forsworn'; and the ode 'On a day, alack the day'. But three are definitely not by Shakespeare: two are by Barnfield, and one, number 11, had been previously published by Bartholomew Griffin in his sequence *Fidessa* in 1596.[4] This last is on the subject of Venus and Adonis, as are the rest of the sonnets not described so far. Also included in the volume is the famous song of dubious authorship often attributed to Marlowe, 'Come live with me and be my love', with an answering stanza.

There is some indication that William Jaggard the publisher became embarrassed about the false implication that all the contents were by Shakespeare. A second printing in the same year as the first edition (of which no full copies survive) included a new title page, inserted oddly in mid-volume, between numbers 15 and 16. It gave no author's name, but said simply 'Sonnets to sundry notes of Musicke'. But what was Jaggard's rationale for assembling the collection in the first place? Could it be that the volume consisted entirely of pieces *by* Shakespeare, or written in rivalry *with* him or in imitation *of* him, or addressed *to* him?

My hypothesis that Jaggard had some rationale for his original ascription of the whole volume to Shakespeare may be questioned. But I believe it is worth treating seriously. The 'Venus and Adonis' poems certainly seem to fall into the category of rivalry or imitation. And turning to Barnfield's contributions to *PP*, we find that one of his poems, the ode 'As it fell upon a day/ In the merry month of May' (number 20), could well be placed in that category also, being so obviously related to Shakespeare's 'On a day, alack the day!/ Love whose month was ever May' (number 16 in *PP*).

It is Barnfield's other poem reprinted from *Poems in Divers Humors* that interests us most, however. 'If musique and sweet poetrie' reappears as number 8 in *PP*, without the epigraph to R.L., but with a heading 'Friendly concord'. The conclusion towards which I should like to press is that this sonnet was originally addressed *to* Shakespeare; and that is why it merited its place in *PP*.

Our next step is to examine Barnfield's collections of poetry. A schedule of his printed works up to 1598 would be useful at this point. His *Greenes Funeralls* appeared in 1594 (Robert Greene, the ostensible subject of all the 'sonnets' contained therein, having died in September 1592). Barnfield's *Affectionate Shepheard* also came out in 1594. Then in 1595 appeared his *Cynthia, with Certaine Sonnets, and the Legend of Cassandra*. And finally in 1598 he published a compendium volume addressed to 'Lady Pecunia', of which *Poems in Divers Humors* (containing the sonnet to R.L.) is the fourth and last work. Our attention will focus first on the preliminaries of *Cynthia* – an epistle to the readers, a dedicatory poem by T.T. Also relevant to the pursuit of R.L. is the title poem of the *Affectionate Shepheard*.[5]

A 'T.T.' contributed a verse dedication to the poem 'Cynthia' and the other poems in the 1595 volume.[6] This T.T. writes tortuous lines that are only half-comprehensible.

> Whylom that in a shepheards gray coate masked,
> (Where masked love the nonage of his skill)
> Reares new Eagle-winged pen, new tasked,
> To scale the by-clift Muse sole-pleasing hill:

> Dropping sweete Nectar poesie from his quill,
> > Admires faire CYNTHIA with his ivory pen
> > Faire CHYTHIA (sic) lov'd, fear'd, of Gods and men.[7]

Who is the subject of the main verb 'admires'? It looks as though we must supply a 'he' after 'whylom' (meaning 'once'). Or could it be that the subject of the verb is 'Whylom' – William? The 'by-clift' would seem to refer to the double peak of Parnassus; but the next stanza, though referring back to 'that mounteine' (i.e. Parnassus) speaks instead of the mountain trod by Pegasus, which in Greek mythology is Mount Helicon. Both were sacred to the Muses, but one poet cannot spring from both at once, as implied, 'decking with *double* grace the neighbour plaines'. A strong whiff of doubleness, in a literal and metaphorical sense, is present. Though the poem is entitled 'Cynthia', as in the 'Aprill' eclogue of the *Shepheardes Calender* a rival to Cynthia appears in the narrative, and seems to win the day.

T.T. next summarizes the story of the other narrative poem in the volume, 'The Legend of Cassandra', ending his stanza with 'Where JANUS-faced Jove, doth lurke disguiz'd'. Jove does not enter Barnfield's 'Cassandra' in person, though Apollo reports his decree. It is a misleading description of the poem, to say the least, unless T.T. means that the poem has reference to a historical person who is 'Jove' to his coterie. Janus is the two-faced Roman god. 'Two-faced' might also apply to the contents of the volume: I have a suspicion that T.T. thinks he is covertly introducing the joint work of two poets, Barnfield and Shakespeare, while on the surface making every phrase apparently applicable to *Cynthia* only. In fact, as we saw, the double publication did not appear until 1599, in the form of *The Passionate Pilgrime*; and then it contained the work of at least one other, Griffin, so it was hardly a twin production. But T.T. might have thought that was the intention behind the 1595 publication.

One common conceit in T.T.'s first stanza and one further fact about T.T. add credibility to the idea of a spider's web of threads connecting the fortunes and interests of Barnfield and Shakespeare.[8] The words 'sweet Nectar', applied by T.T. to the 'poesy', were quite probably short-hand for 'belonging to Shakespeare', who was often described as 'sweet' and 'honeyed', his style as 'mellifluous' and 'nectared'.[9] And it was Thomas Thorpe who published Shakespeare's sonnet sequence of 1609, lending his initials to the mysterious dedication to W.H. It is likely that the 'delphic' 1595 T.T. is the same as the riddling Thomas Thorpe of 1609.

The choice of T.T. by both Shakespeare and Barnfield as publisher has a parallel which deserves attention. Both poets also picked John Danter in

1594 to publish some of their earliest work. Barnfield published his *Greenes Funeralls* and his *Affectionate Shepheard* through Danter. Shakespeare's first published play, *Titus Andronicus*, also came out with Danter in that year.

From these shared paraliterary affiliations, we move to the social affiliations of patronage as revealed within Barnfield's poems. Barnfield belonged unequivocally in the Sidney circle, as has been recognized.[10] But he reveals more about its dynamics than has been realized.

The title poem of the volume *The Affectionate Shepheard* is in two parts of which the first is called 'The Teares of an affectionate Shepheard sicke for Love, or The Complaint of *Daphnis* for the Love of *Ganimede*'. Barnfield does not deny that he himself is Daphnis – indeed, he confirms it in the dedication of the *Affectionate Shepheard* to 'The right excellent and most beautifull Lady, the Ladie Penelope Ritch', which he signs 'Your Honours most affectionate and perpetually devoted Shepheard: DAPHNIS'. He can hardly distance himself, then, from the passionate desire evinced by the author for 'Ganimede' in the first part of the first poem.

> Scarce had the morning Starre hid from the light
> Heavens crimson Canopie with stars bespangled,
> But I began to rue th'unhappy sight
> Of that faire Boy that had my hart intangled;
> > Cursing the Time, the Place, the sense, the sin;
> > I came, I saw, I viewd, I slipped in.
>
> If it be sinne to love a sweet-fac'd Boy,
> (Whose amber locks trust up in golden tramels
> Dangle adowne his lovely cheekes with joy,
> When pearle and flowers his faire haire enamels)
> > If it be sinne to love a lovely Lad;
> > Oh then sinne I, for whom my soule is sad.[11]

The Ganimede whom Daphnis/Barnfield loves (and who does not appear to return his love) was, it transpires in the course of the poem, loved by 'Queen Guendolen'. But Guendolen's love-life was complex: not only was she wooed by a disgustingly old man, but she also loved another young man besides Ganimede. Unfortunately, Death and Love managed to get their respective arrows mixed up in a brawl, the result being that the disgusting old suitor, pierced by a love-arrow fired by Death, won the fair Guendolen; while the beautiful young man, pierced by a death-arrow fired by Love ... died.

Guendolen mourns so much that 'even Ganimede himselfe she would forsake', that very Ganimede 'whose sugred love is full of sweete delight' and '[i]n whose faire eye-balls you may clearly see/ Base Love still staind with foule indignitie' (the two contradictory aspects appearing in one stanza).[12] Daphnis tries to tempt Ganimede to love him with the lure of all pastoral treats imaginable, in language far more erotic than that of his avowed model, Virgil. Then returning to the theme of Guendolen, Daphnis urges Ganimede to leave her because she is 'light in her behaviour, to impaire/ Her honour in her Chastities declining'; and again towards the end of the poem implies that while Guendolen loves Ganimede for his body, the poet loves him for his talents and virtues, and will continue to love him (as she will not) when 'Age drawes on' in 'the December of thy Beauties waning'.[13]

George Klawitter, Barnfield's recent editor, assumes that the poem is not only dedicated to Penelope Rich, but also relates her adventures in love. He is following the consensus that Philip Sidney's *Astrophel and Stella* disguises that poet's love for Penelope, who returned his love. So naturally, when he reaches the passage about the unwanted old suitor and then the one about the deep mourning of Guendolen for a young man who tragically dies, Klawitter maps the Barnfield characters onto the supposed Sidneian historical referents. He registers some concern as he comes up against numerous obstacles to his identifications, but has not appreciated how impossible his scenario is.

A few words about the historical persons will demonstrate the impossibility. Penelope (originally Devereux), who married Robert Rich and caused a scandal by bearing children to her lover Charles Blount, is almost universally believed to have been the Stella to whom Philip Sidney addressed his sonnets, the woman for whom he felt an adulterous passion before and during the earlier part of her marriage. If Penelope was indeed Stella, then a scrupulous reading of 'The Affectionate Shepheard' will force us to conclude that the object of Richard Barnfield's adoration must have been Charles Blount, Penelope's lover, since Daphnis loves the man who loves 'Guendolen'. This is not in itself impossible: Blount was awarded his MA in 1589 at Brasenose as Barnfield was matriculating there. But it would throw every other correlation askew.

Robert Rich cannot be the disgusting old man who was suitor to 'Guendolen'. He was not in fact old: he was about twenty, and Penelope eighteen, when their marriage was settled. Klawitter claims that although he was not literally old, Rich was cast as old by the coterie poets, who disliked him. The language in which the old suitor is described simply will not bear this out.

> But her an Old-Man had beene sutor too,
> That in his age began to doate againe;
> Her would he often pray, and often woo,
> When through old-age enfeebled was his Braine ....[14]

This clearly describes someone who is old, has loved before, and in his dotage decides to look for a new wife. In a later line 'he wipes the drivel from his filthy chin'.[15] The incongruity with the figure of Robert Rich is not the only problem facing Klawitter's interpretation. As he sees it, a very young man (Barnfield) writes extremely erotic verse to an older man warning him against his unchaste woman lover ... and dedicates the verse to this same unchaste rival of his.

The one deduction we can safely make about the poem is that Guendolen is *not* Lady Rich. But does the story not match the story behind *Astrophel and Stella*? Of course it does, and continues it to the death of Philip Sidney, struck down by a death arrow fired by Love. And does Guendolen not map onto Stella? Yes, she does. And is Stella not Lady Rich? Jonathan Crewe has voiced suspicions that Penelope Rich was not Stella, but played the role of a carefully constructed 'screen woman', hiding a worse affair.[16] Crewe is right, I am sure. Let us look at the evidence in Philip's sonnet sequence.

The basis of the 'Rich' hypothesis is puns on the name in sonnets 24, 35 and 37 of *Astrophel and Stella.* In 24, Sidney makes a comparison between rich fools who set their hearts on having more, but at least have the wit to keep what they already have, and a particular rich fool who possesses the richest gem, but fails to hold onto it because of his 'foul abuse' of it and so ends rich only in folly. In 35, he writes '... and now long needy fame/ Doth even grow rich, naming my Stella's name'. In 37, the punning and capitalization are so blatant that it seems no doubt can be admitted but that the 'nymph' in question is Rich. She is 'Rich in all beauties which man's eye can see'; and subsequently

> Rich in the treasure of deserved renown;
> Rich in the riches of a royal heart;
> Rich in those gifts that give the eternal crown;
> Who though most rich in these, and every part
> Which make the patents of true worldly bliss,
> Hath no misfortune, but that Rich she is.
>
> (lines 9–14)

As if that were not proof enough, there is the anecdote sometimes attributed to George Gifford, a puritan clergyman, that a feeling of guilt over Lady

Rich oppressed Sidney shortly before he died, but he overcame it.[17] That the Sidney family and many of his friends intended readers to identify Penelope Rich as Stella I have no doubt. But let us examine the above evidence more critically, and add to it.

The anecdote attributes to Philip a troubling memory of 'a vanity wherein I had taken delight, whereof I had not rid myself. It was my Lady Rich. But I rid myself of it, and presently my joy and comfort returned'.[18] The words 'It was my Lady Rich' occur only in the late manuscript, the Juel-Jensen. The provenance of the document is itself highly doubtful. It appears likely, as Katherine Duncan-Jones says, that the episode was invented or doctored to put Philip in a favourable, almost saintly, light.[19] It is a beautiful instance of Crewe's screen-effect. Because people suspected there was something unsavoury about Philip's past passions, the passions themselves are acknowledged, but in that very act of acknowledgement, one figure, not too scandalous, slides in front of another whose identity, if known, would appal.

The *Astrophel* sequence is all about Astrophel's struggle with an unlawful love. He berates himself again and again, sometimes for not being ruled by reason, but sometimes for not seizing his opportunity to enjoy his love. Sonnet 24 fits the theme perfectly: it is far more natural, in the context of the other sonnets, to read the rich fool as being a description of Astrophel himself, than as an attack on another.

Sonnet 37, in which we have observed the word 'rich' so insistently repeated, was not included in the first or second printing (both of 1591). It first appeared in print in the 'authorized' collected poems of her brother's which Mary Sidney published in 1598. My deduction from this is that the family wanted it in – just as they wanted the death-bed thought to be promulgated. I believe that Sidney discovered by sheer serendipity, from reader reaction to Sonnet 24, that when he used the adjective 'rich', people believed he meant Lord Rich; and that he then put the discovery to good use in later sonnets. The reader reaction would have come from the friends to whom Philip circulated his poems in manuscript, a practice of his well documented by Henry Woudhuysen.[20]

Stella's identification with Penelope may be put in question by an alternative interpretation of a single sentence in Sonnet 35. 'Fame/ Doth even grow rich, naming my Stella's name.' It is universally assumed that Stella is here equated with 'Rich'. But the 'name' of Stella could equally well be 'Fame'. Mary Sidney, Philip's sister, was nick-named 'Fame' or sometimes 'Saint Fame'.[21] Armed with this vital piece of coterie inside knowledge, we can decipher another sonnet in which Stella's name is made mysterious, Sonnet 28.

> You that with allegory's curious frame
> Of others' children changelings use to make,
> With me those pains, for God's sake, do not take;
> I list not dig so deep for brazen fame.
> When I say 'Stella', I do mean the same
> Princess of beauty, for whose only sake
> The reins of love I love, though never slake,
> And joy therein, though nations count it shame.
>   (lines 1–8)

It is natural on a first encounter to read the fifth line as ending in a full stop, and to take it as meaning either 'When I say "Stella", I mean "Stella"', or as referring further back to some antecedent. 'When I say "Stella", I mean the very same thing' … as what? As Brazen Fame. The syntax alters this initial perception, carrying us forward to 'Princess of beauty'. But that does not mean that our initial instinct was not right.

Turning then to the reiterated 'Riches' in Sonnet 37, we discern that the second thing in which Stella is 'Rich' is 'deserved renown', in other words, Fame. To exacerbate suspicion of the overt meaning, there are in this sonnet telling verbal, thematic and methodological echoes of a mysteriously personal passage in Chaucer's *Canterbury Tales*. When the character 'Chaucer' tries to tell the story of Sir Thopas's illicit love for the Elf Queen (which is clearly the author Chaucer's own story as well as the character 'Chaucer's'), he opens with the phrase 'Listeth, lordes'.[22] Astrophel echoes both the words and the theme of an illicit but life-defining secret: 'Listen then, Lordings, with good eare to me/ For of my life I must a riddle tell'. The Chaucer/Thopas of *The Canterbury Tales* is prevented from telling his secret by the Host who presides over the pilgrims' contest as they wend their way to Canterbury. Sidney performs a similar act of censorship on Astrophel – an act of self-censorship exactly equivalent to Chaucer's suppression of 'Chaucer's' story. For Sidney quickly obscures the story of *his* Fairy Queen (who is queenly because she has a 'royal heart' and 'gifts that give the eternal crown', as the same sonnet reports) by screening her with another, with 'Rich'.

Jonathan Crewe demonstrates how precarious this screen is. His most compelling piece of evidence is Sonnet 83. It begins 'Good brother Philip, I have born you long'. The voice is that of the poet, addressing Stella's pet sparrow (sparrows were typically 'Philip' or 'Pip'), jealously telling him to stop taking amorous advantage of the succour Stella gives him, cuddling him in her neck. 'Leave that, Sir Phip', exclaims the poet, though the words sound like Stella's. Duncan-Jones says 'Stella's sparrow is 'brother' to Astrophil because they are rivals for her favour and share a Christian name'. '"Sir" is used here "with contemptuous, ironic or irate force"' she claims, citing the *OED*. 'Sidney's knighthood, which he received in January 1583, is unlikely to be relevant'.[23] But how can a reader avoid hearing a perilous sub-text here? It is natural to hear the opening line as the voice of Stella; and the sparrow's name and title 'sir' reinforce the suspicion that Pip is literally the brother of his loved one.

Other lines and half-lines in the sequence then begin to glow with a peculiarly incestuous light too. There are indications that Astrophel lost this love through his own inadvertence. In sonnet 33, he explains how he 'did miss'. He would not or could not 'see his bliss' when it was available to him. 'No force, no fraud, robbed thee of thy delight ... But to myself myself did give the blow.' Why? He 'could not by rising morn foresee/ How fair a day was near'. Commentators are quick to suppose that Philip must have met Penelope when she was young, and that he failed to see how beautiful she would become when adult. He might have done, of course; but the odd thing is that it was her sister Dorothy to whom he was once betrothed, not Penelope. This fact emerges from a will made by Leicester in 1582.[24]

Sonnet 2, which opens the narrative (Sonnet 1 being a kind of poetic manifesto), does not give the impression that Philip had seen his 'lost love' briefly once or twice, as the proponents of the 'Rich thesis' must necessarily argue. Lines 1 to 4 run:

> Not at first sight, nor with a dribbed shot,
> Love gave the wound which while I breathe will bleed:
> But known worth did in mine of time proceed,
> Till by degrees it had full conquest got.

This sounds more like a close companionship which gradually became something else as the child grew into a woman. Astrophel falls in love 'not at first sight' but gradually with someone whose love he must 'paint' (deceptively); someone with whom he is 'unable quite to pay even nature's rent' (have children); someone in whom he joys 'though nations count it shame'; whose 'rising Morne' he had not known would turn into so 'faire a day' (his sister was seven years younger than he – he watched her grow up); to whom he is 'perhaps' 'somewhat kinne', since 'Thou bear'st the arrow, I the arrow head'.[25]

These scattered hints point to a dire secret. It is not impossible to have children with one's lover when married to someone else – indeed Penelope Rich did just that. But it is impossible to acknowledge children born of sibling incest. (Is that the possibility to which the peculiar opening lines about children and changelings of Sonnet 28 refer?) Nations do not always count it shame to indulge in polygamy, but the taboo on sibling incest is widespread, and Sidney might have taken it to be universal.[26] Sidney's personal seal was an arrowhead: Mary continued to use the Sidney seal after her marriage. In heraldry, the arrow is a 'pheon': the phoenix appellation applied in Sidneian contexts long before Philip's death and 'immortalization' as a phoenix who was to rise from the ashes. There is a 'phoenix Stella' in Sonnet 92, and in *Certaine Sonnets* 24, the poet (Philip) will 'die in Phoenix fire', a highly erotic phrase, for Elizabethan 'die' implies sexual consummation.[27]

This was the dire secret: the Sidney siblings, two phoenixes, were lovers.[28] The secret was well known to contemporaries, and some almost reveal it, whether deliberately or not. Stella is linked with Mary in *The Mourning Muse of Thestylis*, by Ludowick Bryskett: Stella's lament is referred to as 'his [Philip's] noble sister's plaints'.[29] In another of the elegies, Matthew Roydon in speaking of Stella and Philip says 'Tis likely they acquainted soone/ He was a Sun, and she a Moone'.[30] Initially puzzling (again there is a suggestion of an early – childhood? – intimacy), this reference can lead us closer to the heart of the secret.

Stella should be, of course, 'a star', not a moon. A dedication of Thomas Watson's *Amintae Gaudia* to Mary plays on the 'star' derivation, in a way that has not been appreciated, for it too is offering careful readers an insight.[31] The dedication offers Watson's Latin verse to Mary, calling her 'Apollonei soror', 'sister of Apollo', and begging her not to reject 'stellam alteram', 'this second star' or 'stella', for her crown. The implication is that the first stella – the *Astrophel and Stella* of the year before – was also hers. But the clue to Roydon's odd iconography of sun and moon lies in one of the prefaces to *Astrophel and Stella* itself.

It is the one by Thomas Nashe and it was clearly part of the source of the enormous upset caused by the first edition. It uses the mythology of the Olympian gods to refer to Philip and Mary, identifying them (as Roydon does in a veiled way) with Apollo and Artemis – gods of the sun and the moon. This edition, put out by Thomas Newman in the autumn of 1591, was immediately recalled by order of the Chancellor under pressure from the Sidney family, it seems; but was reissued very soon, *minus the dedication and preface*. There is nothing in Newman's dedication to Francis Flower to cause offence, *pace* Warkentin.[32] But in the preface, Nashe, addressing Mary as 'fayre sister of *Phoebus*' (i.e. Artemis to his Apollo), indulges in some rather odd teasing. He exclaims 'Mercury hath Io, and onely Io Paean belongeth to Astrophel'.

'Io paean!' is the traditional Greek cry of exultation, or the celebratory cry of mortals at a visitation of the god Apollo; while plain 'Io' is the name of the poor mortal girl whom Jupiter loved, and Juno jealously turned into a cow. Nashe seems to imply: Astrophel has only glory (being now dead) but someone called Mercury has won Io. This Io had at all costs to be censored out of existence, it appears, for she has also been excised from Sidney's text. A line in Sonnet 69 has undergone a slight but very telling alteration. What most readers read in modern editions, and what all but those lucky few who possessed the illicit first edition would have read in the sixteenth century, is 'I, I, o I may say that she is mine' – a peculiar line of poetry. The wording in the first edition is 'And Io, I may say that she is mine'. So when the Philip character Astrophel sings in Sonnet 63 'Sing then my Muse, now *Io Pean* sing', it is tempting to unearth a double meaning: Sidney's Muse is invited to exult; or, Sidney's Muse *is* Io Paean. The latter reading is consonant with the meaning and context of the censored line of Sonnet 69: 'Stella hath, with words where faith doth shine,/ Of her high heart given me the monarchy;/ And Io, I may say that she is mine'. It is manifest in this latter instance that Stella is Io. And it should be clear from the upshot – the calling in of books, the alterations – that it was the potential identification of Stella with Io by a wider readership that was at the heart of the trouble anticipated by the Sidney family from publication of Newman's first volume.

The Shepheardes Calender provides us with another vital clue. Harry Berger sees that the running subtext to the *Calender* is the story of Io pursued by Jupiter and guarded by Mercury, though he has not related his insight to the addressee of *Astrophel and Stella*.[33] My proposal is that the Ios and Mercuries in these different expressions of the foundational coterie myth be brought into play with each other; and that Barnfield be recognized as a teller of the same story – indeed, as the 'bewrayer' of its inner meaning, his slightly more clumsy narrative being such as to expose the mechanics of concealment of the whole group.

With Barnfield's help, we can fit the coterie's fictional characters to their correct historical referents. The Guendolen weeping for the death of the young man is indeed weeping for Philip: but she is Mary Sidney, not Penelope Rich. The arrow of Death killed Philip instead of *Mary*'s horrible old husband, Henry Herbert, Earl of Pembroke (over forty! and married twice before). But *Mary* still has not given up Ganimede, the beloved of Daphnis. Daphnis therefore casts aspersions on Mary's chastity in his poem, to wean Ganimede away from his female rival. This is the only way to make sense of Barnfield's characters; though as yet Ganimede's part remains a little obscure.

Now, Daphnis was said by the mythologers to be either the son, *or the lover*, of Hermes/Mercury. Herein lies a possible link between Barnfield's fictive-but-real Ganimede and Nashe's fictive-but-real Mercury. Nashe seems to imply that Mercury was successor to Astrophel in Stella/Io's affections. We have good reason to believe that Barnfield's Guendolen was none other than Stella; and she was loved by Ganimede. It seems that Barnfield has substituted the name 'Ganimede' for the name 'Mercury' in retelling the coterie's central myth. He would have done so out of caution, wanting insiders to comprehend what he was about, but fearful of spelling it out for the wider audience his book would reach when printed. He is parasitic on the Astrophel tale, even to the extent of recycling Penelope Rich to defy decoding of the true reference.

'Mercury/Ganimede' does not name a blank space. But who is he? Does either name entail any connection with our quarry, R.L.-as-Shakespeare? I draw on Barnfield's work again to construct some scaffolding for the integration of Ganimede into the composite R.L., and for the inclusion of Shakespeare in Barnfield's literary and social universe.

Klawitter correctly declares that a thematic connection ought to subsist between the earlier and later volumes of Barnfield's poetry, since Barnfield's epigraph for *PDH* deliberately evokes the setting of *The Affectionate Shepheard*.[34] The epigraph 'Trahit sua quemque voluptas' ('each is drawn by his own desire') is taken from that very eclogue of Virgil's that Barnfield declares he was imitating in his *Shepheard*. He was evidently driven to make this declaration because of some adverse reaction to the erotic first poem in that volume of 1594. In an address to the Gentlemen readers prefacing *Cynthia* (1595) we read that 'Some there were, that did interpret *The affectionate Shepheard*, otherwise then (in truth) I meant, touching the subiect thereof, to wit, the love of a Shepheard to a boy; a fault, the which I will not excuse, because I never made. Onely this, I will unshaddow my conceit: being nothing else, but an imitation of *Virgill*, in the second Eglogue of Alexis'.[35]

The highly sexual nature of 'The Complaint of Daphnis' has been noted above. Barnfield is being disingenuous. The fact that he blithely proceeds to utilize the eclogue on the opening page of *PDH* therefore is a promise of further expressions of love for a man. This brings us to our last section, the context of the sonnet to R.L. and finally the sonnet itself.

We are entitled to ask for the rationale for the epigraph from Virgil – where exactly in the later volume does the homoerotic poetry lie? The volume consists of two sonnets (the first to R.L., the second a defence of poetry); a poem of three quatrains plus a six-line stanza, entitled 'A Remembrance of some English Poets' (in which Shakespeare is explicitly praised); the Ode 'As it fell upon a Day' (the one that is reprinted in the *Passionate Pilgrime*), which contrasts true with false friendship; a poem on a portrait of a gentlewoman; an epitaph for Sir Philip Sidney; an epitaph on the poet's aunt (who died in 1594); and a seven-line poem comparing the life of man to a feast. Only the poem to R.L. and the elegy for Philip could conceivably come within the sphere of same-sex passion, I suggest. To have adopted such a tone for the latter would have been markedly inappropriate to the occasion, and Barnfield does not do so. Standing in pride of place, it is the poem for R.L. that has prime claim to embody the sentiment of the epigraph.

This does not make it mandatory to identify the Ganimede of the earlier published volume with the R.L. to whom 'If musique' is dedicated. But Barnfield's statement in a poetic dedication of *PDH* to his Brasenose College friend Nicholas Blackleech that the volume contains the 'fruits of unriper yeares' suggests that the composition of the two works dates from the same period. And that in turn makes it more likely that the beloved is the same individual.

R.L. may be Ganimede: but there is a contra-indication to the other identification I am trying to make, that of Ganimede and Shakespeare. Barnfield addresses Ganimede as a sweet 'Boy' and a 'Lad'. But Shakespeare was ten years older than Barnfield. The objection would apply equally to identification of Charles Blount as Ganimede; or indeed to most contenders, since Barnfield was so young when he wrote his love poems. It is likely, however, that Barnfield's model dictated a format for his love that was not actually mirrored in the situation in which he found himself. He had to seem to copy Virgil, whose eclogues were about love for a boy. But certain lines suggest Barnfield's beloved was actually older than he was. In the 'Affectionate Shepheard', Daphnis promises that because he loves Ganimede for his qualities, not for his beauty, as Guendolen does, he will still be faithful when Ganimede is old.

> But I that lov'd thee for thy gifts divine,
> In the December of thy Beauties waning,
> Will still admire (with joy) those lovely eine,
> That now behold me with their beauties baning.
> (lines 217–20)

If Daphnis looks forward to a metaphorical December of the other's beauty in which, he imagines, he will still love the wintry figure, the likelihood is that he is younger than his beloved.

Another poem from the same volume provides evidence of some prevarication over the age of the hero, whom Barnfield jokingly calls an 'Old

Lad' though he is young. It cannot be proved that the hero of this poem, which is called 'Hellens Rape', masks the same historical person as the Ganimede of the 'Affectionate Shepherd'. But the two poems are bound in the same volume as though they belonged together; and there is also a telling clue to the identity of the woman masked by the poem's heroine, Helen of Troy. She is labelled 'Delia', which is not a title of the mythical Helen. It is, however, a title accorded to Mary Sidney by her coterie poets. Paris the Old Lad stealing away Delia is therefore an analogue of Ganimede courting Guendolen, the link being the real-life relationships that both poems mirror, darkly.

Barnfield's version of the Helen myth is lighthearted, even farcical, told in excruciating hexameters in 'measured verse' (mimicking Latin scansion). Ostensibly it is the tale of Paris stealing Helen from her husband Menelaus. The intrusion of an aunt Amaryllis into the story strikes a false note that further prompts us to suppose that Barnfield is actually relaying tittle-tattle about the Sidneys. Amaryllis featured in Greek and Roman pastoral; but she was also the addressee and subject of many of Edward Dyer's love-poems, and Dyer was a close friend of Philip Sidney's. Barnfield's focus of interest in the myth is the sexual play of 'Delia' and the Young/Old Lad, for that is the point at which he brings his poem to a climax, and abandons it.

> Young Lad, but yet such an old Lad,
> In such a Ladies lappe, at such a slipperie by-blow,
> That in a world so wide, could not be found such a wilie
> Lad: in an Age so old, could not be found such an old lad:
> The Old lad, and bold lad, such a Boy, such a lustie Iuventus.[36]

The fact that the poem ends with this extraordinary emphasis on the oldness of the young lad demands explanation. We saw earlier that Kemp, joking about Macdobeth, alluded to 'a proper upright youth, onely for a little stooping in the shoulders', who seemed to be an old/young Shakespeare. In the next two chapters, we shall follow up other manifestations of the young Old Lad in the works of Thomas Nashe and Robert Armin.

Our hermeneutics of suspicion can now be applied to the sonnet to R.L. This states, innocently enough, that Barnfield loves poetry, R.L. loves music, and since these two things 'agree' together, so must their human aficionados. The logic is faulty, but the argument looks persuasive. Barnfield repeats it at a higher level: because the two great 'gods' of music and poetry love each other, and the mortals each love one of the gods, the mortals must have a like passion for each other.

But that is not all the poem says. Why do we need to know that one specific knight, who is neither of the protagonists, loves both? It suggests a contemporary reference. I suggested above that 'Apollo' alludes to Philip Sidney. Mapping the historical persons onto the innocent-seeming words (with Sir Edward Dyer as the superfluous knight?), we may conclude, and may have been intended to conclude, that the young Barnfield loved Philip Sidney, and Barnfield's beloved loved Philip's sister. The beloved, we note, is not only musical but also endowed with poetic gifts ('both in thee remain'). He looks familiar.

Yet it would not be right to greet Barnfield's R.L. as Shakespeare until we know more about the role of Mercury and Ganimede in the mythology of the coterie. I promised only 'tentative' conclusions in this chapter, and am aware that while much of the material is highly suggestive, it is parasitic on previous argument, and still requires corroboration.

Notes

1   *Poems in Divers Humors* (London: G.S. for J. Jaggard, 1598), E2v. Subsequent citations will be from *Richard Barnfield: The Complete Poems*, ed. George Klawitter (London and Toronto: Associated University Presses, 1990). The poem addressed to R.L. is on p. 181.

2   Klawitter, p. 246. Klawitter appeals also to the discussion by Harry Morris, *Richard Barnfield, Colin's Child* (Tampa: Florida State University Studies (no. 38), 1963), pp. 112–13.

3   For Utterson, Hazlitt and Grosart, see Chapter 3, notes 6, 7, 8. Sidney Lee, *Elizabethan Sonnets*, 2 vols (Westminster: Constable, 1904), 1.cii.

4   Bartholomew Griffin, *Fidessa more chaste than kind* (London: M. Lownes, 1596), sonnet 3.

5   *Greenes Funeralls* (London: J. Danter, 1594); *The Affectionate Shepheard* (London: J. Danter for T. G[ubbins] and E. N[ewman], 1594; *Cynthia. With Certaine Sonnets, and the Legend of Cassandra* (London: Humfrey Lownes, 1595).

6   Klawitter, pp. 113–47.

7   Klawitter, p. 116.

8   Katherine Duncan-Jones descries such a web: see her *Shakespeare's Sonnets*, p. 47.

9   See Sams, *Real Shakespeare*, p. 83.

10   Klawitter and Morris, *passim.*

11   Klawitter, pp. 79–80.

12   Klawitter, p. 82, lines 89–90. The contradiction can be resolved by supposing that Ganimede is only 'base' by birth, and suffers 'foul indignity' for the same reason.

13   Klawitter, p. 84, lines 159–60; p. 85, lines 216–18.

14   Klawitter, p. 80, lines 25–8.

15   Klawitter, p. 81, line 62.

16   Jonathan Crewe, *Hidden Designs: The Critical Profession and Renaissance Literature* (New York and London: Methuen, 1986), pp. 70–88. Jonathan Goldberg, in *Desiring*

Women Writing (Stanford: Stanford University Press, 1997), pp. 114–31, and *Sodometries*, pp. 99–101, appears to accept the erotic nature of the love Mary felt for Philip. He does not consider whether Philip loved Mary. Katrina Bachinger, in *Male Pretense: A Gender Study of Sir Philip Sidney's Life and Texts* (Lampeter: Mellen Press, 1994), recognizes incestuous desire in Philip, but bizarrely concludes that Philip's friend Languet is 'Stella' and the object of Philip's desire in the *Arcadias.*

17   Anon., 'The Manner of Sir Philip Sidney's Death', extant in two manuscripts, BL MS Cotton Vitellius C. 17, fols 382–7; and the Juel-Jensen manuscript. See Duncan-Jones, *Sir Philip Sidney*, pp. 315–18.

18   Ibid., p. 317.

19   Ibid., p. 406.

20   Woudhuysen, *Circulation*, pp. 219–23, and *passim.*

21   McCarthy, 'Milksop Muses'.

22   Geoffrey Chaucer, *The Canterbury Tales*, ed. W.W. Skeat (London: Oxford University Press, 1957), 'Sir Thopas', pp. 502–4.

23   Duncan-Jones, *Sir Philip Sidney*, p. 367.

24   Ibid., p. 227, citing Longleat, Dudley Papers III.56, fol. 11.

25   *Astrophel and Stella*, Sonnets 2, line 1; 18, line 5; 28, line 8; 33, lines 12–13; 65, lines 12–14.

26   See Lord Raglan, *Jocasta's Crime: An Anthropological Study* (London: C.A. Watts, 1940).

27   Philip Sidney, *Certaine Sonnets*, 24, line 27. *Poems*, pp. 135–62, p. 153, line 27.

28   In 'Nabokov's *Ada* and Sidney's *Arcadia*: the Regeneration of a Phoenix', *MLR* 99.1 (January 2004), pp. 17–31, I argue that Vladimir Nabokov knew this, and made it the animating subtext of his *Ada.*

29   Bryskett, 'Mourning Muse', in Spenser, *Works*, p. 552, line 150.

30   Roydon, 'An Elegie', in Spenser, *Works*, p. 557, lines 127 and 131–32.

31   Thomas Watson, *Amintae Gaudia* (London: W. Ponsonby, 1592).

32   Warkentin, 'Patrons and Profiteers', pp. 467–70.

33   Harry Berger, *Revisionary Play: Studies in the Spenserian Dynamics* (Berkeley: University of California, 1988), p. 335.

34   Klawitter, p. 245.

35   Klawitter, pp. 115–16.

36   Klawitter, pp. 110–11, lines 66–70.

Chapter 6

Further Supposes

The Supposes, or personae, who must be tracked down in this chapter are Ganimede, Mercury, and the Old Lad. If it could be shown that these characters are linked with Shakespeare or with R.L. elsewhere in the coterie literature, my speculation in the previous chapter about the identity of Barnfield's R.L. would move into the realm of probability. I shall take each of these characters in turn, pursuing the threads where they may lead through pamphlets, plays, poems, histories and masques dating from 1587 to 1609. The circle of authors participating in the coterie game of allusion will be greatly enlarged, encompassing works by Robert Greene, Christopher Marlowe, George Chapman and Thomas Nashe. Works of unknown authorship also feature. The characteristics of the clown figure in *Locrine* open up the possibility that Shakespeare and his contemporaries indulged in 'guying' of each other. The evidence is to be found in non-dramatic as well as dramatic works, and it would serve no good purpose to make a sharp distinction between different genres.[1]

By 'guying' I mean more than simple parody, though the extent of that practice needs emphasizing too. Citation and verbal parody of a predecessor have been identified and well described, for example by editors of the Arden Shakespeare series and by studies such as that of James Shapiro concerning the relations of Marlowe, Shakespeare and Jonson.[2] But my case is rather that writers presented each other *in person* on stage and *as persons* in their poems and pamphlets. Citation and parody may, of course, be instruments of such presentation.

A work that must be from the pen of one who was in the very heart of the coterie has Ganymede as its protagonist. It is a prose pamphlet entitled *Philippes Venus*, and was published in 1591, under the name of Jo. M.[3] No explanation is given as to why the Venus of the story – a mortal Venus who takes the heavenly Venus's place – is *Philip*'s Venus. Contemporary readers would surely have thought of Philip Sidney as soon as their eyes lighted on the title.

The setting is Olympus, where the gods hold their Council meetings, presided over by Jupiter and Saturn. Jupiter's page Ganymede sports with the ladies. It is highly reminiscent of the *Letter* by R.L., 'the Black Prince', on his duties and amusements at Kenilworth. The Black Prince hinted that the lame Saturn was in fact Ambrose Warwick, and led us to suspect that the 'niece Pallas', who prevented unruly outsiders from getting within the Kenilworth gates, was a real person also. We can justifiably speculate that the author of *Philippes Venus* works within the same conventions. So, although legend dictates that Ganymede was indeed Jupiter's page, knowing readers would have understood a contemporary page and a contemporary Jupiter (Robert Dudley) to be the real targets of the gentle satire.

The author of *Philippes Venus*, whose name is not on the title page, but who signs his dedicatory epistle 'Jo. M.', launches straight into the dedication with mention of good will.

> Good will may be blamed by some curious carpers, that with Gorgon belch forth their venome against the simple, but to such as meane well, Hope to beate downe feare and to overthrowe dispaire, setteth in her foote, to animate the vertuous to persever and goe forward in their well dooinges, confirming the old approved proverb, with this assertion, (though trueth may be blamed saith she), yet shall good will in trueth be never ashamed.[4]

The dedication is ostensibly to a Henry Prannell. But there is a possible subtext. 'This hope of your good liking, hath made me bolde to acquaint and deliver into your hands this small pamphlet, namely, *Phillipes Venus*, but to present *Apollo* with *Pans* Oaten Pipe, or *Diana* with a Distaffe, it were a thing ridiculous....' It is as though Apollo *is* in fact being presented with the work. The title finds its rationale in the identity of the recipient, for Philip (Sidney) is Apollo in the coterie mythology. He was dead by the date of publication, of course, but the setting would seem to be much earlier.

The story in the text is as follows. Wanton Venus is thrown out of heaven. A new chaste Venus is chosen from among the nymphs who attend on Diana. This nymph 'seemed rather a saint than a subject, more like Phoebus sister ...'. The 'nymphs', or ladies waiting while the men are in council, decide to hold a contest to see who can win young Ganymede. They use their wits in a dialogue of love, one praising his beauty, one his wit, and chaste Venus praising his virtue.

At the start, Ganymede is playing at tying love knots and 'making of Puppits'. This may be just what a page would do. But 'puppets' is quite a common term for stage players, and it is interesting to find this Black Prince-like Ganymede involved with something potentially theatrical so early – interesting, too, to find Venus telling him to 'look about Ganymede, and beholde this goodly Theatrum of the heavens' (4r). This Olympus could well be intended to evoke Elizabeth's (Diana's) Council, and this theatrical Ganymede could be the page of its chief luminary Dudley.

The anonymous play *Locrine* has been sometimes attributed to Shakespeare because of the statement on the title page (of 1595) that it had been 'newly set foorth, overseene and corrected' by W.S.[5] Its proletarian character Strumbo has a large role. When Strumbo first appears, he is in a gown and has ink and paper. He is verbose, much given to expressions such as 'not only ... but also ...'. He has a servant called 'Trompart', 'Deceitful Art'. When the character Humber asks Strumbo whether he is a Mercury come to rescue him, Strumbo denies it: 'O alasse sir, ye are deceived, I am not Mercury, I am Strumbo ...' (H2v).

Strumbo may be simply a stock clown; but the specificity of his attributes – especially the ink and paper – prompt the suspicion that he was recognizable to some section of the intended audience, and all the funnier for being so. It may be that the later association of this play with the name of Shakespeare stems less from the initials of its reviser than from the fact that Strumbo represents Shakespeare.

Certain details in the characterization of other comic servants in comedies of the same period are such as to prompt a similar suspicion. Mouse is the servant in the anonymous play *Mucedorus*, which has also been sometimes attributed to Shakespeare.[6] Musidorus, Pyrocles's Arcadian companion, has already appeared in this study among the 'R.L. suspects' in the form of 'Dorus' in Drayton's *Ideas Mirrour*. The Mucedorus of the play is in some sense the same individual as Musidorus in Sidney's *Arcadia*, for he too saves the heroine from a bear. The clownish Mouse (cognate with the hero via Latin 'mus', a mouse) is terrified of *white* bears, i.e., of Dudleys. He is also shown as a tremendous glutton, a characteristic shared with yet another 'Shakespeare-the-clown' figure, Tutch the clown in Robert Armin's play *The Historie of Two Maids of More-clacke*.[7]

As Stephen Orgel has observed, this play is clearly an extended parody of *Hamlet*.[8] Orgel calls it essential reading for anyone interested in how Shakespeare appeared to his contemporaries; from which I deduce that he recognizes that Tutch is a portrait of Shakespeare. (Since he is himself interested only in the play-as-performance, Orgel gives no hints.) Tutch (presumably derived from Touchstone) appears on stage in the act of writing. He is so engaged in this occupation that he is oblivious to those who hail him; but the audience overhears what he is jotting down – a menu: 'Let me see, Capons, Turkies, Small-birds, Beefes, Muttons, Partridge, Plover, Wood-cocks'

(A2v). One of the characters, wanting to know why one of the young suitors used Tutch as messenger, demands why he had made Tutch his 'mercurie' (D1v).

While the plot is modelled on *Hamlet*, with a woman marrying a second husband 'incestuously', much to the disgust of her son, other works by Shakespeare are conspicuously cited. A half-wit, John, is quizzed on the parts of speech, just like the boy William Page in *The Merry Wives of Windsor*.[9] He declares there are eight parts of speech, including 'the vocative, and ablative, caret nominativo' (B4r). Later Tutch disguises himself as John, and he and his interlocutor repeat the joke (G4v). There is citation from *King Lear* ('take you for a ioyne stoole') and also, I think, from *Lucrece* ('Like wax, she'll take any impression').[10] Both utterances belong to Tutch (D2v).

The best clue is possibly a quotation from *Hamlet;* but even if it is not, it has great potential because of its attachment to Tutch, and its appearance in other significant contexts. When he divests himself of another disguise, as a Welshman, Tutch declares 'I am tutch right, hic et ubique, every where' (H1). (The ghost in *Hamlet* is 'hic et ubique', 'here and everywhere'.) It may be that Armin simply quotes Shakespeare for an easy laugh: but I think we should give the witty clown from Shakespeare's company (the Chamberlain's) credit for more wit than that. If Tutch does actually represent Shakespeare, the play is much funnier. Nashe's unlearned poet Humfrey King, addressee of *Lenten Stuffe*, has the same Latin tag 'hic et ubique' attached to him, we saw. And Armin uses the phrase again in his dedication of a poem which invokes an Old Lad, to be examined below. The contexts of all the references strongly suggest the tag attached itself specifically to Shakespeare.

The anonymous play *Guy of Warwick* contains an unmistakable portrait of Shakespeare. Helen Cooper argues that *Guy* may well be Ben Jonson's.[11] It is a comedy by 'B.I.', ('I' being used indifferently for 'J'). It was printed 1661, but probably belongs to the early 1590s or even late 1580s. It is enormously interesting for its comic servant, a character called Sparrow. Questioned as to his parentage and provenance, he boasts that he is no ordinary sparrow. 'I have a fine finical name, I can tell ye, for my name is Sparrow; yet I am no house Sparrow, nor no hedge Sparrow, nor no peaking Sparrow, nor no sneaking Sparrow, but I am a high mounting lofty minded Sparrow.'[12] (Intriguingly, a sparrow is a 'cuddy' in northern rustic speech.) He was born in England, he says, at Stratford upon Avon in Warwickshire.

If Shakespeare had the humble Warwickshire background all suppose, then it is easy to see how the bumptious 'clowns' Strumbo, Mouse or Sparrow could represent him, for 'clown' means 'rustic' as much as 'fool'. Indeed it is probable that in his own plays Shakespeare carried on the joke: the servant Lance in *Two Gentlemen of Verona* and the dim rustic William in *As You Like It* may well be cases of Shakespeare sending himself up. 'Lance' is by no means too outrageous a pun for 'spear'. Ben Jonson used it quite openly in the poem he contributed to the First Folio of Shakespeare's plays – 'he seems to shake a lance'. It is not important to our immediate argument to know whether Mouse and Strumbo are similarly *self*-portraits or not.

'Shakespeare' as a dramatic character is not always incorporated in a clownish or rustic servant figure in contemporary fictions. He appears also in other guises, sometimes under several guises in one play. In my next example, he is hidden under several layers, beneath an Orlando Furioso who appears as a covert Mercury in pursuit of an equally obscured Chloris.

In the Alleyn Library in Dulwich College is a wonderful document, the manuscript part for the character Orlando in Greene's play *Orlando Furioso.* The play was published in quarto in 1594.[13] There are some odd allusions in Orlando's words in the manuscript which do not occur in the quarto. These allusions emanate from the same frame of reference as some speeches in the early scenes in the quarto that have been lost from the manuscript. Having the two versions to compare is immensely instructive.

It is more obvious in the manuscript part than in the printed play that Orlando, driven mad by his suspicions that his beloved Angelica loves wicked Sacrapant, harps on being a poet laureate. This is somewhat odd. We have to bear in mind throughout that Greene had no precedent in his original, the epic poem *Orlando Furioso* by Ludovico Ariosto, for any words spoken by mad Orlando: Ariosto simply has him tear up trees and people, mutely.[14] In Ariosto, he *finds* roundelays – he does not write them. Nor does he in Greene's play, yet Greene makes him a poet. He also makes him low-born. This is quite contrary to Ariosto, whose Orlando was nephew to the Emperor Charlemagne.

Angelica likewise takes on some peculiar aspects. In a scene early in the play missing from the manuscript, the quarto has Angelica's suitors invoking various paragons with whom to compare their beloved. Orlando declares Angelica 'Fairer then … the Nimphe of Mercurie'.[15] The mangled speech that immediately follows shows that the nymph is Chloris: 'Or when bright Phoebus mounteth up his coach,/ And tracts Aurora in her silver steps;/ And sprinkles from the folding of her lap,/ White lilies, roses, and sweet violets'. This was once (before it was deformed) a close translation of Ariosto's lines on Chloris from a context which had nothing at all to do with Orlando and Angelica.[16] It concerned a magic net, the net once used to entrap Venus and Mars, stolen by Mercury to catch Chloris, and subsequently taken to the temple of Anubis at Canopus. At one point in the manuscript, but not in the quarto, Orlando appears to imagine himself as this Mercury, raving 'Lend me the net that <vulc>an trapt for Mars/ < h st>rumpett ven<u>s' (lines 272–3). Yet there is no classical story of any fit of madness suffered by Mercury. Greene appears to have dragged in this imagery gratuitously.

Greene's Orlando thus casts himself implicitly as a 'Mercury', and Angelica explicitly as a 'Chloris'. These are facts we might soon forget, but that the wicked Sacrapant also (in the quarto) casts Angelica as Chloris: 'O Angelica,/ Fairer than Chloris when in all her pride/Bright Maya's sonne intrapt her in the net,/ Wherewith Vulcan intangled the god of warre!'[17] Her Chloris-identity starts to take on something like objective reality.

Greene is, I suspect, twisting mythology to tell a contemporary story. Previous occurrences of Chloris in pastoral and in Smith's sonnets made us suspect that Mary Sidney was the intended referent. Intriguingly, the heroine in George Peele's play *Old Wives Tale*, who is abducted by another wicked Sacrapant and saved by her two brothers, is a Delia (and the coterie Delia, we know, was Mary Sidney).[18] The web of associations raises questions about the extent to which Shakespeare's own Orlando play, *As You Like It*, might have been autobiographical. The play's publication was 'stayed' (blocked by the authorities) in 1600, and unlike two other Shakespeare titles stayed with it, was not published in quarto. One reason might have been the presence of 'scandalous' material in it.

It is commonly believed that Greene was wildly jealous of Shakespeare. My claim that he was on the contrary promoting him as poet laureate in *Orlando* therefore requires some backing. The consensus view stems from the near universal interpretation of Greene's *Groatsworth of Witte* as an attack on an actor who was also a writer, the 'upstart crow' Shakespeare. I side with that minority of critics who see Greene's polemic as aimed solely at *actors*, and specifically at Richard Burbage, who is attacked sharply for thinking himself as good as the writer – namely Shakespeare – whose words he merely mouths.[19] In fact, admiring notice of Shakespeare lurks unnoticed in a host of Greene's pamphlets too.

His early *Perimedes the Blacksmith* has as protagonist a humble Smith who loves Delia.[20] In *Ciceronis Amor* or *Tullies Love* of 1589, Greene sets out to relate the loves of Cicero, which he says (tongue in cheek) Plutarch and Cornelius Nepos left out of their biographies.[21] At the time Marcus Tullius Cicero enters Greene's tale, he is 'a youth of about ye age of twenty yeres'. Quite a-historically, Greene shows him as a playwright, who chides the actor Roscius for arrogating the praise that belongs to the one who invents his lines.

This is in exactly the spirit of the *Groatsworth* attack. Greene constantly harps on Tullie's base parentage, contrary to history: for though Cicero was a 'novus homo', he was far from humbly born. The silly tale was so popular it was reprinted in 1597, 1601, 1605, 1609, 1611, 1616, 1628. I can only think that contemporaries enjoyed the scandal value, since the humble 'Cicero' wins the fair and aristocratic Terentia.

In two other pamphlets, Greene does align Shakespeare with a country fellow. But in the first case, his *Farewell to Folly*, it is done without any obvious attempt to denigrate; and in the second, the posthumously published *Greenes Vision*, it is done in a spirit of homage. The same device is employed in both, and it is arguably the device, not snobbery or hostility, that dictates the allusion to rusticity. The device is that of alluding to a person by including in one's own work some character (fictional or otherwise) from the other's work.

Greene's description of a country fellow in *Farewell to Folly* must be a direct allusion to R.L.'s description of the bumpkin who played the cup-bearer in the country wedding at Kenilworth.

> [H]e was a tall slender youth, cleane made with a good indifferent face, having on his head a strawne hat steeple wise, bound about with a band of blue buckram: he had on his fathers best tawnye worsted jacket: for that this daies exploit stood upon his credit: he was in a pair of hose of red kersie, close trust with a point afore, his mother had lent him a newe muffler for a napkin, & that was tied to his girdle for loosing: he had a pair of harvest gloves on his hands as shewing good husbandry, & a pen and inck-horn at his backe: for the young man was a little bookish, his pumpes were a little too heavie, being trimmed start-ups made of a paire of boote legges ....[22]

There is no requirement in Greene's story that the youth should be bookish, and carry a pen and ink-horn about with him. Greene has added a garment or two, but where there is overlap with the Kenilworth yokel's garments, the similarity is beyond coincidence.

In *Greenes Vision* we find the poet Gower dressed likewise in a *blue* bonnet, a *tawny* short coat that shows his legs, and with a 'napkin'.[23] It is the poet Gower who acts as chorus to Shakespeare's *Pericles*, and on the title page of George Wilkins's *Painfull Adventures of Pericles Prince of Tyre* of 1608 there is a woodcut of ancient Gower himself dressed in his short coat (though without a napkin).[24] I am convinced that underlying the existence of the wood-cut is a long-standing joke on Shakespeare's – that is, the Kenilworth R.L.'s – description of the bumpkin at the mock-wedding. Shakespeare *is* Gower, presenting the play. The introduction to Wilkins's *Painfull Adventures* actually draws attention to the '*habite* of ancient Gower', as Jeffrey Masten notices.[25] Since *Greenes Vision* dates from 1592 at the latest, the reference is strong evidence for the existence of an early *Pericles* by Shakespeare.[26]

Nashe's play *Summers Last Will and Testament* ends with the same joke on clothing.[27] It is Will Summers who acts as 'chorus' throughout; and in the entry in the Stationers' Register, the play is described as 'presented by Will Sommers'. Ostensibly Nashe's character is Henry VIII's fool. But before he leaves the stage at the end, he claims that his coat is too short, and then – if we take the quotation in the text above 'FINIS' to be part of the words the actor spoke – he declaims 'Barbarus hic ego sum, quia non intelligor ulli'. These are Ovid's words, famously uttered in his own voice when he was sent into exile near the Black Sea, and felt himself a 'barbarian' because he could not speak the local language. The play has been presented by a Summers who wears a short cloak and speaks as Ovid, not attributes he possesses elsewhere in literature or anecdote. Nashe calls his piece 'no play ... but a show' (line 75); and G.R. Hibbard states that 'show' implies the presence of topical allusion and satire.[28] Shakespeare was the individual guyed in the persona of Will Summers, I suggest.

The Blind Begger of Alexandria and *Eastward Ho* are both comedies that contain a Mercury among a number of characters who look suspiciously like Shakespeare. The idea that playwrights might indulge in a kind of 'repetitio', whereby several apparently different characters are actually one historical character transmogrified, is a novel one, I think. The first of the two plays, 'sundry times ... publickly acted ... by the Earle of Nottingham, Lord High Admirall, his servants' and printed in 1598, is usually ascribed to Chapman.[29] Yet there is rather strong evidence that it was believed by Shakespeare's own contemporaries to be his. An Edward Pudsey, living in the time of Elizabeth I and James I, kept a notebook, in which he records the titles of some plays.[30] Under a heading 'Pl. Shakesp. Joh.', he lists: 'Mrchaunt of Ve. Shakspear', followed by some extracts from *The Merchant;* 'Irus', followed by extracts from *The Blind Begger*, the protagonist of which is Irus; and then 'Ev'y man out of his humor, Johnson'. 'Irus' is clearly seen as Shakespeare's.

The Blind Begger was enormously successful, according to G.K. Hunter, who thinks little of its merit.[31] It is another of those mysterious cases in which a rather banal work seems to have offered continual delight to contemporary audiences, for some reason other than aesthetic pleasure. The protagonist disguises himself as Irus the beggar, but also as Duke Cleanthes, as Count Hermes, and as Leon the usurer. It cannot be coincidence that Greene's dedication of *Tullies Love* mentions an Irus and a Cleanthis in successive sentences. Count Hermes is clearly a Mercury. We might couple him with the Duke Mercury who appears in the apocryphal Shakespearean play *The Weakest Goeth to the Wall* (1600), and who declaims in vivid language reminiscent of that of the boatswain in *The Tempest.* There is besides these suggestive names in *The Blind Begger* another character Bragadino pretending to be a Spaniard (reminiscent of Jonson's 'Spanish reader' who was a Rodomont, or braggart), and a prince of Arcadia, lovely Doricles (a Dorus/Pericles?).

Eastward Ho, put on in 1599, provides a marvellous compendium of 'Shakespearean' characters, 'Shakespearean' both in the sense of 'like characters in Shakespeare's plays', and 'like Shakespeare'.[32] William Touchstone, a Goldsmith (and therefore a smith), is the protagonist, his apprentices being Golding and Quicksilver (mercury). There is a daughter Gertrude and a footman Hamlet. *As You Like It* and *Hamlet* appear therefore to have been popular enough by 1599 to be good material for parody. Because he is 'William' and a Smith and a Shakespearean character in his own right, this Touchstone looks very like Shakespeare himself.

Eastward Ho was immediately subjected to censorship, causing temporary disgrace and imprisonment for two of its authors, Jonson and Nashe, whom we have already fingered for teasing Shakespeare. Another, John Marston, could be the Jo. M. of *Philippes Venus.*

Evidence for Chapman's implication in the coterie derives not only from his co-authorship of *Eastward Ho*, and rumoured authorship of *The Blind Begger*, but also from his own singly-authored plays. His masking devices for the 'Shakespeare character' in *Monsieur D'Olive* (published in 1607, no doubt acted earlier) include: recognizable characteristics of Shakespeare the individual, citation and parody of Shakespeare's plays and juvenile poems, and a cleverly concealed bilingual multifaceted pun.[33]

The play's protagonist, Monsieur D'Olive himself, is an attractive character, upwardly mobile, self-assured, verbose, 'the perfect model [pattern?] of an impudent upstart: the compound of a poet and a lawyer'.[34] He can speak a little Italian. Planning how to behave when he achieves his new status, D'Olive imagines himself walking up to those who are now his betters, and hailing them with 'Well encountrd noble *Brutus*' – perhaps because his real-life counterpart had written a play on Brutus?[35] A forged letter to D'Olive trying to make him believe a noble lady loves him parodies *Twelfth Night*. 'She' writes to him that he is noble, 'though not by birth, yet by creation', echoing the forged letter to Malvolio stating 'Some are born great, some achieve greatness, and some have greatness thrust upon them'. When Rhodoricke, one of the forgers, writes 'O do but say thou lov'st me', Mugeron his accomplice exclaims 'Soft, there's too many OOs'; to which Rhodoricke answers 'Not a wit: O's but the next doore to P', echoing Malvolio's puzzling over the letters in his missive. The letter ends with the injunction to D'Olive *not* to wear his 'tuft taffeta cloke' or else he 'kills' her, even as Malvolio was urged to wear yellow stockings. When events take a turn for the worse, D'Olive's two servants fall to quoting the November eclogue of the *Shepheardes Calender:* 'Up then Melpomene', 'Dido is dead, And wrapt in lead', 'O heavie hearse'.[36] This would have gained enormously in comic effect if the 'inner circle' had some inkling that D'Olive was Shakespeare, and that his servants were throwing his own juvenile lines at him.

But could they have known? The protagonist's Frenchified name is one of the most unlikely names one could think up. But I suspect that those multilingual auditors, accustomed to secret names and to punning, could have succeeded in tracing a line from 'William' to 'olive' via Greek. 'Elaios/n' means 'made of olive'; 'of olives' – genitive plural – is 'elaiôn'. Elizabethan 'w' was quite soft. So '[w]elaion' could well have stood in for '[W]illiam'. Quick comprehension of bilingual puns was a requisite for audiences of the 'grammar' scenes in *Two Maids of More-clacke* and Shakespeare's *Merry Wives.* And readers of the plays would have had time to work out the joke for themselves.

Another possible Greek homonym for 'William' is 'eleios/eleion', 'pity'. It may already have slipped past our guard at the beginning of the Januarie eclogue of *Shepheardes Calender*, when the young shepherd's boy starts singing in his own voice, 'Ye Gods of love, that pitie lovers payne/ (If any gods the paine of lovers pitie)' in the stanza that ends in an address to Pan, 'Pitie the paines, that thou thy selfe didst prove'. Three 'pity's in one six-line stanza is quite a significant total, particularly as they appear in the very opening of the work. The number is surpassed by four 'pity's in three lines in *Rodomants Infernall*, by Gervase Markham.[37] Markham pretends his poem is a translation from the French of Philippe Desportes, but has the grace to say it is 'paraphrastically translated', which means it is rather far from the original. The ultimate original is Ariosto's *Orlando Furioso*, in which Rodomont is the boastful Saracen leader who pursued Isabella.

Markham's story concerns Rodomant in hell, yearning for his beloved Isabella. Rodomant 'shakt his fire at heaven's gate'. (He is a 'Shakefire'.) He adored an Angel spirit who adored an angel. Though his beloved is called 'Isabella', Markham addresses her as 'Stella' before the end of the poem. His French source does no such thing, even though it, too, is a loose translation.[38] The importance of the 'Angel spirit' lies in the unmistakable echo from Mary

Sidney's dedication to the memory of her brother of the Psalms which she and Philip translated. Mary entitled the dedicatory poem 'To the Angell spirit of the most excellent Sir Phillip Sidney'.

'Rodomont' became the byword for a braggart. Bragadino the Spaniard has crossed our line of vision in the course of this chapter; and earlier we saw a Rodomant parading as the fifth owl in Jonson's masque about Captain Cox. The appearance of these names in their coterie context is to be explained, I think, by the colloquial meaning of Shakespeare's name: a 'shake-spear' is a braggart.

Implicating historical persons by alluding obliquely to them or representing them in disguised form has been recognized as a phenomenon in Elizabethan and early Jacobean pastoral and sonnets. That there is some fairly transparent masking in Spenser's *Shepheardes Calender* has long been part of our critical assumptions, as mentioned above; and it has long been assumed that the 'Rich' puns in Philip Sidney's *Astrophel and Stella* mask Penelope Rich; and that Barnfield's Guendolen masks the same woman. But the phenomenon has not been recognized as ubiquitous. In the case of dramatic representation, the state of critical consensus is similar. It is widely accepted that Jonson engaged in a 'Poets' War' with some contemporaries, Shakespeare included. But the scope of investigation has not extended much beyond that supposed war.[39]

The dominant critical emphasis of recent years on the birth and growth of commercial theatre, on the dramatist as essentially the 'company' writer, on performance, on collaboration, works against the case I am building for the ubiquitous semi-covert representation in drama of rival poets, rival lovers, rival 'courtiers' in an aristocratic coterie.[40] For if it is an adequate description of affairs to say that dramatists effectively belonged to their company and were writing with the short-term aim of supplying plays for stage performances for a fellow-citizen audience, then the dramatists will hardly be seen as harking back, in the 1590s and later, to the heyday of Sidneian power and influence.

I contend that it is not an adequate description. The acting companies were still (up to and even beyond 1600) servants of this or that lord as much as autonomous entrepreneurial acting companies.[41] As late as 1597/98, as Bednarz notes, the 39th Statute of Elizabeth declared players to be legally vagabonds unless they were in the service of a nobleman.[42] Companies were invited to Court *as servants of their patrons* to put on their plays; and title pages of printed plays regularly state whose servants had previously performed them. The genius of English theatre at this time is arguably to be found in the inspired shifting of old plays successfully into their new dual homes of Court and Town.

The 'company playwright' theory that holds sway has created a blind spot about the phenomenon of 'guying' in general, and reference to Shakespeare in particular. I shall add to the examples given earlier three more instances of missed allusion that in their different ways show up the existence of the blind spot rather clearly.

'O that *Ben Jonson* is a pestilent fellow, he brought up *Horace* giving the Poets a pill, but our fellow *Shakespeare* hath given him a purge that made him beray his credit.'[43] Here we have incontrovertible evidence that rival playwrights mocked each other on stage. It is generally agreed that Jonson's *Poetaster* is the play referred to in these lines from the Parnassus Plays. But strangely, while the fact of Jonson's mockery has been recognized, some targets have been mistaken, even though the same piece of evidence refers to *Shakespeare*'s riposte.[44] We ought easily to find Shakespeare in Jonson's character Ovid, acting his own Romeo to a conflated Juliet/Julia in a parody of the balcony scene. (The historical Ovid was according to tradition amorously involved with Julia, the Emperor's daughter.) 'I high, thou low' wails Julia, in Jonson's play, referring presumably to the respective social status of the historical counterparts, as well as the height of the balcony.[45] It is yet another hint of an amorous relationship between Shakespeare and a woman of exalted status. When he published the play, Jonson complained that some lawyers and soldiers had 'conspired to have supprest' it. These could hardly have been common lawyers or soldiers: the play must have caused offence to some powerful people.

Had there been general appreciation of the fact that Chapman guyed Shakespeare in his *Monsieur D'Olive*, there would have been a general readiness to find the same author lampooning the same target in another play, *The Gentleman Usher.*[46] In this comedy, the protagonist serves effectively as steward in a grand household, responsible for all the entertainments and masques That the usher is both a gentleman and 'base', as his proper name Bassiolo implies, is interesting. The hero Vincentio asks himself, concerning Bassiolo, 'now was there ever such a demi-lance?'.[47] 'Vincentio' is the name of the Duke in *Measure for Measure*, according to one stage direction. Taken together, these little details suggest Shakespeare as a possible target: but one would hesitate to assert that it was indeed he without the wider context of *Monsieur D'Olive*, and beyond that of other dramatists who appear to have teased Shakespeare not out of jealousy, but as a spontaneous reaction to his prominence.

Of all the farces that should have been recognized as guying Shakespeare, *Arden of Faversham* (published in 1592) stands out as the one most affected by the blind spot.[48] *Arden*'s plot contains two villains called 'Shakebags' and 'Black Will'. Shakebags was called 'Loosebag' in the historical accounts. Kenneth Muir refers somewhat doubtfully to the possibility that *Arden* might have provided a source for some scenes of *Macbeth*. He picks out the 'conscience-stricken soliloquies of Michael before Arden's murder, Mosbie's soliloquy after the murder, and the knocking at the door', in Act 5, Scene 1.[49] Muir must be right to hear echoes; but he has the wrong author as echo and as source. To attempt to reverse the direction of borrowing seems doomed by the fact that *Arden* was based on a true history – the murder of Arden, recounted by Raphael Holinshed in his *Chronicles* of English royal history.[50]

Holinshed, however, was employed by the Earl of Leicester to write his histories. It is Holinshed who alters the 'Loosebag' of his sources (a manuscript and the Wardmote account of the murder) to 'Shakebags'; and the insertion of the story of the private individual Arden into his history is awkwardly executed. Therefore, I conclude, Holinshed was doing what others in the Leicester entourage are observed doing throughout this book – alluding to the favourite in their patron's circle. That he chose this particular context in which to do so was prompted by the fact that Arden was Shakespeare's mother's family name. The play follows suit.

At least one modern editor sees the play as a farce.[51] The six failed murder attempts cannot fail to provoke increasing laughter, as the audience wonders how the assassins can possibly fail *this* time. Arden is a ludicrously naïve cuckold. Shakebags's part in the plot is greatly increased by the playwright. And where the historical sources, including Holinshed, relate that no-one knew the ultimate fate of Black Will and Shakebags, the play has Will burned 'on a stage' in Flushing – where Leicester had his command in the Low Countries – and Shakebags escaping to Southwark – players' territory, containing the Globe at Bankside. Commentators are quick to tell us that 'on a stage' means 'on a scaffold'. But they are missing the joke.

Our next suspicious Mercury is taken from a narrative poem of Marlowe's. It has become a commonplace to say that Shakespeare had to match himself against the towering genius of Marlowe, who, although the same age, had a head start on him.[52] But John Aubrey, who seems to have known a great deal about what was really going on a hundred years before his time, implies something different. He states that Shakespeare was a butcher's boy who had a rival butcher's boy in town. Shakespeare's father dealt in leather gloves. Marlowe's father also dealt in leather, in shoes. Both trades involve butchering. Aubrey may be enjoying a joke here. And rather than describing a case of the 'anxiety of influence' on Shakespeare's part, he could be describing a rivalry of coevals.[53]

Marlowe's narrative poem *Hero and Leander* incorporates a fable of Mercury, the motivation of which remains unexplained.[54] The poem is divided into six parts – 'sestiads'. Marlowe composed the first two, leaving an unfinished poem at his death in 1593. The last four sestiads and the 'Argument' for each were written by Chapman. In the first sestiad, Marlowe invents a tale of Cupid and Mercury that has no classical authority whatsoever. It purports to explain why the Fates hated Leander. It runs as follows: –

Mercury had fallen in love with a country maid. She set him the task of stealing some nectar from Jove. Mercury did so, and was flung out of heaven in punishment. He complained to Cupid, who took up Mercury's cause against Jove. Cupid forced the Fates to fall in love with Mercury, to whom they offered the shears with which they cut the thread of human life. But all Mercury wanted was the banishment of Jove from heaven, and the reinstatement of Saturn's reign, which the Fates granted. The Golden Age returned, but not for long, as Mercury refused his part of the bargain, and declined to love the Fates, who, furious with him, restored Jove. They could not entirely banish Hermes (as he has become in the course of the tale) from heaven; but they decreed that 'he and Poverty should always kiss'. 'And to this day is every scholar poor.'

Cupid reaped much of the blame for this debacle; and that is why his request to the Fates to speed Leander's love is denied, it is implied. But the gist of the logic is that the Fates hate *Leander* because *Mercury* once cheated them – no logic at all, unless Leander *is* 'Mercury'. So, while I would not claim that Marlowe wrote his poem with the sole ambition of amusing those who knew 'Mercury's' identity with an 'in joke', that may have been part of his aim. Jonson's hilarious parody, the puppet show of Hero and Leander in his *Bartholomew Fair*, would have provided extra entertainment for the coterie, if that is indeed the case.[55] Nashe had enormous fun with the same joke in casting his king of the herrings as Leander in *Nashes Lenten Stuffe*, which we shall examine in the next chapter.

That Jonson colluded in the joke in his *Bartholomew Fair* is a suspicion worth following up. One of Jonson's masques was *Mercury Vindicated from the Alchemists at Court.*[56] The plot is that Mercury (the substance personified) manages to break free from the alchemists who try to bind him in their experiments. From what source could Jonson have dreamed up this wonderful scenario? From his own fruitful imagination? Possibly. But Mary Sidney conducted scientific/ alchemical experiments with her 'laborator' Adrian Gilbert. John Dee the alchemist tutored Philip Sidney. 'Alchemists' at this date have a Sidneian tincture, a fact which might do much to explain Jonson's choice of topic for his play *The Alchemist* (1610).

The above remarks may serve to place Jonson rather more firmly in the early days of the Sidneian circle than is usual – though by the time Robert Sidney was master of Penshurst, it is well known, Jonson was a welcome guest, and advertised the fact with his poem 'To Penshurst'. Marlowe has not been considered part of that literary circle, though it is well established that he must have worked politically for Francis Walsingham, who was Philip Sidney's father-in-law. Could he really have been so intimate with the 'Olympians'? He certainly could, as the dedication of Thomas Watson's *Amintae Gaudia* to Mary Sidney by 'C.M.' strongly suggests. That he actually was, is equally strongly suggested by his tragedy *Edward II.*[57]

Piers Gaveston, Edward's favourite, and the two characters Spencer and Baldock are the foci of suspicion here, on the grounds of the deviations Marlowe makes from the historical facts and the particular choices he makes in describing each, including choices of imagery. Both Gaveston and Spencer are portrayed as of lower birth than their historical counterparts, and lower than either Holinshed or Michael Drayton, who wrote a verse narrative on Piers Gaveston, portrays them. Gaveston is described by the nobles in the play as 'peasant' and 'base groom', but he was in fact the son of a Gascon gentleman.[58] Spencer is shown quite a-historically as a servant of the old Duke of Gloucester, setting out to seek his fortunes with his friend Baldock, and deciding to throw his lot in with the king and Gaveston because the latter had once loved him well. In historical fact and the accounts of Marlowe's contemporaries, Spencer gained the king's favour long after the fall of Gaveston. There was no interaction between him and Gaveston, nor was Spencer the humble follower of Gloucester. He was granted the title 'Earl of Gloucester' by the king quite late in his period of ascendancy.

The character Baldock deviates even further from the historical record, as editors of the play note. He too is shown as a servant of old Gloucester, whereas historically he appeared on the scene later, advanced in his fortunes by the Spencers. The most striking thing about his characterization is his donnish clothing and demeanour, which is justified by nothing in the sources. He appears as a kind of household tutor to Gloucester's daughter, Lady Margaret, to whom he has often read in her youth. He is urged by Spencer to 'cast the scholar off'; and he responds that his drab curate-like attire is misleading – he is 'no common pedant', but one ready to aim for power. Introduced to the king, he proudly states that though he boasts no gentlemanly arms, he fetches his descent from Oxford University.

To see Spencer and his donnish friend appear on stage is to see Edmund Spenser and Gabriel Harvey in the flesh. Though Harvey was chiefly associated with Cambridge, he did have a law degree from Oxford; and in any case, Marlowe would have needed some fig leaf of a defence against the charge of portraying him outright. The play is known to have been performed by the Earl of Pembroke's servants.[59] Here is a case where acknowledging the aristocratic milieu of performance would have allowed its allusions to shine clearly. Lady Margaret is Lady Mary (Sidney); Baldock is none other than Harvey.

I suggested above that Harvey had a project for a series of Leicestrian plays. I now suggest Marlowe was part of that project. The neat distribution of English historical plays among Peele (*Edward I*), Marlowe (*Edward II*), possibly Greene, who fills up the missing gap of Henry III with his *Friar Bacon and Friar Bungay*, Thomas Heywood, who wrote an *Edward IV* and almost got into dire trouble for it, and Shakespeare, who wrote the great majority of them, is not fortuitous. The reigns were parcelled out to the playwrights, who tend not to overlap in subject matter. For example, Shakespeare manages to exclude material from the reign of Edward IV from his *Richard III*, skipping apparently straight from the death of Henry VI to the machinations of Richard Duke of Gloucester as regent to the young Edward V. With varying degrees of subtlety, the dramatists take up the challenge to write 'histories' for the White Bear while simultaneously teasing each other. They show off their skills of plotting and their insider knowledge of the patronage circle at one stroke.

Whom then does Gaveston represent, apart from the historical character? He is compared to Ganymede, but that is a mandatory comparison in a work that centres on love between men. He refers to himself in the opening scene as a Leander, wanting to swim the channel to be reunited with his love. This too fits perfectly naturally in its context; yet for those who knew the hidden reference in Marlowe's narrative poem, it could have figured as a clue to the contemporary referent. He once loved Spencer, and so was in a position to advance him: perhaps the William Smith who seemed to be the one patronized *by* Edmund Spenser, in fact mediated *for* him from his position as darling of the Sidneys.

Gaveston's clothes send the strongest signal as to whom he masks in reality. Though historically a Gascon living in an age before Italian tours were *de rigueur*, Gaveston wears a short Italian hooded cloak, and a Tuscan cap.[60] This may of course simply be Marlowe's anachronistic notion of the dandified favourite. But granted that Marlowe has presented by means of the Earl of Pembroke's servants in the Earl of Pembroke's household two of the Earl of Pembroke's wife's familiars, there is no good reason to resist the supposition that he portrays a third such familiar in Gaveston. That third is the fellow who is often shown with a short cloak, and to whom Harvey also attributed

'Tuscanism'. He is the one adored by 'the king' of the coterie and his niece. He is Leicester's servant William Shakespeare.

Startling as the suggestion that Gaveston masks Shakespeare may be, it is confirmed by the evidence of a prose Letter, part of a work entitled 'Polimanteia', by William Covell.[61] There Covell eulogizes his contemporaries from the two universities (Oxford and Cambridge) who shone in the field of literature. Shakespeare is praised in the margins of the group from Cambridge, alongside Samuel Daniel: that is, he is present in a *printed* marginal note that runs beside praise of Samuel Daniel in the text. The note is therefore contemporaneous with the first printing of 1595.

> All praise worthy Lucrecia Sweet Shakspeare. Eloquent Gaveston. Wanton Adonis. Watsons heyre. So well graced Anthonie deserveth immortall praise from the hand of that divine Lady who like Corinna contending with Pindarus was oft victorious. (R2v)

It is universally held that nothing after 'Watsons heyre' relates to Shakespeare, for the simple reason that it will not match the Shakespeare we think we know. The remains of the apostrophe are supposed to apply to some new unmentioned person, or perhaps to Anthony Chute, author of 'Tabaco'. Critics make no attempt to explain why Shakespeare is a Gaveston, to identify Corinna, or to work out the identity of the poet whom (says Covell diplomatically) she often out-performed in poetic song.

Let me spell out what Covell's passage implies. It implies that Shakespeare, who is author of *Lucrece* and *Venus and Adonis*, is not only Watson's heir, but also a Gaveston and an Antony. His patroness is a rival poet. There is no justification for dividing the passage into disparate references: it is an extended conceit naming Shakespeare after either his own literary creatures or those of others who encoded him in their literary works. To make 'Antony' refer to a historical person called Anthony (Chute) would ruin the conceit, and is anyway extremely unlikely: Chute was not a good enough poet to be seen as a Pindar singing in competition with his Corinna.

But Shakespeare *was* a Pindar. Ovid's mistress was also supposedly Corinna, so those who already thought of Shakespeare as an Ovid might well have conflated the two male poets. The only woman of the age widely acknowledged as a poet in public was Mary Sidney. Both Shakespeare and Mary Sidney wrote plays on Antony and Cleopatra. Samuel Daniel and Fulke Greville joined this contest, Daniel with a *Cleopatra* and Greville with an *Antony*. Possibly each of the male writers in the dramatic contest (for that is what it seems to be) imagined himself as Antony to Mary's Cleopatra. But Covell set that wreath on Shakespeare's head.

Covell's other names for Shakespeare are arguably just as apt. If he was 'Watson's heir', he could have inherited the pen-name 'Amintas', on which Watson presumably has first claim as the author of *Amintae Gaudia*. The question of whose identity is concealed under this name is somewhat contested and worth disentangling.

At the end of his *Pierce Penilesse* (1592), Nashe launches into ecstatic praise of '*Ioves Eagle-borne Ganimed*, thrice noble *Amyntas*'. Oddly, no commentator takes this to be Watson: but that may be because all assume that this 'magnificent rewarder of vertue' must be a nobleman. They duly pick the nobleman of their choice, Ferdinand Stanley, Earl of Derby, or Francis Walsingham or the Earl of Southampton.[62] But besides failing to account for the purloining of Watson's nickname, the critics fail to notice that a 'patron and Benefactor' is not necessarily well-born. Richard Lichfield, the subject of the next chapter, is twice referred to as 'patron' by Nashe, we shall see. Nashe also calls Humfrey King his 'patron' in the Epistle prefacing *Lenten Stuffe*. Compare Harvey's use of the word in *Pierces Supererogation*: he lists 'M. Apis Lapis, Greene, Marlow, Chettle and whom not' as Nashe's 'favorablest Patrons'.[63]

The Amyntas whom Spenser mourns as recently dead in his *Colin Clouts Come Home Againe* of 1595 does indeed look like Watson. Watson died in 1592, and his work was dedicated to Mary Sidney. Spenser claims his Amyntas was the 'floure of Shepheards pride' (one of the Sidneian shepherds, I take it), and 'maintained' other singers (lines 435–42), just like Nashe's benefactor in *Pierce Penilesse*. But the date of Watson's death counts against his being the patron to whom Nashe refers. Watson was buried early in the September of 1592. Nashe's book went into a second and third edition in the same year as the first, which was entered in the Register on 8 August 1592. Yet when he adds a new preface for the second edition, Nashe nowhere states that his benefactor has died since he penned his praises. I assume that he would have done so, and therefore that his benefactor is not Watson.

Nashe provides the key to his true identity in something he implies but does not spell out. 'Oh decus atque aevi gloria summa tui', he exclaims, quoting Ovid's *Heroides* 15, line 94, 'Oh ornament and chief glory of your day'.[64] The immediate context of Ovid's poem is the clue here, the line preceding the one quoted being 'Nec adhuc iuvenis, nec iam puer, utilis aetas': 'Not yet a young man, but no longer a boy – a useful age'. In other words, he is an Old Lad.

This description fits neither Watson nor Shakespeare literally, but does serve to denominate Shakespeare metaphorically. A difficulty for my solution is the fact that Nashe does want to give the impression that his benefactor is a 'renoumed Lord'. He deplores Spenser's failure to give this 'Lord' his due credit in the *Faerie Queene* dedications. But why could neither Spenser nor Nashe name him? I suggest he was too humble, a Lord in faerie world only, just as Spenser becomes 'Sir' Scudamor in that world. I would give more weight to the conjunction of 'Ganimede' and 'Amyntas' in Nashe's eulogy, and the reflection that Watson might always have intended Shakespeare for 'Amyntas'. Watson could have been following the coterie practice of praising the darling of the Sidney circle: 'Amintas' joys' may have been Shakespeare's.

The opening lines of Armin's poetic translation of a popular tale, *The Italian Taylor and His Boy*, are also strongly evocative of the Old Lad.[65] Armin purports to be translating an Italian tale which is known to be by Giovanni Straparola. In his dedication to Viscount Haddington and his wife Lady Fitzwater, Armin appears to refer to Straparola as his 'Italian Poet', a Maecenas of poets. This is doubly odd. Straparola wrote 'novelle', that is, *prose* stories. And a Maecenas is usually a living patron who aids the author financially, not the source of one's work, however richly he may have furnished subsequent generations of writers with materials. Armin allows that the original work was unpolished, but stones that come rough from the quarry can be polished up, he declares. His own translation may have its weaknesses: yet 'I beseech you, call to question my Weaknes, and my Will, will answere in my behalfe' (A3).

A second dedication, to the reader, is headed 'Ad lectorem hic et ubiq:' (A4). There is something odd about this too. Though many dedications are framed 'To the Reader', the 'hic et ubique' of this one makes the readers in effect plural. Why did Armin not simply say 'Ad lectores'? Possibly it is because he was addressing not ordinary readers, but a Reader to whom the tag 'hic et ubique' particularly attached – the Spanish Reader of Jonson's *Masque of Owles*.

Armin ends his second dedication: 'bid this welcome for his sake to whom it is dedicated, which we may all rejoyce in, if his happie hand be duly considered. Fare-well'. It was ostensibly dedicated to two people, one of them female. It is not clear why two have shrunk to one, why all should rejoice in Viscount Haddington, or why he has a happy hand. But if he is merely a front man, if the dedications secretly refer to Shakespeare throughout, the sentiment becomes comprehensible. It is Fair Well, the 'Italian' poet, who has a happy hand. He is the Maecenas who helps Armin, as he may have helped Nashe. It is in homage to his talent that Armin offers him the work: 'I but light a Taper at his Torch'.

Armin describes the Italian tailor's boy in rather contradictory terms.

> The Boy was yong, yet wits persuade
> His yeares were many more:
>
> How ever, he's reported young,
> Though old in apprehention.
>   (B2r)

This looks like our friend the Old Lad. And though the rest of the poem veers off into magic, without any hint of a connection with the real world, the damage has been done. We cannot but suspect that it teases Shakespeare, and that a knowing readership would have gleaned extra pleasure from this fact.

My claims concerning the magnitude and extent of Shakespeare's reputation among his sixteenth-century peers, while more far-reaching than previous claims, are in tune with those of Lukas Erne.[66] Erne points out, correctly, that extracts from Shakespeare's plays greatly outnumber extracts taken from other plays in *England's Parnassus* and *Belvedere, or the Garden of the Muses*, anthologies claiming to assemble 'the choysest Flowers of our Moderne Poets'. Both were published in 1600. The dramatic extracts are placed alongside extracts from supposedly 'elevated' poetic genres, the sonnets, epic poems, lyric songs, histories of renowned authors such as Sidney, Spenser, and Drayton.

More controversially, Erne suggests that it was Francis Meres who was chiefly responsible for the new acclaim for Shakespeare as an equal to Samuel Daniel, William Warner and the three prestigious poets mentioned in the last paragraph. Erne notes that Shakespeare's name starts to appear on the title page of his printed plays from the date of the appearance of Meres' *Palladis Tamia* (1598). I applaud the shift of Shakespeare's fame back in time, but it is too timorous. I see Meres's work as part of a tidal wave of approbation for Shakespeare, a wave that had already been gathering momentum for two decades. And I see Nashe, to whom we now turn, as an even more important instrument in the construction of 'Shakespeare the bard'. But let us give Meres credit for the secrets he uncovers: not only did he reveal the equivalence of Cuddy, Ovid and Shakespeare, I suggested earlier, but the title of his work means 'O steward of Pallas'. If Shakespeare was indeed the Gentleman Usher of Chapman's play, he was a steward, a Sidneian steward, perhaps Minerva's steward.

Notes

1   The playwrights themselves did not make such a distinction: Jonson's foreword to his printed play *Every Man out of his Humour* refers to it as his 'poem'. Ben Jonson, *Every Man Out of his Humour* (London: [A. Islip] also [P. Short] for W. Holme, 1600). *Works*, 3.420–598, 421.

2   James Shapiro, *Rival Playwrights: Marlowe, Jonson, Shakespeare* (New York: Columbia University Press, 1991).

3   Jo. M., *Philippes Venus* (London: John Perrin, 1591).

4   *Philippes Venus*, A2r–v.

5   *The lamentable tragedie of Locrine. Newly set foorth, overseene and corrected, By W.S.* (London: Thomas Creede, 1595).

6   *A most pleasant comedie of Mucedorus the kings sonne of Valentia* ... (London: William Jones, 1598).

7   Robert Armin, *The Historie of Two Maids of More-clacke* (London: N.O. for Thomas Archer, 1609).

8   Stephen Orgel, *Imagining Shakespeare: A History of Texts and Visions* (Basingstoke: Palgrave Macmillan, 2003), p. 30.

9   *Merry Wives*, IV.1.

10 *King Lear*, III.6.55. *Lucrece*, line 1240–6.

11 Helen Cooper, 'Guy of Warwick, Upstart Crows and Mounting Sparrows', in *Shakespeare, Marlowe, Jonson: New Directions in Biography*, ed. J.R. Mulryne and Takashi Kozuka (forthcoming from Ashgate).

12 I.B. (Ben Ionson?), *The tragical historie ... of Guy of Warwick* (London: Thomas Vere and William Gilbertson, 1661), V.2.

13 Dulwich College MSS., 'The Henslowe Papers', MS 1. 138. Robert Greene, *The Historie of Orlando Furioso* (London: John Danter for Cuthbert Burby, 1594). Greene, *Works*, 13.111–98. W.W. Greg, ed., *Two Elizabethan Stage Abridgements: The Battle of Alcazar and Orlando Furioso* (Oxford: Clarendon Press, 1923).

14 Ludovico Ariosto, *Orlando Furioso* (1516), ed. Lanfranco Caretti (Milan and Naples: R. Ricciardi, 1954).

15 Greene, *Works*, 13.121, lines 106–10.

16 Ariosto, *Orlando Furioso*, trans. Barbara Reynolds (1975; London: Penguin, 1981), Bk. 15, stanzas 56–58, 1.461.

17 Greene, *Works*, 13.130, lines 314–7.

18 George Peele, *Old Wives Tale* (London: J. Danter sold by J. Hardie and R. Hancocke, 1595).

19 See Winifred Frazer, 'William Kemp as "Upstart Crow"', *The Upstart Crow* 15 (1995), pp. 140–42; Jay Hoster, *Tiger's Heart: What Really Happened in the 'Groatsworth of Wit' Controversy of 1592* (Columbus, OH: Ravine, 1993); Fleissner, '"The Upstart Crow" Reclawed'. I take from Honan, *Shakespeare*, p. 159, the idea that Greene was attacking Richard Burbage with a pun on the 'burs' who batten off writers.

20 Robert Greene, *Perimedes the Blacksmith* (London: John Wolfe for Edward White, 1588). *Works*, 7.1–93.

21 Robert Greene, *Ciceronis Amor* Or *Tullies Love* (London: Robert Robinson for Thomas Newman and John Winnington, 1589). *Works*, 7.95–216.

22 Robert Greene, *Farewell to Folly* (London: T. Scarlet for T. Gubbins and T. Newman, 1591), D4. *Works*, 9.223–348, 265.

23   Robert Greene, *Greenes Vision* (London: Thomas Newman, n.d.), C1v. *Works*, 12.189–281, 210.

24   George Wilkins, *The Painfull Aduentures of Pericles Prince of Tyre* (London: T. P[urser], 1608). The first quarto of Shakespeare's *Pericles* was published in 1609 by Henry Gosson.

25   Wilkins, *Adventures*, A2r–v. Masten, *Textual Intercourse*, p. 93. Masten takes the reference to apply to the 'clothing' in print of the staged play.

26   John Dryden implies that *Pericles* was the experimentation of a young poet trying to find his feet: see Suzanne Gossett, ed., *Pericles* (London: Arden, 2004), intro., p. 15. Thomas Pavier's project to publish Shakespeare's plays (in 1619) began with *The Whole Contention*, Parts 1 and 2 (the 'Bad Quartos' of *Henry VI, Parts 2* and *3*) together with *Pericles*, as though he were proceeding chronologically. Gossett and most other editors assume a date of composition close to date of first overt mention – 1608.The existence of an 'Ur-Pericles' has often been mooted, but only Eric Sams in recent years has promoted the notion of a *Shakespearean* Ur-Pericles (*Real Shakespeare*, pp. 171–2, 189–90).

27   Thomas Nashe, *A pleasant comedie, called Summers last will and testament* (?1592; London: S. Stafford for W. Burre, 1600). Zachary Lesser argues that Walter Burre made a specialty of publishing plays that had failed on stage: 'Walter Burre's "The Knight of the Burning Pestle"', *ELR* 29.1 (Winter 1999), pp. 22–43. Burre's preface to *The Knight* mentions the 'privie ironies' that had not been appreciated by the general public. I suspect his specialty was in plays that were too subtly satirical to be understood beyond a small coterie.

28   G.R. Hibbard, *Thomas Nashe: A Critical Introduction* (Cambridge: Harvard University Press, 1962), p. 85.

29   [George Chapman], *The blind begger of Alexandria* (London: [J. Roberts] for William Jones, 1598).

30   *Shakespearean Extracts from 'Edward Pudsey's Booke'*, ed. Richard Savage (Stratford: John Smith; London: Simpkin and Marshall, n.d.), pp. 7–9.

31   G.K. Hunter, *English Drama, 1586–1642: The Age of Shakespeare* (Oxford: Clarendon Press, 1997), p. 301.

32   It was published by William Aspley for Thomas Thorpe in 1605. Thorpe used Aspley for publication of *Shakespeare's Sonnets.*

33   George Chapman, *Monsieur D'Olive* (London: T.C. for William Homes, 1606). *The Plays of George Chapman. The Comedies*, ed. A. Holaday and M. Kiernan (Urbana: University of Illinois, 1970), pp. 397–457.

34   *D'Olive*, I.ii.195.

35   *D'Olive*, II.ii.335; III.ii.15–16.

36   *D'Olive*, IV.ii.176–230.

37   Gervase Markham, *Rodomanths Infernall or, The Divell Conquered* (London, V. S[immes] for Nicholas Ling, 1607). 'Paraphrastically translated' from Philip Desportes' translation of Ariosto's *Orlando Furioso.*

38   Philippe Desportes, 'La Mort de Rodomont' in *Les Imitations de l'Arioste* (1572) (Paris: Droz, 1936), pp. 36–75.

39   My point applies strictly to the guying of fellow *writers.* Richard Dutton, in *Mastering the Revels: The Regulation and Censorship of English Renaissance Drama* (Iowa City: University of Iowa Press, 1991), pp. 127–36, esp. 132, suggests that lampooning of fellow citizens, and of nobles, was widespread in the 1590s. Allusion to the Queen is a separate issue, which I address in Chapter 9.

40 Two relevant studies are: Scott McMillin and Sally-Beth Maclean, *The Queen's Men and their Plays* (Cambridge: Cambridge University Press, 1998); Masten, *Textual Intercourse*.

41 See A.J. Cook, *The Privileged Playgoers of Shakespeare's London, 1576–1642* (Princeton: Princeton University Press, 1981), pp. 99–105.

42 James Bednarz, *Shakespeare and the Poets' War* (New York: Columbia University Press, 2001), p. 29.

43 *The Three Parnassus Plays*, c.1598–1601, ed. J.B. Leishman (London: Nicholson and Watson, 1949), p. 337.

44 Bednarz makes a strong case that Shakespeare retaliates against Jonson in the person of Ajax in *Troilus and Cressida*. See *Poets' War*, pp. 38–9.

45 Ben Jonson, *Poetaster* (London: R. Braddock, for M. L[ownes], 1602), IV.9.5. *Works*, 4.197–324, 286.

46 George Chapman, *The Gentleman Usher* (London: V.S. for T. Thorpe, 1606). *Comedies*, pp. 131–209.

47 *Usher*, II.ii.109–111; IV.ii.77.

48 Peter Levi is an exception. See his *Life and Times of William Shakespeare* (New York: Henry Holt, 1988), pp. 61–2.

49 Muir, ed., *Macbeth*, intro., p. xli.

50 Raphael Holinshed, *Chronicles* (London: John Harrison, 1577, 1587), 2.1703–1708.

51 *The lamentable and true tragedy of M. Arden of Feversham* (London: Edward White, 1592). *The Tragedy of Master Arden of Faversham*, ed. M.L. Wine (London: Methuen, 1973).

52 Jonathan Bate, *The Genius of Shakespeare* (London: Picador, 1997), pp. 13–14, 104–32.

53 Compare Ernst Honigmann, 'Shakespeare's Life', in *The Cambridge Companion to Shakespeare*, ed. Margareta de Grazia and Stanley Wells (Cambridge: Cambridge University Press, 2001), pp. 1–12, 5.

54 Marlowe, *Hero and Leander* (London: F. Kingston for P. Linley, 1598). *Marlowe: Plays and Poems*, ed. M.R. Ridley (1909; London: Dent, 1958), pp. 374–433.

55 Ben Jonson, *Bartholomew Fair* (1614) (London: I.B. for Robert Allot, 1635). *Works*, 6.1–141.

56 *Works*, 7.409–17.

57 Christopher Marlowe, *Edward II* (London: R. Bradocke for W. Jones, 1593). References are taken from Ridley's *Marlowe*.

58 I.2.230; I.4.293.

59 See the Stationers' Register entry and the title page of the Eliot Court edition of 1622.

60 I.4.413.

61 William Covell, *A Letter from England to her Three Daughters*, in *Polimanteia* (Cambridge: John Legate, 1595).

62 McKerrow, note on *Pierce Penilesse*, *Works*, IV.150–51. Stephen Hilliard, *The Singularity of Thomas Nashe* (Lincoln and London: University of Nebraska Press, 1986), p. 97.

63 Harvey, *Pierces Supererogation*. *Works*, 2.1–346, 322 (114).

64 *Works*, I.243.

65 Robert Armin, *The Italian Taylor and His Boy* (London: T. P[avier], 1609).

66 Lukas Erne, *Shakespeare as Literary Dramatist* (Cambridge: Cambridge University Press, 2003), pp. 65–77.

Chapter 7

Fourth Candidate – Dick of Lichfield

Thomas Nashe's Quarrel with Gabriel Harvey was a long-running affair, and its true aims are hard to discern. It was conducted through a series of prose pamphlets. Nashe's side of the Quarrel was adumbrated in *Strange Newes*,[1] and presented extensively in *Have With You to Saffron Walden*. The latter is addressed to a 'Richard Lichfield', about whose identity there is reason to be suspicious. Richard Lichfield answers in his own pamphlet, *The Trimming of Thomas Nashe*, the authorship of which has never been settled.[2]

This chapter examines the identity of the R.L. who was 'Richard Lichfield'. It will be argued that the 'Apis Lapis' who is addressed in *Strange Newes* is in reality the same person; and that the addressee of a third pamphlet of Nashe's, Humfrey King, is yet another manifestation of R.L. Humfrey, whom we have encountered in earlier chapters, is not only addressed on the title page of *Lenten Stuffe*, but is also, covertly, the hero of the whole work. The three pamphlets constitute one extended programme that had three main aims (apart from those of expressing Nashe's own delight in extravagant writing, and demonstrating his skill to his patrons and public): to ridicule Harvey, to attack Mary Sidney, and to promote the work of Shakespeare. Only the first has been widely recognized, and will be ignored here. I have argued elsewhere that Mary Sidney was the woman Harvey claimed as his 'championess', and Nashe was covertly attacking her through her protégé.[3] The third claim is the one relevant to the overall theme of this book, the one I shall attempt to make good.[4]

Richard Lichfield is not only the addressee of *Have With You to Saffron Walden*, he is its subject throughout. Only through close reading does this become apparent. Nashe hails him as the barber of Trinity College, Cambridge (which was Harvey's college). There really was a barber at Trinity called Richard Lichfield, who provides Nashe with the metaphor he needs for his jokes, most of which are variations on 'trimming'. The bombastic heading to the pamphlet describes Dick the barber as 'the most Orthodoxall and reverent Corrector of staring haires, the sincere & finigraphicall rarifier of prolixious rough barbarisme, the thrice egregious and censoriall animadvertiser of vagrant moustachios …' and so on in similar vein right up to the grand title 'Don Richardo Barbarossa de Caesario'.[5] 'Barba rossa' is, of course, Red Beard.

The Latin 'caesaries' means a luxuriant growth of hair. Strictly speaking, the title 'Caesar' meant the Emperor's 'heir', while 'Augustus' was reserved for the Emperor himself. I presume Nashe, a good classical scholar, built all these 'hair' puns into the comical title.

But Dick has admirable attributes that go beyond his barbering skills. In the opening apostrophe the phrase 'rarifier of prolixious rough barbarism' already hints as much – he sounds somewhat literary. He is also 'paraphrasticall gallant Patron Dick ... curteous Dicke, comicall Dicke, lively Dicke, lovely Dicke, learned Dicke'.[6] And Nashe exhorts him to be more ambitious: 'Be not a horse to forget thy own worth: thou art in a place where thou maist promote thy selfe; do not close-prison and eclipse thy/ vertues in the narrow glasse lanthorne of thy Barbers shop, but reflect them up and down the Realme'.[7] In the main text, we learn that Dick is a translator: 'one *Dick Litchfield*, the barber of *Trinity Colledge*, a rare ingenuous odde merry Greeke, who (as I have heard) hath translated my *Piers Pennilesse* into the *Macaronicall* tongue'.[8]

Dick's literary credentials are part of the point of the allusions, it seems. It is unlikely that a simple college barber should have been in a position to spread his fame throughout the realm; unless, as McKerrow was rather inclined to believe, the barber was building a reputation with his smart repartee, and actually wrote *The Trimming* with the help of some academic wit. But McKerrow did not consider how flat the 'hair' jokes would fall if they were directed at a real barber. There must be a *double entendre* in them, which we might be able to ferret out by worrying at other phrases Nashe uses to describe various 'Dicks'.

Nashe opens with a roll-call of Dicks whom he declares *not* to be his Dick. But by mentioning them, he naturally calls them to the reader's attention. There is 'old Dick of the Castle'; there is 'Dick Swash, or Desperate Dick, that's such a terrible Cutter at a chyne of beefe, and devoures more meate at Ordinaries in discoursing of his fraies and deep acting of his slashing and hewing, than would serve halfe a dozen Brewers Dray-men'.[9] Both these sound suspiciously like Falstaff. The first recalls 'Oldcastle', the original of the character Falstaff. He is not necessarily the character in Shakespeare's drama – though Shakespeare does call his Falstaff 'my old lad of the castle' in *Henry IV, Part 1*.[10] The second, however, is so like the play's character as to seem modelled on him. The scene evoked in the passage above is exactly like the scene in the Boar's Head Tavern in Act 2, Scene 4, in which Falstaff boasts of his exploits.

This 'rarifier of barbarism' is probably the same as the 'purifier' of poetry who appears in the body of the main text of *Have With You*. Attacking Harvey's behaviour before the Queen at Saffron Walden, when she was on a Progress there in 1578, Nashe writes of Harvey:

> [H]e ... would make no bones to take the wall of *Sir Philip Sidney* and another honourable Knight (his companion) about Court yet attending; to whom I wish no better fortune than the fore lockes of Fortune he had hold of in his youth, & no higher fame than hee hath purchast himselfe by his pen; being the first (in our language) I have encountred, that repurified Poetrie from Arts pedantisme, & that instructed it to speake courtly. Our Patron, our *Phoebus*, our first *Orpheus* or quintessence of invention he is.[11]

McKerrow believes that 'his companion' means 'Sidney's companion', and looking for a knight to fit the bill, comes up with Sidney's great friend Fulke Greville. It is not clear that the words do not refer to a companion of Harvey's rather than Sidney's; but this is immaterial. What is clear is that Nashe could not have been speaking of Greville, for a number of reasons.

Greville had published no poetry at this date except for elegies for Philip Sidney in the collection called *Exequiae*,[12] and one poem in the hastily cancelled first edition of *Astrophel and Stella.* Even if he had been admired within the Sidney coterie for poems in manuscript (there is no evidence that he was: he was even omitted from the very inclusive lists in Meres' *Palladis Tamia*) this would hardly count as 'purchasing fame by his pen'. The same disqualification would apply to Sir Edward Dyer, another of Sidney's poet friends who was a knight. Dyer was more admired, but not more published.

There is likewise no reason why Nashe should say that Greville or Dyer had hold of the forelocks of Fortune in their youth. Nashe was much younger than Greville, and Dyer was older than either: what could Nashe have known of their youthful fame?

Above all, Nashe was an excellent literary critic. It is inconceivable that he could have considered Greville's obscure poetry as exemplified in *Caelica*, which contains the very poems Greville was writing in his youth, as the rescuing of English verse from pedantry. Dyer's poetry was better, but his engagement with transferring classical metre to English verse does little to enrol him among the enemies of pedantry – rather the opposite.

Who, then, is the *Have With You* 'Patron', 'paraphrasticall gallant Patron Dick', in real life? Some clues relating to his past life and personal characteristics are given us in the Epistle. The miserable wages of clerks are mentioned. 'Thou hast long served as a Clarke in the *crowne* office' to win '*bare* wages (yea as bare as my nayle, I faith)' says Nashe to Dick.[13] The italics are Nashe's, and not much ingenuity is required to read a pun in '*bare* wages' (the Bear and Ragged Staff being the Dudley *impresa*). Further, in the 'Neoterick' tongues he professes, Dick's pronunciation varies markedly from 'old Tooly's'.[14] This is an obscure joke, to be sure, but it does sound like yet another jibe at R.L.'s pronunciation of English.

Another type of clue altogether is found in the form of allusion to and opaque quotation of two works of Shakespeare's, *Henry IV*, both parts, and the *Sonnets*. These occur throughout *Have With You*, though many are packed into the Epistle.

The very Falstaffian Dick of the Castle and Dick Swash have already been brandished before our eyes by Nashe, before being whipped away on the pretext that these are not the Dick he means to address. Yet Nashe returns within a page or two to copious parallels with Shakespeare's *Henry IV*. John Tobin has argued in a series of articles that this is to be explained by Shakespeare's habit of absorption from Nashe, whose vocabulary and phraseology he so admired that he utilized it continually.[15] I shall argue the opposite: Nashe's admiration for Shakespeare led him to quote the other copiously. Since the dates of the two *Henry IV* plays are generally accepted to be 1598 for Part 1 and 1600 for Part 2, this is a radical claim. I shall start with the particular examples of echoes from *Henry IV* before making a more general case for the direction of the borrowings, turning finally to the *Sonnets*.

In the Epistle of *Have With You*, Nashe expresses his scorn for Gabriel Harvey's (truly awful) hexameter verses. 'Indeed, in old King Harrie sinceritie, a kinde of verse it is hee hath been enfeoft in from his minoritie, for, as I have bin faithfully informed, hee first cryde in that verse in the verie moment of his birth.'[16] In *Henry IV, Part 1*, the old King Henry (King Harrie) scornfully describes how Richard II when he was king 'enfoeffed himself to popularity'.[17]

In the body of the text, Nashe has great fun attacking Harvey's *Supererogation* for its inflated style. 'O, tis an unconscionable vast gorbellied Volume, bigger bulkt than a Dutch Hoy, &/ farre more boystrous and cumbersome than a payre of *Swissers* omnipotent galeaze breeches. But it shuld seeme he is asham'd of the incomprehensible corpulencie thereof himself, for at the ende of the 199. Page hee beginnes with 100. againe, to make it seeme little.'[18] (This last fact is perfectly true: such mistakes in printing were quite common.)

These two contiguous sentences contain numerous striking words from different scenes of the *Henry IV* plays. To take four of them: 'Most *omnipotent* villain' 'a goodly portly man, i' faith, and a *corpulent*' appear as descriptions of Falstaff.[19] Abundant evidence of 'the *incomprehensible* lies that this same foul rogue will tell'[20] is given throughout both parts of *Henry IV* and throughout *The Merry Wives of Windsor*, which is parodied in *Lenten Stuffe*. It is the anti-hero himself who exclaims 'Hang ye *gorbellied* knaves'.[21]

The conceit with which Nashe is playing, obviously, is that of the *Supererogation* as an enormous fat man. On the same page, he describes the same book as 'so fulsome a fat *Bonarobe*', and considers hooping it about 'like the tree at *Grayes-Inne* gate' to prevent its bursting (italics in the original).[22] It is in *Henry IV, Part 2* that Justice Shallow associates himself with the Inns of Court where, in his youth, he knew where the bonarobas were, and fought behind Gray's Inn.

These are parallels that have long been noted ... and discussed, I was about to write, but in fact they have been treated rather strangely by critics. J. Dover Wilson drew up a list of them in 1946, but said in conclusion that he could not account for them.[23] His paralysis is telling. For after all, they must be either coincidence, or imitation; and if the latter, either Nashe imitates Shakespeare, or Shakespeare imitates Nashe. No one supposes they are coincidence. So why did Dover Wilson not conclude that Shakespeare imitates Nashe?

John Tobin does so conclude, citing parallels distributed over almost the whole of Nashe's oeuvre and many of Shakespeare's histories and comedies. *Titus Andronicus, Richard III, Henry IV, Henry V, Julius Caesar, Troilus and Cressida, Macbeth, Romeo and Juliet, Merchant of Venice, Hamlet, Othello, King Lear, All's Well that Ends Well, Measure for Measure, Merry Wives of Windsor* have all been drawn into the complex of what Tobin believes is Shakespeare's habit of absorbing words and phrases from Nashe and weaving them into the texture and structure of his plays. This has become the consensus view. The work of those who believe in an 'early start' for Shakespeare's writing has not, as far as I know, disrupted that consensus. I shall show that the chronological evidence is against Tobin in three cases on which he relies. I shall also challenge one of his chief axioms and demonstrate that another of his axioms works *against* his case.

For credible parallels in *Titus Andronicus* and Nashe's *Christs Teares over Jerusalem*, in *Merry Wives* and *Lenten Stuffe*, and (the case in question) the *Henry IV* plays and *Have With You*, there is very strong, strong and good evidence that the plays antedated the pamphlets – that is, that the Shakespeare play had been written and performed, but most probably not published, before Nashe composed his echoing piece in each case. To ward off the objection that Nashe too might have composed long before publishing, I must point out that Nashe was working to a much closer timetable than Shakespeare, who had no particular need to publish. Nashe was keeping step with Gabriel

Harvey's serial attack on him: therefore, unusually, we can posit a short interval between composition and publication in Nashe's case. He himself sometimes corroborates this. Towards the end of *Have With You*, for example, Nashe's derogatory remarks about Harvey's 'Venus' refer to recent print publication on Harvey's part. '*He puts her in print for a* Venus, *yet desires to see her a* Venus *in print; publisheth her for a strumpet ....*'[24] This must have been written after Harvey actually published *Supererogation* in 1593: and indeed, Nashe confesses to his 1596 reader that he had been pondering his retaliation for about three years before settling down to write it.

The first extant quarto of *Titus Andronicus* is dated 1594. It was entered in the Stationers' Register on 6 February of that year. Philip Henslowe's diary notes performances on 23 and 28 January as well as 6 February.[25] What is clear is that *Andronicus* had been on stage well before 1594. Arguing from the number of companies who are listed on the title page as having previously played it; from signs of textual revision; from the evidence of Ben Jonson in his induction to *Bartholomew Fair*, that *TA* was on stage twenty-five or thirty years before 1614; from an allusion in the anonymous *A Knack to Know a Knave* of 1592 to a scene in *TA* which has no counterpart in the prose history or the ballad of *Titus Andronicus*, Harold Metz concludes that Shakespeare's play antedates Nashe's pamphlet, and that Nashe is consciously echoing Shakespeare.[26]

Chronological evidence favours the same relation between the two authors in the cases of *Merry Wives*, and *Henry IV*. As Tobin allows, it is commonly supposed that *Merry Wives* (first quarto 1602) was written for a court occasion in 1597. So to believe that Nashe provides material in his 1599 *Lenten Stuffe* for a play composed in 1597, Tobin has to suppose that Shakespeare altered his original text a good deal, for some reason incorporating Nashean material, before the play was printed in 1602 – which he duly proceeds to believe.[27]

As regards the *Henry IV* plays, Harvey provides some evidence for their existence before 1593 or 1592. In the 1593 *Supererogation*, he includes in a long list of satirists 'a lusty ladd of the Castell, that will binde Beares, and ride golden Asses to death'.[28] As Seymour Pitcher says, this must be must be a composite *literary* reference.[29] In his *Foure Letters and Certaine Sonnets* Harvey wrote: 'Never childe so delighted in his rattling baby; as some old Lads of the Castell have sported themselves with their rappinge bable'.[30] 'Lads of the Castle' looks like a reference to Oldcastle, Falstaff's original; but the allusion is plainly to recent times. Unless critics can show that 'Lads of the Castle' was a common phrase for roisterers, it is legitimate to suppose that Harvey is using the literary vocabulary of Shakespeare's play to refer to his own contemporaries.

Tobin proposes some criteria for determining whether a word or phrase is an echo or a foreshadowing of a parallel in the text of another. One proposed criterion is historical motivation: the author who has a particular history or person as his subject, and is tied to using appropriate markers for that subject, ought to be seen as the originator. The one who is free to invent yet has the same phrases as the 'tied' author will be the echoer. So, for example, where Nashe is attacking Gabriel Harvey in *Have With You* and has jokes about ropes and hangmen, it must be because Harvey's father was a rope maker: the language is correctly motivated by the historical facts. But if Shakespeare has Hal promise Falstaff that when Hal's rule comes, Falstaff will be granted the post of hangman (*1 Henry IV*, I.2.63–5), the association 'fat man – hangman' is unmotivated by the play's plot, claims Tobin, and must derive from Nashe's pamphlet.[31]

But I would argue that though the principle is a good one, this scene in Shakespeare does not exemplify it. Shakespeare often utilizes the notion of the hangman as the lowest public office – see *Pericles* IV.6.75 or *Othello* I.1.34. That demotion, from best friend to lowest officer, is exactly what Falstaff fears at Hal's hands, and has no necessary connection with Nashe's vocabulary or conceit.

When the same principle is applied to other parallels, it does not support Tobin's chronology, but undermines it. In a play about Julius Caesar, Shakespeare must *of necessity* include the repeated offering of a crown to a god-like Caesar. He can hardly avoid mentioning the Ides of March: the historical records demand it. Nashe's hilarious Red Herring in *Lenten Stuffe* is offered a coronet by the sea creatures and thrice refuses it; and he is god-like. Lent is usually mostly in March, and Nashe says of *Lenten Stuffe* itself that he had no mind for 'such a mighty March brewage'.[32] But to suppose that Shakespeare comes at his March via Nashe's Lent, his crown-refusing god-like Caesar via other Nashean passages, as Tobin implies, is absurd.[33]

Another principle of Tobin's is that words and word-clusters that are rare or unique in Shakespeare's canon, but occur repeatedly in particular passages of Nashe, must be in origin Nashe's words and word clusters. Tobin does not always tell us whether these are also rare in the whole of Nashe's oeuvre. But even in the cases where the suspect item is common in Nashe and rare or unique in Shakespeare, I do not accept his corollary. Take for example the phrase 'rasher on the coals'. Shakespeare has it once, in *Merchant* (III.5.25–6): Launcelot Gobbo says 'If we grow all to be pork-eaters, we shall not shortly have a rasher on the coals for money'. Nashe has it twice. In the introduction to *The Unfortunate Traveller* (1594) he offers his epistle to the pages as an appetiser to the work itself 'as a rasher on the coles is to pull on a cup of Wine …'.[34] On the very next page, the first page of the text proper, he describes Jack Wilton his hero as 'Lord high regent of rashers of the coles'. Why does Shakespeare have a promised dearth of rashers on the coals? Because if every Jew converts, there will be not enough rashers to go round. Why does he have it only once? Because he has only one Jewish play. Why does Nashe have the phrase? Obviously to make a joke, since it is repeated, and is a mock title at its second occurrence. What kind of joke? Parody.

As with words, phrases, and conjunctions of words, so with whole plays. Traces of Nashe's *Pierce Penilesse, Terrors of the Night, Have With You, Lenten Stuffe*, and the play *Summer's Last Will and Testament* have been descried by Tobin in Shakespeare's *Hamlet*.[35] Arguing his 'frequency' principle, that numerous scattered instances in Nashe result in a concretization of echoed material in one single play of Shakespeare's because of Shakespeare's peculiar receptivity to Nashe's language, Tobin makes Nashe the origin and *Hamlet* the echo.

It is hard to imagine the process by which scraps of *five* of Nashe's works kept floating into Shakespeare's head, and eventually forced their way into the diction of a play with such a huge freight of apparently personal emotion and its own constraints as to coherence and the existing legend. Conversely, we know that Nashe's practice was to keep common-place books (as did many Elizabethans) in which he jotted down striking phrases from others' works. 'Of my note-books and all books else here in the countrey I am bereaved, whereby I might enamell and hatchover this device more artificially and masterly … had I my topickes by me in stead of my learned counsell to assist me, I might perhaps marshall my termes in better array.'[36] We know too that plays were among the works from which he borrowed. 'I borrowed this sentence out of a play. The Theater, Poets hall, hath many more such proverbs ….'[37] Therefore, I would urge the plausibility of the opposite of Tobin's concretization theory – a scatter effect caused by one vivid play impressing itself so forcibly on Nashe that he echoes its words again and again. He likes to consult his common-place book to reassemble the shards into his parodies: but he can sometimes manage without it, so forcibly has he been struck by the original phrasing.

To these counter-arguments to Tobin's axioms, or their application, we might add one new axiom, one old axiom drawn from thermodynamics, and some pure common sense.

The new axiom I suggest is that in determining the vector of imitation of one author by another, one should consider what makes for the funnier joke. Just as when trying to determine which of two disputed readings in a text is more likely to be correct, the principle of 'lectio difficilior' is adopted (accept the phrasing least likely to have been substituted by a copier making a slip or guessing a missing word), so we should always go for the 'lectio facetior', the wittier reading.

Take Nashe's odd detail that the herring when smoked 'will smile upon no man'.[38] Tobin suggests a connection with the unsmiling mien of Cassius in *Julius Caesar*, which is plausible in view of the contiguity of other *JC* markers in Nashe's story. But which connection? Nashe's unsmiling coronet-rejecting herring would seem funny even if read to a six-year-old who knew nothing of the history of Julius Caesar. It would appear funnier to an educated Elizabethan who had just returned from years abroad in 1599 and picked up *Lenten Stuffe* in St Paul's. It would be funniest, however, to those who knew Shakespeare's play, and had its phrases ringing in their ears. The funniest connection would be Nashean parody of a Shakespearean original.

The same principle should operate in the case of the barbering jokes in *Have With You.* The lathering, trimming, hairbrained jibes are a little banal if the barber addressed actually practised such things, funnier if they are pure metaphor relating to the pseudo-barber. For the joke in 'rarifier of prolixious rough barbarisme' to function, Dick should be a pretend cutter of 'barbae', beards, but a real purifier of the language of the tribe. Nashe's observation that 'hair the more it is cut the more it comes' is quite funny offered as a translation of 'Prolixior est brevitate sua', but funnier still if it parodies Shakespeare's 'the camomile the more it is trodden on the faster it grows'.[39] And the same will be true for numerous exaggerations perpetrated by Nashe. The threat to rape a woman on the corpse of her dead husband can only be felt as *comical* if it echoes a threat in a well-known play (*Titus Andronicus*).[40] Half Nashe's wit will be lost if we do not credit him with having utilized Shakespeare's fat Falstaff in order to joke on Harvey-conflated-with-his-overblown-book.

Tobin believes, conversely, that the figure of the Nashean Harvey, a kind of unregenerate old man/ Bacchus/ bragging soldier figure, worked as a magnetic core to attract Shakespeare's shreds of thoughts into a Falstaff cluster. 'Clearly Harvey's excessive literary bulk has allowed Shakespeare to describe more easily the corpulent Falstaff.'[41] The second law of thermodynamics suggests that it is extremely unlikely that from the chaos of Nashe's remarks there should emerge the solid figure of Falstaff. And what exactly does Tobin mean by 'describe *more easily*'? That Shakespeare had after all thought of Falstaff independently, but needed Nashe's words to conjure him onto stage? The same kind of thinking (which is really a capitulation to the notion of Shakespearean independence) seems to be behind Tobin's remark that Shakespeare gratefully used the Nashean *Julius Caesar* material in 1599 'as soon as it was available to him'. Tobin is in thrall not only to the notion that where there are Shakespeare/ Nashe parallels, Nashe must have anticipated Shakespeare, but also to the assumption that Shakespeare would have written his play shortly before its first mention. (The first mention is that of Thomas Platter who saw it at the Globe on 21 September 1599.) But even granted that assumption (which is in fact quite untenable), it is an odd thought that, having pondered over his play and included the obligatory scenes, Shakespeare should have let scraps of *Lenten Stuffe* infiltrate his vocabulary at the last moment before publication.

Common sense should be the touchstone when considering Shakespeare's and Nashe's diverse aims. Nashe's *Strange Newes*, *Have With You*, and *Lenten Stuffe* are meant to be comical/satirical. Shakespeare's comedies were meant to be comical, to be sure, but his tragedies were not. The farcical nature of Nashe's herring would surely have been something Shakespeare would have wanted to avoid evoking in *Julius Caesar*, if *Lenten Stuffe* had been known to him at the time of writing. The pathos of the deep division between the families of the lovers in *Romeo and Juliet* resulting in both their deaths is undermined if Shakespeare had to borrow from Nashe the thought that (in the case of the fishy Hero and Leander in *Lenten Stuffe*) 'in their parents the most division rested' and the fact their respective towns were bitter enemies.[42] With antennae alerted by direct parody of *Merry Wives* in the sentence 'the churlish frampold waves gave him [Leander] his belly full of fishe-broath, ere out of their laundry or washe-house they would graunt him his coquet or *transire*' – 'frampold', 'bellyfull' and the bundling of Falstaff into a laundry basket being words or features of the play – one can hardly shut down one's reception of Shakespearean parody when the same paragraph ends 'shee dreamed that Leander and shee were playing at checkestone with pearles in the bottome of the sea'.[43] Who could fail to see Miranda and Ferdinand (to whom Ariel sings of his father drowned 'full fathom five' and with pearls for eyes) playing chess at the end of *The Tempest*? And when Nashe starts the next paragraph with a disquisition on dreams, which are '*reaking* vapours of no impression', is he not making the connection clear as day, recalling for us Prospero's beautiful 'We are such stuff as dreams are made on' and his actor spirits who melt 'into air, into thin air' leaving 'not a *rack* behind'?

Fortified by these examples, we can turn back to *Have With You*, and recognize that both the 'motivation' axiom and common sense demand that if we find in the Epistle no less than three echoes from the first seventeen of Shakespeare's *Sonnets*, we can justifiably surmise that Nashe is echoing Shakespeare, even though the *Sonnets* were published in 1609. Striving to answer the demands of his material with its own emotional charge, in a difficult form, with deeply-thought-out abstruse metaphors, Shakespeare would not have been looking for inspiration to a prose pamphlet written in comic mode.

One echo from the *Sonnets* has already been quoted, but it is well camouflaged, and probably passed unnoticed by the reader, as it always has done. The exhortation to Dick not to 'close prison' his virtues in a narrow glass is strongly reminiscent of Sonnet 5's 'liquid prisoner pent in walls of glasse'. The phrase '*lines* of life' is dragged into a joke about Gabriel's brother Richard Harvey: and Shakespeare in Sonnet 16 writes 'So should the lines of life that life repaire'. Thirdly, there is a whole half-line which should not have been missed. 'Be not self-wild' occurs in both Nashe's Epistle and Sonnet 6. And what is more, in Nashe it is followed by a battery of words applicable to Shakespeare's situation. 'Be not self-wild, but insist in my precepts, and I will tutour thee so Pythagoreanly how to husband them in al companies, that even *Willington* himselfe, thy fellow Barber in *Cambridge* ... shalbe constrained to worship and offer to thee.'[44]

'Husbandry' is a theme word in the early sonnets, in which Shakespeare urges a young man both literally to be a husband and metaphorically to sow his seed. The odd use of the plural 'companies', rather than 'in all (kinds of) company', may hint at players' companies. Could 'Pythagoreanly' have something to do with the love *triangle* in the *Sonnets*? At the end of the dialogue, Nashe himself gives us a clue that the repetition of 'self-wild' in 'will' and 'Willington' are deliberate and significant. The clue is in a pseudo-index of faults escaped in the printing, which is far too vague to be of any use, and contains some covert jokes.

> Spectatores, *the faults escaped in the Printing I wish may likewise escape you in reading. In the Epistle Dedicatorie correct* Willington *and put in* Williamson: *in the midst of the Booke* vide *make* vidi: *about the latter end* stellified stalified, *and* Sunius Surius: *with as many other words or letters too much or too-wanting as ye will.*[45]

Some of the items to be corrected were no doubt genuine misprints. But the original instance of 'stellified' was no mistake. It occurred when Nashe was scorning Harvey for implying that the great and the good wanted 'to stellifie him [Harvey] above the cloudes and make him shine next to Mercury'.[46] We are already suspicious of 'Mercury' and 'Stella'. And to change the (perfectly correct) 'stellify', meaning 'to turn into a star', to the (non-existent) 'stalify', presumably connected with 'stale' meaning 'urine', is to insult the holder of the name 'Stella'. To fuss over the name of the Barber is perhaps to draw attention to the fact that the last syllables are unimportant: it is the 'Will' that matters.

So, let's boldly conclude, not just because of the puns, but in view of the frequent quotation from works of Shakespeare, *Have With You* addresses Shakespeare. *Ergo*, Richard Lichfield is Shakespeare.

Verbal allusion to Shakespeare's works may also serve to identify Apis Lapis (mentioned by Harvey as one of Nashe's 'patrons') with Shakespeare. In *Strange Newes*, addressing Maister Apis Lapis ('Bee Stone'?), Nashe twits him about his 'dudgen dagger'.[47] Macbeth, we remember, sees gouts of blood on the blade and dudgeon of the imaginary dagger, in a scene which seems to have struck Shakespeare's contemporaries as much as it does us. Nashe continues his teasing with a joke on the 'Stilliard'. He pretends that Apis Lapis was concerned about where the stilliard or distillery (for the students' beer drinking) was to be moved when the law courts had to be moved to Hertfordshire out of London because of plague. But he deliberately associates the stilliard question with Apis's dagger, which is, of course, a 'steel yard': 'you fell into a great studie and care by your selfe' – presumably in a monologue – 'to what place the Stilliard should be remooved'.[48] He seems to conflate Apis with the character Macbeth here, in that mode of allusion noted before, by which an author's fictional character is taken to stand for the author himself. In view of Chapman's joke on the upstart poet and lawyer D'Olive, it is interesting that Apis is associated with the courts.

Later in the pamphlet Nashe returns to his theme: 'one of my fellowes, *Will. Monox* (Hast thou never heard of him and his great dagger?)'[49] That someone called 'Will' is associated with this great dagger is quite startling. The explication of the surname Monox and the nick-name Bee-stone must wait awhile.

The dedication of the Epistle and its first sentence raise echoes of another play.

To the most copious Carminist
of our time, and famous persecutor of *Priscian*, his
verie friend Maister *Apis lapis: Tho. Nashe* wish-
eth new strings to his old tawnie Purse, and
all honourable increase of acquain-
tance in the Cellar.

Gentle M. William, that learned writer Rhenish wine & Sugar, in the first booke of his comment upon Red-noses, hath this saying ... .[50]

It almost seems as though Gentle M. William is the same person as the addressee, for one naturally reads on in the vocative from the heading ... but then one has to realign 'Gentle M. William' as the subject of a new sentence. And what a sentence! The combination of 'Rhenish wine & Sugar', 'first book' and red noses is highly evocative of *Henry IV, Part 1* (i.e. first book), in which Sir John Sack and Sugar (Falstaff) comments on Bardolph's red nose. I suggest the syntactical false alley is deliberate: we are meant to hear M. William as addressee. But even disallowing that supposition, the notion that Apis Lapis is Shakespeare becomes more plausible within a page of text with the *Macbeth* allusions noted above.

The reason that these allusions, and the later one to Will. Monox, have not been previously connected with plays of Shakespeare's lies not only in the accepted dating of the plays, but arguably also on a quirk of human cognition noted by Stuart Sutherland.[51] Given a certain number of clues pointing to a particular conclusion, we can be deflected from drawing that conclusion by the addition of more items which seem to us unconnected. I rather unfairly left off the end of the first quotation from the epistle to Apis Lapis: '... hath this saying: veterem ferendo iniuriam invitas novam'. In the *Henry IV* we have, no-one says that ignoring an injury lays one open to more injury. Therefore we check an initial impulse to make the identification with Shakespeare and his play, thereby wasting valuable potential evidence that does match. Yet Shakespeare could have altered lines of the play before publication. And to reject the identification involves belief in an odd chain of events. Nashe must have implicated one William with sack and sugar, red noses, and a book with parts; another William with daggers; and an Apis Lapis we suspect may be Maister William he implicates with dudgen daggers and solitary musings. Later, Shakespeare (another William) must have come across these references, and worked one into *Henry IV* (into the first part, presumably on some subconscious prompting that it ought to be in a Part One of something) and the others into *Macbeth*.

Such a concatenation of events is highly unlikely to have occurred. To add to the strong presumption that it was Nashe who echoed Shakespeare, there is a welter of small pointers to the person of Shakespeare in all three Nashean pamphlets. Some personal allusions to Shakespeare in the *Have With You* epistle have already been noted above. *Lenten Stuffe*, we saw, is dedicated to 'Lustie Humfrey, King of Tobacconists *hic et ubique*', an *unlearned* lover of poetry, and a poet himself. Nashe urges him to publish his *Hermit's Tale* – an extraordinary linkage back to the Woodstock festivities of 1575, for which no-one has offered an explanation. *Strange Newes* is addressed to Apis Lapis, a 'copious carminist' and a 'famous persecutor of Priscian'. A productive poet is unlikely to be a tormentor of grammar – yet there is one who, we know, strained grammar to its limits – William Shakespeare.

An appeal to Lapis in the Epistle throws up a number of further pointers.

> What say you, Maister Apis Lapis, will you with your eloquence and credit shield me from carpers? Have you anie odde shreds of Latine to make this letter-munger [Harvey] a cockscombe of?
>
> It stands you in hande to arme your selfe against him: for he speaks against Connicatchers, and you are a Conni-catcher, as Connicatching is divided into three parts; the Verser, the Setter, and the Barnacle.[52]

Lapis is eloquent. He may have shreds of Latin – and Shakespeare had 'small Latin and less Greek', according to Ben Jonson. He is a coney-catcher, a joke which may find its explanation in one of Robert Greene's pamphlets, *A Defence of Conny-catching* (1592). Rather naïvely, commentators have accepted at face value Greene's attacks on urban rogues. They have failed to see the coterie game played out within the texts.

Greene tells one tale of a trickster, or coney-catcher, who was a 'holy brother' in search of a wife. This brother was, we learn, 'a scholastical panyon [companion] nourst up onely at Grammer-scoole, least going to the Universitie, through his nimble witte, too much learning should make him mad … He pronounced his words like a bragout …'.[53] A later tale concerns Will Summers; and another, a man who married sixteen wives and wooed a maid 'whom we will call Marian', of good family. It turns out that he was a taylor 'whom we will call William'. The whole takes place in Wiltshire.[54] The descriptions are strangely specific. My suspicion is that under the guise of a number of different tales, Greene is telling a continuous tale about a single person. We have a joke on the lack of further education combined with learning and wit, faults in pronunciation, and braggadoccio. The 'taylor' is reminiscent of Armin's Taylor's Boy, and he is a William. The dramatic use of Will Summers to refer to a later dramatic William was observed in Chapter 6. Wilton in Wiltshire was the home of Mary Sidney (a 'Marian' of good family). All this fits R.L. to a 'T', or a 'W.S.'[55]

In the case of *Lenten Stuffe*, both the male protagonist, the herring King of Fishes, and the objects of his wooing, Hero and Lady Turbot, cry out to be unmasked. Nashe calls Hero Leander's 'Mistris or Delia' which Margaret Hannay has suggested would not endear him to the one who was often addressed as Delia – Mary Sidney.[56] Hannay does not, however, suppose that

Nashe was insinuating a relationship between the protagonist of *Lenten Stuffe* and the Countess of Pembroke. Yet the insinuation is there, in numerous tiny details, some internal to the text, some external.

The herring (as Leander) woos first Hero, then Lady Turbot. Between these two tales, there is an abortive story of Madam Celina Cornificia (Heavenly Bestower of Horns). The same narrative technique as Greene's is skilfully deployed by Nashe, I suggest. The pretence of telling disparate tales masks the fact that all the tales are one tale. The Celina episode is lost in a long expostulation by Nashe against those 'mice-eyed decipherers' who try to read too much into his words and then denounce him to the noblemen they think he has offended. 'Talke I of a beare, O, it is such a man that emblazons him in his armes.'[57] Returning to the story of Lady Turbot, Nashe parodies his own style to make it quite incomprehensible to such decipherers. Lady Turbot's reaction to the Herring's wooing is a prime example:

> This speech was no spireable odor to the *Achelous* of her audience; wherefore she charged him by the extreame lineaments of the Erimanthian beare, and by the privy fistula of the *Pierides*, to committee no more such excruciating sillables to the yeelding ayre, for she would sooner make her a French-hood of a cowsharde and a gown of spiders webbes, with the sleeves drawn out with cabbages, than be so contaminated any more with his abortive loathely motives ....[58]

Nashe has cleverly pre-empted the reader's natural instinct to cry 'Erimanthian *boar*, not bear!', and to conclude he alludes to the Dudley family – which is what he surely *is* doing. Another clue to the covert reference has been inserted by a sleight-of-hand typical of the best conjurors' tricks. On the pretence that an act has not yet begun, a conjuror will perform the vital move. So it is in the very sentence that introduces the riddling account of the wooing: 'though there be neither rime nor reason in it, (as by my good will there shal not,) they, according to their accustomed gentle favors, whether I wil or no, shall supply it with either, and runne over al the peeres of the land in peevish moralizing and anatomizing it'.[59] 'Good Will' and a disguised 'willy nilly' lurk not far below the surface.

That the fishy stories are not sheer nonsense can be further divined by items in the Epistle and on the title page; by the publication licence; and by cross-referencing the pamphlet with the source text of the tale of wooing, acknowledged by Nashe to be Marlowe's *Hero and Leander.*

In the Epistle, the king of herrings is explicitly connected with the Humfrey King to whom the whole is dedicated. 'A King thou art by name, and a King of good fellowshippe by nature, whereby I ominate this Encomion of the king of fishes was predestinate to thee from thy swaddling clothes.'[60] It is therefore interesting that Nicholas Breton – whose affiliation to the Sidney circle no one would dispute – should dedicate to the same Humfrey his advice on how to woo and win the ideal woman in his *Pasquil's Mistresse* (1600).[61] Wooing and Humfrey go hand-in-hand at this period, it seems. Both *Lenten Stuffe* and Breton's text were subjected to demands for 'lawful authorization' before the grant of a publication licence. Again the question arises: *Whose* authorization was in question, besides the normal ecclesiastical?

An inscription on the title page of *Lenten Stuffe* declares: 'Fitte of all Clearkes of Noblemens Kitchins to be read: and not unnecessary by all Serving men that have short boord-wages, to be remembred'. 'Remembered'? The Clerk of the Council Chamber Door was in a position to remember the kitchens of Kenilworth where he used to find his morning 'manchet' of bread. The addressee Humfrey King is being sketched quite deliberately into the same background as that young 'Clerk'.

The emblem on the title page of *Lenten Stuffe* is 'Famam peto per undas'. The Latin motto could mean 'I pursue fame across the waves': but it might also mean 'I hound Fame even over the water', i.e., across the Hellespont as in the story of Hero. Investigating allusion to Mary Sidney in the Quarrel, I found that both Nashe and Harvey tend to allude to her as 'Saint Fame'.[62] The Bishops' Ban of 1599 followed on the heels of the publication of *Lenten Stuff*, calling in many works and prohibiting Harvey and Nashe from publishing ever again. Viewing these facts in relation to each other and to the subtle puns on 'fame' in *Astrophel and Stella* is highly instructive.[63]

Finally, in his 'Hero and Leander' parody in *Lenten Stuffe*, Nashe shows in-depth knowledge of the 'implications' Chapman said Marlowe 'did implie' in his poem of Hero and Leander. For where Marlowe had the *non-sequitur* of the Fates hating *Leander* because *Mercury* had cheated the Fates, Nashe has Jupiter hating *Ganimede* his cup-bearer because the latter was so like Leander. (In what way he was similar, we are not told.) Nashe does cook up another reason: that all the gods were so sorrowful at the drowning of Leander, they could no longer stand liquids. But the real reason is the web of inter-reference that leads from Mercury to Ganimede. In this connection, it is significant that Nashe declares at the end of his *Lenten Stuffe* that the pamphlet is no more absurd than '*Philips his Venus*', whose protagonist is the child Ganimede.[64]

It is rather unlikely, on reflection, that Nashe deeply admired a writer (Humfrey King) of whose works none survived except the unimpressive poem the *Hermites Tale.* For Nashe had set himself up as a literary critic from his first moments in print, with his survey of other writers in the preface to Greene's *Menaphon* and in his *Anatomie of Absurditie*. Humfrey falls into the same category as William Smith and A.W. – a writer admired by the best poets and critics among his contemporaries, who mysteriously fades from view or rather, fails to float into focus. It is also against the odds that Nashe should have found the same exceptional qualities in three quite distinct and equally mysterious writers, Apis Lapis, Dick Lichfield and Humfrey King. It is far more likely that one man with three pseudonyms – or four, if the Amyntas identification is accepted – was the object of Nashe's admiration, and also his gratitude for 'benefits received', as he puts it in *Pierce Penilesse*.

Nashe urged this person repeatedly not to hide his talent, but blazon it out as he had done in his early youth. The constant allusion to Shakespeare's plays makes it plausible to regard Nashe's programme as unexpectedly unified. Under cover of his effervescence, he is urging Shakespeare to publish all his works. (Perhaps the wretched *Hermites Tale* – because it was the only piece that would not give away Shakespeare's identity to a wider readership? – is a joke cipher for 'your works'.) It is therefore significant that the first of Shakespeare's plays to reach print came out with John Danter's press. For Nashe had published many of his pamphlets with Danter, and had actually worked for him, it appears. Many present-day scholars would claim to the contrary that it is not significant at all that *Titus Andronicus* was printed by Danter (or that Danter published *Romeo and Juliet* in 1597). Plays became the property of the acting companies, they would claim, and authors had no say in the sale of their texts to the printing houses. But this is demonstrably not universally true.[65] Shakespeare had good reason to approach Danter – the recommendation of his deepest admirer, Nashe.

Richard Lichfield's own work in response to Nashe appeared between the publication of Nashe's *Have With You* and his *Lenten Stuffe*. 'The Trimming *of Thomas Nashe Gentleman*, by the high-tituled patron *Don Richardo de Medico campo*, Barber chirurgion to Trinitie Colledge in Cambridge', reads the title page, with 'London: Printed for Philip Scarlet, 1597' at its foot. In the centre is a wood-cut picture of Thomas Nashe in chains, and a motto: 'Faber quas fecit compedes ipse gestat', a Latin proverb meaning 'The smith is wearing the shackles he himself forged'. The word 'faber' may have been innocently chosen. On the other hand it may have been chosen with ulterior motive, to align this Richard with 'A.W. Artificer', that suspicious Smith who has featured in previous chapters. 'Medico campo' looks like a clue to a true identity, but turns out to be re-mystification in another language: 'leech-field'. There are various ways of translating 'compedes': 'shackles', 'chains', 'fetters', 'bonds'.

But the first might be the most appropriate in this context, for it too may be intended as a beacon, to light up the hidden identity of the author.

The work is often ascribed to Gabriel Harvey. But in the opinion of McKerrow it is much funnier than Harvey could have made it, and in a different style from the run of Harvey's extant attacks on Nashe, such as *Pierces Supererogation* and *Foure Letters*.[66] McKerrow points out that Dick features mainly in the Epistle of *Have With You*, and the author of *The Trimming* answers the Epistle, not the long attack on Harvey in the body of the text. This author speaks of Harvey as 'the partie against whom thou writest' (G2v), patently distancing himself from Harvey.

On the verso of the title page is written 'To the Learned: Eme, lege, nec te precii poenitebit. To the simple. Buy mee, read me through, and thou wilt not repente thee of thy cost'. Next comes a preface To the Gentle Reader: 'Proface gentle Gentlemen, I am sorry I have no better Cates to present you with: but pardon I pray you, for this which I have heere provided, was bred in Lent, and Lent (you know) is said of *leane*, because it macerates & makes leane the bodye' (A2).

What could 'mice-eyed decipherers' make of these two pages? The first word of the whole tract is one that recalls Ro. La. of Kenilworth, who hurried on from his short historical preface with 'Thus proface ye with the preface'. On the next page may be found another reminder: 'Your favours happily might adde strength unto it, and stirre up the faint creeping steps to a more lively pace: it by hard hap being denied of the progresse, keeping at home hath grown somewhat greater' (A2v). We were inclined to suspect that 'The Pastime of the Progress' was the title under which 'Langham's Letter' was originally known. This 'denial' and 'keeping at home' might well be deciphered as a reference to that act of censoring.

It would be satisfying to be able to say that *The Trimming* is the most brilliant of pamphlets. Unfortunately, it would not be true. Dick of Lichfield has some excuse: 'His Epistle I expected any time these three yeares, but this mine aunswer *sine suco loquar*, though it be not worthy to bee called the worke of one well spent houre) I have wrought foorth out of the stolne houres of three weekes' (A2r–v). I am inclined to believe he did dash it off, adding (so McKerrow believes) a rather unpleasant section on Nashe's imprisonment for his part in the writing of the troubled play the *Isle of Dogs*. To joke on a friend's imprisonment is perhaps permissible. But when the jokes allude to the risk of having one's ears cropped, they have an unpleasant ring to them: 'Therefore thou deservedst to loose thine eares for naming the Bishop of *Ely* and of *Lincolne*, and for writing of *Christs teares over Ierusalem*' (G1v).

It may be that Dick was genuinely angry with Nashe for the references he deplores. Nashe had deliberately picked out the Bishop of Ely in *Have With You* as an example of a College Visitor.[67] Dick might have felt it gave his identity away: for the Bishop of Ely is prominent at the opening of *Henry V.* He might equally have been hurt by *Christs Teares*, for it is possible, given the coterie joke in the naming of Marian as William's bride in Greene's *Defence of Conny-catching*, that the attack on the Miriam of Jerusalem was intended by Nashe as an attack on Mary Sidney.[68]

However rushed *The Trimming* may have been, there are some lovely Shakespearean touches in it. One is a story about a dog who was a brilliant actor, pretending to die of poison, and reviving pat on cue. Shakespeare's early *Two Gentlemen of Verona* has comparable comic scenes with Lance (Spear?) and his dog. There are silly puns, as one might expect. Nashe's Epistle is said to be too bright and glittering, but 'vestured with this Caule & rare-wrought garme(n)t, it loseth part of it [sic] hurting vigour, & therefore is cald to be seen againe' (A3r). There are also some telling ones. The words 'Patronage', 'Patron' (capitalized) and 'patronize' and 'patterne' are so insisted on over the space of two pages (B1-B1v) that they start to cause a nervous reaction in readers who wonder where on earth the joke lies. I suggest it lies in the surname of the man under whose cloak Ro. La. hid – William Patten.

Dick has enormous fun with the conventions of printing. He misuses the marginal note like a street urchin, to address Nashe directly, or to crow at his own cleverness. 'Ha ha ha', he crows; 'How I bewich the[e] with facunditie'; 'Marke this secret allegorie'; 'O eloquence'; 'Wel put in'. He makes fun of the convention: 'I began to marke the note which you adioyned to your notes that they might be noted, there tossing and turning your booke upside downe, when the west end of it hapned to be upward, me thought your note seemed a *D*, ah *Dunce, Dolt, Dotterell*, quoth I' (B3v). And he uses the note to dismantle his text: 'that one lye I make of thee in this booke is presently washed away with repentance', with a marginal note to direct us to where it is washed away, 'Pag: 6' (C3). The 'repentance' here and on the verso of the title page may be a deliberate reference to Greene's *Groatsworth*, which was 'bought with a million of repentance'.

The long and apparently idiotic coinages are equally delightful: 'To the polypragmaticall, parasitupocriticall, and pantophainoudendeconticall Puppie Thomas Nashe'; 'God save you (right glossomachicall *Thomas*)' (B2v). To have 'less Greek' is a relative term in the 1590s: this writer both knows Greek words ('polypragmos' means 'busybody') and can combine Greek roots in non-existent compendia that are nevertheless apt descriptions. The longest one may give the main reason for Dick's anger, for it seems to mean 'someone who reveals everything when it is absolutely inappropriate to do so'.

It must have been subject to many strains, this friendship we think we have uncovered between the two literary giants, Nashe and Shakespeare. Mary Sidney especially must have been a cause of friction between the two, hated by one, loved by the other. The consensus belief, based on the substantial preface Nashe contributed to Greene's prose romance *Menaphon*, in 1589, is that the relationship was antagonistic from the start. But this is to misinterpret Nashe's diatribe in that preface: as Lorna Hutson has correctly argued, it is the pedantic graduates whom Nashe abhors, in contrast with the simple Menaphon. Described in tones of admiration and linked to the world of theatre in all the prefatory material, Menaphon *is* Shakespeare.[69]

Nashe's death seems to have occurred in 1600 or 1601, not long after the Bishops' interdiction on the publication of any more of his works. It may be that Nashe's status of *persona non grata* to the authorities inhibited his friends from voicing their tributes in public. But it turns out that they voiced them in private. In 1995, Katherine Duncan-Jones made public a bifolium manuscript from the Berkeley Castle Muniments.[70] It contains two pages of elegies for Nashe followed by a dedication offering Humphrey King's *Hermites Tale* to a patron. The first elegy is by Ben Jonson. Then on fol. 1v is a Latin elegy – eight lines of hexameter verse – and an English one, and another in English follows on fol. 2r. The two English elegies are light-hearted and witty, referring to wonders such as herrings mourning in black and Harvey weeping at Nashe's death. They are followed by the poem dedicating the *Hermites Tale* to a patron, in sonnet form with an appended couplet containing (possibly) a self-advertising pun: 'True honorable Lord respect his will/who only lives to doe you duties still'. The Lord, though unnamed, must be one of the Carey/Hunsdon family, owners of Berkeley Castle, and patrons to Nashe. It is not clear, says Duncan-Jones, whether the three poems preceding King's dedication are also by King. She thinks the short Latin one is bad enough to be by this unskilled home-brewed poet.

> Indoctus doctum celebrare poeta poetam
> Incipio; doctum celebravit Naso Catullum
> Naso poeta bonus, vates fuit ipse Catullus.
> Ast ego si doctum celebrarem carmine Nashum
> Indoctus; notum quis sciret carmine Nashum?
> Sed satis ingenio quum Nashe sis notus acuto
> Incipio tantum (quo me est (dolor o) penes unum)
> Ignotus notum deflere poeta poetam.
>
> fol 1v.

fol.2r

fol.1v

7.1 Berkeley Castle Muniments. General Miscellaneous Papers 31/10, fols 1v and 2r. By permission of the Berkeley Will Trust

To celebrate a scholar-poet, I, a simple verser
Take up my pen, as Ovid did to celebrate Catullus.
Yet Ovid was a poet fine, Catullus was a bard:
With my poor skill to sing of Nashe, his glory may be marred.
Yet Nashe since you are throughly known a poet of great wit,
I take my pen, 'tis all, alas, for which my powers are fit,
A mute inglorious poet here bemoans a glorious one.

Anon.

In my translation, I take the liberty of assuming that the 'quo' in the penultimate line should be 'quod' – 'a thing which'.[71] This makes sense where 'quo' does not. My 'Anon.' is an attempt to show the ambiguity of 'ignotus' in the last line. In Chapter 4, the possibility was raised that 'William Smith' called himself Ignoto, and the *Calender*'s Colin was 'uncouthe' because he was Ignoto, the Unknown.

Ovid did not in truth write an elegy for Catullus. Ovid was born in 43 BCE: Catullus died in the decade before. But the writer of Nashe's Latin elegy saw himself as Ovid, because that is what everyone else called him. I think we may safely conclude that he *is* the same poet as Humphrey King, and that is why these poems have been transcribed in such close proximity to each other. There is only one poet we know of who was called Ovid, Humphrey King and Ignoto. He was the one who supposedly had 'small Latin'. His skill was enough for simple tasks, though, such as composing a punning elegy in Latin to show off his lack of learning (!) and to mourn his constant friend, Nashe, who had always shown faith in his talent.

Notes

1   Thomas Nashe, *Strange Newes* (running title 'Foure Letters Confuted') (London: [J. Danter], 1592). *Works*, I.253–335.
2   'Richard Lichfield', *The Trimming of Thomas Nashe* (London: Philip Scarlet, 1597). It can be found in Grosart's *Works of Gabriel Harvey*, 3.1–72. I shall give the original folio references.
3   McCarthy, 'Milksop Muses'.
4   Some of my argumentation is given in 'Some *quises* and *quems*: Shakespeare's True Debt to Nashe', in *New Studies in the Shakespearean Heroine*, ed. Douglas Brooks (Lampeter: Mellon, 2004), pp. 175–92.
5   Nashe, *Works*, III.5.
6   *Works*, III.5–6.
7   *Works*, III.13.35–14.2.
8   *Works*, III.33.

9   *Works*, III.5.
10 *1Henry IV*, I.2.41.
11 Nashe, *Works*, III.76.33–77.7.
12 *Exequiae Illustrissimi Equitis, D. Philippi Sidnaei* ... (Oxford: J. Barnes, 1587), D2v, E1v–E3r.
13 Nashe, *Works*, III.6.
14 *Works*, III.14.
15 A useful starting point is J.J.M. Tobin, 'Nashe and Shakespeare: Some Further Borrowings', *N&Q* 219 (1992), pp. 309–20, where citations are given to his previous articles.
16 Nashe, *Works*, III.7.
17 *Works*, III.2.69.
18 *Works*, III.35.
19 I.2.109; II.4.421.
20 I.2.187.
21 II.2.85.
22 Nashe, *Works*, III.35–6.
23 J. Dover Wilson, ed., *1 Henry IV* (Cambridge: Cambridge University Press, 1946), pp. 191–6.
24 Nashe, *Works*, III.121.
25 *Henslowe's Diary*, 2nd edn, ed. R.A. Foakes (Cambridge: Cambridge University Press, 2002), p. 21 (fol. 8).
26 Metz, *Shakespeare's Earliest Tragedy*, chs 6 and 9.
27 J.J.M. Tobin, 'Texture as Well as Structure: More Sources for the Riverside Shakespeare', in Thomas Moisin and Douglas Bruster, eds, *In the Company of Shakespeare: Essays on English Renaissance Literature in Honor of G. Blakemore Evans* (London: Associated University Presses, 2002), pp. 197–10.
28 Harvey, *Works*, 2.44 (B2v).
29 Seymour M. Pitcher, *The Case for Shakespeare's Authorship of The Famous Victories* (New York: Alwin Redman, 1961), p. 164.
30 Gabriel Harvey, *Foure Letters and Certaine Sonnets* (London: J. Wolfe, 1592). Harvey, *Works*, 1.225 (G3).
31 His argument is implicit in 'Texture as Well as Structure'. It was spelled out more clearly in 'Nomenclature and the Dating of "Titus Andronicus"', *N&Q* 229 (1984), pp. 186–7, and in a paper presented to the World Shakespeare Congress at Valencia, 18–23 April 2001.
32 Nashe, *Works*, III.175.
33 See Tobin, 1992, pp. 317–19. Similarly unconvincing is James Shapiro's discussion of a parallel between Marlowe's *Massacre at Paris* and Shakespeare's *Julius Caesar*. He ascribes to *Marlowe* priority for the repeated phrase 'Caesar shall go forth'. See Shapiro, pp. 122–5.
34 Thomas Nashe, *The Unfortunate Traveller* (London: T. Scarlet for C. Burby, 1594). *Works*, III.199–328, 208.
35 J.J.M. Tobin, 'Nashe and *Hamlet* Yet Again', *Hamlet Studies* 2.1 (1980), pp. 35–46.
36 Nashe, *Works*, III.175–6.
37 *Works*, I.271–2.
38 *Works*, III.191.
39 *Works*, III.8, A4; *1Henry IV*, II.4.400–01.
40 *Works*, II.292, *Titus Andronicus* II.3.130.
41 Tobin, 2002, p. 102.

42 Nashe, *Works*, III.195–6.
43 *Works*, III.179.
44 *Works*, III.14.
45 *Works*, III.139.
46 *Works*, III.107.
47 *Works*, I.256.
48 *Works*, I.256.
49 *Works*, I.287.
50 *Works*, I.255.
51 Stuart Sutherland, *Irrationality, The Enemy Within* (London: Penguin, 1992), pp. 202–4.
52 Nashe, *Works*, I.257.
53 Robert Greene, *The Defence of Conny-catching* (London: A.I. for Thomas Gubbins, sold by John Busbie, 1592), C4. Greene, *Works*, 11.39–104, 79–80.
54 *Works*, 11.87 (D2–D2v).
55 An R.L. joined in the coney-catching pamphleteering. *Robin the devil, his two peni-worth of Wit in Half a penni-worth of Paper. By Robert Lee, a famous Fencer of London, alias Robin the Devil* printed by Nicholas Ling appeared in 1607. We have only the shadow of this R.L.: all that remains of him is the title of the work in Hazlitt's *Handbook*, p. 318, s.v. King (Humphrey). The 'penny-worth' allusion connects the work to the *Hermites Tale* as much as to Greene's well-known *Groatsworth of Witte.* Hazlitt believed that *Robin the Devil* was an earlier edition of the former
56 Nashe, *Works*, III.195. Hannay, *Philip's Phoenix*, p. 142.
57 *Works*, III.214.
58 *Works*, III.217.
59 *Works*, III.216.
60 *Works*, III.149.
61 Nicholas Breton, *Pasquils Mistresse* (London: Thomas Fisher, 1600).
62 See footnote 3 above.
63 See Chapter 5.
64 *Works*, III.146–226.
65 Ioppolo, *Revising Shakespeare;* Douglas Brooks, *From Playhouse to Printing House: Drama and Authorship in Early Modern England* (Cambridge: Cambridge University Press, 2000); Joseph Loewenstein, *The Author's Due: Printing and the Prehistory of Copyright* (Chicago and London: University of Chicago Press, 2002).
66 McKerrow, *Nashe, Works*, vol. 5, intro., section 3, 'The Harvey-Nashe Quarrel', pp. 65–110, esp. 107–10.
67 *Works*, III.16.
68 Thomas Nashe, *Christs Teares Over Jerusalem* (London: James Roberts for Andrew Wise, 1593). *Works*, II.1–186, 71–7.
69 Thomas Nashe, preface to *Menaphon*, by Robert Greene (London: T. O[rwin] for Sampson Clarke, 1589), A2– B4. *Works*, 3.309–25. Lorna Hutson, *Thomas Nashe in Context* (Oxford: Clarendon Press, 1989), pp. 64–5. See also McCarthy, 'Some *quises*', pp. 184–6.
70 Katherine Duncan-Jones, 'Jonson's Epitaph on Nashe', *TLS* (7 July 1995), pp. 4–6. The document she labelled 'Berkeley Castle Muniments 31R' is now General Miscellaneous Papers 31/10.
71 It is 'quo' in the manuscript.

Chapter 8

Last Supposes

There is one very distinctive pseudonym – it could hardly be anything else – outstanding from the last chapter: 'Apis Lapis'. Someone is encoded as 'Bee Stone'. This someone is apparently conflated by Nashe with Gentle M. William of sack-and-sugar associations, author of a two-part 'ballad' on red noses – *Henry IV*? He is also implicated with a dudgen dagger and a soliloquy – and therefore, we supposed, with *Macbeth*. But as McKerrow points out, this someone can hardly be William Beestone the actor. The Apis Lapis of *Strange Newes* is clearly a *poet*, with a style Nashe greatly admires; and besides, the real Beestone would have been a mere child in 1592. The pursuit of Bee-Stone in this chapter will lead to re-investigation of some works already glanced at: Nashe's *Christs Teares* and *Have With You*; Harvey's *Pierces Supererogation*; Armin's *The Italian Taylor and His Boy*; Shakespeare's *Merry Wives*. It will move on to a poem of John Davies's, Nicholas Breton's *Wil of Wit* and his *Wits Trenchmour*, and John Lyly's *Euphues*. 'Wit' is added to the string of pseudonyms of R.L. A new interpretation of Shakespeare's tombstone is offered.

In *Pierces Supererogation*, Harvey complains that Nashe 'hath robbed William Conqueror of his surname, and in the very first page of his Straunge Newes, choppeth-off the head of foure Letters at a blow'.[1] What can this mean?

We know that Shakespeare was supposed to have called himself 'William the Conqueror'. While playing the part of Richard III in Shakespeare's play, the story ran, Richard Burbage had made an assignation with some woman. When he came knocking at her door, Shakespeare was already with the woman and sent the message that William the Conqueror was before Richard III.[2] The gentle Maister William in *Strange Newes* is given no surname: perhaps he has been deprived of his title 'the Conqueror'. Now Harvey states definitely that 'four letters' on the first page of *Strange Newes* lost their head. Might he mean: Nashe left off the first 'L' of 'Lapis Lapis', so that this William became apparently 'Bee stone', though his 'real' nickname was 'Stone stone' or 'Stones'?

McKerrow, Nashe's editor, has noticed how often 'the fool Stones' is mentioned by Nashe. He crops up on the very first page of the dialogue of *Have With You*, where one participant exclaims: 'No *aqua fortis*, if you love me, for it almost poysoned and spoyled the fashion of *Stones* the fooles nose'.[3]

And yet Stones the Fool is a shadowy creature. No one else mentions him. Or do they?

Why did Armin so ingenuously remark that his work was but rough stones from the quarry, in his introduction to *The Italian Taylor and His Boy*, a dedication that we suspected did not address Lady Fitzwater at all, but paid compliments to its true addressee, William Shakespeare? Why does John Davies of Hereford refer mysteriously to a STONE in an epigram on Edward Herbert, Earl of Montgomery? He reproves his addressee: 'Some say (bolde Britaine Knight) thou wert too blame/ To fetch that STONE thou foundst in *Dangers* Mouth'.[4] Davies then absolves this Herbert on the grounds that his faulty deed was done 'to follow Fames SUNNES'. It was to William and Philip, sons of Mary Sidney (Fame), that Shakespeare's First Folio was dedicated by Heminge and Condell, in words that imply a relationship of close patronage. Their lordships had 'prosequuted both [the works], and their Author living, with so much favour'; he was 'your *servant* Shakespeare'.[5] It sounds as though Edward Herbert was criticized by Davies for lending his patronage to one, STONE, who was tainted with 'danger', a word implying subversion and the risk of scandal.

Nashe may have invented this crude nickname for Shakespeare, perhaps reasoning that since 'spear' is slang for 'penis', and 'stones' are testicles, the latter name would serve as well. Another rationale was suggested to me recently on reading a poem of Robert Pinsky's, 'In Defence of Allusion'.[6] He draws the etymology of Shakespeare's name from 'Jacques-Pierre', which he reads as 'Jack-Peter'. It might equally be 'Jacques Stone'. Then again, the alchemical 'philosopher's stone' is mercury, and we have seen grounds for suspecting both Mercury and allusions to alchemy.[7] Whatever the nickname's provenance, Nashe utilized it, I believe, as a hidden motif in his long pamphlet *Christs Teares Over Jerusalem*. It is 'hidden' in the now-familiar sense that it lies on the surface of things so obviously that it cannot be seen. It is the main term in the biblical text on which Nashe constructs his theological diatribe.

The work is a sermon against the evils of London, couched in terms of Christ's weeping over Jerusalem for its sins, and abandoning it to its fate – the sacking carried out by the Romans in 70 CE. Nashe takes for his text a passage of Matthew's gospel: '*O Ierusalem, Ierusalem, which killest the Prophets. And stonest them that are sent unto thee. How often would I have gathered thy Chyldren together, as the Henne gathereth her Chickins together under her wings, and ye would not!* How often would I have revokt, reduced, & brought you into the right way, *But you would not? Therefore your habitation shall be left desolate*' (Nashe's wording, taken from Matthew 24, verses 37 and 38).

After a dedication to Lady Elizabeth Carey, and a note to the reader containing conciliatory words to Gabriel Harvey, Nashe embarks on his work warning London (sometimes 'England') to repent, by offering the example of the punishment of Jerusalem. He leads up to the point at which Christ uttered the words above, and then continues with an invented 'oration' by Jesus. After many pages of this, in which the key words of his text – 'stones', 'gathered', and 'desolation' – gather to themselves other scriptural and everyday accretions, he describes the sacking of Jerusalem in quite a peculiar tone (as we shall see), and then turns to excoriate London in similar terms, for a great many more pages.

We have some insight into how the work was received, for Nashe substituted a new Letter to the Reader in the second edition, of 1594, in which he alludes to some reader reaction to the first edition of 1593. He mentions the 'heavie penance my poore Teares here have endured, to turne them cleane unto tares'; he says his style was scorned; and he confesses that he has a tendency to stir whirlwinds of trouble: 'let me but touch a peece of paper, there arise such stormes and tempestes about my eares as is admirable'.[8] We may wonder why the work proved so contentious, if it was conciliatory to Harvey, and deeply pious.

The answer lies partly in its tone, partly in its encoded words. Read with an ear open for irony, it does not sound like a call to virtue, but more like a spoof sermon. In the 'London' part of the text, Nashe offers us the key to his own practice by sending himself up as an ignorant sermonizer.

> Scripture we hotch-potch together, & doe not place it like Pearle and Gold-lace on a garment, heere and there to adorne, but pile it and dunge it up on heapes, without use or edification. We care not howe we mispeake it, so we have it to speake. Out it flyes East and West; though we loose it all it is nothing, for more have we of it then we can well tell what to doe withall. Violent are the most of our packe-horse Pulpit-men in vomiting theyr duncery.[9]

There is more in the same vein. Then suddenly: 'Thys is erring from my scope: of the true use of the Scripture I am to talke'. It is a very clever double-layering, for Nashe first accurately describes what he was doing in his oration attributed to Christ, then falls into precisely the same preachifying all over again as he tells his audience how ridiculous preachifying is. And indeed it was ridiculous in Christ's oration. Nashe piled and dunged up in heaps his instances of 'stones' in the scriptures: 'the very *stones* in the streete shall ryse up in judgement against thee'; 'he that had blasphemed ... was *stoned* to death by the Prophets and Elders'; 'for this thou shalt grinde the *stones* in the Myll with *Sampson*, and whet thy teeth upon the *stones* for hunger', 'there shall be no David any more amongst you, that with a *stone* sent out of a sling, shall strike the chiefe Champion of the Philistines in the for-head'; and more ill-assorted texts.

Quotation becomes even more ridiculous in the case of the next key-word, 'gather'. The word's meaning slithers from the scriptural gathering together of obedient souls, like sheep, or like the chickens of the gospel text, through 'garnering' the kingdom of heaven (quite unexceptionable); *gathering* for the poor, i.e. collecting alms; the *gathering* of grains of corn into one to make bread and the *gathering* of geese and of bees to make flocks and hives; stars shining *together*; the necessity for the parts of man's body to hold *together* if there is to be a body; likewise the particles of the sea and the earth; to being *gathered* as equivalent to being 'tamed' (which it is not); through the failure of the children of Israel to '*gather*' manna ... and so on and on. Into the exposition of 'gather' we suddenly find an alien word intruding, namely '*echo*', as though it was one of the key words in the sermon text requiring exposition. But it was not: more likely it is the nymph Echo of Sidneian pastoral poetry to whom Nashe is making such oblique allusion. Far from having had a sudden rush of piety to the head, he is attacking the Sidneys and 'Stones' under the guise of attacking the depravity of Jerusalem.

To make the judgement that Nashe is being deliberately silly involves a difficult assessment of tone, and will inevitably be partly subjective. Yet some suspicion of Nashe's style is justified. For Christ to say that he has 'wasted myne eye-bals well-neere to pinnes-heads with weeping (as a Barber wasteth his Ball in the Water)' is pure bathos.[10] The mismatch of style to subject-matter becomes clearer still in the scenes from the sacking of Jerusalem. 'Scarce could one friende in commoning [gossiping] heere another, for the howling, wringing of hands, sobbing, & yelling of men, women, & chyldren':[11] which is to say, in effect, 'My dear, I could hardly hear myself *think*, what with the massacring, slaughtering ...'.

If we ask why he chose the text he did, why it was ill-received, and why Richard Lichfield the Barber of Pembroke College was so angry about it in his *Trimming of Thomas Nashe*, we might light on the following rationale. The work proclaims a very clear message, namely: 'Stones gather desolation' (in connection with the non-scriptural Echo). It was 'Stones' who reacted so angrily. And Nashe does in fact drop indirect hints that he wrote in a mood of alienation from Shakespeare/Stones. For in the dedicatory epistle he has some adverse comment on 'wit'.

To the Elizabethans, 'wit' and 'will' went hand in hand, roughly equivalent to our modern 'hearts and minds', but reversed. To find the word 'wit' behaving in a suspiciously referential way in Sidney coterie writers besides Nashe, we could turn to Nicholas Breton and to John Lyly.

The Wil of Wit, Wits Will, or Wils Wit, chuse you whether (i.e. 'What You Will') is an early work of Breton's. Entered in 1580, it must have been published in a first edition before 1582, for it is mentioned in that year by the Leicestrian protégé Richard Madox as though it were well known. The first extant edition is the one of 1597.[12] It had been reprinted five times by 1606. The work personifies Will and Wit, two friends. Jean Robertson, in her useful compilation of Breton's previously unpublished works, is at great pains to deny that the 'will' pun could have anything to do with Will Shakespeare, in spite of the presence of a dedicatory poem signed W.S.[13]

Some secret meaning is hinted at by the typography of this poem: W.S.'s second stanza begins 'Why? What his *UUit*? Proceed and aske his *VVill,/* Why? What his *Will*? proceed and aske his *Wit*'. The 'W's of the first line are printed as first double 'U', then double 'V'. The fact that there is a reference in Harvey's *Pierces Supererogation* (actually in the pamphlet inserted in the middle of that work, *An Advertisement for Papp-hatchett, and Martin Mar-prelate*, dated 1589) to someone called 'Double V' makes it all the more likely that W.S. or Breton insisted on the typography to point up the reference. Harvey says of Double V that he was 'like an other Doctor Faustus', and that his phrases, like 'Tarletons trickes, Eldertons Ballats, Greenes Pamflets, Euphues Similes', are 'too-well knowen, to go unknown'.[14] A second Marlowe, a writer renowned for his phrases – what more do we need to associate Double V with VVilliam Shakespeare?

In the case of another work of Breton's, *Wit's Trenchmour*, it is the relation of the 'Wit' of the title to the contents of the work that demands explanation. The prose work was published in 1597, in the form of a dialogue between a Scholar and an Angler.[15] The consensus is that it sketches the story of Breton's disgrace and expulsion from Mary Sidney's Eden. The fact that it is dedicated to William Herbert is one indicator of its affiliation. And the heroines of both the embedded stories are described in terms that led even Grosart to suspect that Mary Sidney underlies both.[16] The first, Fianta, picks up her book of 'Daplisses' to take on her walk in the garden, which, as Jean Robertson notes, must be (at least) a compliment to Mary who translated Du Plessis' *Discourse of Life and Death* in 1592.[17] In the next story the lady is one whose house is 'in a maner a kind of little Court'.

Grosart also suspected glancing allusion to something in the real world in the tale of the Scholar's downfall, for the details are too ridiculous to be realistic. By 'the faction of the malicious', he fell out of favour with the Lady, and left her court to travel. 'In a cold snowy day passing over an unknowne plaine ... [he] fell so deepe downe into a Saw-pitte, that he shall repent the fall while he lives: for never since daring to presume, but in prayers to think on his faire Princesse.'

Let me suggest a Carpenter motivated the reference to a saw-pit. Edmond Bollifant changed his name to Carpenter. And Edmond Bollifant was the publisher of *Chloris* in 1596, a publication that might well have infuriated Mary Sidney, if our identifications of Chloris and Corin are correct. Robertson assumes that Breton conceals himself under the persona of the Scholar. But Breton rather carefully distinguishes himself from the protagonist by the device of including 'a certeine odde Diogenes', one who has overheard the whole dialogue and writes it down after the Scholar and Angler depart.

And who was the Angler, with whom the Scholar converses? Another publisher, or rather, future publisher, Thomas Fisher. In June 1600, a number of drapers, Thomas Fisher among them, were sworn and admitted freemen of the Stationers' Company.[18] Fisher was not a printer, but a bookseller – of sorts. He sold a grand total of two books on his own account in 1600, and two shared with Matthew Lownes in 1602. One of the 1600 publications was Breton's *Pasquils Mistresse*: the other was Shakespeare's *Midsummer Night's Dream*. The idea that the two 1600 publications are related in some way is quite an attractive one, given these facts. They may have been hard to place with more established booksellers. It is a pattern of publication replicated by Andrew Wise, who was 'everything but an established publisher', according to Erne.[19] He printed five of Shakespeare's plays between 1597 and 1600 (including two that had been 'stayed', or delayed) but only six other works in total, before disappearing from the bookselling world. Two of the six are the 1593 and 1594 editions of Nashe's *Christs Teares*.

It is vaguely recognized that John Lyly's books *Euphues. The Anatomy of Wyt* (1578) and the enlarged edition of that work *Euphues and his England* (1580) have a coterie resonance, since they are explicitly set in that 'Silexedra' to which Thomas Lodge's *Rosalynde* and Greene's *Menaphon* refer on their title pages.[20] *Menaphon*'s alternative title is 'Camilla's Alarm to Slumbering Euphues, in his Melancholy Cell at Silexedra'. The preliminaries to the 1592 edition of *Rosalynde* also refer to Camilla, who is apparently married to a 'Philautus', and has sons (A3v). Camilla and Euphues play roles in Lyly's elaborate dialogues.

The dialogues are generally taken to be anodyne exercises in the elaborate style Lyly was making his own – Euphuism. His Epistle to the Earl of Oxford in *Euphues his England* suggests otherwise. There Lyly worries that 'Euphues would be carped of some curious reader'. For 'curious', understand 'one who sees further into the matter than he or she should do'.

So accepted has 'euphuism' become in our vocabulary that it is easy to be incurious about its derivation. The Greek 'euphues' translates as Elizabethan 'witty', to be sure, but some of the overtones of that word may escape a modern reader. The Greek refers to someone 'naturally' clever as opposed to the 'gegumnasmenos', the trained or educated person. Lyly's protagonist is not an abstract personification of a quality, I believe: he is a real member of the coterie, one who was naturally brilliant, but not university educated.

If, as early as 1578, Lyly means to allude to the presence of Shakespeare in this coterie by 'anatomizing' Wit, that brings out a feature of the phenomenon of contemporary reference to Shakespeare that I have not sufficiently stressed. I have written as though other writers alluded to Shakespeare out of pure admiration for his work. But by 1578, Shakespeare could not have achieved much that Lyly sincerely thought was superlative. Reading the courtly dialogues of Lyly and his imitator Greene makes one aware that flattery of their patrons was an essential part of their aim, and they could not have afforded to ignore a favourite of those patrons.

Current criticism, particularly of Greene, lays far too much stress on his independence and 'modern book market' character. It would be better to consider both him and Lyly as transitional beings between two ages, that of pure patronage and that of the market. They set out in the spirit of the first age, as though they were renaissance Italian courtiers in the court of Urbino for instance, where Castiglione set his 'Courtier', or the court of the Gonzagas of Mantua, to which Greene often alludes. But they then turned their writings to commercial effect, suddenly aware that their tittle-tattle about great families was saleable. They were trying to make ends meet in the harsh modern age – certainly in Greene's case (and he failed, dying in poverty). The point as it applies to Breton's and Lyly's praise of wit is that at the time of writing, they could not have left the person Wit out of their works because young Wit was the court favourite.

To return then to *Christs Teares*: 'Wit hath his dregs, as wel as wine', Nashe remarks to Lady Elizabeth, before embarking on a paragraph full of 'wills' and 'wits' that describes, obliquely, the recent falling-out between Nashe and his friend.

> A young imperfect practitioner am I in Christs schoole. Christ accepteth the will for the deede. Weake are my deedes, great is my will. O that our deedes onely should be seene, and our wil die invisible! / Long hath my intended will (renowned Madam) beene addressed to adore you. But words, to that my

resolved will, were negligent servaunts. My woe-infirmed witte conspired against me with my fortune. My impotent care-crazed stile cast of his light wings and betooke him to wodden stilts. All agility it forgot, and graveld it selfe in grosse-braind formallitie.[21]

On the surface, Nashe excuses himself for not having written something worthy of his patroness, owing to his 'woe'. Covertly, with his harping on the words 'will' and 'wit', he excuses another. The wooden stilts and clumsy grossness refer to some actual work, it is clear; and probably not his own previous work. The 'stile' that cast off his wings is possibly a leaden Mercury. Shakespeare did eventually win a way into the favours of the Carey family through Nashe's promotion, it seems. That is why his tributes to Nashe in the voice of Humphrey King found their way into the Berkeley Castle manuscript, in close proximity to a dedication of the *Hermites Tale*. Was *this* the 'wodden' work to which Nashe refers?

Ending his address to the readers of *Christs Teares*, Nashe bids farewell to all those that wish him well – 'others wish I more wit to'. At the beginning of the main text, he declares 'Mine own wit I cleane disinherite', ostensibly to ask for divine inspiration in writing, rather than rely on his own brain. It seems in truth to mark a low point in the relationship between Nashe and his dear Stones the fool.

Did Shakespeare ever acknowledge his nickname 'Stones'? I believe so, in connection with his childhood, and with his death. In *Merry Wives*, little William Page is put through his paces in Latin grammar, as observed on p. 122 above. Jonathan Bate suggests that the scene recalls the childhood of William the author of the play, and there is an example in it that backs his Suppose.[22] The child William is asked: 'What is *lapis*, William?' and replies correctly 'A stone'. 'Lapis' was the exemplar for the third declension of nouns in the grammar book used in Elizabethan schools. It lends itself to innuendo – 'stone' meant 'testicle'; and indeed, other grammatical terms mentioned by William or Evans are made the subject of bawdy interpretation by Mistress Page. So the scene had its own intrinsic humour. Yet for insiders, the spectacle of little William solemnly reciting his own later nickname would have added to the hilarity.

The inscription on Shakespeare's tombstone has puzzled generations of Shakespeare's biographers. It seems so artless, so frivolous.

GOOD FREND FOR JESUS SAKE FORBEARE,
TO DIGG THE DUST ENCLOSED HERE:
BLESTE BE YE MAN YT SPARES THESE STONES,
AND CURST BE HE YT MOVES MY BONES.

Yet Schoenbaum records that a number of seventeenth-century commentators say that Shakespeare himself devised it and ordered it to be cut on his tombstone.[23] If so, it was his last joke. (If not, a joke on the part of his friends.) For 'these Stones' are equivalent to 'my bones'. 'Here lies Stones', is what the stone says.

Notes

1   Harvey, *Works*, 2.49 (14).
2   *The Diary of John Manningham of the Middle Temple 1602–1603*, ed. R.P. Sorlien (Hanover: N.H., 1976), fol. 29b, pp. 75, 328.
3   Nashe, *Works*, III.25.
4   Davies, *Scourge of Folly*, p. 107, epigram 223. *Works*, 2k, p. 33.
5   Donna Hamilton remarks on this in *Shakespeare and the Politics of Protestant England* (New York: Harvester, 1992), p. 28. David Bergeron describes the vocabulary of the dedication as exemplifying 'the *older* system of patronage': but possibly it was also the system still current in 1623. David Bergeron, 'The King's Men's king's men: Shakespeare and folio patronage', in *Shakespeare and Theatrical Patronage*, ed. Paul Whitfield White and Suzanne Westfall (Cambridge: Cambridge University Press, 2002), pp. 45–63.
6   *LRB*, 22 May (2003), p. 8.
7   For Shakespeare's own interest in the figure of Mercury, see Joseph Porter, *Shakespeare's Mercutio: His History and Drama* (Chapel Hill and London: University of North Carolina Press, 1988), p. 80.
8   Nashe, *Works*, II. 186.
9   *Works*, II.127.
10 *Works*, II.36.
11 *Works*, II. 67.
12 Nicholas Breton, *The Wil of Wit* (London: Thomas Creede, 1597).
13 Jean Robertson, ed., *Poems by Nicholas Breton (not hitherto reprinted)* (Liverpool at the University Press, 1952), intro., p. xli. Grosart thinks the pun is indicative of Shakespeare's authorship: *The Works in Prose and Verse of Nicholas Breton*, ed. A.B. Grosart, 2 vols (Edinburgh: privately printed, 1879), I.2c, 6 (A4), and memorial introduction, p. liv.
14 Harvey, *Works*, 2.206 (131), 2.217 (136).
15 Nicholas Breton, *Wits Trenchmour* (London: J. Roberts for N. Ling, 1597). Breton, *Works*, I.2b.
16 Grosart, memorial introduction, pp. xxvi–xxvii.
17 Robertson, *Breton*, intro., p. xxvi.
18 *Transcript of the Register of the Company of Stationers*, 4 vols (London: privately printed, 1875), 2.725.
19 Erne, *Literary Dramatist*, p. 88. Wise inherited his business and its imprint from John Perrin. Perrin printed *Philippes Venus.* The fact that 'Perrin' kept cropping up in the pastoral poetry studied in Chapter 4 may be coincidental.
20 John Lyly, *Euphues: The Anatomy of Wit* (London: J. Cawood, 1578), and *Euphues and His England* (London: Thomas East for Gabriell Cawood, 1580). Thomas Lodge, *Rosalynde* (London: T. Orwin for T. Gubbins and J. Busbie, 1590).

21 Nashe, *Works*, II.10.
22 Bate, *Genius*, p. 8.
23 Reproduced in Schoenbaum, *Compact Documentary Life*, p. 306.

Chapter 9

R.L.'s Biography

It is time to weave into a coherent web the string of clues gathered in the labyrinth comprising works by and works referring to R.L. It would be useful to have a simple narrative of what R.L. wrote and when; and an outline account of his doings and whereabouts at various stages of his writing life. Conceptually, we are dealing with the biographical aspect of the writing entity or author R.L., be he Borgesian King, Traveller, servant, or lion. At ground level, we have reason to believe we shall be dealing with the biography of William Shakespeare. We start with the 'William Smith' persona.

'Why Brand They Us with Base?'

As in the case of the life of Tristram Shandy, one vital part of the life of William Smith is to be found nine months before his birth. Let us review and enlarge on the facts about the William Smiths of Shakespeare's generation in Stratford.

The younger William of the two Williams in the family of Alderman William Smith the mercer was born, so Fripp tells us, in 1564.[1] So was William Shakespeare; and Fripp supposed that he received the name William from his godfather, a different William Smith, the haberdasher of Henley Street. Shakespeare's birth was registered in April 1564; the younger William Smith's birth was registered in November of that year, according to the consensus.

A William, son of Alderman Smith, was bequeathed a copy of *Aesop's Fables* and a copy of Erasmus' *Apophthegmata* by the Stratford schoolmaster Brechtgirdle, in 1565. A Richard, a Robert, a John, and a Thomas Smith also received books from the schoolmaster, while the daughter Margaret and the youngest William received a shilling each.

The Alderman's will of 1578 listed his sons as 'William Smythe my eldest sonne', Richard Smyth, John Smyth, Thomas Smyth and 'Willm Smythe my youngest sonne'; and mentioned his daughter Margaret.[2] The baptism register, which dates from 1597 when Elizabeth ordered the compilation of all parish registers from the beginning of her reign, and whose data therefore go back as far as 1558, contains: Lewis Smith, 18 August 1558, son to William Smith;

i)

ii)

9.1   **Stratford-on-Avon Baptism Register: i) entry of William Shakespeare's birth, 26 April 1564; ii) entry of W. filius W. Smith, 22 November 1564**

Robert Smith, 1 June 1559, son to William Smith; Margareta filia Gulielmi Smith, 15 September 1561; Thomas Smith, 11 November 1563, filius Gulielmi Smith; and W. filius W. Smith, 22 November 1564.[3]

There is confusion in the records between Richard and Robert, which I shall leave aside. It is the last entry that most concerns us; and 'Lewis' is also of some interest. 'W. filius W.' is quite anomalous, in that both son and father are given only initials, which stand for the names in English. All entries since page 3 of the register, dating from 1560/61, had been in Latin. (English becomes intermixed with Latin again around 1566/67). Only two previous babies and three previous fathers had been entered with initial plus surname, never combined in one entry; and one previous father had been entered as '[blank] cultellari' – a trade description.

Concerning the youngest William, Fripp believes him to be the W. of November 1564. But this is where the anomalies start to become exciting. We approach them through a brother-in-law of the Alderman.

John Watson, Bishop of Winchester, brother of Alderman Smith's second wife, bequeathed twenty marks each to his two nephews the William Smith brothers.[4] He described the younger one as 'scholar at the College'. Watson died in October 1583, but since the will contains codicils, one of which is dated January 1583, we may suppose that it was actually drawn up well before his death, when the younger William was still at Winchester College. By October 1583, this William had entered Exeter College, Oxford, as we shall see.

The Winchester College records show a William Smyth 'de Stratford upon Avon' (without noting his father's name) enrolled on 7 November, 1580.[5] The entries give the boys' ages in terms of the number of years they will reach by the following Michaelmas. William Smith's is given as '12 yeres' by the next Michaelmas, i.e. by September 1581. It was the custom at the College for all scholars to take an oath when they had reached the mature age of fifteen. William Smyth did so, it is recorded, in February 1582/83.[6] The dates are inconsistent: he seems to have gained at least a year over the course of two years, for one who would still be twelve in September 1581 could not have attained the age of fifteen by February 1583. But more importantly, he could not have been born in November 1564, which he should have been if his identity at birth is to connect with his identity at the ages of (roughly) twelve and (roughly) fifteen.

There is, however, a peculiar entry in the Stratford baptism register, which may come to our rescue. On page 13, against 3 August 1566, is the entry 'Gulielmus filius Vincenti faber ferrarii'. There is no other entry like it, as Richard Savage the editor of the printed Register observes. Who is Vincent the

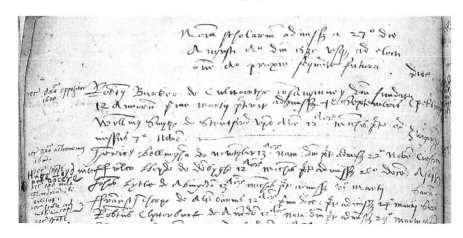

i)

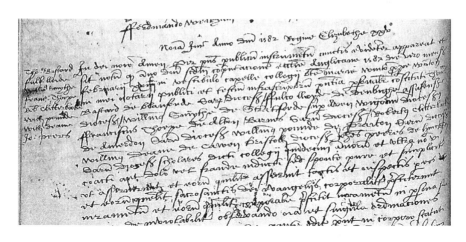

ii)

9.2   **Winchester College Fellows' Library: i) First Register of Scholars, 7 November 1580. MS. Registrum Primum Wint. Coll., p. 94; ii) record of oaths, February 1582/3. MS. Liber prothocollorum de iuramentis Wint. Coll., p. 58. Reproduced by permission of the Warden and Scholars of Winchester College**

9.3 Stratford-on-Avon Baptism Register. Entry of Gulielmus filius Vincenti faber ferrarii, 3 August 1566

Blacksmith? Why does he not have a proper surname? Of course he *does*: it must be 'Smith'. He is apparently not too keen to be recognized as the father of a William in 1566. He was perhaps not too keen to be perspicuous in November 1564 either, when he declared the second William as a W. claiming a W.

I suspect that by August 1566 Alderman Smith already had two Williams. I think the baby W. entered on November 1564 was not newly born, but had been entered in April of that year. He already had a father, John Shakespeare: he ends up with a second father. I suspect, too, that the baby William born legitimately but entered in a covert manner in the 1566 register had to go through his early life being a little reticent about his age. He could pass as eleven or twelve at Winchester in 1580, when he was perhaps actually thirteen or fourteen. He then passed as eighteen on matriculation at Exeter College, Oxford in 1583, when he must have been seventeen. The records show a William Smyth entering Exeter College Oxford on 11 October 1583. He is 'Smythe, William; Worc. (i.e. of Worcester, where the Stratford Smith family had moved in 1578), pleb f. (i.e. son of a commoner) 18'.[7] If the record is meant to register the age attained, this entry aligns this William perfectly with W., the baby registered in November 1564; and that might be why the student William made the claim. But I do not think he was that baby.

It could be that those charged with the transcribing of the existing parish records in 1597 were aware of the old scandal of an excess of Williams in Alderman Smith's family. 'Lewis' does not occur elsewhere in the records. He comes just where the elder William should appear, and in the very year the author of *Gemma fabri* claimed to have been born.[8] A well-meaning attempt to avoid embarrassment could be behind the inscribing of 'Lewis' for 'William', as Alderman Smith's eldest son. Unfortunately, or rather, fortunately, the transcribers picked the wrong entry to tamper with.

Obviously, considering the plethora of Stratford Smiths and the imperfect nature of the records, I cannot prove that the above account is true. As previously mentioned, one clan usefully rules itself out of the reckoning because a third William Smith in the generation before Shakespeare's, the corviser Smith, is always inscribed as 'alias Hoode' (sometimes 'Whood' or 'Wood'). Interesting to note is the frequency with which aliases occur in the records: it was not uncommon to go through life with two surnames. All I have done here is to show the possibility that William Smith, the poet in whom we are so interested, did so. To put it more plainly, I have sketched possible grounds for a vindication of William *Shakespeare's* claim to belong to the gentlemanly Smiths.

The secret of William Shakespeare's birth was not a huge secret to his contemporaries. He himself was partly proud of it when young, partly ashamed, it seems. The literary evidence for both statements is quite strong.

Wilhelm Schrickx noted that George Chapman (whose plays, we have seen, reveal knowledge of Shakespeare's early life) offers a misleading gloss on a 'double-fathered son' in his poem *Shadow of the Night* (1594).[9] This poem is so obscure that to quote it will hardly help to bring out the peculiarity that Schrickx noted. The lines that give rise to the gloss are nevertheless important:

> Come Goddess come, the double fathered sonne
> Shall dare no more amongst thy traine to runne
> Nor with polluted handes to touch thy vaile:
> His death was darted from the Scorpions taile,
> For which her forme to endlesse memorie
> With other lamps, doth lend the heavens an eye,
> And he that showd such great presumption,
> Is hidden now, beneath a little stone.
>
> (E1r)

The gloss given by Chapman himself is this: 'The double-fathered sonne is Orion, so cald since he was the sunne of Iove and Appollo, borne of their seede enclosed in a Bulls hide ...'. But, says Schrickx, the legend as given in Natalis

Comes, from whom Chapman derives it, gives Orion three fathers, not two. 'Orion fuit Neptuni & Iovis & Apollonis filius.' Why does Chapman alter the legend? To refer to Shakespeare, according to Schrickx, who connects it with the fact that in the 1603 quarto of *Hamlet*, Hamlet calls Claudius 'father'.

Schrickx must be right to search for some motivation for the switch to two fathers, but his explanation does not convince.[10] I would look instead to William Shakespeare's paternity. Something has likewise been altered in Chapman's account of Orion's fate. He becomes not the constellation, but someone hidden beneath a little stone. This may be because the historical person intended by Chapman went through life as a humble Stone.

Chapman's play *The Gentleman Usher* shows a similar knowledge, or knowing-ness. The lord called Vincentio asks lowly Bassiolo the usher to call him 'Vince', 'As they call Iacke or Will, 'tis now in use/ Twixt men of no equallity or kindnesse'.[11] 'Kindness' can mean 'kinship': the joke may point beyond the confines of the play to a kinship between Vincentio – the name of the mysterious Stratford 'Blacksmith' – and Jack or Will. The 'poesie' from 'August' on the occasion of Cuddie's carrying off the prize comes to mind: 'Vincenti gloria victi'. In Chapman's *Monsieur D'Olive* we find Rhodoricke saying to D'Olive: 'Goe too, we must have you follow the lanthorne of your forefathers'. Mugeron remarks 'His forefathers? S'body had hee more fathers then one', pretending to have misheard 'four fathers'.[12] It could be a feeble joke, following on from a series of jokes about D'Olive's father being a bachelor and a cuckold. But it could be a joke about the real-life person who underlies the dramatic character D'Olive, the too-richly-fathered 'Elaion'.

To Chapman's evidence we can add a remark of Nashe's addressed to Richard Lichfield. He speaks of 'the redundance of thy honorable Familie, and how affluent and copious thy name is in all places, though *Erasmus* in his *Copia verborum* never mentions it'.[13] Nashe has smoothed his joke seamlessly into his text so that it appears to make perfect sense to move to Erasmus' book *De Copia* via 'copiousness'. Yet it may be his reference was motivated by his understanding of the Spenserian joke about 'Erasimus' the good old father. Being used to Nashe's exuberant style, we also tend to grant him the word 'redundance' in this context, assuming he means to link it with the word 'honourable', to give the sense 'superabundant in honour'. But 'the redundance of thy family' strictly means 'the superabundance of your family'. He is addressing the man we believe (on other grounds) to be Shakespeare. And the fact that he ascribes a superfluity of family to Shakespeare is significant.

Nashe may be revealing inner knowledge of Shakespeare's family again when he drags into his *Unfortunate Traveller* the fact that 'Cato, one of the wisest men in Romane Histories canonised, was not borne till his father was four score yeres olde'.[14] If this was a commonly known fact about Cato the Elder, he could have functioned as a useful figure for the aged but polyphiloprogenitive Alderman Smith. It is suggestive that Edmond Bollifant published a translation of 'the short sentenc'ez of Cato' by the William Bullokar who so concerned himself with English orthography. The work took the form of poetic advice from Cato the Elder to his son, and was appended to the *Aesopz Fablz* translated by Bullokar in 1585. The Register of the Stationers records a decree of December 1595, fining Bollifant and his partners for the 'disorderly' printing of 'CATO', and imprisoning Bollifant himself.[15] This is rather draconian, and by the same token rather puzzling. We are at the furthest reaches of speculation here, peering through the cobwebs of association between Aesop and Cato, Cato and Erasmus.

E.K./Spenser, when speaking of the ungodliness of old men in his gloss to Cuddie's motto in 'Februarie', mentioned in one breath Aesop and 'Erasimus' that 'great clerke', a good father who construed things so fatherly. The irregularities in the Stratford baptism register go some way to underpinning these insinuations concerning Cuddie. William Smith the Alderman was the most highly educated 'clerkly' man in his home town. One of his two (or three) sons called William came into possession of *Aesop's Fables* and Erasmus' *Apophthegmata.* We cannot ever *know* which William Smith kept possession of which of the Stratford schoolmaster's gifts. But it is strange that the younger William, like the only girl in the family, was bequeathed a shilling rather than a precious book. Most of the other boys in the family were also of pre-school age, and therefore not pupils known personally to Brechtgirdle.[16] Perhaps the girl and the bastard shared a lower status.

It may be that the tendency of those who wrote in Shakespeare's praise to insist he was 'Nature's child' should be subjected to more searching scrutiny. A natural child is an illegitimate child. Ben Jonson's tribute in the First Folio mentions Nature four times in eleven lines as Shakespeare's progenitor. Equally, when Jonson turns to the subject of family likeness, what we have read metaphorically could in fact be far more knowing and literal.

> For a good *Poet's* made, as well as borne.
> And such wert thou. Look how the fathers face
> Lives in his issue, even so, the race
> Of Shakespeare's minde, and manners brightly shines
> In his well torned, and true-filed lines.
>
> (lines 64–8)

We naturally take the 'children' of this trope to be Shakespeare's lines, bearing his lineaments in their faces. But notice how uncertain it is whether Jonson considers Shakespeare more 'made' than 'born' a poet. Covertly, Jonson could be saying that Shakespeare's (true) father's character shines in the son. The metaphors of good 'turning' and 'filing' often applied to writing would, when literalized, have special applicability to Smiths.

· The shift from the parentage of works (overt meaning) to the parentage of the author (concealed meaning) is present, I am convinced, in Immerito's envoi 'To his booke' at the opening of the *Shepheardes Calender.* The book was sent 'as child whose parent is unkent' to present itself to its patron. 'But if that any aske thy name,/ Say thou wert base begot with blame:/ For thy thereof thou takest shame'.[17] There is no reason to deprecate the little book quite so much: why should it be 'base begot', 'blameworthy' and 'shamed'? Because the concealed author, the one responsible for the best lyrics in the work, fits that description.

Shakespeare's pride in his more elevated family appears in the fact that he used the surname Smith when he was a humble servitor offering Mary Sidney his New Year manuscripts, and when publishing *Chloris.* I believe that his *King John* displays the same feeling. It has already been suggested that *The Troublesome Reign* (its antecedent) is Shakespeare's, and has the marks of the militant Protestantism of his patrons, being violently anti-Catholic – indeed *King John* itself is moderately so. I deduce that he was very young when he wrote it: and it is therefore interesting that the Bastard Faulconbridge's attitude to his paternity is unashamed. He exonerates his mother completely for succumbing to a man of great talent and high standing. He claims his high parentage at the cost of his potential inheritance from his nominal father.

Faulconbridge was (historically) the son of Richard Coeur de Lion. Critics have been puzzled by his role in the drama, larger than life (and than Faulconbridge's historical role) and somewhat inconsistent.[18] To suppose that Shakespeare projects himself into the character is to offer a plausible explanation for the exaggerations, an explanation in keeping with his adoption of the falcon (later) for the Shakespeare coat of arms. Possibly he even played the part before the aristocrats who first saw the play, making an in joke dependent on others' knowledge of his personal aspirations. I am convinced he played the part of another 'Faulconbridge', the Lord Talbot of *Henry VI, Part 1*. Critics have been a little puzzled by the long roll-call of Talbot's titles, of which 'Faulconbridge' is one, given by the character Sir William Lucy at Talbot's death. So extreme is it that another character is made to mock it. But no one has evinced much puzzlement at the Countess's description of Talbot as 'a child, a silly dwarf ... a weak and writhled shrimp' (II.3.21–2). There is simply no justification in history for this extreme belittling of Talbot. Both anomalies find their rationale in extra-dramatic circumstances, I suggest. If Talbot was played by the writer/actor calling himself 'Faulconbridge', and if that actor himself was still an adolescent, the motivation for the title and the description becomes clear.

Shakespeare's unabashed confidence that blue-blood trumps bastardy suffered some knocks, it seems. Or perhaps he was always ambivalent, and his plays express now one response to his circumstances, now another. (I believe the former is nearer the mark.)

King Lear's Edmund is Gloucester's illegitimate son, and much weight is placed on the moment of his conception (I.1.11–23), many lines given to Edmund himself to ponder why bastardy should be called 'base', why it should not be an enviable status, arising as it does out of true passion, not dull marital duty (I.2.1–22). The emphasis does not perhaps go beyond the needs of rendering the character lifelike: but there is one factor in Edmund's circumstances that goes beyond dramatic necessity, and is in fact puzzling. Edmund complains that he has been deprived of his inheritance because of his illegitimacy, when he is also a younger son who on that count alone would not have inherited. Critics have noticed this, but not pressed the point.[19] Yet it requires pressing to reveal how the logic of the situation fails to match the text's logic.

Shakespeare contrives to obfuscate not only which brother is the elder, but also where the fault of adultery lies. Was Edmund born as a result of his father's or his mother's adultery? Gloucester's first words in answer to the question 'Is not this your son, my Lord?' are 'His breeding, Sir, hath been at my charge' – which one expects to be followed by something like 'but he is not mine by blood'. His next words reinforce that impression: he states that Edmund's mother 'had a son for a cradle ere she had a husband for a bed'. Yet towards the end of the play, Edgar tells his dying half-brother that Gloucester's blinding was the price paid for his begetting of Edmund. When Lear reflects that Gloucester's bastard son was kinder to his father than his own legitimate daughters were to him, he hints at the first interpretation of Edmund's relationship to Gloucester once again: the question for debate *ought* to be the question of blood relationship versus nurture.

If Gloucester's wife had her illegitimate child before she had a husband, then Edmund was the older of the two brothers. Yet immediately after making that pleasantry, Gloucester describes his true-born son as a being a year older than Edmund. Edmund is, I think, *both* the younger and the older son; both adopted by his father, and misbegotten by his father. He offers a realistic picture of Shakespeare's two states, one overlaid on the other, in his two families.

But Edgar reflects that same state. Philip Sidney's parallel story to that of Edgar and Gloucester in the *New Arcadia* (in Book 2.10) has as protagonists the blind king of Paphlagonia and his son, Leonatus. 'Leo-natus' is 'son of the Lion' – like Faulconbridge the son of Coeur de Lion.

There was an earlier *Lear, The True Chronicle History of King Leir*, which is known to have been both entered for publication and performed (as *King Leare*) in 1594. Strong arguments for seeing these two as one and the same play by Shakespeare have been made by E.B. Everitt and R.L. Armstrong.[20] To their evidence we might add that the printer Jane Bell assumed a right to print Shakespeare's (later) *King Lear* in 1655 on the basis of a right she held to print the anonymous *King Leir*.[21] I claim, therefore, that Shakespeare's first composition of his plays on ancient Britain (*Lear, Cymbeline* and *Macbeth*) come from the same period as each other – very early in his writing career.

The darker responses to a mother's infidelity come with *Hamlet.* The horror Hamlet feels at his mother's liaison with Claudius is vividly expressed. Many readers have felt a weight of meaning in the play, and particularly in that aspect of it, that goes beyond the requirements of dramatic necessity. Did the child author, as he grew in moral stature, come to think more deeply about his adoptive father's disgrace and suffering, and for that reason, start to identify himself as a Shakespeare rather than a Smith as he had done during adolescence? Did he project into the play his fantasies of avenging his 'father' John Shakespeare?

One who was sent out as a page early in life would have lost touch with his mother; and that may account for the marked absence of mothers in Shakespeare's plays. But there may be more to it: a deliberate elision of mothers, owing to the early trauma of knowing his mother unfaithful and himself illegitimate. I reserve for a moment those romances in which a mother *re*appears clothed in a saintly aura.

'A Mercer Ye Wot az We Be'

The Kenilworth R.L. insisted on his affiliation with mercers. He had to, of course, since he was posing as Robert Langham, who was in the Company. But the stress on the fact seems overdone: at the end of the *Letter*, he devotes more than a page to showing off his knowledge of St Paul's and St Antony's (Mercers' schools), and his acquaintance with a large number of prestigious

Table 9.1   Captain Cox's Library and Shakespeare's Memory

Cox's Library	*Shakespeare's memory*
Gargantua	*AYLI*, III.2.210. Gargantua's mouth
Malory's *Morte d'Arthur*	Mistress Quickly: *Henry V* II.3.9 et seq.
The Squire of Low Degree	Fluellen: *Henry V*, V.1.34
Sir Eglamour	*Two Gentlemen of Verona*, IV.3
A Hundred Merry Tales	Beatrice: *Much Ado*, II.1.112–13
Robin Hood	*Two Gentlemen of Verona*, IV.1.36; *2 Henry IV*, V.3.102; *AYLI*, I.1.106–9
Adam Bell	*Much Ado*, I.1.224
The Wife Wrapped in a Morell Skin	Motif of *Taming of the Shrew*
Song 'Hey ding a ding'	*AYLI*, V.3.14 et seq.

as well as minor individual mercers. Possibly his motive was to insist on his more elevated paternity, for William Smith the Alderman of Stratford was a draper and mercer. Sons were frequently taken into their father's guild. Indeed, in Elizabeth's time, the guilds were already packed with honorary members who were not practising their respective crafts. I am not suggesting that this William Smith/Shakespeare ever did join the Mercers; simply that he saw himself as 'belonging' to them when he was a child.[22]

The store-house of the child R.L.'s brain is intriguing. Much of it came from the library of Captain Cox. Edgar Fripp observes that much of Shakespeare's did too.[23]

Some of these tales would have been well known to all, of course. The connection between *Frederyck of Jennen*, seen by R.L. in Cox's library, and Shakespeare's *Cymbeline* is more singular. The parallels are highlighted by J.M. Nosworthy.[24] Shakespeare follows the old story closely, sometimes preferring its version to that of the same folk-tale in Boccaccio.[25] His play mirrors incidents in *The Rare Triumphs of Love and Fortune*, which was apparently performed in 1582, and was printed in 1589. 'Precisely what led Shakespeare to this ramshackle old play' Nosworthy does not pretend to know, but he is sure the parallels are non-coincidental.[26] One possibility that has not been considered is that the ramshackle play was Shakespeare's first version of what became the *Cymbeline* whose earliest mention is in 1611, and whose date of composition has accordingly been placed in 1608/09. I offer the following arguments for very early composition of the play.

One of the episodes in *Cymbeline*, that of the old man and his sons holding a narrow track against the might of Rome, comes from the chronicle histories of *Macbeth*. This alone inclines me to place the two plays in the same period of Shakespeare's imaginative growth.

Then *Cymbeline*'s author is rather ignorant about the state of Europe in Roman times. Though Holinshed's account of Cymbeline's reign is confused and uncertain, it does not present us with the simultaneous existence of Italians, Frenchmen, Dutch, Spaniards and *Romans*, as Shakespeare does. Young Shakespeare is equally ignorant of Roman naming practice: if 'Leonatus' was the protagonist Posthumus's father's cognomen, it would have been a personal tribute and would not have become the son's first name. This ignorance contrasts with the more mature understanding of the Roman world displayed in *Julius Caesar*, *Antony and Cleopatra* and *Coriolanus*, whose author does understand that Caius Marcus Coriolanus won his cognomen at Corioli.

The political tone of the play is likewise indicative of the Sidneian era. Rome is set against Britain. The Romans invade via Milford Haven, which is historically where Henry VII landed to institute the Tudor reign. The 'Romans' of the play, I therefore suggest, stand for the alien Tudors. Posthumus the lowly orphaned gentleman beloved by the heroine Imogen finds himself on both sides. He mediates between Romans (Tudors) and Britons. The 'Britons', then, are the Tudors' opponents, the Dudleys.

If we recall how Jonson portrayed Mercury as breaking free of his masters the Alchemists, and how Armin had the Tailor's Boy break from his master, I think we may descry in *Cymbeline* a trace of a conflict Shakespeare experienced between his upbringing as a Leicestrian and a strong desire he felt that the Elizabethan settlement should succeed. Whether this was due to a reconciling temperament, or because John Shakespeare was a Catholic (if he was), or through revulsion from the Dudleian crimes he had witnessed, or because he had actually served the Queen, who requisitioned Leicester's best players on forming her own company in 1583, I shall not attempt to decide.

Most striking, in view of the leonine connections of the Bastard Faulconbridge and Edgar, is Posthumus' family name, Leonatus – the 'lion-born'. *Why* Shakespeare saw his secret self as a lion or lion descendant is necessarily a matter of speculation. I speculate that it was overdetermined.[27] He perhaps saw himself as Guy of Warwick, an irremediably proletarian character (unlike most other heroes, who turn out to be princes in disguise), who according to legend was accompanied by a lion. 'Our Mercury' in alchemical lore was the Green Lion, sometimes shown uniting with the Moon in an act of 'Coitus'.[28] Shakespeare, we have argued, was seen as 'Mercury'.

The figure of the Green Lion might be useful in explaining two debated lines in Shakespeare's Sonnet 112: 'For what care I who calles me well or ill/ So you ore-greene my bad, my good allow?' This is the sonnet, interestingly, in which he speaks of the 'vulgar scandal' with which his brow is stamped – the scandal of illegitimacy? I think so: reread the first of those lines thus: 'For what care I who calls me Will or Will', i.e. Will Smith or Will Shakespeare.

That Shakespeare did encode himself as a lion is made incontrovertible, in my opinion, by his Sonnet 94, 'They that have power to hurt and will do none'. Embedded in the opening line is the emblem 'posse et nolle virtutis' – 'it is the part of a virtuous man to have power, but not exercise it'. That was the emblem of the family of Sir John Salusbury of Lleweni – the White Lion. The sonnet closes with the line 'Lilies that fester smell far worse than weeds', a proverb uttered in those identical words by the Countess of *Salisbury* in Shakespeare's *Edward III.* Intermediate lines of the sonnet refer to those 'who do not do the thing they most do show' – like those who portray bloody deeds on stage; who 'moving others, are themselves as stone' – as Stone, who moves others with his tragedies; and who are lords and owners of themselves, while *others* are merely stewards of their excellence – implying a reversal of expectations, an arrogation of a noble virtue on the part of one who was an usher or steward.

The Sonnet is not in fact number 94, but number XCIV. In a recent article, Marjorie Garber has demonstrated how Elizabethans played 'crossword-like' games with Roman numerals.[29] I advocate reading the numerals of the sonnet backwards, as WI–SX, i.e. Wi[lliam] Shks. It was Shakespeare's emblem sonnet, his 'manifesto'.

That Salusbury connection would seem to be woven intricately into the texture of Shakespeare's early works, both in the plays mentioned above, and in a work I think was also Shakespeare's. In *Loves Martyr* or *Rosalins Complaint*, written ostensibly by the Robert Chester who was in John Salusbury's circle, there is embedded a poetic history of Arthur.[30] It deals with the period of history of Lear and Cymbeline: Lucius the Roman consul demands tribute, and the kings of the various principalities of Britain, including the King of 'Albania' (Albany or Scotland) and the Duke of Cornwall, urge Arthur to resist. The history is in iambics, and is headed with its own preface to the 'curteous Reader', set off from the rest and given particular prominence by the title page of the whole, which advertises 'the first *Essay* of a new *Brytish* Poet'. (For 'British', read 'not Roman/Tudor but Dudleian'.) It seems plain to me that the author of the Essay and the author of the whole are being flagged as different individuals.

There is not space here to demonstrate how the publication uses Chester and Salusbury simply as front-men for a collection that was deeply Sidneian (published by Field and Blount, and with appended poems by Jonson, Chapman, Marston, Ignoto and Shakespeare), and had reference to Philip's death and the Turtle Dove Robert Sidney's love for the female phoenix, his sister Mary, or 'Rosalin'. Nor can I do more than sketch grounds for considering whether the witty Euphues of Lyly's, Greene's and Lodge's work, who dwelt in his lone cell at Silexedra, was at one time in his life in service with the Salusburys of Denbigh, which is almost Flintshire (silex-hedra). Potential evidence lies in a manuscript poem addressed to John Salusbury, discussed by Tom Lloyd-Roberts and Jeremy Griffiths.[31] The two-part poem is signed 'Danielle' after each part, probably playing on the notion of Daniel in the lions' den. Lloyd-Roberts and Griffiths adduce much circumstantial evidence, the first arguing for Shakespeare's authorship, the second sceptical. What they have not observed is that 'goodwill' appears twice in the penultimate stanza of the second part of the poem; and perhaps more significantly, in the margin of the first part, John Salusbury himself wrote four lines of doggerel verse of which the last two lines are: 'defende mee from my enimies/ And from ther raginge will'.

It should not be surprising that investigation of the lion motif should have led us directly to the phoenix motif. The quintessential sixteenth-century phoenixes were the Sidneys. In *Cymbeline*, Leonatus the lion-born loves a phoenix, as editors all note, for Imogen is a phoenix, 'alone th' Arabian bird' (I.7.17). Posthumus' vision contains a cedar tree symbolizing Cymbeline, and Nosworthy makes it plain that the Elizabethans connected this tree (and the sun, to which King Cymbeline is also compared) to the Phoenix and its tree in the city of the sun, Heliopolis. At that point in his commentary, Nosworthy turns for confirmation to a sonnet of … William Smith!

> The Phoenix fair which rich Arabia breeds,
> When wasting time expires her tragedy;
> No more on Phoebus' radiant rayes she feeds:
> But heapeth up great store of spicery;
> And on a lofty tow'ring cedar tree,
> With heavenly substance, she herself consumes.[32]

Armed with knowledge of the way these leonine manifestations of Shakespeare often occur in phoenix contexts, we can face again some of the mysteries of *Lear*. The playwright consciously evokes the Oedipus story, in having Edgar lead his blinded father to the 'right' place for his death (as in Sophocles' *Oedipus Coloneus*), and Cordelia immured and then hanged (as in *Antigone*). Seneca's *Thebais*, the medium through which Shakespeare would probably have known the story, opens with a scene in which blind Oedipus asks Antigone to let him stumble over a precipice. The target of these evocations is the incestuous Sidney family. I indicated above that Shakespeare also wove his own story (a leonine one) into the play. The two aspects – the secrets of his patrons and the intensely personal – come together in the names of Cordelia and Lear himself. Cordelia's legendary name was Cordeill, Cordeilla, or Cordell – not the same as 'Cor de lia', which is aurally a 'cor de lion'. Lear is a 'leo'.

Transition

What has to be accommodated next into R.L.'s biography if he is to fit exactly into Shakespeare's profile are his polishing in Italy, and his staging of the dramas of the more recent history of England.

Nashe provides useful links from page to traveller to English (rather than British) dramatist, in the person of his Jack Wilton, the hero of *The Unfortunate Traveller*. Nashe opens with an 'Induction' (surely a very theatrical term) to 'the dapper Mounsier Pages of the Court', in which their fellow Jack Wilton, the protagonist, is labelled the 'king of Pages'. Every time the pages pass a stationers' shop, Nashe declares, they should revere their 'grand printed Capitano' (sc. a printed 'page') who is there entombed. There is probably more to the pun than a mere verbal quibble: Jack is supreme among pages or books – 'a literary master'.

Jack is at one and the same moment a young page and a man performing acts of derring-do, first in France as a camp-follower. 'About that time that the terror of the world and feaver quartane of the French, *Henrie* the eight (the onely true subiect of Chronicles), advanced his standard against the two hundred and fifty towers of *Turney* and *Turwin* ... I, *Iacke Wilton*, (a Gentleman at least,) was a certain kind of an appendix or page, belonging or appertaining in or unto the confines of the English court.'[33] Later he accompanies his master round Italy, steals his mistress, and has various adventures during which scenes and lines from plays of Shakespeare are parodied to great effect.

Harvey's Letterbook, studied above, indicated the existence of a dramatic programme for the Leicestrian coterie around 1580: to 'exemplify' the acts of the English kings. When discussing Marlowe's *Edward II*, I proposed that a number of dramatists, Shakespeare most prolific among them, carried out that programme. The proposal needs further argument before we examine whether Shakespeare's history plays can be convincingly fitted into such a schema.

Peele's *dramatis personae* in his *Edward I* constitute a roll call of Dudley names and ancestors. The opening scene has Edward I asking for money to found a 'colledge' for soldiers wounded abroad. This is a complete anachronism: but Robert Dudley did found such a hospital in Amsterdam in 1587. Peele is quietly mapping the figure of Dudley onto that of Edward. Many have questioned whether Peele puns on Shakespeare's name in the lines 'Shake thy speres in honour of his name'.[34] It may be that Shakespeare was seen as the prime mover in the overall project, and that is why the others insert covert reference to him in their plays. If this is correct, it might explain something in a work of Francis Bacon's which has lent great support to those who think Bacon was the real Shakespeare. On the title page of Bacon's prose *Henry VII* – a work that fills what would otherwise be a gap in the English history series – is an illustration showing a figure in actor's buskins, grasping a spear. It is tempting to see in this an allusion to a 'player' who is associated with a spear. The allusion may be to Shakespeare as 'author' in the Elizabethan sense of 'inspirer' of the work.

How could Shakespeare's history plays fit the pro-Dudley, anti-Elizabeth programme? Leah Marcus has demonstrated how Joan of Arc in *Henry VI, Part 1* is clearly meant to embody Elizabeth.[35] Towards the end of the play, Joan is called 'Astraea's daughter': Elizabeth was often portrayed as Astraea. 'Almost incredibly' remarks Marcus, 'the two Frenchmen she [Joan] confesses to have taken as lovers are the duke of Alençon and the duke of Anjou (Reignier) – precisely the names of the two noblemen Elizabeth had come closest to marrying … These highly charged details are not to be found in Shakespeare's source', she notes. The play was not printed in quarto, probably because it was too 'daungerous'. Nor was *King John*, in which the villain king also masks Elizabeth (though the anonymous *Troublesome Reign of King John* was printed). Honigmann logs the parallels, including the excommunication of the monarch by the Pope; the fact that the monarch was barred from the crown by a will (supporters of Lady Jane Grey had claimed the same at Mary Tudor's accession, and by extension, it would apply to Elizabeth); and the Armada-like wrecking of the ships of a would-be invader.[36]

It is commonly believed that the Queen herself believed that Shakespeare portrayed her as Richard in his *Richard II.* And *Henry IV* and *Henry V* would map easily onto Sidney history. Young Hal as a Philip figure, consorting with low-life characters such as Shakespeare himself, before taking on princely responsibilities, is arguably young Sidney. Many critics have felt tempted to identify Falstaff with Shakespeare. Empson, for example, feels a quasi-tragic depth of meaning in Falstaff's prophecy that Hal will throw him over when he becomes King; and a truly tragic moment in the fulfilment of the prophecy.[37] That strength of feeling could be due to the absolute reality of Shakespeare's fear. The shape of the name 'Fall-staff', like a limp version of 'Shake-spear', has been remarked on by Fleissner.[38] And we have seen above that as an old lad, Shakespeare was readily identifiable with the Old Lad of the Castle, Oldcastle, whose name Shakespeare was constrained to alter to 'Falstaff'.

The Salic Law discussed so earnestly at the opening of *Henry V* matches Philip Sidney's insistence in his 'Defence of Leicester' on his own high descent on his *mother*'s side (the Dudley side).[39] Sidney glosses over the question of whether the Dudleys really derived from the noble Suttons at all; and claims that 'in law of heraldry', as opposed to 'the quiddities of our law', descent should be traced through the eldest daughter. This is a dart aimed at the Queen's claim to rule postulated on her inheritance through the male line of the Tudors. Sidney's 'Defence' is patently *not* what it was supposed to be – a rebuttal of the allegations in the anonymous *Leicesters Commonwealth* (1584) that Leicester was plotting to seize power – but a vindication of his uncle's fitness to rule.[40]

In *Henry VIII*, a clever sleight of hand is performed: Henry stands in for Elizabeth. Wolsey's plan to marry the king to the Duchess of Alençon cannot but be pertinent to Burleigh's plan for Elizabeth to marry the Duc d'Alençon. Nashe's remark about Henry VIII being the only true subject of chronicles is evidence that Shakespeare's 'All is True' – the alternative title for his *Henry VIII* – existed in 1594, though modern editors place it close to 1613.[41] Yet Henslowe's Diary provides evidence for a *Henry VIII* of about 1600. There is an entry in a detailed list of stage props for 'Hary ye viii gowne', which R. A. Foakes dates to 1598 or 1602.[42]

'The reversion to the epic chronicle at the end of Shakespeare's career is odd', admits E. K. Chambers.[43] It would have been, had it happened. But *Henry VIII* must have been an old Shakespearean play, turned over to Fletcher to rewrite close to 1613. The extraordinary absence of Edmund and John Dudley, Robert Dudley's grandfather and father, from the cast of Henry's advisers suggests strenuous rewriting of history on Shakespeare's part. Shakespeare's Dudleys, I believe, were already encoded elsewhere in his play. The emphasis on granting Ann Boleyn the title 'Countess of Pembroke' points us to the true Dudleian element. The grant is historically accurate: but a different Countess of Pembroke was probably in Shakespeare's mind. For when the nurse in *Henry VIII* announces the birth of a child to Ann, the Countess, her first words imply, remarkably, that Henry has been blessed with a son. Of course the baby was not a son, but the daughter Elizabeth. Yet that instant of puzzlement allows an audience to see into the author's motives. He was insinuating that Mary Sidney's child, William Pembroke (born in 1580), was to be the future ruler of England. The child is praised effusively as a Phoenix, in a long speech of prophecy by Cranmer into which are wound the themes of the sun and the cedar tree, as in *Cymbeline.* By this time the baby has been identified as Elizabeth. But these phoenix markers suggest to me that the speech subtly insinuates a hoped-for Dudley history in place of the actual Tudor history, and is part of the original play, not inserted later in the hope that Elizabeth would be taken as the referent.

The Dudleian servant R.L. could not by 1580 have written all or perhaps any of those Shakespearean plays *as we have them.* But he could have written their prototypes, then or soon thereafter. In more recent history, the Argentine poet Juan Gelman published his first volume of poems at the age of eleven. Rimbaud wrote the poem 'Le soleil était encore chaud' aged ten, and by nineteen had produced his best work and stopped writing. As for the sixteenth-century, Michael Drayton's ambitions at the age of ten are instructive. He came to his tutor, he relates, when he was 'a proper goodly page,/ (Much like a pigmy, scarce ten years of age)', and begged him: 'Can you/Make me a poet? Do it if you can,/And you shall see I'll quickly be a man'.[44]

Schoolmaster in the Country

John Aubrey thought Shakespeare was a schoolmaster in the country in his youth.[45] And so he was, as Thomas Howell reveals. Howell, who dedicated *H. his Devices* to Mary Sidney in 1581, addresses a sonnet in answer to four bitter lines penned by A.W. about the poverty and hard work he endures.

> If nipping neede Legittimus constraynde,
> in hande to grype the heauie Hammer great;
> With whiche through wante his Princely corps he paynde,
> on stythie hard, in Vulcans trade to beat.
> If he (I say) of crowned king the sonne,
> by fate was forste such bitter blastes to bide:
> Dispaire not thou thy wrackfull race to runne,
> for welth as shade from eche estate doth hide.
> Pluck up thy harte, thy hap not yet so harde,
> since Princes great haue felt a fall more deepe:
> King Dionise from regall rule debarde,
> for his reliefe a Grammer schoole did keepe.

By which thou mayste thy wandring minde suffise,
That fortunes wheele now up, now down doth rise.[46]

Howell is implying that since 'Legittimus' had to labour like a smith, and Dionysus had to teach at a grammar school, A.W., who is *illegitimate* and a Smith, must resign himself to Dionysus' fate. The school in question, however, was not in Lancashire and the poor teacher was not William Shakeshafte.[47] It was on the Essex/Hertfordshire borders, and the poor teacher was William Smith, alias A.W. We take up the trail once more with Nashe, and with Harvey.

Not all school teachers were graduates; but Shakespeare came very close to taking a degree at Cambridge under the aegis of Gabriel Harvey. We saw that Covell writes him *into the margins* of Cambridge – which is exactly where he belongs. Nashe, pretending to be speaking of Harvey, shows us that Shakespeare almost 'disputed for his degree' there.

> So it is that a good Gowne and a well pruned paire of moustachios, having studied sixteene yeare to make thirteen ill english Hexameters, came to the University Court regentum & non, to sue for a commission to carry two faces in a hoode: they not using to deny honour to any man that deserved it, bad him performe all the schollerlike ceremonies and disputative right appertaining thereto, and he should be installed.
>
> *Noli me tangere*: he likt none of that.
>
> A stripling that hath an indifferent prety stocke of reputation abroad in the worlde already, and some credit amongst his neighbours, as he thinketh, would be loth to ieoperd all at one throwe at the dice.
>
> If hee should have disputed for his degree, discended *in arenam et pulverem Philosophicum*, and have beene foild, Aih me, quoth Wit in lamentable sort, what should have become of him? hee might have beene shot through ere hee were aware, with a Sillogisme.[48]

This is manifestly more about a stripling of sixteen (Wit?) who has already impressed those around him with his poetic essays than it is about Harvey. Wit tries to slip past in another's hood – Harvey's hood, in fact, as so often before in the *Familiar Letters* – under the name 'Master G.H.'

That failure to present for a degree did not prevent our hero from setting out boldly into the country to teach in 1580. We see Harvey at the end of the second Commendable letter sending out into the world a protégé, *not* his addressee Spenser, since he is describing *to* Spenser this third person. Harvey has high hopes for this fellow, 'il pellegrino' ('the traveller'), who enjoys 'My Lords

Honor, the expectation of his friendes, his owne credit and preferment'. He harps on 'travellers' and 'travel' a good while longer, prompting the suspicion that for him, this descriptive had a particular referent in the world.

Could this be Nashe's unfortunate traveller? It could indeed. Appended to Harvey's last letter are some poems in Latin, whose relevance is at first utterly mysterious. The first poem was made by Doctor Norton for Thomas Sackford; the next (also in Latin) was made by Doctor Gouldingham at the request of 'olde M. Withypoll of Ipswiche'. The next two are English translations of the verses, one by old Maister Withypol himself, one by 'Master G.H., at M. Peter Withypolles request, for his Father'.

Edmund Withypoll lived in Ipswich at the time, but with his father Paul he had purchased the 'Rectory and Church of Walcomstowe [Walthamstow] and the patronage of the Vicarage of the Parish Church of Walcomstowe' in 1544.[49] He and his son Peter (born 1549) were excellent scholars. The family had received their grant of the 'Rectory Manor', as the Walthamstow property was called, from Henry VIII. It had previously belonged to George Monoux, also called Monox, who had founded a school there in 1527. It still exists as the George Monoux School.

After the Reformation, the first schoolmaster in the parish of whom there is any record is John Matthew, who died in 1609/10. We would dearly like to know who served as masters before him. The information is not available: but there is a useful lacuna in the records concerning the vicar. The vicar used to hold the Vicarage Fields as 'copyhold' of the Rectory Manor: each vicar on entering his post had to seek admission and pay a fine. The Court Records show that by 28 April 1578, the vicar George Johnson was dead and 'no one came to take up that land and make fine for the sume according to the custom of this Manor'.[50] The land was not taken up again until November 1601, when John Reynolds was admitted to their possession. A note says that Reynolds was vicar from 1583–1612. How the copyhold practice lapsed is of less interest than the question: Who was vicar between 1578 and 1583? Why do the records not contain his name?

We have a candidate to fill that gap, if certain assumptions are allowed. It is likely that the early vicars taught the children in the George Monoux school, as Brechtgirdle taught in Stratford. If there was some kind of hiatus in the appointment of a vicar in Walthamstow in 1578, the children would still have needed a schoolmaster. The Withypolls, responsible for the school, would have asked their learned acquaintances for a suitable candidate. In 'Master G.H.'s' paraphrastical variation of 'Olde Maister Withypol's' translation, we may have the job application of Harvey's protégé.

This candidate stands rather on his pride, for in an envoy to the exercise, he adds 'Virtuti, non tibi Feci': 'I have done this for virtue (to show my virtuosity?), not for you'; not, that is, for Peter Withypoll. But the latter replies: 'Et Virtuti, et mihi:/ Virtuti, ad laudem:/ Mihi, ad usum', meaning 'For both – for virtue, to earn praise; and for me, for a practical reason'. The 'practical reason', I suggest, was to show the Withypolls that he had enough learning to be the schoolmaster of their school. The name of the founder of the school is written 'Monoux' or 'Monox'. The rationale for Nashe's Will of the great dagger being nick-named 'Will Monox' becomes blindingly clear.

Since the boundary between Hertfordshire and Essex shifted frequently, Waltham, Walthamstow, and Waltham Cross found themselves now in one county, now the other. A passage in Harvey's third Familiar Letter introducing his poem *Speculum Tuscanismi* revealingly links a certain *Hertfordshire* gentleman to the subject of the poem, the plain swain who had so perfected his manners after twelve months in Italy. 'Il secondo, et famoso Poeta, Messer Immerito' is expected to respond to the 'Satyricall Libell' (the *Speculum*) which Harvey has devised 'at the instaunce of a certayne worshipfull Hartefordshyre Gentleman, of myne olde acquayntaunce: *in Gratiam quorundam Illustrium Anglofrancitalorum, hic et ubique apud nos volitantium*' ('to please certain elevated Anglo-frenchified Italians, fluttering here, there and everywhere around us'). That Harvey should imply the existence of a *second* Immerito vindicates the Suppose that there were two Immeritos. We have here the earliest instance of the catch-phrase 'hic et ubique' which so haunts potential references to Shakespeare. It begins to look as though Harvey's 'Libell' is in fact the other half of the job application for the post at the George Monox school. Harvey recommends his 'scholler' for the post. The scholar succeeds and sets up as a 'country gentleman', as Harvey puts it elsewhere in that third Letter.

It may not have been only to Harvey that Shakespeare owed his appointment. The network of Sidneians in Walthamstow and its environs is surprisingly dense.[51] George Gascoigne came into property in Walthamstow through his marriage to the widowed mother of Nicholas Breton, and Nicholas was probably brought up partly there. Sir Edward Denny, a close friend of Philip Sidney, lived at Walthamstow, where he has a grandiose monument in the church, with a puzzling inscription that we shall investigate. The Manners family, Earls of Rutland, had lands at Walthamstow: Shakespeare and Richard Burbage made an *impresa* in 1613 for the sixth Earl, Francis, who was married to Elizabeth Sidney, Philip's daughter. It is usually supposed that this was done for purely mercenary reasons, or that it came about partly as a result of the Earl of Southampton's friendship with Manners. If we can instal Shakespeare firmly in Walthamstow in 1580, clearly there might have been more personal reasons for him to have undertaken the unusual task.

A letter of Philip Sidney's to Denny, and the Denny monument in Walthamstow, aid that installation.[52] When Denny set out with Lord Grey to Ireland in 1580, Philip wrote to his friend from Wilton on 22 May, advising him on his reading, and passing on various messages.[53] Interest has been roused by the wording of one sentence that might refer to Spenser, who was also serving Lord Grey in Ireland: 'good will carries mee on to this impudence to write my councell to him that (to say nothing of your good selfe) hath my L. Grayes company'. It seems to me plain that that Sidney is considering writing his good counsel to someone *besides* Denny, and this someone could well be Spenser. But what is of more interest here is the potential pun in 'good will': it is the matter of whose messages Sidney is passing on *from* England. At the end of his letter, he writes: 'remember wth your good voyce to singe my songes for they will one well become another. My L of Pembrook, my sister, & your charge thanke you with many thankes'. Here again is 'will', reduplicated and emphasized. Arguably, '*Will*' is the 'charge' Denny undertook before leaving for Ireland.

Denny's grandiose monument in Waltham Abbey Church, next to the ruins of Walthamstow Abbey, was erected after his death in early 1600. It contains a long inscription in English, which is unusual in the period. Other aspects of the wording are odd. It begins with a self-description: 'An epitaph upon ye death of ye Right Worthie Sir Edward Denny …'. It continues, after giving Denny's parentage and appointments to high office, with the words: 'He is offered to ye view and consideration of ye Discreete reader a spectacle of Pietie and Pittie, the Pittie kindly proceeding from a vertuous Ladie' his wife, who 'hath out of meane fortune but no meane affection produced this Monument dedicate to the remembrance of her deare hysband'. But this wife of straitened means who erected such a massive stone and marble monument, complete with coats of arms and the ten Denny children in effigy, and who is described in the third person, yields towards the end of the inscription to the 'I' in whose voice the whole is uttered: 'I finally refer inquisitive searchers into men's fame to ye true Report even of the most malitious …'.

Who erected this monument? The inscription reads at first like a title page: 'An epitaph upon'. Critical acumen is demanded of the 'discreet reader': 'discreet, wise to perceive' is one meaning of the word given by the *OED*. The one who takes responsibility is the one who emerges as the 'I' at the end. We may have a clue to his identity in the operations of the 'Pietie and Pittie', which appear to malfunction in their reference. The 'Pittie' proceeds from the wife who produced the monument out of affection, 'dedicate to the remembrance of her deare hysband'. This sounds a good deal more like piety than pity. The 'Pietie' is described as something that 'must inwardly be conceyved and considered': it cannot be spelled out … but it is, as something that sounds a good deal more like pity. It 'must inwardly be conceyved and considered in ye person of ye dead carkeys here interred cut off like a plesunt fruite before perfect ripeness'.

Let me suggest that Piety and Pity (whom the engraver perhaps muddled after their first occurrences) are in fact the poverty-stricken wife and a good friend of the family known as 'Pity' – a literary friend used to devising literary works.

Apart from the historical indications of the presence of Shakespeare at Walthamstow, we have literary references which are as telling. Greene in his *Defence of Conny-catching* had, among the tales we passed over to study the case of William who coney-catched for a wife, a tale of a miller and an Alewives Boy of Edmonton.[54] Edmonton is close by in Essex. The trick of Greene's pamphlet, we realized, was to tell a number of tales that seem disconnected except for the fact that all contain trickery, when in fact the tales all concern the same person under different disguises.

'Edmonton' stands in as a sign for 'Essex' in other covert references to our hero. The play *The Merry Devil of Edmonton* was published in 1608. No author was given, but the play was acted by Shakespeare's company: 'as it hath been sundry times Acted, by his maiesties Servants, at the Globe, on the bank-side'. Its hero is the host of the George at Waltham, who declares 'away with puntillioes, and Orthography'. There is a 'Goodman Smug the honest Smith of Edmonton'. The play was immensely popular, which must be incomprehensible to anyone unaware of the resonance of Essex, Waltham, orthography, or Smiths. It was reprinted in 1612, 1617, 1626, 1631 and 1655.

A later play *The Witch of Edmonton* tries to cash in on the genre, with an appealing character called Cuddy Banks, and a hobby horse. Beaumont's anonymously published *Knight of the Burning Pestle* (1613, possibly first performed in 1607) tries the same ploy. Its hero Jasper is found at one point in Waltham Forest, quoting *Macbeth.* There is a wicked barber, Barbarossa (one of the names Nashe gives Dick Lichfield). 'Jasper' is of course a Stone. And Beaumont had a track record of imitating Shakespeare: his *Philaster* (a lover of Stella?), co-authored with Fletcher, imitated *Cymbeline.*

More literary allusions to school-mastering are made by Nashe, who describes Apis Lapis with 'the high countenance you show unto Schollers'.[55] This, I imagine, refers to him sitting on his elevated desk above his schoolchildren. The fictional Nashe of the Parnassus Plays is equally revealing.

As 'Ingenioso', Nashe says to 'Philomusus': 'take heede I take you not napping twentie yeeres hence in a viccars seate ... or els interpretinge Pueriles confabulationes to a companie of seavn yeare olde apes'.[56] Philomusus becomes a sexton (alluding to his counterpart's post of vicar?) and a clerk. But he is also said to have 'gone into the countrie to teache', as has his companion Studioso.[57]

There is firm historical evidence that the William Smith who attended Oxford was a schoolmaster in Loughton (Essex), and in Waltham Cross, and claimed to be again of Loughton in 1589. Leslie Hotson, in his *Shakespeare's Sonnets Dated*, gives us the following information from the Consistory Court of London.[58] On 12 May 1589, William Smith gave a deposition.

> William Smithe of the parish of Lucton [Loughton] in the county of Essex, schoolmaster, Bachelor of Arts, where he lived for about one year, and before that in the parish of Waltham Holy Cross, where he lived for about one year, and before that in the University of Oxford, where he studied letters for two years. Born in Stretford upon haven in the county of Warwick, aged 24 years or thereabouts.

Hotson puzzles over this, and makes a surprising suggestion. 'Is it possible that old Beeston' (William Beeston, whose father Christopher had been an actor in Shakespeare's company, was Aubrey's authority for the piece of information) 'unwittingly transferred the youthful schoolmastering activities of this contemporary William Smith of Stratford to William Shakespeare?' A moment's reflection will show that it is extremely unlikely that old Beeston could have been so confused; and another moment may serve to show the opposite! He could easily have been so confused, *if* there were two William Smiths from Stratford, of a similar age, and with the same father, and if one of them was Shakespeare. And yet I think he was not confused: *both* young men (Philomusus *and* Studioso) were schoolmasters in the same county.

Ajax's Man

What did William Smith do after 1583, when a newly appointed vicar took over at Walthamstow? I am sure he wrote or polished many of the Leicestrian histories and many of his comedies in this period, such that Nashe and Greene knew him as an accomplished playwright by 1589. As William Shakespeare, he married in a rush by special licence in 1582. Perhaps it was the marriage that ended his Walthamstow teaching career. He had a child in 1583; twins followed in 1585. Perhaps he wrote and worked with the newly formed Queen's Men, who had no home base, but were 'travellers'. There *was* a William Smith in the Queen's Men; but he was still with them in 1598 when Shakespeare, one would think, was deeply involved with Burbage and the Globe.[59] Possibly he was much at Lleweni.[60] The poem by 'Danielle' of deeply affectionate farewell to John Salusbury can be dated unambiguously between October 1593 and April 1594, which would fit well with Shakespeare's taking up a formal position with the Chamberlain's Men in 1594.

A hint as to R.L.'s affiliations before 1597 is given by a remark of the Trinity College barber Dick Lichfield, who claims in *The Trimming of Thomas Nashe* that mighty Ajax gave him protection (D4). 'Ajax' must be Sir John Harington, who wrote *The Metamorphosis of Ajax*, which he published in 1596.[61] Harington was the Queen's cousin, and highly placed in society. In church matters, he was for tolerance and reconciliation. He was a connoisseur of poetry, and a good critic. His family had a literary commonplace book, into which he transcribed many of the early versions of Philip Sidney's poems. Mary Sidney sent him three of her translated Psalms. He knew the *Taming of the Shrew* before 1596, and he had a number of copies of Shakespeare's plays in his library.[62]

The *Metamorphosis of Ajax* contains, amid a great deal of satire, scurrility and politics, a design for the article that works as the metaphor for the whole – a flushing privy ('a jakes'). There are sketches for this invention included in the text, which, we are given to understand, are the work of Harington's man Master Thomas Combe. The title page of one section of the *Metamorphosis*, 'The Anatomie', claims to be written by 'T.C. Traveller. Aprentice in Poetrie, Practiser in Musicke, professor of Painting'; and T.C. Traveller also signs the design of the stinkless privy.[63] But the way in which this Maister T.C. is mystified and joked about (he is aligned with another M.T.C., Marcus Tullius Cicero, whom he calls his 'cosin M. Tomas Cicero'[64]) makes him suspect, even though Harington did indeed have an educated servant called Thomas Combe in his household.

'The Anatomie' is really by Harington himself. I deduce this from three things: the entry in the Stationers' Register, which describes the Metamorphosis, Anatomy and Apologie – the three parts of the work – as 'written by Mysacmos', not as 'by Mysacmos [Harington's name for himself] and T.C.';[65] the similarity of the illustrations in Harington's part of the work and the part supposedly by Combe; and 'Combe's' defence of *himself* for having called Ajax 'Stercutius', when it was Harington who did so in the first part of the work.[66]

Combe's defence of himself over the *faux pas* of using the crude word 'Stercutius' ('dungy') and describing Ajax as a 'Nowne Adjective' is a ploy to make us turn back to the relevant section, where we find that the discussion as to whether Stercutius was properly a substantive or an adjective involved a boy William being quizzed on the parts of speech – yet another reflection of that popular scene in *Merry Wives.*[67]

In the description 'Combe' gives of his likeness to his master Harington, there is an extraordinary emphasis on plays and playing that requires explanation, for the real Thomas Combe's writings extended no further than emblem books.

> We have playd, and bene playd with, for our writings. *Si quis quod fecit, patiatur ius erit aequum.* If you do take but such as you give, it is one for another, but if they that play so, would give us but a peece of gold for everie good verse we thinke we have made; we should leave some of them, but poore felowes. But soft, if I shold tell all, he wold say, I am of kin to *Sauntus Ablabius.* It is no matter, since he makes me to write of *Sauntus Acacchius.*[68]

Something is being concealed here, as the last two sentences show. The two saints were mentioned earlier as heretics. 'Combe' puns on their names, pretending to fear Harington will call him *a blab* if he expresses himself any more clearly in the course of writing on '*cacare*' – 'to shit'.

The dark hints, the unexplained title 'Traveller' (compare Harvey's 'pellegrino' and Nashe's surreal character), the connection with Cicero (compare Greene's pamphlet *Tullies Love*), the invoking of the pupil William in a scene about grammar, the stress on 'playing', all point towards Shakespeare. But in a list of autobiographical features given before the passage quoted, there are items that map onto Combe's known life and not onto Shakespeare's. For instance, 'Combe' claims that both he and his master have been 'beyond sea, but never out of the Queenes dominions'. Thomas Combe had apparently accompanied Harington to Ireland; but Shakespeare, so I have argued, had travelled to Italy. And 'Combe' draws a parallel between himself and Harington which seems to rule out Shakespeare: 'one of my kin did teach him at Eaton, & one of his kin taught me at Oxford'.[69]

The problem we face is that of interpreting one who is writing 'in the skin' of another, as happened with R.L.'s account of Kenilworth, written in the guise of Robert Langham. Which details will be true of the false persona, and which of the real person? I interpret Harington as having a double-layered pretence. He falsely suggests Combe is the author of the Anatomy, and accordingly gives some details that are true of Combe. All the while, he is insinuating that under Combe's mask lurks Shakespeare, and plants information that can be true only of Shakespeare. He paves the way for the subtle shift from Combe's characteristics to Shakespeare's with a bridging sentence: 'we are taken for true men, and have holpe to hang theeves'.[70] Harington, as a Justice of the Peace, had 'helped' to hang thieves; Shakespeare, as Falstaff, had 'hoped' to hang thieves.

In the case of such a playful text, it is not possible to insist that one reading is right and all others wrong. But the guess that Maister T.C. is Shakespeare receives startling confirmation from the Parnassus Plays. In Act 3, Scene 4, Ajax appears with his servant Immerito. The ensuing dialogue corroborates the suspicion that the servant is the *second* Immerito, Shakespeare. He is asked 'What is a parson' (either 'person' or 'parson') 'that was never at university?' He is ironically praised for his proficiency in poetry, which extends to reciting 'Thirty days hath September'. He is then asked, 'How many miles from Waltham to London?' 'Twelve Sir', he answers. He should know: he must have made the journey hundreds of times, from home to court or theatre.

Theatre Proprietor

A William Smith of Waltham Cross made that journey frequently during the winter of 1598/99, and during certain court cases which resulted from an operation carried out on 28 December, 1598. The operation was the dismantling of the Burbages' theatre at Shoreditch and the transporting of it wholesale to the south bank of the Thames, where it was rebuilt as the Globe. It happened as follows.[71]

Cuthbert and Richard Burbage and their father James had long had an agreement with Giles Allen, who had leased the Shoreditch site to the Burbage family. The land was Allen's and the structure was the Burbages'. The lease was coming up for renewal in the April of 1597, and there were wrangles about the price of a new lease, the acceptability of Richard, the actor son, as surety, and whether the Burbages had properly maintained the Theatre. Clearly Allen was not too keen to renew. Nothing was settled; the Chamberlain's Company tried and failed to set up in Blackfriars; the Theatre in Shoreditch lay deserted.

Towards the very end of 1598, Richard, Cuthbert, Peter Street a carpenter, William Smith the brothers' backer, and others took down the Theatre at Shoreditch timber by timber, at dead of night, and transported it to a site on the Bankside. The Burbages, we learn from a much later case in the Court of

Requests, Witter v. Heminges and Condell, of 1619,[72] then took out a thirty-one year lease for their new/old theatre, now the Globe. (This lease was not formally signed until 21 February 1599, but was backdated to 25 December 1598.) The land belonged to a Nicholas Brend, who had inherited it from his father Thomas Brend. Thomas Brend owned land in Walthamstow – it could be that William Smith the mysterious backer had approached his Essex neighbours (perhaps Nicholas the son, since Thomas died in 1597) for help, with a view to leasing this prime site near the Rose Theatre on the south bank.

Allen sued, issuing a Bill of Complaint at the Queen's Bench, for £800 worth of materials and for trespass.[73] The case was brought in the Trinity (Summer) Term, but deferred for Cuthbert Burbage to bring in his own complaint against Allen in the Court of Requests in January next year. The case in the Court of Requests, spread out over the year 1600, throws a fascinating light on the venture, and on William Smith, who gave a deposition in evidence.[74] The Burbage team won the case on 18 October. Allen counter-sued in the Star Chamber in 1601.[75] (He lost again.) Comparing that record with deeds concerning the tenancy of the land the Brends had leased throws yet more light on the matter.

Allen's complaint, we learn from the Star Chamber record, was that Peter Street and sixteen others including the two Burbage brothers had 'riotously assembled' to tear down the theatre in Shoreditch, and 'riotously resisted' those who tried to stop them. One Shakespearean biographer, Holden, cannot resist adding to the demolition team: 'including, we can but hope, Shakespeare'.[76] For not only was the venture that of the Chamberlain's Company, to which Shakespeare and Richard Burbage belonged, but the new lease, a complex affair, had Shakespeare as holder of a fifth of one half of all the shares. (The Burbage brothers held the other half.) And when Thomas Brend's assets were declared in Chancery after his death, in a document of 16 May 1599, the site of the Globe, 'newly built', was said to be 'in occupatione Willielmi Shakespeare et aliorum', which, as Park Honan notes, 'implies that in May 1599 Shakespeare was thought to be the most prominent Globe tenant'.[77]

But it was William Smith who had played the vital role in the enterprise. In the Star Chamber record, Allen refers to the past history as 'the sayd sute betweene your subject and the sayd Cuthbert Burbage … prosecuted agaynst your Subjecte by the malicious procurement and the unlawfull mayntenance of the aforesayd William Smyth (he t[he sayd] William unlawfullye [bringing]e the sayd sutes for th[e sayd] Cuthbert Burbage a[nd th]en unlawfullye expen[din]g and layeing out divers forms of money in the same for and in the behalfe of the sayd Cuthbert Burbage …'.

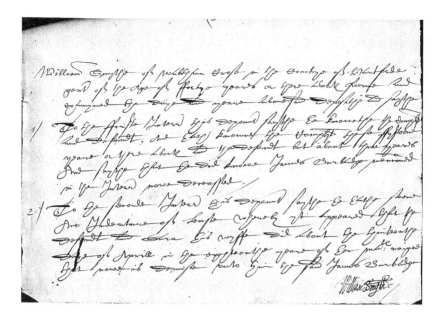

9.4   PRO Req. 2/184/45. A page of William Smyth's deposition, Court of Requests, 5 June 1600

Two historians have been properly puzzled by the role of William Smith in the affair. Charlotte Stopes demands to know why this person enters the Globe story as such an intrinsic part of it, and is then never heard of again.[78] Hotson poses the following question about William Smith the Waltham Cross schoolmaster: 'Is he to be identified with Richard Burbage's otherwise unknown friend William Smith of Waltham Cross, gentleman, who on December 28 was present when the Burbages' workmen tore down The Theatre?' 'Like what song the sirens sang,' he muses, 'these are puzzling questions'.[79]

We do know something about this unknown friend from the deposition of witnesses for Cuthbert Burbage on 5 June 1600 in the Court of Requests. (Cuthbert brought the case on 26 January 1600; Allen answered on 6 February; the list of witnesses for either side, containing one signature 'William Smyth, gen.', was drawn up on 9 April.) The document Req. 2/184/45 contains William Smith's deposition in answer to nine interrogatories. He signs every page (five of them) in a neat italic 'William Smyth'. He is stated to be 'William Smythe of Waltham Cross in the County of Hertfordshire gent of the age of forty yeares or there aboute' (but for some reason he is twice referred to as 'Thomas Smith'). To the first interrogatory, he answered that he had known the complainant (Cuthbert Burbage) for 'these fyfteene yeares or there aboute'. This would take us back to 1595 or so (Shakespeare having joined the Chamberlain's Company in 1594). To other interrogatories, Smith replied that he had known James Burbage; had seen an indenture of his original lease at Shoreditch; knew that Sara Burbage, Cuthbert's mother, had approved the dismantling of the Theatre there; that he had himself been present and approved it; that he had seen in James Burbage's book of accounts not only sums for normal wear and tear but also additional sums amounting to more than two hundred pounds spent on the building. His evidence must have contributed substantially to the finding for his side on 18 October.

Yet when shares were allotted, no Smith was partaker in ownership of the Globe. Did one of the driving forces behind the move to the new site and chief defender of that move in the courts get nothing out of his support of the Burbages?[80]

We noticed that from its inception, the new theatre was said to be in the possession of 'William Shakespeare and others'. There must be a reason why Shakespeare was thought so prominent, because that document concerning Thomas Brend's holdings is at odds with the terms of the lease of the Globe, in which Shakespeare owned only a tenth (a fifth of half) of the shares. Two mortgage documents drawn up in 1601 concerning this Brend family property, the Globe site, also cite William Shakespeare, Gent., together with Richard Burbage as the tenants.

Perhaps it was due to his social status that Shakespeare was mentioned first in connection with ownership of the Globe: but perhaps he had the over-riding moral claim to be recognized as joint owner, on the grounds that he was that very William Smith of Waltham Cross who had motivated, financed and supported the brothers throughout.

A Winter's Tale

I have argued that Lions figured largely in Shakespeare's self-representation, and Leonati of various kinds might have carried a freight of personal meaning for him. It would seem that the author of *The Blind Begger*, whether or not he was Shakespeare, knew of the self- identification, since the last of the characters into which the 'Shakespeare figure' in that play transmogrifies is Leon the usurer.[81] Still to be accounted for among prominent Shakespearean characters with related names are the father of Hero in *Much Ado About Nothing*, whose name is Leonato, and the jealous king Leontes in *The Winter's Tale*.

Winter's Tale is a fitting place at which to draw R.L.'s biography to a close, since 'R.L.' stands for the writing entity, not the historical person. The writing and revision of many of the sonnets for the 1609 publication *Shakespeare's Sonnets* may indeed have postdated the *Winter's Tale*; but their story is long and complicated, and belongs in another study.

The reason I antedate *Winter's Tale*, normally dated a little before its *terminus ante quem* in 1611, when Simon Forman saw a performance of it at the Globe on 15 May,[82] is its relation to *Mucedorus* (1598) and to Greene's *Pandosto* (1588).[83] The Arden editor of *Winter's Tale*, J.H.P. Pafford, holds that Shakespeare 'certainly knew the popular comedy *Mucedorus*', since the episode of being chased by a bear is replicated, and the reflections of Polixenes on the grafting of stronger humbler stock is contained in brief in *Mucedorus*' 'My mind is grafted on an humbler stock'.[84] Granted the parodic nature of *Mucedorus* as I sketched it earlier, if the parallels are indeed strong enough to be echoes, they are likely to be the anonymous author's echoes of Shakespeare, rather than the other way round.

That would place *Winter's Tale* before 1598, which to my mind is entirely likely, since it would have been perverse of Shakespeare to have waited twenty years before writing a riposte to Greene's *Pandosto*, as he obviously does: he not only switches the courts of Bohemia and Sicily, but he alters the whole tone of Greene's romance by 'resuscitating' the Queen.

But what exactly are the indications that either *Much Ado* or *Winter's Tale* is driven by deeply personal imperatives? After all, such tales were generally loved, and they gave writers opportunities for high drama. This does not prevent us from asking why a particular dramatist loved the theme and reverted to it often. Shakespeare took it upon himself to write a series of tales in which virtuous women – sometimes after suffering calumny – are hidden away as though dead, and then reappear. *Pericles* and *Comedy of Errors* (in which Aegeon's wife is hidden away as a holy abbess), *Much Ado* and *All's Well* fall within the definition. I speculate that the theme of the long-maligned woman had such a grip on Shakespeare because of the circumstances of his birth, and the light in which it cast his mother.

The leonine names are the first pieces of evidence. The Italian name 'Leonato' appears in one of Shakespeare's sources for *Much Ado*, Bandello, who has the Hero figure's father's name as 'Lionato de' Lionati'.[85] But the motivation of *The Winter's Tale*'s 'Leontes', where Greene had 'Pandosto', has not been explained.

Hero herself is called 'Fenicia' (a phoenix?) in Bandello; but she is 'Genevra' in Ariosto's version of the story (in *Orlando Furioso*, which

Harington translated in 1591). That name 'Genevra' alone might well have stirred R.L.'s imagination. He saw himself as Dom Diego, adoring a Ginevra. It is striking that (apart from the oblique relation of his Orlando in *As You Like It* to Ariosto's hero) this is the sole occasion on which Shakespeare borrows from Ariosto.[86]

A similar motivation may have led Shakespeare to the tale of Boccaccio's that underlies the *Cymbeline* plot, in which the name of the Imogen figure is 'Zinevra'. The name 'Imogen' itself may then have taken on a similar resonance. For in the quarto stage directions for Act 1, Scene 1 of *Much Ado* is a character following in Leonato's train called 'Innogen his wife'; and 'his wife' is listed in the directions for Act 2, Scene 1. Yet no wife features in the quarto plot. This vindicates John Dover Wilson's belief that there was an earlier Shakespearean *Much Ado* with some differences in plot.[87]

Where there is a Hero, there is often a Leander, as editors of *Much Ado* observe before declaring that in this case, no such person is invoked. Yet Shakespeare's motivation for naming his heroine Hero must be queried: he could either be joking that his heroine was really a hero – himself at the time of his wedding, suspected of unchastity and forced to marry Ann Hathaway – or he could be invoking Leander after all – himself as he appears in Marlowe's poem and Nashe's parody of it. That is, Claudio is a concealed Leander, Leander being yet another leonine name.

In *Winter's Tale*, we find a cluster of 'Mercurial' names. 'Hermione', the name Shakespeare gives his queen in place of Greene's 'Bellaria', is derived from 'Hermes', as Joseph Porter points out.[88] Autolycus, the play's trickster, draws attention to his own descent from Mercury, which explains, he says, is why he is snatcher-up of unconsidered trifles. I suspect this may be a self-referential joke: Shakespeare as Mercury has snatched up the unconsidered trifle of Greene's *Pandosto*, and almost in spite of himself, turned it to good, echoing Autolycus's behaviour. I do not quite know what to make of the fact that Simon Forman's notice of the play, on 15 May 1611, has the sign of Mercury against the entry.[89] May 15 was a Wednesday that year, and Wednesday is Mercury's day; but the inclusion of the symbol is still a little strange.

Sicily has been deliberately made the setting for the main plot of *Winter's Tale*, reversing Greene's localities. The pastoral part of the play has been resituated in Bohemia, though Theocritean shepherds are normally found in Sicily. Sicily is also the setting for *Much Ado*, by tradition (and history – there really were Sicilian Leonati). Possibly the name of Leonatus Posthumus' father, Sicilius, has some bearing on Shakespeare's choice of Sicily for the place of both disaster and triumph in *Winter's Tale*. There was a play described as a 'matter of Panecia' performed by Leicester's Men at Court on New Year's Day 1575, and A.R. Humphreys suggests 'Panecia' could be a confused 'Fenicia', Bandello's heroine.[90] The play is lost and its contents are unknown. It would be marvellous to think that Shakespeare's last play was also his first, but it is an unwarranted supposition, on the evidence.

It is not only the proper names that connect the plays to each other. Pafford traces many characteristics common to *Cymbeline*'s Posthumus Leonatus and *Winter's Tale*'s Leontes. 'In each the Leo-character behaves weakly and foolishly; each is overcome by jealousy, each wills the death of his wife and actually thinks that he has caused it, and each is shown his criminal folly, becomes remorseful, and is united to and reconciled with his wife.'[91]

I am far from suggesting a one-to-one mapping of Shakespeare's family members onto characters in the three plays. Shakespeare wove his themes too intricately, and out of diverse sources. But two elements of *Winter's Tale*, the matter of the Queen's guilt and the names of her two children, may be invoked to strengthen the suggestion of personal investment on Shakespeare's part.

Howard Felperin thinks critics have not allowed themselves to be puzzled enough by the problem of whether Hermione was really innocent of adultery with Leontes' friend Polixenes.[92] Not that he means to argue for her guilt. But he means to show that Shakespeare intended us to worry over her warm behaviour to Polixenes, over the ambiguities of numerous words and expressions, especially the word 'friend', for that could mean a lover. Felperin postpones certitude to the moment the oracle makes its clear pronouncement of her innocence; and even then, he would have us maintain a sense of insecurity.

Felperin does notice that the last sentence of the unwontedly clear oracle, 'The king shall live without an heir until that which was lost is found' contains the only ambiguous phrasing. But like every spectator or reader from Forman onwards, he thinks it has direct reference to Perdita, 'the lost one', the baby whose birth to the Queen nine months after the arrival of Leontes' old friend had done most to spark Leontes' violent accusations. I suggest it *remains* ambiguous: 'that which was lost' could also mean 'marital trust', or even 'the Queen's chastity'. The entire history of oracles, after all, is one of misprision.

Leontes' jealousy is shown by the reaction of most other characters to be wildly unreasonable. Only Antigonus just before his death, and, I think, the hesitant Bohemian courtiers at the play's opening, who imply their lord has received excessive hospitality, contradict this impression. And yet ... I think we are meant to accept the impossible paradox that Hermione is both unfaithful to Leontes, and chaste. A 'winter's tale' is an old wives' tale, something quite incredible. Yet as Ernest Schanzer says, the insistence that the queen's 'resurrection' is like an old tale has the effect of 'strengthen[ing] the listeners' *belief*, not their disbelief.' 'And' he goes on to observe, 'the same seems to have been Shakespeare's purpose in devising the play's title and in likening its most marvellous events to an old tale.'[93]

This is wonderfully put, and of wider application than Schanzer probably intended. Within the play, the winter's tale that never gets told (the story young Mamillius had just started to tell when his furious father burst in) seems comparable to the story of the whole play. Shakespeare's own winter's tale is incredible too, but it happened. The title is a double-bluff.

Etymologically, the children of Hermione have switched names and gender. 'Mamillius' should mean a child at the breast. Shakespeare was a child at the breast, we can presume, when his father claimed the six-month-old as a Smith, and his other father, John Shakespeare, suffered the shock of knowing his wife adulterous and his child another's. The Perdita of *Winter's Tale* is the female babe. Yet I wonder whether she has been trans-gendered in her author's imagination. Is 'she' really 'Perditus', the 'lost' young boy, living under the shadow of bastardy (as Perdita does in the play), with no 'true' mother?

John Shakespeare's reaction to his shock can only be imagined: perhaps it was analogous to the irruption of Leontes into the room where the young Mamillius was beginning his story: 'There was a man ... dwelt by a churchyard'. 'I will tell it softly', he said – and Shakespeare told his own winter's tale so softly, we hardly hear it.

Redemption in *The Winter's Tale* works at three levels: restoration of the mother to innocence; 'restoration' of fatherhood to Leontes; psychological restoration for the teller of the tale that is the play. It was this last who was truly 'Perditus', but who found himself again. After such a triumph of reconciliation with the ghosts of his own past, perhaps *The Winter's Tale*'s author found no further need for play-writing.

Notes

1   For Fripp, see above, Chapter 3, p. 64, and note 48. No Shakespearean biographers doubt Fripp's identification of the youngest Smith's date of birth.
2   Worcester Probate 1578/111, referenced 008.7, in Worcestershire Record Office. Will made 4 December 1578; probate granted 17 January 1578/79.
3   Stratford-on-Avon Registers, consulted on microfilm in the Society of Genealogists library. See *Stratford-on-Avon Registers c.1558–1652*, transcribed by Richard Savage, 2 vols (London: privately printed., 1897), 1.1–13.

4   P.C.C. 1 Watson. See Fripp, *Shakespeare Studies*, p. 60.

5   MS. Registrum Primum Wint. Coll. (Record of admissions), p. 94. See also *Winchester Scholars*, ed. T.F. Kirby (London: Henry Frowde and Winchester: P. and G. Wells, 1888), p. 149.

6   MS. Liber prothocollorum de iuramentis (Record of oaths at Winchester College), p. 58.

7   *Register of the University of Oxford*, 2 vols (Oxford: Clarendon Press, 1887), 2:ii.129.

8   See above, pp. 85–6.

9   W. Schrickx, *Shakespeare's Early Contemporaries* (Antwerpen: Nederlandische Boekhandel, 1956), pp. 47–8. George Chapman, *The Shadow of the Night: Containing Two Poeticall Hymnes* (London: R. F[ield] for William Ponsonby, 1594).

10 But see Barbara Everett, 'Whirligig', *LRB* (2 September 2004), pp. 19–23. She lays stress on Hamlet's 'two fathers' and describes him as 'too complexly fathered'.

11 *Usher*, III.2.110–11. The play was often called 'Vincentio and Margaret'.

12 *D'Olive*, I.2.178–80.

13 Nashe, *Works*, III.6 (A2v).

14 *Works*, II.237.

15 *Transcript*, vol. 2. 824. (fol. 394b).

16 The youngest William, the one who attended Winchester College, had not yet been born by the time of Brechtgirdle's death, if my reasoning is correct.

17 Spenser, *Works*, p. 416, lines 13–15.

18 John Roe, *Shakespeare and Machiavelli* (Cambridge: D.S. Brewer, 2002), pp. 97–106, argues that the Bastard's Machiavellian character dissolves the contradictions.

19 David Thatcher, *Begging to Differ: Modes of Discrepancy in Shakespeare* (New York: Peter Lang, 1999), pp. 295–8, raises many possible implications of legitimacy, illegitimacy and inheritance as represented in *Lear*, but does not attempt not distinguish which of them were Shakespeare's implications.

20 E.B. Everitt and R.L. Armstrong, *Six Early Plays Related to the Shakespeare Canon* (Copenhagen: 1965), orig. article in *Anglistika* 14 (1965).

21 Loewenstein, *Author's Due*, p. 101.

22 As A.W., he contributed a commendation to the *Spirituall Song* of Roger Cotton 'of the worshipful company of Drapers' in 1596, presumably only because he was socially obliged to do so, since his praise is very muted. See Roger Cotton, *A Spirituall Song* ... (London: G. Simson and W. White, 1596), A4r–A4v.

23 Fripp, *Man and Artist*, pp. 122–3.

24 J.M. Nosworthy, ed., *Cymbeline* (London: Methuen, 1955), pp. 191–204.

25 Giovanni Boccaccio, *Il Decameron* (1349–51?) (Florence: I Giunti, 1573), Giornata seconda, Novella nona, pp. 120–29.

26 Nosworthy, *Cymbeline*, intro., xxv.

27 For many writers, there exists some such personal emblem that has more than one determinant. See my arguments about Nabokov and the phoenix symbol in 'Nabokov's *Ada*'.

28 BL Additional MS 29, 895, f.119v, reproduced in *The Mirror of Alchemy*, Gareth Roberts (London: British Library, 1994), plate VIII. See also Stanislas Klossowski de Rola, *Alchemy the Secret Art* (London: Thames and Hudson, 1973), p. 110, figures VII and VIII, the Leo Viridis, reproduced from MS. 974, Bibliothèque de l'Arsenal, Paris.

29 Marjorie Garber, 'Roman Numerals', *In the Company of Shakespeare*, pp. 233–50.

30   Robert Chester, *Loves Martyr* (London: R. Field for E. Blount, 1601), pp. 42–85. For Chester's affiliation, see *The Poems of John Salusbury and Robert Chester*, ed. F. Carleton Brown (London: Kegan Paul, 1913/14).
31   Tom Lloyd-Roberts, 'Bard of Lleweni? Shakespeare's Welsh connection', *New Welsh Review* 23 (Winter 1993–94), pp. 11–18. Jeremy Griffiths, '"Loose Sheets and Idle Scribblings": The Case against Shakespeare's Lleweni Connection', *New Welsh Review* 25 (Summer 1994), pp. 52–7. The document is MS Christ Church Library, Oxford, 184, fols 82–83.
32   Smith, *Chloris*, Sonnet 23, lines 1–6.
33   Nashe, *Works*, II.209.
34   George Peele, *Edward I* (c. 1589) (London: A. Jeffes sold by William Barley, 1593), 3, line 72. *The Dramatic Works of George Peele*, ed. A.H. Bullen, 2 vols (London: J. Nimmo, 1888), 1.75–217, 117.
35   Marcus, *Puzzling Shakespeare*, pp. 52–3, 66–96.
36   E.A. Honigmann, ed., *King John* (London: Methuen, 1954), intro., p. xxix.
37   William Empson, 'They That Have Power', *Some Versions of Pastoral* (1950; London: Chatto, 1968), pp. 89–115, 104–9.
38   Fleissner, *Names, Titles*, p. 48.
39   Philip Sidney, 'The Defence of Leicester' (1585?) first printed in *Letters and Memorials of State*, 2 vols, ed. Arthur Collins (London: T. Osborne, 1746), I.62–8. See *Miscellaneous Prose*, pp. 129–41, esp. 134–9.
40   *Leicesters Commonwealth* (1584), ed. D. Peck (Athens, Ohio: Ohio State University Press, 1985).
41   R.A. Foakes, ed., *Henry VIII* (1957; London: Methuen, 1986), intro., pp. xxviii–xxx.
42   Dulwich College MS IX. *Henslowe's Diary*, p. 291, article 30.
43   E.K. Chambers, *William Shakespeare. A Study of Facts and Problems*, 2 vols (Oxford: Clarendon Press, 1930), 1.497.
44   Michael Drayton, *Elegies upon Sundry Occasions* (London: William Lee, 1627). *Works*, 3.203–43, 226, lines 17–30.
45   Aubrey, *Brief Lives*, p. 291.
46   Thomas Howell, *H. his Devices* (London: [W. How?] for H. Jackson, 1581), G2r.
47   E.A. Honigmann, *Shakespeare: The Lost Years* (1985; Manchester: Manchester University Press, 1998). Richard Wilson, 'Shakespeare and the Jesuits: New Connections Supporting the Theory of the Lost Years in Lancashire', *TLS* (19 December 1997), pp. 11–13.
48   Nashe, *Works*, I.278.
49   P.H. Reaney, *Court Rolls of the Rectory Manor Walthamstow* (Waltham Antiquarian Society, 37, 1939), p. 9. G.C. Moore Smith (revised by P.H. Reaney) *The Family of Withypoll* (Waltham Antiquarian Society, 34, 1936). These two pamphlets are the main sources for the information on Walthamstow that follows.
50   Reaney, *Court Rolls*, p. 19.
51   George Edward Roebuck, *The Walthamstow Armorial* (Waltham Antiquarian Society, 26, 1932).
52   For the Denny family in Walthamstow, see H.L.L. Denny, *Biography of Sir Edward Denny*, Transactions of the East Hertfordshire Archaeological Society, 2 (1902–4), pp. 247–60.
53   The letter came to light in 1972. See John Buxton, 'An Elizabethan reading-list: An unpublished letter from Sir Philip Sidney', *TLS* (24 March 1972), pp. 343–4.
54   Greene, *Works*, 11.64–70 (B4–C1).
55   Nashe, *Works*, I.255.

56 *Parnassus Plays*, pp. 121–2.

57 Ibid., p. 186.

58 Leslie Hotson, *Shakespeare's Sonnets Dated and Other Essays* (London: Hart-Davis, 1949), p. 131. *Cur. Cons. Lond. Respons. Personalia Testium*, 1581–93, Bk 3.

59 See McMillin and Maclean, *Queen's Men*, pp. 29, 51, 196.

60 One of Tutch's disguises in Armin's *Two Maids* is that of a Welshman (F1).

61 Sir John Harington, *A New Discourse of a Stale Subject, called the Metamorphosis of Ajax* (London: R. Field, 1596). References will be to E. Story Donno, ed., *Harington's Metamorphosis of Ajax* (London: Routledge, 1962).

62 See F.J. Furnivall, 'Sir John Harington's Shakespere (sic) Quartos', *N&Q* 7th series, IX 1890 (17 May), pp. 382–3.

63 *Harington's Metamorphosis*, pp. 195, 196 for the sketches; 187 for title page; 197 for the signature.

64 Ibid., pp. 199, 202.

65 *Transcript*, III.73.

66 *Harington's Metamorphosis*, pp. 179, 198.

67 The theory that Harington's staged scene echoes the play involves antedating the play. *Merry Wives* could have been written any time after the visit of Count Mömpelgard to England in 1592. See H.J. Oliver, ed., *The Merry Wives of Windsor* (1971; London: Arden, 1996), intro., pp. xlvi–xlvii.

68 *Harington's Metamorphosis*, pp. 203–4.

69 Ibid., p. 202.

70 Ibid., p. 203.

71 Key accounts are those of Charlotte Carmichael Stopes, *Burbage and Shakespeare's Stage* (London: De la More Press, 1913); Charles William Wallace, *The First London Theatre* (University of Nebraska Studies 13, 1913), esp. 276–89; Herbert Berry, *Shakespeare's Playhouses* (New York: AMS, 1987).

72 Discovered by Wallace in 1909.

73 PRO Coram rege 1362. R. 587.

74 PRO Req. 1/198 is a list of witnesses drawn up on 9 April, containing a signature of William Smyth. PRO Req. 2/184/45 comprises various depositions, including five pages of William Smyth's deposition with signatures on each page.

75 PRO Stac. 12/35.

76 Holden, *Shakespeare*, p. 168.

77 Honan, p. 268. PRO Chancery, Inquisitions Post Mortem, C.142/257/68.

78 Stopes, *Burbage and Shakespeare's Stage*, p. 76.

79 Hotson, *Shakespeare's Sonnets*, p. 132.

80 See Stopes, *Burbage and Shakespeare's Stage*, p. 77.

81 See above, p. 126.

82 Details are given by J.H.P. Pafford, ed., *The Winter's Tale* (1963; London: Arden, 2002), intro., p. xxi.

83 Robert Greene, *Pandosto: The Triumph of Time* (London: Thomas Orwin for Thomas Cadman, 1588). *Works*, 4.225–317.

84 *Winter's Tale*, IV.4.92–7. Pafford, p. xxxv. *Mucedorus*, I.1.48.

85 Bandello, *Novelle*, I. 22.

86 Thomas Moisan shows how Shakespeare interweaves Bandello's and Ariosto's versions in 'Deforming Sources: Literary Antecedents and Their Traits in *Much Ado About Nothing*', *Shakespeare Studies* 31 (2003), pp. 165–83.

87 John Dover Wilson, joint ed., *Much Ado About Nothing* (Cambridge at the University Press, 1923), pp. 92–107. Wilson's other arguments are less convincing.

88 Porter, *Shakespeare's Mercutio*, p. 115.

89 See Pafford, intro., p. xxi, citing Ashmole MS 208, fol. 201v.

90 A.R. Humphreys, ed., *Much Ado About Nothing* (1981; London: Arden, 2002), intro., pp. 5–6. Dover Wilson anticipated him.

91 Pafford, appendix, p. 164.

92 Howard Felperin, '"Tongue-tied our Queen?" The Deconstruction of Presence in *The Winter's Tale*', in *Shakespeare and the Question of Theory*, ed. Patricia Parker and Geoffrey Hartman (New York and London: Methuen, 1985), pp. 3–18.

93 Ernest Shanzer, ed., *The Winter's Tale* (1969; London: Penguin, 1996), intro., p. 8.

Envoi

If each and every one of the Supposes argued for in this book were correct, there would be effects of various kinds on scholarship in various fields of early modern studies. I shall sketch here what I think would be the main ones, without assuming that the final picture will turn out to be exactly as I have described, but without pausing to qualify every remark as being under the sign of the initial 'if' of this envoi. (It is more the logicians' 'iff': 'if and only if'.)

My study has elevated the notion of coterie and patronage to a central position with great explanatory potential; and it is from these two notions that an assessment of effects should start. I have implied the need for new criteria for identifying a coterie circle or a sphere of patronage, which in turn implies slightly altered understandings of coterie's (and patronage's) effects, whether one is working in the purely literary field, the paraliterary, the social, the political, historical or biographical. The first three fields can be treated under the aegis of 'coterie'; 'patronage' can come in at the level of 'the social' and go on to encompass the political, historical and biographical. Theoretical concerns belong in both sections.

More particular effects may be felt in specific arenas of study: effects on the dating of various works, presenting a challenge to stylometricians; on currently held notions of censorship, collaboration, topicality (including satire), source and influence; on the current conception of indirection, of anonymity and pseudonyms. My study may contribute to the discussion on authorial revision; alter the conception of the growth of Shakespeare's reputation; extend and alter the notion of coterie names. The concept of authoring a work will be affected, as will the interpretation of particular authors, markedly so in the case of Shakespeare, Nashe, and Spenser; to a lesser degree in the case of Gascoigne, Greene, Marlowe, Lyly, Harvey, Chapman; diminishing further with Harington, Holinshed, Jonson and so for all the other writers whom I have suspected of referring to R.L. R.L. himself will need consideration as an author previously unknown to criticism (or known only piecemeal), and as Shakespeare's juvenile self.

A final reflection on 'motivation' in some of its senses will sum up the way my approach differs from that of other critics.

Coterie

The centrality of the Dudley/Sidney coterie to sixteenth-century literary culture has of course long been recognized. Robert Dudley's general patronage of the arts has been examined and well described by Henry Woudhuysen and others; and the angling of Spenser's and Harvey's works to flatter and impress Dudley and his nephew Philip Sidney are integral to Woudhuysen's study. The frequent dedication of works of poetry and translations to the older Mary Sidney is not news; nor the enormous influence of Philip on the writers in his circle; nor the example and patronage of the younger Mary Sidney, and later the patronage of her son, William Herbert.[1]

What has been underestimated is the impact that belonging to a coterie has on the literary practice of its members. While *some* punning, *some* contemporary reference encoded in classical names, *some* point to the use of a source or a classical allusion, *some* teasing and satirizing of fellow writers, has been 'seen and allowed' in modern criticism, the tricks and encoding of persons have not been seen as the almost ubiquitous phenomena they were.

I have ventured to suggest the presence of extremely puerile puns, bilingual puns, unvoiced puns, puns that are heard rather than read ('pattern', 'patron', 'patten'). This aspect of my study has been facilitated by the work of Anne Ferry and Patricia Parker. Ferry shows how the Elizabethans heard near-homonyms as 'the same word' rather than as a pun because of the contemporary fluidity of pronunciation and orthography.[2] This habit of theirs would have simultaneously occluded the fact that a joke was being perpetrated, and helped them to connect words that we would not instinctively connect. 'Posies' and 'poesies', for example, were supposed to be radically connected, even though Elizabethans knew the latter derived from the Greek 'poiesis' (making).

Parker's work on puns and word-play has opened up a way for me to formulate the possibility of unvoiced and 'hard-to-read' puns.[3] My bilingual puns are usually not as 'given' as hers are, but have to be sought in the reader's competence in other languages, and dragged into consciousness. ('Pity', 'olive' and 'William' are not readily identified.) And I hope I have extended the range of the puerile.

Other devices in the coterie repertoire are newly identified in my study. There is the double-bluffing metaphor, in which the literal sense may be the true point, as when the *Shepheardes Calende*r is sent forth 'as child whose parent is unkent'. There is the 'two-persons-under-one-hood' trick, which occurs both within texts and in a paraliterary way to disguise shared or distributed authorship: the doubling of 'Immerito', whether as a character or an author sign, is a good example. The variant pseudonym and the simple pseudonym can each be seen in the same dual light. As paraliterary markers, R.L., R. Lynche, and Richard Lichfield baffle identification – do they denote one or many or no historical persons? But the names can also provide an excuse for play *within* the text, as when R.L. of Kenilworth refers to himself as Ro. La., R.L., and Laneham, and when jokes on 'Dick' are made in Nashe's *Have With You*. There is the repeated use of non-classical *topoi* to encode a secret – the dress of the oafish Kenilworth groom, for example, or the Old Lad, whose identity is once hinted at by quotation from the classics, but more often in other ways. Slightly off-key geographical markers – Flintshire for Denbighshire, any old Essex town for Walthamstow – can flag a coterie secret. There is the significance of differential spelling, and of verse form. There is the tag standing as a personal marker ('hic et ubique'). Epigraphs, marginal notes and glosses can 'convey' (smuggle in) more information than has been previously realized. If they have been persuaded that these tricks inhere in Elizabethan literature, future critics may investigate the same and other works of the period with a keener ear for subterfuge, and produce new readings of them.

'Coterie' was identified by the markers I am calling paraliterary by Arthur Marotti in the case of John Donne.[4] Marotti took the external evidence of manuscript exchange to show Donne as a member of a learned, witty group of men with similar tastes and outlook. The contents of prefaces and dedications are often applied to the same end by modern critics. (Nashe prefaces Greene's *Menaphon*, and deductions are then drawn about a group of 'University Wits'.) The paraliterary factors of printer, publisher and seller have received attention in previous studies.

I have laid far more stress on internal markers of coterie membership, to the extent of admitting into the Sidney coterie some whose presence there has not been suspected, purely on the basis of modes of allusion they share with the coterie. Marlowe, Lyly, and Greene may be the most unexpected writers appearing in this category.[5] I have, however, also relied on external paraliterary markers. I have supposed that the choice of Danter and Wise for the publication of some of Shakespeare's plays has a previously ignored significance. The publishers Jhones, Bollifant, Wolfe, Islip, Fisher and Burre and the booksellers Olney and Thorpe have also served as beacons to secret links between affiliated persons and personae. This may alter current perceptions of the kind of collusion that existed between author and printer or bookseller. And I have mined prefaces and dedications for their covert meanings, rather than their overt statements of fealty.

In fact, it is descrying the *process of rendering covert* that is my prime hermeneutic tool throughout the study. For it is only items with 'scandal potential' (and that includes the politically subversive) that require concealing. The examination of modes of conveying in a subtext a meaning contrary to that of the overt text, so vital to my study, was pioneered by Leo Strauss.[6]

The obverse of this process of self-censorship is an external power's attempt to render an author unheard because unread. Annabel Patterson has applied Strauss's analysis when investigating reasons for political censorship in early modern England. Censorship (by the licensers, Privy Council, Bishops) can be an extremely useful beacon flagging a dangerous subtext, in cases where it is not obvious what aspect of a text caused offence. Building on this work, and on studies of 'scandal' such as Warkentin's in the case of the *Astrophel and Stella* publication, and Clegg's in other cases, I have recommended seeing the demand for 'lawfull auchthorization' as an indicator of potential embarrassment for a powerful family (always, in this study, the Dudley clan). I have suggested that more scandalous matter than previously supposed lies hidden in Shakespeare's works, both canonical and those I have attributed to him, and in the works of his Sidneian fellows, including the Sidney siblings.

The work of Marcy North includes pseudonyms and coterie codes in the wider perspective of 'anonymity'. But her critical tools are directed towards a different end from mine. While she discusses the usefulness, uses, and types of this kind of 'indirection', North is not much concerned to find out which historical person lurked under a pseudonym, or what secrets were being transmitted. My angle has been more positivistic, my interest arising not out of the general phenomenon of pseudonymity, but out of particular puzzles posed by particular texts assigned to one pseudonymous writer.

Future investigators of Elizabethan pseudonyms may want to assess my claim that it can be useful to treat a name as specifically referential and as constant over different works, genres and authors. I have adapted Germaine Warkentin's hypothesis about coterie naming. She claims that 'the names adopted by sonneteers in England and on the continent are not ones intended to conceal; rather they are well-known academic designations or symbolic coinages designed to reveal the identity of the poet and the lady to an initiated group'.[7] I have replaced 'academic' with 'coterie', and extended her dictum beyond the sonnet. She refers to personae *within* the sonnet or love lyric, typically the beloved and the speaking lover. I have proposed that the reference spreads beyond a single work; beyond even the lyric and prose romance allowed by some other critics. It has been allowed that Astrophil and Philisides (both meaning 'Star-lover') apply to Philip Sidney in his own lyrics, sonnets and prose romance, and the poems of others who refer to him. But that a lyrical or romance nickname might remain constant through genres as diverse as narrative poem, marginal note, pamphlet and play has not been envisaged as a possibility.

I have claimed that the critical consensus has drastically misidentified some coterie names – Amintas, Menaphon, Stella. This is all the more surprising because the work of Jonathan Crewe on front-men has been widely praised, and is crucial to my study – and Stella was one of his subjects. My reading of the work of Richard Barnfield supports his identification.

The claim that one person can appear under a large number of different pseudonyms and still be recognized will also need assessing.

I hope less credence will be given to Masten's claim that anonymity was not a functional concept in the sixteenth century because authorship was not one. Neither claim seems to me correct: they only too obviously answer to a currently popular anti-elitism that takes the death of the author as something more than a trope, and invests in the idea of 'collaboration' to a peculiar degree. My investigation of the *Poetical Rhapsody* reveals a marked contemporary concern for a single historical author's wishes, ambitions and rights as a writer.

The currently fashionable conception of collaboration marks a point of divergence between my conception of shared authorship and peer support and that of postmodern critics and those whose interest in stage performance is so intense as to make all study of 'poiesis' irrelevant, in their judgement (unless more than one author is involved, when it mysteriously becomes a matter of great interest). Critics of these persuasions tend to treat absolutely everyone involved in the process of 'making public', whether through print or stage performance, up to and including the printers' devils who filled up the ink-wells, as co-creators of the work.[8]

My evidence for the antedating of plays that Shakespeare is believed to have collaborated on should undercut the exponents of this kind of collaboration. Some of Shakespeare's supposed collaborators turn out to have been too young to have co-authored the plays they are declared to have shared with him. Thomas Middleton, often invoked as a collaborator for *Macbeth*, and increasingly put forward as co-author for other Shakespearean plays, was born in 1580.[9] I contend that Shakespeare wrote *Macbeth* and other history plays well before 1592, when Nashe starts to quote from them. It is not impossible that history repeated itself: Shakespeare, impressed with the budding genius Middleton, appealed to the child to help him write his plays. I think it unlikely.

'Collaboration' in my study is something different. I have suggested that the young R.L. was aided and indeed educated as a poet by his elders in the Sidney coterie. That is one type of collaboration, reinforced by the same elders' promoting him by 'embedding' his works in theirs, getting him into print with printers to whom they had access, liberally sprinkling those printed works with clues and hints as to their true joint authorship, and encoding him as a young prodigy in their own singly-authored works. Shakespeare's coevals too similarly encouraged him, urged him to print, introduced him to their printer friends, paid him the homage of citing him and frequently representing him in disguise in their writings. I have presented him, conversely, as collaborating with others to complete a series (individually authored) of English history plays to promote his patron's political ambitions.

I do not rule out the possibility that Shakespeare occasionally recast a play with the help of another, years after he had first written it. *Two Noble Kinsmen* and *Henry VIII* are obvious candidates. If unmistakable traces of the hand of another are found in some of his other plays, I shall suppose likewise that this other helped in the revision. But I remain suspicious of the stylometricians' findings, blasphemous though this sounds in the present climate of their ascendancy. Again, it is partly my antedating that challenges their findings; though it is always open to them to say that they have the serial order of Shakespeare's perfected plays, if not the decade of composition, correct. However, *iff* my 'maturation' principle is allowed, and naïve plays antedate mature ones, 'Senecan' antedate 'confident vernacular', even this claim of theirs will be weakened. My principle is likely to be a good one, if the author is *not* dead, but embodied in a historical person. Allowing the possibility that the poet could grow in technical skill implies, too, the possibility and utility for the critic of evaluating a work on aesthetic grounds. Such evaluations find no place in deconstructivist, psychoanalytic, and most historicist studies.

The strongest arguments for my case against the conclusions of stylometrics in Shakespeare's case are less speculative. If R.L.'s corpus, William Smith's works, three lyrics in the *Shepheardes Calender*, some verse in the Familiar Letters, 'Robert Chester's' Arthurian narrative, half the *Poetical Rhapsody*, Humfrey King's work, and A.W.'s immature *Remedie* are indeed to be added to the Shakespearean corpus, the stylometricians' database for Shakespeare's practice has hitherto been woefully incomplete. Conversely, their database for Philip Sidney and Spenser has been contaminated by alien matter.

My next point may be simply a rephrasing of the preceding paragraph, but is worth spelling out: I have found Shakespeare's lost lyrical poetry and early sonnets, and presented him as a multifaceted writer, not a dramatist who turned occasionally to narrative verse or sonnets when the theatres were closed for plague.[10] Though it is not made a sufficient criterion, aesthetic evaluation also plays a role in identifying R.L., A.W. and William Smith with this youthful Shakespeare. Their works generally show literary talent, or promise, or, at their weakest, enormous inventiveness of vocabulary and vigour of expression.

My 'anti-collaborationist' case rests not only on the evidence rehearsed above, but also on a particular conception of authorship. I have postulated a continuous subjectivity for my R.L.: he has been treated as an author-function inextricably entwined with a historical person, capable of maturation and change, with an individual memory and imagination, interests and attitudes, however much the last two, in particular, were overlaid with those of his society. My demonstration of the degree to which in proto-Mozartian fashion he wove his life into his work has aimed to vindicate such a humanistic approach. I have never believed that the notion of Shakespeare writing two or three intense and complex plays a year from scratch throughout the 1590s was at all credible. The onus rests now with those who believe that is what he did to produce more compelling evidence for their belief, and to counter my evidence to the contrary.

Such a positivistic approach has to run foul of postmodernist indeterminacy of all kinds. It is essential to my position to be able to *rule out* some interpretations as misguided or wrong. One example from my book will suffice to show the necessity of raising such matters as half-understanding or misunderstanding a text, and the doubtful validity of reception theories that assign to readers the power to decide an author's meaning. Lorna Hutson has opened up the question of Nashe's attitudes to graduate and non-graduate writers, as presented (obliquely) in his preface to Greene's *Menaphon*. But her insight – that Nashe favours non-graduates – has been ignored, and critics and biographers of both Nashe and Shakespeare continue to assert that the University Wits (Nashe, Greene and some others) scorned Shakespeare for attempting to write while lacking a higher education. It was necessary for me to be able to assert that Hutson is right, other critics wrong, and it is the Nashean text itself that offers us the means of reading it correctly. Even if no contemporary of Nashe's had understood him, and Hutson had never written, it would still be true that the words on the page mean that Nashe scorned graduates, not a certain non-graduate. I appeal to the enormous utility of positivistic studies such as that of James Hirsh on soliloquies, which should have a lasting effect on our understanding of Elizabethan subjectivity.[11]

My readings will affect the conception of the literary/social world in which Shakespeare moved. In many of the cases of contemporary reference to him that I have chosen to examine, the results appear at first sight rather bland. Of course Jonson knew him. Of course Armin would have known him – he was in his company. Is it at all surprising that Chapman knew him? – surely not. But I have added a particular dimension to this knowledge: these writers not only knew Shakespeare socially, they knew his origins; they knew his extraordinarily ambivalent social standing in the coterie. I hope also that I have cleared a way for future radical re-readings of Spenser's *Faerie Queene* and Philip Sidney's *Arcadia*, with Shakespeare as part of their social and literary environs. Work on Greene's *Menaphon* (whose subtext mirrors that of Shakespeare's *Venus and Adonis*) and on Henry Chettle's *Kind Hartes Dreame* (1592), which has much light to throw on the supposed scorn of Greene for the upstart crow, will also be required as a priority. For other aspects of the social, we move on to the concept of patronage.

Patronage

Late sixteenth-century England should be seen more as a patronage society with disparate power centres than as 'Elizabethan' with everything centred on the Court, I have argued. Alan Sinfield was ahead of the field in arguing that there were tensions under the calm surface of the Elizabethan settlement. David Norbrook sees Elizabeth as merely 'prime inter pares', first among equals. The work of Suzanne Westfall and Paul Whitfield White and the collected essays in their joint collection have delved further.[12] In her own essay in the volume, Westfall historicizes patronage, seeing it, correctly, as inflecting *all* social relations in the Elizabethan age. She also usefully draws attention to opposition to the Queen expressed through performance sponsored by powerful lords, as does White for an earlier period.[13] There are three aspects of patronage concerned here that it might be useful to distinguish, even though they are interwoven in practice: that of the social world of each client writer; that of the limited world of the theatre; and that of power games on the national scale.

The effects on an individual's social life of being born in an era of patronage have still to be internalized in many critics' thinking. We should not still be speaking of a young man's 'leaving Stratford to go to London' *tout court*, as though London, and not the houses of the great lords, were the centre of the universe for ambitious proletarians in the 1580s. We should appreciate better the strength of the tie, life-long or extremely hard to break, that bound patron and client. Donna Hamilton has noted that not only was Shakespeare referred to in the First Folio as William and Philip Herbert's 'servant' whom they had always prosecuted with favour, but also that Shakespeare's changing attitude to ecclesiastical matters seems to map that of the Dudley faction.[14] Andrew Gurr highlights the continuity of allegiance shown by Edward Alleyn and by James Burbage in the early 1590s: Alleyn continued to wear the livery of Lord Howard, patron of the Admiral's Men, during the three years he worked with Strange's Men, and Burbage likewise 'flaunted' Henry Carey's livery, before the latter became Lord Chamberlain and patron of the Chamberlain's Men, even though Burbage had stopped acting and was running his own theatre.[15] Gurr sees these instances both as 'unique arrangements' and as clear signs of personal allegiance and 'old loyalty'. I suppose that they were not unique, but the norm, and therefore include them in 'social life' rather than in 'world of the theatre'.

My study may contribute to the elucidation of these more obscure aspects of the functioning of patronage. It may help remind us of the hierarchical nature of that society. But I hope it will point up a less-noticed and paradoxical aspect, the levelling effect of coteries in terms of social rank. The patrons were also patrons in the sense of *cognoscenti*, and they searched out the best craftsmen and artists to attract to their own 'courts'. Leeds Barroll, a guiding spirit in recent patronage studies, concludes that many lords (and ladies such as the countesses of Pembroke, Essex, Derby and Bedford) granted their patronage to acting companies in the same spirit as they did to other artists, simply as connoisseurs and amateurs of good art.[16] Though I have some reservations about this view, it is helpful to an implicit finding of my study – the peculiar equality of standing between aristocratic artists and plebeian ones. Cuddie, the herdsman's boy, adjudicates Willy's (Philip Sidney's) contest with Perigot, and then 'overgoes' both. Nor is that all: the intimacy bred by such coterie activity plays out in personal relations, whether homosocial or heterosexual, to a 'scandalous' degree. Aspiring poets seek and receive the friendship and love of highly placed men and women. Or they engage as enemies on equal ground: Nashe dared to attack Mary Sidney without regard to her aristocratic status.

My reservations about Barroll's view move us into the narrower arena of theatrical patronage. Too much emphasis on connoisseurship will understate the aristocrats' political games played out in dramatic presentation (and in printed non-dramatic works, which urgently need bringing into the picture). It will lead us to ignore the possibility that 'home-grown' artists, actual servants of this or that noble, often expressed the attitudes and interests of their lord or lady when they turned to artistic production.[17] Too much emphasis on the 'fluidity' of patronage, discerned by Barroll in the search of companies for new patrons and the passing on of artists by recommendation from one patron to another, will obscure the existence of life-long ties between client and patron. As a corollary, we may lose sight of the fact that commercial plays may have had a long 'pre-life' as coterie plays, and saleable pamphlets a 'pre-life' as coterie dialogues.

I welcome the new emphasis on the possibility of tension between the nobles and the pinnacle of patronage, the monarch. But concentrating hard on the fact that plays had to be selected for Court performance at Christmas, many critics still trace unbroken lines of allegiance from humble actors and playwrights right up to the Queen. This is obviously so in the case where it most requires challenging – that of Robert Dudley's patronage. Though it is recognized that he urged his own marriage suit on the Queen, together with his own puritan objectives in home and foreign policy, through masques and tragedies such as *Gorboduc* (played under his presidency as Christmas lord of the Inner Temple), it has not been suggested that he turned his patronage to treasonous purposes, or that his country-wide influence exercised through Leicester's Men and his clear interference in the affairs of the Queen's Men was other than benign.[18]

Susan Frye's findings of tension between Elizabeth I and the Dudleys expressed in R.L.'s and in George Gascoigne's accounts of the Kenilworth visit point the way towards more questioning of Dudley loyalty to Elizabeth. A great deal more could be done to follow up David Norbrook's acute observation that the old Fairy Queen of folklore was the black-faced, disreputable underworld queen who opposes the real queen.[19] It is not only for the understanding of the *personal* affairs of the Sidneys that I urge the re-evaluation of Spenser's *Faerie Queene* and Philip Sidney's *Arcadia.* Jean Wilson's study is a striking contribution to what should become a serious debate about long-held Dudley opposition to the monarch.

Modern historians, I remarked, have made light of the accusations in *Leicesters Commonwealth.* They discount the possibility that Robert Dudley was plotting to take the throne, on the grounds that the work probably emanated from a Catholic source. The possibility that it could be both partisan and mainly true seems not to have occurred to them. Yet the Earl of Talbot believed in Dudley's treason. On the flyleaf of his copy of the *Commonwealth* is a simple poem containing the lines: 'The Ragged-staffe that stay was to the state,/ As some men thought, is bent another way,/ As here is taught.'[20] My study does some of the ground-work for a study of 'The Leicester Coterie and its Treasonous Literary Programme', which I hope someone will write soon.

It is only possible to admit the political into discussion of literature if one is not too deconstructivist in approach. 'If authorial intention has a substantial and under-acknowledged political element, to ignore the intention is effectively to depoliticize', observes Norbrook.[21] The same applies to eroticism in a text: one may de-eroticize a narrative by speaking too glibly of the 'erotics of the text', rather than of the writer.[22] Much of my discussion of Shakespeare's and others' programme of Dudleian political advancement would have been ruled out of court by too deconstructivist an approach. And my analysis of the 'envie' that surrounded the poet – which was not envy of his talent on the part of other writers, but potential outrage on the part of the more elevated section of society at the amorous liaisons obliquely described in his own and others' verse – would have been ruled out by too Lacanian an approach.

Topical reference falls squarely within the social/historical field in the broader compass of literary studies. I have proposed that some of Shakespeare's plays (*Cymbeline*, *Macbeth*) obliquely refer to events in decades earlier than those proposed by other critics. I doubt if there could be any intrinsic marks of better or worse ascriptions of topicality: a piece of definitive external evidence must always trump the supposed match of a dramatic item to a historical item. It must do so not only because it is fatally easy to conjure up events or scenarios from *any* decade to match a dramatic incident; it is also because it is easy to assume that a historical document that seems too good a match to ignore must have triggered its apparent fictional counterpart. Many critics are adamant that William Strachey's account of the adventures of the ship Sea Venture of 1609 is a source for *The Tempest*.[23] I would feel justified on the sole basis of Nashe's parody in supposing rather that Strachey echoed the play. Luckily, the history of the Strachey publication supports this proposition, as does the odd literariness of the historical account, and the fact that Strachey was a sharer in a theatrical company, and presumably familiar with plays. His account was not published until 1625, though he wrote a private letter about it in 1610. Supporters of Shakespeare's indebtedness to Strachey therefore have to postulate that the letter was widely circulated and that Shakespeare saw it – the kind of argument they would never countenance in an opponent challenging the consensus date. Arthur Kinney, like Kenneth Muir before him, has doubted whether the Strachey letter has the slightest connection with *The Tempest*.[24]

Where no accommodation is possible between the critic who finds a correlation too good to ignore and the critic who is sure that some reference by a third party fixes the date of composition *before* the historical event in question, appeal might be made to authorial revision: topical lines may have been added to a play originally written and performed much earlier. Indeed, the author himself or his company or a potential audience may suddenly have seen a new relevance in an old play – as when a private performance of *Richard II* was specially commissioned before Essex's departure for Ireland. My study has strengthened the likelihood that authorial revision was often required and practised.

A new conception of 'source' complicates the notion of topicality. Many critics now demote literary sources in favour of seeing the total cultural environment of the writer as *sources* of his or her production. This is precariously dependent on not making false deductions from the *terminus ante quem* or being tempted by an alluring historical correlation. It ignores the fact that writers are peculiarly susceptible to the *poiesis* of others (Derrida himself stresses this). And in flattening out the landscape of influence, it is liable to miss irony and humour, which are particularly effective when they are achieved through verbal quotation and misquotation.

The satirizing of writers by each other is, I have claimed, ubiquitous in the works studied. By combining the notion of the 'Poets War' already on the radar of critics with the suggestion of Richard Dutton that by the 1590s, impersonation of people of high and middling social standing had become so widespread that the censorship could not keep up with them, I can increase the credibility of my argument and the scope of the phenomenon – well beyond the dramatic.[25]

Changes to Shakespeare's biography are indicated by my study. The amount of autobiographical reference in his plays needs re-assessing. Much will have to be subtracted from some biographies of Marlowe, Bacon, the Earl of Oxford and whoever else has been proposed as the 'real' Shakespeare. Various motivations have been ascribed to those who do not accept that William Shakespeare of Stratford wrote the plays commonly known as Shakespeare's. I think their doubts about the consensus story were justified. I hope my account has answered those doubts – chiefly, doubts about Shakespeare's education, knowledge of things Italian, and sympathy with the aristocratic view-point.

My study has emerged out of my conviction that everything in a text is motivated. Choice of pseudonym is motivated. Reference to the classics is motivated not merely by a desire to show off learning, but to manipulate the lines cited to a present purpose. A single name can motivate diverse works: 'Ginevra' may have motivated Shakespeare's interest in the old tales underlying *Cymbeline* and *Much Ado*. The choice of one word over another, one dialect, one language, one register, one orthography, one example over another – all are motivated. Choice of a number for a sonnet in a sequence can be motivated. Choice of verse form is highly significant.

My motive was not originally to find out about the historical Shakespeare. It was to understand puzzling texts and their motivation. And texts are sometimes incomprehensible, at least in part, until correctly 'placed' in relation to the acting and experiencing entity whom we call 'the author'. This 'placing' is of course done by extracting clues from texts. This may look circular, but it is not viciously so, even in cases where the texts are those of the author in question. Where one can 'triangulate' from other authors, it is not vicious at all.

The study of early modern English literature remains a humanistic study, I hope. And it is only human to want to find the person in the work. That has been part of my motivation, too. Petrarch's feeling for classical authors was so personal as to be a passionate friendship. Joseph Brodsky's first thought on getting out of Soviet Russia was to search out W.H. Auden in person. There is nothing to be lost, and something to be gained, by approaching our authors in this spirit.

Notes

1   See Michael Brennan, Katherine Duncan-Jones, Margaret Hannay, Mary Ellen Lamb and Gary Waller in the bibliography.
2   Anne Ferry, *The Art of Naming* (Chicago and London: University of Chicago Press, 1988), pp. 1–48.
3   Patricia Parker, *Literary Fat Ladies: Rhetoric, Gender, Property* (London: Methuen, 1987); 'On the Tongue: Cross-gendering, Effeminacy and the Art of Words', *Style*, 23 (Fall 1989), pp. 445–65; *Shakespeare from the Margins: Language, Culture, Context* (Chicago: University of Chicago Press, 1996).
4   Arthur Marotti, *John Donne: Coterie Poet* (Madison: University of Wisconsin Press, 1986).
5   I am not ignoring the fact that Lyly also enjoyed the Earl of Oxford's patronage.
6   Leo Strauss, *Persecution and the Art of Writing* (1952; Chicago and London: University of Chicago Press, 1980).
7   Germaine Warkentin, 'The Meeting of the Muses: Sidney and the Mid-Tudor Poets', in *Sir Philip Sidney and the Interpretation of Renaissance Culture: The Poet in his Time and in Ours*, ed. Gary Waller and Michael Moore (London: Croom Helm, 1984), pp. 17–33.
8   The work of Jerome McGann has been influential: Jerome McGann, *A Critique of Modern Textual Criticism* (Chicago: University of Chicago Press, 1983).
9   See Gary Taylor's ascription of *Macbeth*, *Timon of Athens* and *Measure for Measure* to Middleton in his Oxford edition of the poet; and the work of Brian Vickers, especially *Shakespeare, Co-author: A Historical Study of Five Collaborative Plays* (Oxford: Oxford University Press, 2002).
10   Patrick Cheney's *Shakespeare, National Poet-Playwright* (Cambridge: Cambridge University Press, 2004) came out too late for me to absorb its arguments here.
11   James Hirsh, *Shakespeare and the History of Soliloquies* (London: Associated University Presses, 2003).

12   Alan Sinfield, 'Power and Ideology: An Outline Theory and Sidney's *Arcadia*', *ELH* 52 (1985), pp. 259–79. David Norbrook, intro., *The Penguin Book of Renaissance Verse, 1509–1569*, ed. Henry Woudhuysen (London: Penguin, 1992), p. 21. See also Woudhuysen, 'Leicester's Literary Patronage'; Suzanne Westfall, *Patrons and Performance: Early Tudor Household Revels* (Oxford: Clarendon Press, 1990); Paul Whitfield White, *Theatre and Reformation: Protestantism, Patronage and Playing in Tudor England* (Cambridge: Cambridge University Press, 1993). Details of the collection were given above in Chapter 8, note 5.

13   Suzanne Westfall, "'The useless dearness of the diamond: theories of patronage theatre' in White and Westfall, pp. 13–42, 13–14, 26. White, *Theatre and Reformation*, pp. 12–27.

14   Hamilton, *Shakespeare*, pp. xi–xii, 23.

15   Andrew Gurr, 'Privy Councillors as Theatre Patrons', in White and Westfall, pp. 221–45, 237–8.

16   Leeds Barroll, 'Shakespeare, Noble Patrons, and the Pleasures of "Common" Playing', in White and Westfall, pp. 90–121.

17   Though the caveats of Richard Dutton should be accepted: clients did not always reflect or even concur with their patrons' views. (*Mastering the Revels*, pp. 70–73.)

18   Alan Sinfield, *Literature in Protestant England, 1560–1660: Religious Anxiety from Spenser to Milton* (London: Croom Helm, 1983), p. 23 et seq., sees Sidney advancing Leicester's puritan programme. But Sally-Beth MacLean, 'Tracking Leicester's Men: The Patronage of a Performance Troupe', in White and Westfall, pp. 246–71, finds no political intent.

19   Norbrook, *Poetry and Politics in the English Renaissance* (London: Routledge, 1984), p. 115.

20   See Dugdale, *Kenilworth Illustrated*, p. 28.

21   Norbrook, *Poetry and Politics*, p. 8.

22   Goldberg recognizes this, I think: *Sodometries*, pp. 74–5.

23   Virginia Mason Vaughan and Alden T. Vaughan, eds, *The Tempest* (1999; London: Arden, 2003), intro., pp. 41–2.

24   Arthur Kinney, 'Revisiting "The Tempest"' *MP* 93 (1995), pp. 161–77.

25   Dutton, *Mastering the Revels*, pp. 127–36, esp. 132.

Bibliography

Primary Sources

Manuscripts

Berkeley Castle Muniments, General Miscellaneous Papers 31/10.
Bodleian Library, Malone MS 348.
British Library, MS Cotton Vitellius C. 17.
British Library, Additional MS 29,895.
British Library, Additional MS 35186.
British Library, N. Tab. 2026/25 (19).
British Library, Harleian MS 280.
British Library, Sloane MS 93.
Dulwich College MSS, 'The Henslowe Papers'. MS I, Orlando's part for Robert
 Greene's Orlando Furioso.
Dulwich College MSS, 'The Henslowe Papers'. MS IX, Henslowe's Diary.
Oxford. Christ Church Library, MS 184.
Public Record Office, P.C.C. 1 Watson.
Public Record Office, Chancery Inquisitions post mortem C.142/257/68.
Public Record Office, Coram rege 1362. R. 587.
Public Record Office, Req. 1/198.
Public Record Office, Req. 2/184/45.
Public Record Office, Stac. 12/35.
Winchester College, Registrum prothocollorum de iuramenti Wint. Coll. (Record of
 oaths).
Winchester College, Registrum Primum Wint. Coll. (First Register of admissions).
Worcester County Records, Probate 1578/111. 008.7.
Stratford-on-Avon Baptism Register.

Printed Archives

Acts of the Privy Council. Edited by J.R. Dasent, 32 vols. London: HMSO, 1890–1907.
 n.s. 11.
Calendar of State Papers, Spanish.
Letters and Memorials of State. Edited by Arthur Collins. London: T. Osborne,
 1746.
*Minutes and Accounts of the Corporation of Stratford-upon-Avon and Other Records:
 1553–1620*. Edited and transcribed by Richard Savage, with notes by Edgar Fripp.
 Oxford: Ed. Hall for the Dugdale Society, 1921.

Envoi 1 Half-page image of Bear with Lance. © British Library 190d13.
(Taken from *Kenilworth Illustrated*, ed. C. Whittingham (Chiswick:
1821), 6th leaf.)

Records of the Court of the Stationers' Company. Edited by W.W. Greg and E. Boswell. 5 vols. London: Bibliographical Society, 1930.

Register of the University of Oxford. 2 vols. Oxford: Clarendon Press, 1887.

Shakespeare in the Public Records. London: HMSO, 1964.

STC, Short Title Catalogue of English Books, 1475–1640. Edited by A.W. Pollard and G. Redgrave. 2nd edn revised by W. Jackson and F. Ferguson, completed by K. Pantzer. 3 vols. Oxford: Oxford University Press, 1986.

Stratford-on-Avon Registers c.1558–1652. Transcribed by Richard Savage. 2 vols. London: privately printed, 1897.

Transcript of the Registers of the Company of Stationers in London. Edited by E. Arber. 5 vols. London: privately printed, 1875–94.

Winchester Scholars. Edited by T.F. Kirby. London: Henry Frowde and Winchester: P. and G. Wells, 1888.

Arden of Feversham, The lamentable and true tragedy of. London: Edward White, 1592.

—. *The Tragedy of Master Arden of Faversham*. Edited by M.L. Wine. London: Methuen, 1973.

Ariosto, Ludovico. *Orlando Furioso*. 1516. Edited by Lanfranco Caretti. Milan and Naples: R. Ricciardi, 1954.

—. *Orlando Furioso*. Translated by Barbara Reynolds. 2nd edn, London: Penguin, 1981.

Armin, Robert. *Italian Taylor and His Boy, The*. London: T. P[avier], 1609.

—. *Two Maids of More-clacke, The Historie of*. London: N.O. for Thomas Archer, 1609.

Aubrey, John. *Brief Lives*. 1669–96. Edited by A. Clark. Oxford: Clarendon Press, 1898.

—. *John Aubrey: Brief Lives*. Edited by J. Buchanan-Brown. London: Penguin, 2000.

Bandello, Matteo. *Novelle*. 1554. 3 vols. Venice: C. Franceschini, 1566.

Barnfield, Richard. *Affectionate Shepheard, The*. London: J. Danter for T.G[ubbins] and E. N[ewman], 1594.

—. *Greenes Funeralls*. London: John Danter, 1594.

—. *Cynthia. With Certaine Sonnets, and the Legend of Cassandra*. London: Humfrey Lownes, 1595.

—. *Poems in Divers Humors (being the fourth part of 'The Encomion of Lady Pecunia')*. London: G.S. for J. Jaggard, 1598.

—. *Complete Poems, The*. Edited by George Klawitter. London and Toronto: Associated University Presses, 1990.

Belleforest, François. *Histoires Tragiques*, vol. 2. Anvers: J. Waesberghe, 1567.

—. *The French Bandello*. Edited with an introduction by Frank S. Hook. Columbia: University of Missouri Studies, 1948.

Blind Begger of Alexandria, The. London: [J. Roberts] for William Jones, 1598.

Boccaccio, Giovanni. *Il Decameron*. Florence: I Giunti, 1573.

Borges, Jorge Luis. *Obras Completas*. 4 vols. Barcelona: Emecé, 1996.

——. *The Aleph*. Translated by Andrew Hurley. London: Penguin, 1998.

Breton, Nicholas. *Wil of Wit, Wils Wit or Wits Will, The*. London: Thomas Creede, 1597.

——. *Wits Trenchmour*. London: J. Roberts for N. Ling, 1597.

——. *Pasquils Mistresse: or the worthie and unworthie woman*. London: T. Fisher, 1599.

——. *Works in Prose and Verse of Nicholas Breton, The*. Edited by A.B. Grosart. 2 vols. Edinburgh: privately printed, 1879.

——. *Poems of Nicholas Breton (not hitherto reprinted), The*. Edited with an introduction by Jean Robertson. Liverpool at the University Press, 1952.

Brydges, Egerton. See *Poetical Rapsodie*.

Bryskett, Ludowick. 'The Mourning Muse of Thestylis'. 1595. In *Astrophel*, by Edmund Spenser, q.v.

Bullokar, William, trans. *Aesopz Fablz*. London: E. Bollifant, 1585.

Cartari, Vincenzo. *Le imagini de I dei de gli antichi*. Venice [Venetia]: F. Marcolini, 1556.

Chapman, George. *Shadow of the Night, The: Containing Two Poeticall Hymnes*. London: R. F[ield] for William Ponsonby, 1594.

—— et al. *Eastward Ho*. Circa 1599. London: W. Aspley for T. Thorpe, 1605.

——. *Gentleman Usher, The*. London: V. S[immes] for T. Thorpe, 1606.

——. *Monsieur D'Olive*. London: T.C. for William Homes, 1606.

——. attributed, *The Blind Begger of Alexandria*, q.v.

——. *Plays of George Chapman, The. The Comedies*. Edited by A. Holaday and M. Kiernan. Urbana: University of Illinois Press, 1970.

Chaucer, Geoffrey. *The Canterbury Tales*. Edited by W.W. Skeat. London: Oxford University Press, 1957.

Chester, Robert [?pseud.]. *Loves Martyr, or Rosalins Complaint*. London: R. Field for William Blount, 1601.

——. *R. Chester's Loves Martyr, or, Rosalins Complaint (1601)*. Edited with introduction, notes and illustrations by A.B. Grosart. London: Bungay for The New Shakespere Society, 1878.

——. *The Poems of John Salusbury and Robert Chester*. Edited by F. Carleton Brown. London: Kegan Paul, 1913/14.

Chute, Anthony. *Tabaco. Gathered by A.C.* London: A. Islip for F. Barlow (Barley), 1595.

——. *Tabacco*. Edited with an introduction by F.P. Wilson. Oxford: Basil Blackwell, 1961.

Cinthio. See Giraldi, Giovanni Battista.

Collins, Arthur. See *Letters and Memorials of State*, under Printed Archives.

Coryat, Thomas. *Coryates Crudities*. London: William Stansby, 1611.

Cotton, Roger. *A Spirituall Song*. London: G. Simson and W. White, 1596.

Covell, William. *A Letter from England to her Three Daughters*. In *Polimanteia*. Cambridge: John Legate, 1595.

Davies, John (of Hereford). *The Scourge of Folly*. London: E. Allde for F. Redmer, c. 1611.

—. *Complete Works of John Davies of Hereford, The*. Edited by A.B. Grosart. 2 vols. Edinburgh: Chertsey Worthies' Library, 1878.

Davison, Francis. See *Poetical Rapsody*.

Dekker, Thomas and Webster, John. *The Famous History of Sir Thomas Wyat*. London: E[dward] A[llde] for Thomas Archer, 1607.

—. Edited by John S. Farmer. Tudor Facsimile Texts London. British Museum, 1914.

Desportes, Philippe. *Les Imitations de l'Arioste*. 1572. Reprint. Paris: Droz, 1936.

Drayton, Michael. *Ideas Mirrour*. London: J. Roberts for N. Ling, 1594.

—. *Matilda*. London: J. Roberts for J. Busby, 1594.

—. *Robert Duke of Normandy* (including *Matilda* and *Piers Gaveston*). London: J. Roberts for N. Ling, 1596.

—. *Elegies upon Sundry Occasions*. London: William Lee, 1627.

—. *Works*. Edited by J.W. Hebel. 5 vols. 1931–41. Reprint. Oxford: Basil Blackwell, 1961.

Dugdale, William. *The Antiquities of Warwickshire*. London: Thomas Warren, 1656.

Eastward Ho. See under Chapman, George.

Englands Helicon (1600). London: [Thomas Snodham] for Richard More, 1614.

—. 1614 edition. Edited by H. Macdonald. London: Routledge, 1949.

Exequiae illustrissimi equitis, D. Philippi Sidnaei .... Edited by W. Gager. Oxford: J. Barnes, 1587.

Fenton, Geoffrey, trans. *Certaine Tragicall Discourses of Bandello*. London: Thomas Marshe, 1567.

—. *Certaine Tragicall Discourses of Bandello. Translated into English by Geoffrey Fenton, anno 1567*. Edited by R.L. Douglas. 3 vols. London: D. Nutt, 1898.

Gascoigne, George. *The Princely Pleaures at the Courte at Kenelwoorth*. London: Richard Jhones, 1576.

—. *The Whole Woorkes of George Gascoigne*. London: Abel Jeffes, 1587.

—. *The Complete Works of George Gascoigne*. Edited by John W. Cunliffe. 2 vols. Cambridge: Cambridge University Press, 1907–10.

Giraldi, Giovanni Battista [Cinthio]. *Gli Hecatommithi*. Monte Regale [Mendovi]: L. Torrentino, 1565.

Greene, Robert. *Pandosto: The Triumph of Time*. London: Thomas Orwin for Thomas Cadman, 1588.

—. *Perimedes the Blacksmith*. London: John Wolfe for Edward White, 1588.

—. *Ciceronis Amor or Tullies Love*. London: Robert Robinson for Thomas Newman and John Winnington, 1589.

—. *Menaphon*. London: T. O[rwin] for Sampson Clarke, 1589.

—. *Farewell to Folly*. London: T. Scarlet for T. Gubbins and T. Newman, 1591.

—. *The Defence of Conny-catching*. London: A.I. for Thomas Gubbins, 1592.

—. *Greenes Groats-Worth of Witte, bought with a million of Repentance*. London: William Wright, 1592.

—. *Historie of Orlando Furioso, The*. London: John Danter for Cuthbert Burby, 1594.

—. *Greenes Vision: Written at the instant of his death*. London: Thomas Newman, n.d.

—. *Life and Complete Works*. Edited by A.B. Grosart. 15 vols. Huth Library. Manchester: privately printed, 1881–6.

—. *Robert Greene: Menaphon*. Edited by Brenda Cantar. Ottawa: Dovehouse, 1996.

Greville, Fulke, *Certaine learned and elegant workes*. London: E.P. for Henry Seyle, 1633.

—. *Poems and Dramas of Fulke Greville, First Lord Brooke*. Edited by G. Bullough. 2 vols. Edinburgh and London: Oliver and Boyd, 1939.

Griffin, Bartholomew. *Fidessa more chaste than kind*. London: M. Lownes, 1596.

Halle, Edward. *The Union of the Two Noble and illustrate Famelies of Lancastre & Yorke*. 1548. 2nd edn. London: R. Grafton, 1550.

—. *The Union of the Two Noble Families of Lancaster and York*. Menston: Scolar Press, 1970.

Harington, Sir John. *New Discourse of a Stale Subject, called the Metamorphosis of Ajax, A*. London: R. Field, 1596.

—. *Letters and Epigrams of Sir John Harington, The*. Edited by N. McLure. Philadelphia: University of Pennsylvania Press, 1930.

—. *Harington's Metamorphosis of Ajax*. Edited with an introduction by Elizabeth Story Donno. London: Routledge, 1962.

Harvey, Gabriel. *Foure Letters and Certaine Sonnets*. London: J. Wolfe, 1592.

—. *Pierces Supererogation*. London: J. Wolfe, 1593.

—. *Three Proper and Wittie Familiar Letters*. See under Spenser, Edmund.

—. *Letterbook of Gabriel Harvey*. Edited by Edward J.L. Scott. London: Camden Society, 1874. cf. BL Sloane MS 93.

—. *Complete Works of Gabriel Harvey, The*. Edited by A.B. Grosart. 3 vols. Huth Library. Manchester: privately printed, 1884–5.

Henslowe, Philip. Diary in Dulwich College Archive.

—. *Henslowe's Diary*. 2nd edn. Edited by R.A. Foakes. Cambridge: Cambridge University Press, 2002.

Herbert, Mary. See Sidney, Mary.

Heywood, Thomas. *Fair Maid of the West or, A Girl Worth Gold*. London: Richard Royston, 1631.

Holinshed, Rafael. *Chronicles*, vols 2 and 3. London: John Harrison, 1577, 1587.

Hoskyns, John (Sir). *The Life, Letters and Writings of John Hoskyns: 1566–1638*. Edited by L.B. Osborn. Hamden, CN: Archon, 1973.

Howell, Thomas. H. his Devices. London: [W. How?] for H. Jackson, 1581.

I., B. (Ben Jonson?). *The Tragical History, Admirable Atchievements and Various Events of Guy of Warwick*. London: Thomas Vere and William Gilbertson, 1661.

Jonson, Ben. *Every Man out of his Humour*. London: [A. Islip] also [P. Short] for W. Holme, 1600.

—. *Poetaster*. London: R. Braddock for M. L[ownes], 1602.

—. *Alchemist, The*. London: Thomas Snodham for Walter Burre, 1612.

—. Dedicatory poem: 'To the memory of my beloved The Author Mr. William Shakespeare: And what he hath left us'. In the First Folio of Shakespeare's Works. 1623.

—. *Bartholomew Fair*. London: I.B. for Robert Allott, 1631 for inclusion in 2nd Jonson Folio. See below: *Workes of Benjamin Jonson: The Second Volume*.

—. *Masque of Owles at Kenilworth, A*. In *The Workes of Benjamin Jonson. The Second Volume*. London: Richard Meighen, 1640.

—. *Ben Jonson*. Edited by C. Herford, P. Simpson and E. Simpson. 11 vols. Oxford: Clarendon Press, 1925–50.

Kemp, William. *Kemps Nine Daies Wonder*. London: E. Allde for N. Ling, 1600.

—. Edited by G.B. Harrison. New York: Dutton, 1923.

Kenilworth Illustrated. Chiswick: C. Whittingham, 1821.

King, Humfrey, *An Half-penny-worth of Wit, in a Penny-worth of Paper, or, The Hermites Tale*. London: Thomas Thorpe, 1613.

L., R. *A Letter whearin, part of the entertainment untoo the Queenz Maiesty, at Killingwoorth Castl, in warwik Sheer, in this soomerz Progress. 1575, iz signified: from a freend officer attendant in Coourt, untoo hiz freend a Citizen, and Merchaunt of London.*

—. *Diella, Certaine Sonnets, adioyned to the amorous Poeme of Dom Diego and Gyneura*. London: James Roberts for Henry Olney, 1596.

—. Edited by Edwd. V. Utterson. London: Beldornie Press, J.N. Lyall for Edwd. V. Utterson, 1841.

—. Edited by A.B. Grosart. *Occasional Issues of Unique or Very Rare Books*. 17 Vols. Edinburgh: privately printed, 1877.

—. *Robert Laneham: A Letter (1575)*. Edited by R.C. Alston. Menston: Scolar Press, 1968.

—. *Robert Langham, A Letter*. Edited with an introduction by R.J.P. Kuin, q.v.

See also Linche, Richard; Lichfield, Richard; Lynche, Richard.

Lakatos, Imré. 'Changes in the Problem of Inductive Logic'. 1968. Reprint in *Mathematics, Science and Epistemology*. Philosophical Papers. Edited by J. Worrall and G. Currie, vol. 2. Cambridge: Cambridge University Press, 1978.

Langham or Laneham, Robert. See under Kuin, and L., R.

Leicesters Common-wealth. 1584.

—. *Leicester's Commonwealth*. Edited by D. Peck. Athens, Ohio and London: Ohio State University Press, 1985.

Linche, Richard [?pseud.], trans. *The Fountaine of Ancient Fiction*. London: Adam Islip, 1599.

Lichfield, Richard [pseud.] *The Trimming of Thomas Nashe*. London: Philip Scarlet, 1597.

—. *Complete Works of Gabriel Harvey*. 3.1–72.

Lloyd, David. *The Statesmen and Favourites of England Since the Reformation*. London: J.C. for Samuel Speed, 1665.

Locrine. See under S., W.

Lodge, Thomas. *Rosalynde*. London: T. Orwin for T. Gubbins and J. Busbie, 1590.

—. *Complete Works of Thomas Lodge, The*. Edited by E.W. Gosse. 4 vols. Glasgow: Hunterian Club, 1883.

Lyly, John. *Euphues: The Anatomy of Wyt*. London: J. Cawood, 1578.

—. *Euphues and His England*. London: Thomas East for Gabriell Cawood, 1580.

—. *Euphues*. Edited by E. Arber. London: Alex Murray, 1868.

Lynche, Richard [?pseud.]. *An Historical Treatise of the Travels of Noah into Europe*. London: Adam Islip, 1601.

M., Jo. [?John Marston] *Philippes Venus*. London: John Perrin, 1591.

Madox, Richard. *An Elizabethan in 1582: The Diary of Richard Madox, Fellow of All Souls*. Edited by Elizabeth Story Donno. London: The Hakluyt Society, series 2, vol. 147 (1976).

'Manner of Sir Philip Sidney's Death, The'. British Library MS Cotton Vitellius C. 17. Printed in *The Miscellaneous Prose of Sir Philip Sidney*, pp. 166–72. See under Sidney, Philip.

Manningham, John. *The Diary of John Manningham of the Middle Temple 1602–1603*. Edited by R.P. Sorlien. University Press of New England: Hanover, NH, for the University of Rhode Island, 1976.

Markham, Gervase. *Rodomanths Infernall or, The Divell Conquered*. London: V. S[immes] for Nicholas Ling, 1607.

Marlowe, Christopher. *Edward II*. London: R. Bradocke for W. Jones, 1593.

—. *Hero and Leander*. London: F. Kingston for P. Linley, 1598.

—. *Plays and Poems*. Edited by M.R. Ridley. 1909. Reprint. London: Dent, 1958.

Meres, Francis. *Palladis Tamia: Wits Treasurie. Being the Second part of Wits Commonwealth*. London: P. Short for C. Busbie, 1598.

Mirror for Magistrates. 1563 edn. Edited by Lily B. Campbell from the Huntington Manuscript. Cambridge: Cambridge University Press, 1938.

Molyneux, Edmund. *Historical Remembrances of the Sidneys, father and son*. In Holinshed's *Chronicles*, vol. 3. 1587.

—. In *Sir Philip Sidney*, pp. 311–14. See under Sidney, Philip.

Mucedorus, A most pleasant comedie of. London: William Jones, 1598.

Nabokov, Vladimir. *Ada or Ardor: A Family Chronicle*. London: Penguin, 1969.

Nashe, Thomas. Preface to Robert Greene's *Menaphon* (1589).

—. *Pierce Penilesse His Supplication to the Divell*. London: A. Jeffes for John Busbie, 1592; Richard Jones, 1592.

—. *Strange Newes* (running title 'Foure Letters Confuted'). London: [J. Danter], 1592.

—. *Christs Teares Over Jerusalem*. London: James Roberts for Andrew Wise, 1593.

—. *The Terrors of the Night*. London: J. Danter, 1594.

—. *The Unfortunate Traveller*. London: T. Scarlet for C. Burby, 1594.

—. *Have With You to Saffron Walden*. London: John Danter, 1596.

—. *Nashes Lenten Stuffe*. London: N.L. for C.B., 1599.

—. *Summers Last Will and Testament*. London: S. Stafford for W. Burre, 1600.

—. *Works*. Edited by R.B. McKerrow. 5 vols. 1904–10. Revised by F.P. Wilson. Oxford: Basil Blackwell, 1958.

Nichols, J., ed. *The Progresses ... of Queen Elizabeth*. London: J. Nichols, 1788.

Painter, William. *Palace of Pleasure, The*. 2 vols. London: H. Bynneman for N. England, 1567.

—. *Paradyce of Dayntie Devises, A*. London: R. Jones for H. Disle, 1576.

—. *The Paradise of Dainty Devices*. Edited by Hyder E. Rollins. Cambridge, MA: Harvard University Press, 1927.

Parnassus Plays. *The Three Parnassus Plays, c. 1598–1601*. Edited by J.B. Leishman. London: Nicholson and Watson, 1949.

Patten, William. *The Calender of Scripture*. London: R. Jugge, 1575.

—. *The Expedicion into Scotlande of ... Edward, Duke of Somerset*. London: R. Grafton, 1548.

Peele, George. *Edward I*. London: A. Jeffes sold by William Barley, 1593.

—. *Old Wives Tale, The*. London: John Danter sold by J. Hardie and R. Hancocke, 1595.

—. *Dramatic Works of George Peele, The*. Edited by A.H. Bullen. 2 vols. London: J. Nimmo, 1888.

Pembroke, Countess of. See Sidney, Mary.

Peplus Illustrissimi viri D. Philippi Sidnaei supremis honoribus dicatus. Edited by J. Lloyd. Oxford: J Barnes, 1587.

Pinsky, Robert. 'In Defence of Allusion'. Poem printed in *LRB*, 22 May 2003, p. 8.

Poetical Rapsody. Edited and co-authored by Francis Davison. London: Valentine Simmes for John Baily, 1602.

—. 2nd edn with alterations. *A Poetical Rapsodie*. London: Nicholas Okes for Roger Jackson, 1608.

—. *A Poetical Rapsodie*. Edited by Egerton Brydges, 3 vols. Kent: Lee Priory Press, 1814–17.

—. *A Poetical Rhapsody, 1602–21*. Edited by Hyder E. Rollins, 2 vols. Cambridge MA: Harvard University Press, 1931–2.

Pollard, Alfred W., ed. *The Queen's Majesty's Entertainment at Woodstock, 1575*. 1903. Reprint. Oxford: Daniel and Hart, 1910.

Pudsey, Edward. See *Shakespearean Extracts*.

Puttenham, George. *The Arte of English Poesie*. London: Richard Field, 1589.

—. *The Arte of English Poesie*. Edited by Willcock, Gladys and Walker, Alice. 1936. Cambridge: Cambridge University Press, 1970.

Queenes Majesties entertainment at Woodstocke, 1575, The. London: Thomas Cadman, 1585.

—. See also under Pollard.

Roydon, Matthew. 'An Elegie, or friend's passion, for his Astrophil'. In *Astrophel,* by Edmund Spenser.

S.,W. *The Lamentable tragedie of Locrine. Newly set foorth, overseene and corrected*. London: Thomas Creede, 1595.

Salusbury, Sir John. *Poems*. See under Chester, Robert.

Sanford, John. 'A Sceleton or bare Anatomie of the *Punctures and Junctures of Mr.* Thomas *Coryate* of Odcombe'. In *Coryates Crudities*. See Coryat, Thomas.

Scott, Sir Walter. *Kenilworth*. 1821. Edited by Ernest Rhys, Everyman edition. 1906. London: Dent, 1929.

Shakespeare, William. *Complete Works*. Edited by W.J. Craig. 1905. Reprint. London: Oxford University Press, 1955.

Individual Arden Editions

All's Well that Ends Well.
The Comedy of Errors.
Cymbeline.
Henry IV, Part 1.
Henry IV, Part 2.
Henry V.
Henry VI.
Henry VIII.
King John.
King Lear.
Julius Caesar.
Love's Labour's Lost.
Macbeth.
Measure for Measure.
The Merchant of Venice.
The Merry Wives of Windsor.
A Midsummer Night's Dream.
Much Ado About Nothing.
Pericles.
Richard III.
Sonnets.
The Taming of the Shrew.

The Tempest.
Titus Andronicus.
The Two Gentlemen of Verona.
The Winter's Tale.

Other Editions

Edward III. Edited by Eric Sams. London: Yale University Press, 1996.

Hamlet. New Variorum. Edited by H.H. Furness. 2 vols. 1817. Revised by H.H. Furness, Jr. Philadelphia and London: J.B. Lippincott, 1918.

Henry IV, Part 1. Cambridge New Shakespeare. Edited by J. Dover Wilson. Cambridge: Cambridge University Press, 1946.

Macbeth. New Variorum. Revised by H.H. Furness, Jr. Philadelphia and London: J.B. Lippincott, 1915.

Much Ado About Nothing. Edited by A. Quiller-Couch and J. Dover Wilson. Cambridge New Shakespeare. Cambridge at the University Press, 1923.

Rape of Lucrece, The. London: Richard Field, 1593.

Shakespeare: The Narrative Poems. Edited by Maurice Evans. London: Penguin, 1989.

Sonnets and a Lover's Complaint, The. Edited with an introduction by J. Kerrigan. London: Penguin, 1986.

Winter's Tale, The. Edited with an introduction by Ernest Schanzer. 1969. Reprint. London: Penguin, 1996.

Shakespearean Extracts from 'Edward Pudsey's Booke'. Edited by Richard Savage. Stratford: John Smith; and London: Simpkin and Marshall, n.d.

Sidney, Mary (Herbert, Countess of Pembroke). *The Collected Works of Mary Sidney Herbert, Countess of Pembroke.* Edited by M. Hannay, N. Kinnamon and M. Brennan, 2 vols. Oxford: Clarendon Press, 1998.

Sidney, Philip. 'The Defence of Leicester'. c.1585. In *Letters and Memorials of State*, I. 62–8, and *Miscellaneous Prose*, pp. 129–41.

—. *Countess of Pembrookes Arcadia, The.* Otherwise *The New Arcadia.* London: William Ponsonby, 1590, 1593, 1598.

—. *Astrophel and Stella.* London: Thomas Newman, 1591.

—. *An Apology for Poetrie.* London: Henry Olney, 1595. Otherwise *The Defence of Poesie.* London: William Ponsonby, 1595.

—. *Certaine Sonnets.* In *The Countess of Pembrookes Arcadia*, q.v.

—. *The Poems of Sir Philip Sidney.* Edited by W. Ringler. Oxford: Clarendon, 1962.

—. *Old Arcadia, The.* c. 1580. Edited by A. Feuillerat. *Prose Works of Philip Sidney.* Vol. 4. 1912. Reprint. Cambridge: Cambridge University Press, 1963.

—. *Miscellaneous Prose.* Edited by Katherine Duncan–Jones and Jan van Dorsten. Oxford: Clarendon Press, 1973.

—. *Countess of Pembroke's Arcadia, The*. Edited by Maurice Evans. Harmondsworth: Penguin, 1977.

Smith, William (1). 'A newyeares Guifte made upon certen Flowers.' (BL Additional MS 35186.)

—. *Chloris, or The Complaint of the passionate despised Shepheard*. London: Edmond Bollifant, 1596.

—. *Chloris*. In *Occasional Issues*, 3c. See under Grosart.

—. 'Allegory of Time.' Yale University Library. Osborn MS. Printed as 'An Elizabethan Allegory of Time.' Edited by Kent Talbot van den Bergen. *ELR* 6 (Winter 1976), pp. 40–59.

Smith, William (2). (as Smyth) *Gemma fabri*. London: F. Kingston for J. Porter, 1598.

—. *The Blacksmith*. London: Ed. Allde for Martin Clarke, 1606.

Spenser, Edmund. *A Theatre ... Devised by S. John vander Noodt*. London: Henry Binneman, 1569. Printed as *Epigrams and Sonnets* in *Works*, pp. 605–8.

—. *The Shepheardes Calender*. London: Hugh Singleton, 1579.

—. *Three Proper and Wittie Familiar Letters* (with Gabriel Harvey). London: Henry Binneman, 1580.

—. *Astrophèl*. In *Colin Clouts Come Home Againe*. London: T. Creede for William Ponsonby, 1595.

—. *Poetical Works*. Edited by J.C. Smith and E. De Selincourt. 1912. Reprint. Oxford: Oxford University Press, 1989.

Three Collections of English Poetry of the Latter Part of the Sixteenth Century. London: 1578–9. In the Earl of Northumberland's Library at Alnwick. Reprinted by The Shakespeare Press. William Nicol for the Roxburghe Press, 1844.

Virgil: The Eclogues and Georgics. Edited by R.D. Williams. 1979. London: Duckworth for the Bristol Classical Press, 1996.

W., A . *A Speciall Remedie, Against the Furious Force of Lawlesse Love*. London: Richard Jones, 1579. Also in *Three Collections of English Poetry*, q.v.

—. co-author, *Poetical Rhapsody*, q.v.

Watson, Thomas. *Amintae Gaudia*. London: W. Ponsonby, 1592.

Webster, John., *The Famous History of Sir Thomas Wyat*. See under Dekker, Thomas.

Whetstone, George. *Sir Philip Sidney, His Honorable Life, His Valiant Death, and True Virtues*. London: Thomas Cadman, n.d.

Wilkins, George. *The Painfull Aduentures of Pericles Prince of Tyre*. London: T. P[urser], 1608.

Secondary Sources

Amnaeus, Daniel. *The Mystery of Macbeth*. Alhambra, Calif.: Primrose, 1983.

Armstrong, R.L. See under Everitt, E.B.

Bachinger, Katrina. *Male Pretense: A Gender Study of Sir Philip Sidney's Life and Texts*. Lampeter: Mellen, 1994.

Barroll, Leeds. 'Shakespeare, Noble Patrons, and the Pleasures of "Common" Playing'. In *Shakespeare and Theatrical Patronage*. Edited by Paul Whitfield White and Suzanne Westfall. Cambridge: Cambridge University Press, 2002, pp. 90–121. Cited hereafter as 'White and Westfall'.

Bate, Jonathan. *The Genius of Shakespeare*. London: Picador, 1997.

Bednarz, James. *Shakespeare and the Poets' War*. New York: Columbia University Press, 2001.

Berger, Harry. *Revisionary Play: Studies in the Spenserian Dynamics*. Berkeley: University of California Press, 1988.

Bergeron, David. 'The King's Men's King's Men: Shakespeare and Folio Patronage'. In White and Westfall, pp. 45–63.

Berry, Herbert. *Shakespeare's Playhouses*. New York: AMS, 1987.

de Biase, Carmine. 'The Decline of Euphuism: Robert Greene's Struggle Against Popular Taste'. In *Critical Approaches to English Prose Fiction, 1520–1640*. Edited by Donald Beecher. Ottawa: Dovehouse, 1998.

Blayney, Peter. 'The Publication of Playbooks'. In *A New History of Early English Drama*, q.v., pp. 383–422.

—. *The First Folio of Shakespeare*. Washington: Folger Library Publications, 1991.

Booth, Roy. See (1) *Elizabethan Sonnets*.

Bradbrook, Muriel. *The Rise of the Common Player: A Study of Actor and Society in Shakespeare's England*. London: Chatto and Windus, 1962.

Brennan, Michael. *Literary Patronage in the English Renaissance: The Pembroke Family*. London: Routledge, 1988.

—. See also under Sidney, Mary.

British Stage, The, vol. 6. 1821. London: F. Marshall, 1822.

Brooks, Douglas. *From Playhouse to Printing House: Drama and Authorship in Early Modern England*. Cambridge: Cambridge University Press, 2000.

Bruster, Douglas. *Quoting Shakespeare: Form and Culture in Early Modern Drama*. Lincoln, NE: University of Nebraska Press, 2000.

—. See also under Moisan, Thomas.

Buxton, John. 'An Elizabethan Reading–List: An Unpublished Letter from Sir Philip Sidney'. *TLS*, March 24 1972, pp. 343–4.

Cambridge Companion to Shakespeare, The. Edited by Margareta de Grazia and Stanley Wells. Cambridge: Cambridge University Press, 2001.

Chambers, E.K. *Elizabethan Stage, The*. 4 vols. Oxford: Clarendon Press, 1923.

—. *William Shakespeare: A Study of Facts and Problems*. 2 vols. Oxford: Clarendon Press, 1930.

—. *Sir Henry Lee*. Oxford: Clarendon Press, 1936.

Cheney, Patrick. *Spenser's Famous Flight: A Renaissance Idea of a Literary Career*. Toronto and London: Toronto University Press, 1993.

—. 'Shakespeare's Sonnet 106, Spenser's National Epic, and Counter-Petrarchism'. *ELR* 31 (Autumn 2001), pp. 331–64.

Clegg, Cyndia Susan. *Press Censorship in Elizabethan England*. Cambridge: Cambridge University Press, 1997.

Cook, Ann Jennalie. *The Privileged Playgoers of Shakespeare's London, 1576–1642*. Princeton: Princeton University Press, 1981.

Cooper, Helen. 'Guy of Warwick, Upstart Crows and Mounting Sparrows'. In *Shakespeare, Marlowe, Jonson: New Directions in Biography*. Edited by J.R. Mulryne and Takashi Kozuka. Aldershot and Burlington, VT: Ashgate, forthcoming.

Cory, Herbert E. *Edmund Spenser: A Critical Study*. Berkeley: University of California Press, 1917.

Crawford, Charles. '"Greenes Funeralls", 1594, and Nicholas Breton'. *SP* extra series 1 (May 1929), pp. 1–39.

Crewe, Jonathan. *Hidden Designs: The Critical Profession and Renaissance Literature*. New York and London: Methuen, 1986.

Denny, H.L.L. 'Biography of Sir Edward Denny'. *Transactions of the East Hertfordshire Archaeological Society* 2 (1902–4), pp. 247–60.

Dobson, E.J. *English Pronunciation 1500–1700*. 1957. Reprint. 2 vols. Oxford: Clarendon Press, 1968.

Dorsten, J. van. See under Sidney, Philip.

Dover Wilson, John. Introduction and appendices to *Henry IV, Part 1* by William Shakespeare. Cambridge: Cambridge University Press, 1946.

Dronke, Peter. *The Medieval Lyric*. 1968. Reprint. Cambridge: D.S. Brewer, 1996.

Duncan-Jones, Katherine. *Sir Philip Sidney*. Oxford: Oxford University Press, 1989.

—. *Sir Philip Sidney: Courtier Poet*. London: Hamish Hamilton, 1991.

—. 'Jonson's Epitaph on Nashe'. *TLS*, 7 July 1995, pp. 4–6.

—. Introduction to the Arden *Shakespeare's Sonnets*. 1997. London: Thomas Nelson, 1998.

—. See also under Sidney, Philip.

Dutton, Richard. *Mastering the Revels: The Regulation and Censorship of English Renaissance Drama*. Iowa City: University of Iowa Press, 1991.

(1) *Elizabethan Sonnets*. Edited by Sidney Lee, 2 vols. Westminster: Constable, 1904.

(2) *Elizabethan Sonnets*. Edited by Maurice Evans. 1977. 2nd edn, revised by Roy Booth. London: Dent, 1994.

Empson, William. *Some Versions of Pastoral*. 1935. Reprint. Harmondsworth: Penguin in association with Chatto and Windus, 1966.

Erne, Lukas. *Shakespeare as Literary Dramatist*. Cambridge: Cambridge University Press, 2003.

Evans, Maurice. See under (2) Elizabethan Sonnets; *Shakespeare, The Narrative Poems*; and *The Countess of Pembroke's Arcadia* by Philip Sidney.

Everett, Barbara. 'Whirligig'. *LRB*, September 2004, pp. 19–23.

Everitt, E.B. and Armstrong, R.L. *Six Early Plays Related to the Shakespeare Canon.* Anglistika, vol. 14. Copenhagen: 1965.

Felperin, Howard. '"Tongue-tied our Queen?" The Deconstruction of Presence in *The Winter's Tale*'. In *Shakespeare and the Question of Theory*. Edited by Patricia Parker and Geoffrey Hartmann, pp. 3–18. New York and London: Methuen, 1985.

Ferry, Anne. *The Art of Naming.* Chicago and London: University of Chicago Press, 1988.

Fleissner, Robert. *Shakespeare and the Matter of the Crux: Textual, Topical, Onomastic, Authorial, and Other Puzzlement.* Lampeter: Edwin Mellen, 1991.

—. 'The "Upstart Crow" Reclawed: Was it Kemp, Wilson, Alleyn, or Shakespeare?' *The Upstart Crow* 15 (1995), pp. 143–9.

—. *Names, Titles, and Characters by Literary Writers – Shakespeare, 19th and 20th Century Authors.* Lampeter: Edwin Mellen, 2001.

Fletcher, Angus. 'On Shakespeare and Theory'. In the *Shakespearean International Yearbook*. Edited by W.R. Elton and John M. Mucciolo. 2 vols. Aldershot: Ashgate, 2002. 2, pp. 3–19.

Foakes, R.A. Introduction to the Arden *Henry VIII*. 1957. Reprint. London and New York: Methuen, 1986.

—. See also under Henslowe.

Frazer, Winifred. 'William Kemp as "Upstart Crow"'. *The Upstart Crow* 15 (1995), pp. 140–42.

Fripp, Edgar. *Shakespeare's Stratford.* London: Oxford University Press, 1928.

—. *Shakespeare Studies.* London: Oxford University Press, 1930.

—. *Shakespeare Man and Artist.* 2 vols. 1938. Reprint. London: Oxford University Press, 1964.

—. ed. *Minutes and Accounts of the Corporation of Stratford-upon-Avon.* See under Printed Archives.

Frye, Susan. *The Competition for Representation.* New York and Oxford: Oxford University Press, 1993.

Furnivall, F.J. 'Sir John Harington's Shakspeare [sic] Quartos'. *N&Q* (17 May 1890), pp. 382–3.

Garber, Marjorie. 'Roman Numerals'. In *In the Company of Shakespeare*. Edited by Thomas Moisan, q.v., and Douglas Bruster, pp. 233–50.

Gilvary, Kevin. *Twelfth Night, A Midsummer's Dream and the Earl of Oxford.* De Vere Society Publication, 2002.

Goldberg, Jonathan. *Sodometries: Renaissance Texts, Modern Sexualities.* Stanford, CA: Stanford University Press, 1992.

—. *Desiring Women Writing.* Stanford, CA: Stanford University Press, 1997.

Gossett, Suzanne. Introduction to the Arden *Pericles*. London: Thompson, 2004.

Greg, W.W., ed. *Two Elizabethan Stage Abridgements: The Battle of Alcazar & Orlando Furioso.* Oxford: Clarendon Press, 1923.

Griffiths, Jeremy. '"Loose Sheets and Idle Scribblings": The Case Against Shakespeare'. *New Welsh Review* 25 (Summer 1994), pp. 52–7.

Grosart, A.B., ed. *Occasional Issues of Unique or Very Rare Books*. 17 vols. Edinburgh: privately printed, 1877.

Gurr, Andrew. 'Privy Councillors as Theatre Patrons'. In White and Westfall, pp. 221–45.

Halliday, F. *A Shakespeare Companion: 1550–1950*. London: Duckworth, 1952.

Hamilton, A.C. Introduction to *Spenser: The Faerie Queene*. London: Longman, 1977.

Hamilton, Donna. *Shakespeare and the Politics of Protestant England*. New York: Harvester, 1992.

Hannay, Margaret. *Philip's Phoenix: Mary Sidney, Countess of Pembroke*. New York and Oxford: Oxford University Press, 1990.

Hazlitt, W.C. *Hand-book to the Popular, Poetical and Dramatic Literature of Great Britain*. London: John Russell Smith, 1867.

Hibbard, G.R. *Thomas Nashe: A Critical Introduction*. Cambridge: Harvard University Press, 1962.

Hilliard, Stephen. *The Singularity of Thomas Nashe*. Lincoln, Nebraska and London: University of Nebraska Press, 1986.

Hirsh, James. *Shakespeare and the History of Soliloquies*. London: Associated University Presses, 2003.

Holden, Anthony. *William Shakespeare: His Life and Work*. 1999. Reprint. London: Abacus, 2000.

Honan, Park. *Shakespeare: A Life*. Oxford: Oxford University Press, 1999.

Honigmann, E.A. Introduction to the Arden *King John*. London: Methuen, 1954.

—. 'Shakespeare's Life'. In *The Cambridge Companion to Shakespeare*, pp. 1–12.

—. *The Stability of Shakespeare's Text*. Lincoln, Nebraska: University of Nebraska Press, 1965.

—. *Shakespeare: The Lost Years*. 1985. Reprint. Manchester: Manchester University Press, 1998.

Hoster, Jay. *Tiger's Heart: What Really Happened in the 'Groatsworth of Wit' Controversy of 1592*. Columbus, OH: Ravine, 1993.

Hotson, Leslie. *Shakespeare's Sonnets Dated and Other Essays*. London: Hart-Davis, 1949.

Humphreys, A.R. Introduction to the Arden *Much Ado about Nothing*. 1981. Reprint. London: Thompson, 2002.

Hunter, G.K. *English Drama, 1558–1642: The Age of Shakespeare*. Oxford: Clarendon Press, 1997.

Hutson, Lorna. *Thomas Nashe in Context*. Oxford: Clarendon Press, 1989.

Ioppolo, Grace. *Revising Shakespeare*. Cambridge, MA and London: Harvard University Press, 1991.

Jackson, William A. *The Carl H. Pforzheimer Library. English Literature 1475–1700*, 3 vols. New York: privately printed, 1940.

Kingsley-Smith, Jane. *Shakespeare's Drama of Exile*. Basingstoke: Palgrave Macmillan, 2003.

Kinney, Arthur. 'Revisiting *The Tempest*'. *MP* 93 (1995), pp. 161–77.

Klossowski de Rola, Stanislas. *Alchemy the Secret Art*. London: Thames and Hudson, 1973.

Kuin, R.J.P. Introduction and notes to *Robert Langham, A Letter*. Leiden: E.J. Brill, 1983.

—. 'The Purloined Letter: Evidence and Probability Regarding Robert Langham's Authorship'. *The Library*, 6th series, vol. 7.2 (June 1985), pp. 115–25.

Lamb, Mary Ellen, *Gender and Authorship in the Sidney Circle*. Madison: University of Wisconsin Press, 1990.

Lesser, Zachary. 'Walter Burre's *The Knight of the Burning Pestle*'. *ELR* 29 (1999), pp. 22–43.

Levi, Peter. *The Life and Times of William Shakespeare*. New York: Henry Holt, 1988.

Lloyd-Roberts, Tom. 'Bard of Lleweni? Shakespeare's Welsh Connection'. *New Welsh Review* 23 (1993–94), pp. 11–18.

Loewenstein, Joseph. *The Author's Due: Printing and the Prehistory of Copyright*. Chicago: University of Chicago Press, 2002.

Maclean, Sally-Beth. 'Tracking Leicester's Men: The Patronage of a Performance troupe'. In White and Westfall, pp. 246–71.

—, ed. *The Queen's Men and Their Plays*. See under McMillin, Scott.

Malcolm, Noel. *The Origins of English Nonsense*. London: Fontana, 1997.

Marcus, Leah. *Puzzling Shakespeare: Local Reading and its Discontents*. Berkeley: University of California Press, 1988.

Marotti, Arthur. *John Donne: Coterie Poet*. Madison: University of Wisconsin Press, 1986.

Masten, Jeffrey. *Textual Intercourse: Collaboration, Authorship, and Sexualities in Renaissance Drama*. Cambridge: Cambridge University Press, 1997.

McCarthy, Penny. 'E.K. Was Only the Postman'. *N&Q* n.s. 47.1 (March 2000), pp. 28–31.

—. '"Milksop Muses" or Why Not Mary?'. *SEL* 40 (Winter 2000), pp. 21–39.

—. 'Nabokov's *Ada* and Sidney's *Arcadia*'. *MLR* 99 (January 2004), pp. 17–31.

—. 'Some *quises* and *quems:* Shakespeare's True Debt to Nashe'. In *New Studies in the Shakespearean Heroine*. Edited by Douglas Brooks. Lampeter: Edwin Mellen, 2004. *Shakespeare Yearbook*, vol. 14, pp. 175–92.

McCoy, Richard. 'Eulogies to Elegies: Poetic Distance in the April Eclogue'. In *Soundings of Things Done: Essays in Early Modern Literature in Honor of S.K. Heninger Jr*. Edited by P. Medine and J. Wittreich, pp. 52–69. London: Associated University Presses, 1997.

McGann, Jerome. *A Critique of Modern Textual Criticism*. Chicago: University of Chicago Press, 1983.

McKerrow, Ronald B. *Printers' and Publishers' Devices in England and Scotland, 1485–1640*. London: Chiswick, 1913.

McLane, Paul. *Spenser's 'Shepheards Calender': A Study in Elizabethan Allegory*. Notre Dame, IL: University of Notre Dame Press, 1961.

McMillin, Scott, and Maclean, Sally-Beth. *The Queen's Men and Their Plays*. Cambridge: Cambridge University Press, 1998.

McMullan, Gordon. 'The Invention of Late Writing: Shakespeare, Biography, Death'. Paper, read at the Shakespeare Association of America Conference, March 2002.

Mehl, Dieter. 'Shakespeare Reference Books'. In *The Cambridge Companion to Shakespeare*, q.v., pp. 297–313.

Metz, G. Harold. *Shakespeare's Earliest Tragedy: Studies in 'Titus Andronicus'*. London: Associated University Presses, 1996.

Miller, Edwin Havilland. 'The Relationship of Robert Greene and Thomas Nashe (1580–92)'. *PQ* 33 (October 1954), pp. 353–6.

Miola, Robert. *Shakespeare's Reading*. Oxford: Oxford University Press, 2000.

Moisan, Thomas, ed. with Bruster, Douglas. *In the Company of Shakespeare: Essays on English Renaissance Literature in Honor of G. Blakemore Evans*. London: Associated University Presses, 2002.

—. 'Deforming Sources: Literary Antecedents and Their Traits in *Much Ado About Nothing*'. *Shakespeare Studies* 31 (2003), pp. 165–83.

Moore Smith, G.C. *The Family of Withypoll*. Revised by P.H. Reaney. Waltham Antiquarian Society 34, 1936.

Morris, Harry. *Richard Barnfield, Colin's Child*. Tampa: Florida State University Studies, 1963.

Muir, Kenneth. Introduction to the Arden *Macbeth*. 1962 and 1984. Reprint. London: Thompson, 2001.

Mulryan, John. 'Shakespeare and the Italian Mythographers'. In the *Shakespearean International Yearbook*, 2 vols. Aldershot: Ashgate, 2002. 2, pp. 305–17.

New History of Early English Drama, A. Edited by John Cox and David Scott Kastan. New York: Columbia University Press, 1997.

Norbrook, David. *Poetry and Politics in the English Renaissance*. London: Routledge, 1984.

—. Introduction to the *Penguin Book of Renaissance Verse, 1509–1659*. Edited by Henry Woudhuysen. London: Penguin, 1992.

North, Marcy. *The Anonymous Renaissance: Cultures of Discretion in Tudor-Stuart England*. Chicago and London: University of Chicago Press, 2003.

Nosworthy, J.M. Introduction and notes to the Arden *Cymbeline*. London: Methuen, 1955.

O'Kill, Brian. 'The Printed Works of William Patten (c. 1510–c.1600)'. *TCBS* 7.1 (1977), pp. 28–45.

Orgel, Stephen. *Imagining Shakespeare: A History of Texts and Vision*. Basingstoke: Palgrave Macmillan, 2003.

Pafford, J.H.P. Introduction to the Arden *Winters Tale*. 1963. Reprint. London: Thompson, 2002.

Parker, Patricia. *Literary Fat Ladies: Rhetoric, Gender, Property*. London: Methuen, 1987.

—. 'On the Tongue: Crossgendering, Effeminacy and the Art of Words'. *Style* 23 (Fall 1989), pp. 445–65.

—. *Shakespeare from the Margins: Language, Culture, Context*. Chicago: Chicago University Press, 1996.

Patterson, Annabel. *Censorship and Interpretation: The Conditions of Writing and Reading in Early Modern England*. Madison: University of Wisconsin Press, 1984.

Pitcher, Seymour M. *The Case for Shakespeare's Authorship of 'The Famous Victories'*. New York: Alwin Redman, 1961.

Porter, Joseph. *Shakespeare's Mercutio: His History and Drama*. Chapel Hill and London: University of North Carolina Press, 1988.

Raglan (Lord). *Jocasta's Crime: An Anthropological Study*. London: C.A. Watts for The Thinker's Library, 1940.

Rambuss, Richard. *Spenser's Secret Career*. Cambridge: Cambridge University Press, 1993.

Rampton, David. *Vladimir Nabokov*. Basingstoke: Macmillan, 1993.

Reaney, P.H. *Court Rolls of the Rectory Manor Walthamstow*. Waltham Antiquarian Society, 37, 1939. See also under Moore Smith.

Roberts, Gareth. *The Mirror of Alchemy*. London: British Library, 1994.

Roe, John. *Shakespeare and Machiavelli*. Cambridge: D.S. Brewer, 2002.

Roebuck, George. Edward. *The Walthamstow Armorial*. Waltham Antiquarian Society, 26, 1932.

Sams, Eric. *The Real Shakespeare: Retrieving the Early Years, 1564–1594*. New Haven and London: Yale University Press, 1995.

Savage, Richard. See *Minutes and Accounts; Shakespearean Extracts; Stratford-on-Avon Registers*.

Schoenbaum, Samuel. *William Shakespeare: A Compact Documentary Life*. 1977. Reprint. New York and Oxford: Oxford University Press, 1987.

Schrickx, W. *Shakespeare's Early Contemporaries: The Background of the Harvey–Nashe Polemic and 'Love's Labour's Lost'*. Antwerp: Nederlandische Boeckhandel, 1956.

Scott, David. 'William Patten and the Authorship of "Robert Laneham's *Letter*" (1575)'. *ELR* 7 (Autumn 1977), pp. 297–306.

Shakspere Allusion Book, A. 1591–1700. Compiled by C.M Ingleby et al. London: Oxford University Press. 1932.

Shapiro, James. *Rival Playwrights: Marlowe, Jonson, Shakespeare*. New York: Columbia University Press, 1991.

Sinfield, Alan. *Literature in Protestant England, 1560–1660: Religious Anxiety from Spenser to Milton*. London: Croom Helm, 1983.

—. 'Power and Ideology: An Outline Theory and Sidney's *Arcadia*'. *ELH* 52 (1985), pp. 259–79.

Skura, Meredith. *Shakespeare the Actor and the Purposes of Playing*. Chicago: University of Chicago Press, 1993.

Spurgeon, Caroline. *Shakespeare's Imagery*. 1935. Reprint. Cambridge: Cambridge University Press, 1965.

Staunton, H. 'A Mistaken Allusion to Shakespeare'. *The Athenaeum*, 2415, 7 February 1874, pp. 193–4.

Stern, Virginia. *Gabriel Harvey: His Life, Marginalia and Library*. Oxford: Clarendon Press, 1979.

Stopes, Charlotte Carmichael. *Burbage and Shakespeare's Stage*. London: De la More Press, 1913.

Strauss, Leo. *Persecution and the Art of Writing*. 1952. Reprint. Chicago and London: University of Chicago Press, 1980.

Sutherland, Stuart. *Irrationality: The Enemy Within*. London: Penguin, 1992.

Thatcher, David. *Begging to Differ: Modes of Discrepancy in Shakespeare*. New York: Peter Lang, 1999.

Tobin, J.J.M. 'Nashe and *Hamlet* Yet Again'. *Hamlet Studies* 2 (1980), pp. 35–46.

—. 'Nomenclature and the Dating of *Titus Andronicus*'. *N&Q* 229 (1984), pp. 186–7.

—. 'Nashe and Shakespeare: Some Further Borrowings'. *N&Q* 219 (1992), pp. 309–20.

—. 'Texture as Well as Structure: More Sources for the Riverside Shakespeare'. In *In the Company of Shakespeare* (2002). Edited by Moisan and Bruster, pp. 97–110.

Vaughan, Virginia Mason and Vaughan, Alden T. Introduction to the Arden *Tempest*. 1999. London: Thompson, 2003.

Vickers, Brian. *Shakespeare, Co-author: A Historical Study of Five Collaborative Plays*. Oxford: Oxford University Press, 2002.

Wallace, Charles William. *The First London Theatre*. University of Nebraska Studies 13, 1913.

Waller, Gary. *Mary Sidney, Countess of Pembroke: A Critical Study of her Writings and Literary Milieu*. Salzburg: University of Salzburg Press, 1979.

Warkentin, Germaine. 'The Meeting of the Muses: Sidney and the Mid-Tudor Poets'. In *Sir Philip Sidney and the Interpretation of Renaissance Culture: The Poet in his Time and in Ours*. Edited by Gary Waller and Michael Moore, pp. 17–33. London: Croom Helm, 1984.

—. 'Patrons and Profiteers: Thomas Newman and the "Violent Enlargement" of *Astrophil and Stella*'. *The Book Collector* 34 (1985), pp. 461–87.

Westfall, Suzanne. *Patrons and Performance: Early Tudor Household Revels*. Oxford: Clarendon Press, 1990.

—. ed. *Shakespeare and Theatrical Patronage*. See Whitfield White, Paul.

—. 'The Useful Dearness of the Diamond: Theories of Patronage Theatre'. In White and Westfall, pp. 13–42.

Whitfield White, Paul. *Theatre and Reformation: Protestantism, Patronage and Playing in Tudor England.* Cambridge: Cambridge University Press, 1993.

—, ed. with Suzanne Westfall. *Shakespeare and Theatrical Patronage.* Cambridge: Cambridge University Press, 2002.

Wilson, Derek. *Sweet Robin: A Biography of Robert Dudley, Earl of Leicester.* 1981. Reprint. London: Allison and Busby, 1997.

Wilson, Ian. *Shakespeare: The Evidence.* London: Headline, 1993.

Wilson, Jean. 'Why Fotheringhay? The Location of the Trial and Execution of Mary, Queen of Scots'. *Renaissance Journal* 2.2 (June 2004), pp. 3–31.

Wilson, Richard. 'Shakespeare and the Jesuits: New Connections Supporting the Theory of the Lost Years in Lancashire'. *TLS*, 19 December 1997, pp. 11–13.

Woudhuysen, Henry. 'Leicester's literary patronage: a study of the English Court'. D.Phil. dissertation, University of Oxford, 1980.

—. *Sir Philip Sidney and the Circulation of Manuscripts, 1558–1640.* Oxford: Clarendon Press, 1996.

Yates, Francis. *Astraea: The Imperial Theme in the Sixteenth Century.* London: Routledge, 1975.

Index